THE SOCIALIST REGISTER 1999

GLOBAL CAPITALISM VERSUS DEMOCRACY

SOCIALIST REGISTER 1999

Edited by LEO PANITCH and COLIN LEYS

MERLIN PRESS UK
MONTHLY REVIEW NY

First published in 1999
by The Merlin Press Ltd
2 Rendlesham Mews, Rendlesham
Nr. Woodbridge, Suffolk
IP12 2SZ

Published in the US by:
Monthly Review Press
122 West 27 Street
New York
NY 10001

Published in Canada by:
Fernwood Publishing Co.
P.O. Box 9409
Station A
Halifax
Nova Scotia
B3K 5S3

British Library Cataloguing in Publication Data

The Socialist Register. — 1999
1. Socialism — 1999
I. Panitch, Leo
355'.005

UK ISBN 0-85036-480-9 Pbk
0-85036-481-7 Hbk
US ISBN 0-85345-948-7

Typesetting by
Creative Print and Design, Harmondsworth, Middlesex

Printed in Finland by WSOY

TABLE OF CONTENTS

PREFACE

One of the hallmarks of *The Socialist Register* has been its critique of the illusions that have attended capitalism's triumphal global march over the last two decades. If our analysis of the contradictions of 'globalisation' has been necessary and distinctive, this is equally true of this present volume, the *Register*'s thirty-fifth, which has been completed amidst general recognition that global capitalism has entered an era of global crisis. 'The collapse of the emerging markets and its ricochet effect on advanced economies may not be the end of globalisation. But it is certainly the end of an era,' writes Jeffrey Sachs in *The Economist* of September 12, 1998. The mantra of the day among capitalists themselves is that globalisation has gone 'too far, too fast' and that 'the 90s are over'. 'Investors have begun to treat "global" as a bad word,' the *New York Times* tells us. Suddenly, even the *Wall Street Journal* and the *Financial Times* feature sober articles giving credence to the relevance – even the necessity – of capital and exchange controls, while pressures that the US Treasury and the IMF exerted only a few months back for further capital liberalisation and currency convertibility measures are now derided as having been other-worldly.

What has made the *Socialist Register*'s approach distinctive over the past decade has been its demonstration that the contradictions of contemporary capitalism have not disappeared b ut have been playing themselves out both within the new forces generating globalisation and in the various forms which the process of globalisation has taken. This stands in contrast to the arguments advanced both by those who have minimised globalisation's novelty or significance, and by those who have only seen it as unstoppable force, sweeping away a century of socialist ideals and institutions, and even transcending the nation state. One of the *Register's* main accomplishments has been to have explained why states remain central actors, and to have shown how they have reorganised themselves, however unevenly, to try to both advance and harness the processes generating globalisation. Just as the current global crisis will not have surprised *Register* readers, nor led them to imagine that it means the end of globalisation, so would they have understood that processes that developed under the neo-liberal ideological aegis of the new right will increasingly be revealed as depending heavily on the role of states for their continuance and stabilisation.

But increased – or at least more visible – regulation, even under the aegis of social democratic elites, must also mean an acceleration in the political contradictions of global capitalism. A further achievement of the *Register* in this respect has been to pierce the predominant illusions that have governed left strategies in the 1990s, from the vague search for a new international civil society, to the apparently sober pursuit of 'progressive competitive' strategies by social democratic parties. The latter, in particular, have been shown not only to have failed the test of socialist ethics, in seeking to export their unemployment to less competitive regions, but also to have failed practically: the attempt by every state to compete for capital inflows, while limiting its imports and promoting exports, generates a vicious circle of 'competitive austerity', growing inequality and financial instability.

In these conditions, far from the socialist aspiration for democratic economic planning being passe, it has never been more relevant; and the *Register* has also been distinctive in its endeavour to offer at least the rudimentary basis of an alternative response (beginning with, but hardly limited to, capital controls). This has entailed constructive thinking about strategic direction on the basis of our authors' more realistic and complex view of capitalist and state restructuring. This important thread, combined with a stream of essays which have explicitly focussed on organisational alternatives, has meant that thinking about agency and strategy has been a consistent feature of the *Register*'s engagement with the globalisation phenomenon.

This volume takes the analysis further, both in examining the changing contours of global capitalism at the end of the century, and in demonstrating that no democracy worth the name can any longer be conceived except in terms of a fundamental break with it. In the process, it exposes many illusory responses to globalisation. The essays published here on the contradictions that have been undermining the Swedish, Rhineland and East Asian 'models' go far towards showing how vacuous are the currently fashionable proposals for a 'third way' (even those advanced in Cuba). But it is not only the crisis of all models implicated in globalisation that concerns us here. The essays in this volume also reveal the shallowness and growing instability of the 'democracy' peddled and often put in place by global capitalism's ideologues and state functionaries from Latin America to Russia. That it was always a serious error to take East Asia as offering a 'progressive' model of any kind was very clear long before the economic cataclysm that has now engulfed that region. But even in the core capitalist countries, as several of the essays here also show, democracy is increasingly thin, the public sphere and the autonomy of the state having been drastically curtailed by market forces, and the social democratic parties having been hollowed out by the very political elites who pretend that their 'third way' is a solution to, rather than a symptom of, the crisis of the left.

Yet there is no easy way forward. Among the obstacles examined by the contributors to this volume are, for example, the western working classes' complex implication in globalisation through their pension funds as well as through trade union support for 'progressive competitiveness', and the readiness of some left intellectuals to embrace the idea of a new non-material 'cyber-economy'. Many such problems will have to be confronted and overcome before effective movements able to challenge and transcend the forces that have brought us globalisation will be able to emerge and develop strategies, not only for democratising the economy and the state, but for reconstructing a public sphere where socialist voices can once again be heard. Such movements will need to discover how to make democracy simultaneously meaningful and effective at the local, national and global levels, not least by building new linkages between these levels.

This volume thus bridges the theme of the *Socialist Register 1998*, which drew on the socialist legacy by taking as its focus 'The Communist Manifesto Now', and that of our forthcoming volume for the year 2000, on the theme of 'Necessary Utopias', in which we hope to contribute to the task of developing viable alternatives for socialist democracy in the new century. *The Socialist Register 2000* will appear in the fall of 1999.

Among the contributors to the current volume, Hugo Radice teaches in the Division of Industrial and Labour Studies at the Leeds University Business School. Ursula Huws is a writer and researcher who is Associate Fellow at the Institute for Employment Studies in London and Director of the independent social and economic research consultancy, Analytica. Konstantinos Tsoukalas is Professor of Political

Science at the University of Athens, and Wally Seccombe teaches at the Ontario Institute for Studies in Education in Toronto. David Coates is Director of the International Centre for Labour Studies at the University of Manchester. Birgit Mahnkopf teaches at the Fachhochschule fur Wirtschaft, Berlin, and Mitchell Bernard is in the Department of Political Science at York University, Toronto. Atilio Boron teaches political science at the University of Buenos Aires, and Haroldo Dilla is a researcher and writer in Havana. Adam Tickell teaches Geography at the University of Southampton, England, and Joachim Hirsch teaches Sociology at Johann-Wolfgang-Goethe Universitaet in Frankfurt, Germany. Boris Kagarlitsky is an independent writer and political activist in Moscow, and Sheila Rowbotham is at the Department of Sociology at the University of Manchester.

We want to express our appreciation to all the contributors for the effort they put into this volume, while reminding readers that neither the contributors nor the editors necessarily agree with everything in it. Thanks are also due to Mike Gonzales for his translation of haroldo Dilla's essay from the Spanish, and to Johanna Liddle and Mark-Oliver Johnson for their translations of the essays by Birgit Mahnkopf and Joachim Hirsch from the German. In addition to the advice and help we have received from the *Register*'s Manchester and Toronto Collectives and our Corresponding Editors, the preparation of this volume has been immensely facilitated by the energy, commitment and editorial skills of the *Register*'s assistant at York University, Alan Zuege. We are also grateful to Marsha Niemeijer of York University for her help with proofreading. Dave Timms provided us with invaluable creative help in promoting the *Register* throughout 1998, and we are especially grateful to Sheila Rowbotham and him for organising the *Register*'s celebration of the Communist Manifesto at Conway Hall in London on May 9, 1998. We are proud to conclude this year's volume with 'A Tale That Never Ends' – the remarkable text that Sheila prepared for four outstanding actors to read that evening.

Above all, we want to thank Martin Eve of Merlin Press, our publisher throughout the 35 year history of the *Register*. Martin's dedication to the *Register*'s project, and the skills he brings to it, were never more evident than over the past year. This volume is dedicated to him with deep affection and gratitude.

September 1998 L.P.
C.L.

TAKING GLOBALISATION SERIOUSLY

Hugo Radice

I. INTRODUCTION

More than thirty years ago, the expansion of US corporations abroad through foreign direct investment was already giving rise to a substantial literature on the origins, behaviour and consequences of what were then usually called multinational corporations (e.g. Kindleberger 1970, Vernon 1971). The conventional social sciences responded quickly to these new developments. In international economics, a new sub-discipline arose on the economics of MNCs; in business and management studies, the new field was labelled 'international business'; while international relations and politics specialists created the field of 'international political economy', centered on the international politics of the evolving world economy. At the same time, the reemergence of a more vigorous left from the deep-freeze of the Cold War was generating a body of radical scholarship, especially in the social sciences, which looked at the new phenomenon of MNCs in the framework of revitalised theories of accumulation and imperialism (e.g. Magdoff 1969, Murray 1972, Radice 1975).

Thus, while the term 'globalisation' scarcely existed ten years ago and has enjoyed a meteoric rise as a focus for debate both in academia and in the world at large (Waters 1995, p. 2), its central social institutions and processes – MNCs (now usually renamed TNCs), cross-border flows of foreign investments, technologies and tastes, governmental and intergovernmental policies towards these flows – have in fact been under intensive study for a long time. Indeed, many of the current debates around globalisation, not least its effects upon the nation-state, are clearly prefigured in the 1960s and 1970s (e.g. Servan-Schreiber 1968, Tugendhat 1971, Levinson 1971 in addition to those already cited). Some of the fiercest of these debates, for example about the real extent and significance of globalisation, were in fact being conducted with equal ferocity and on almost exactly the same lines more than twenty years previously.

So what has changed? Why has a hitherto rather distant and esoteric subject suddenly become such a hot intellectual property? The simple answer might be that Foreign Direct Investment (FDI) and other measurable activities have become much more important, and have therefore attracted more attention. But two other factors are also important. First, these activities have intrinsically posed important challenges to established orders, both in the 'real world' of politics and business, and in the theories of the social sciences, and hence those of us who argued for their significance faced a lot of scepticism and resistance. This sort of process is understood well enough in the sociology of knowledge, and it persists to this day.

Secondly, and more importantly, the practices of international business helped to undermine the ability of governments to manage their economies along the established post-war Keynesian lines, and thus contributed to creating the economic crises and the crises of economic policy of the 1970s and 1980s. Indeed, the leaders of international business and international finance have almost without exception lauded and sustained the abandonment of welfare-state Keynesianism in favour of what we now call 'neoliberalism'. Since 1970, we have seen the shift from Keynesianism to monetarism; the breakdown of Bretton Woods; the Reagan/Thatcher assault on labour, the welfare state, and public ownership; and more recently the apparent resurgence of 'flexible', 'Anglo-Saxon' capitalism as against 'Eurosclerosis' and East Asian 'croneyism'. All these may be experienced, from a national perspective within each country, as victories of right over left, market over state, capital over labour; but it is the practices of international business, the core economics and politics of globalisation, that have transmitted, reproduced and refined these shifts.

A decade of debate around the idea of globalisation is at last giving rise to a promising response which can challenge the swaggering triumph of neoliberalism. This essay reviews the debates within the framework of conventional international political economy, in which the central issue is the relationship between the global economy and the nation-state; suggests a critique of this framework, based on a less state-centred analysis of global capitalism; and, finally, briefly points to the political conclusions that flow from this critique.

II. THE GLOBALISATION DEBATE IN INTERNATIONAL POLITICAL ECONOMY

What is globalisation? Most commonly, it is defined as a process through which an increasing proportion of economic, social and cultural transactions take place directly or indirectly between parties in different countries[1]; the term is then synonymous with 'internationalisation'. This sort of definition, used for example by Hirst and Thompson (1996), presupposes an 'original condition', a starting-point for the process, in which the world is made up of distinct and self-sufficient national economies, each under the jurisdiction of an independent nation-state. It leads to the hypotheses that if globalisation proceeds 'far enough' it must lead to the replacement of an 'inter-national' world economy by a single integrated global economy; and that the globalisation process confronts, threatens or undermines the nation-state.

This way of looking at globalisation raises a number of methodological issues. First, the implicit 'national' starting-point makes no long-term historical sense, since 'international' transactions have been crucial to economic and political dynamics in many parts of the world since centuries before the development of industrial capitalism. Secondly, attempts to measure globalisation in the above sense founder on the choice of measures, the availability of data and the time period considered. Such measures are also heavily dependent on the chances of political history and geography, so that international transactions are inevitably more significant for nations that are small, resource-poor, or subject to colonial or other forms of external domination. Thirdly, although a review of these measures quickly reveals enormous quantitative and qualitiative differences in the way different nations are internationally integrated, and of course huge inequalities of condition as well, the model of globalisation in itself abstracts from these differences and inequalities. Fourthly, as a starting-point for analysing the dynamics of the world economy today, this approach falsely counterposes the global to the national, and thus paves the way to seeing the central political issue as one of 'globalisation versus the (national) state'.

Nonetheless, a lot of the debates about the extent and significance of globalisation take place within this framework. In particular, contributors such as Gordon (1988), Hirst and Thompson (1996), Ruigrok and van Tulder (1995), Wade (1996), Zysman (1996) and Weiss (1998) have argued that globalisation has been greatly exaggerated. Eight main conclusions arise from this sceptical literature. Taking these points in turn, but remaining within the same framework of analysis:

1. The extent of globalisation

If we accept as meaningful measures such as trade/GDP or FDI/GDP, and accept the available data, then globalisation may not have occurred between the 1890s and the 1990s, but it *has* occurred between the 1940s and the 1990s. The historical data suggest that since around 1970, the global character of capitalism (measured in these ways) has been substantively restored, after 40 years in which the industrial core – and to some extent other zones – was fragmented into more autonomous national economies. With regard to the core elements of trade, finance and direct investment, this is the conclusion reached in a thorough review of the empirical evidence by Perraton et al (1997) which will not be repeated here. It suggests that globalisation, as a process of change through time, is very much a reality in recent times.

2. 'International' versus 'global'

The counterposition of these two models is abstract and artificial. Historically, the paths of 'national' economic development in *every* country over the last several centuries have been created – consciously or unconsciously, by individuals or states – in a global context. World markets in labour, finance and products have created or denied opportunities for structural transformation to national business leaders and other elite groups; world politics, diplomacy and warfare have shaped the capacities and policies of national governments to direct such transformations. National economies are better seen as zones of relatively deeper economic integration within a single, highly-differentiated world economy; and nation-states as interdependent political entities in a complex inter-state system. On the whole, economic and political interdependence appear to have increased since the 1940s, in line with trends in trade, finance and investment, but the 'system as a whole' has always been both national and global. This argument cannot be pursued further within a framework that automatically counterposes 'state' and 'market', and so will be taken up again in section 3 below.

3. Globalisation or regionalisation

There is a further pointless counterposition in the sceptical account, between globalisation and regionalisation. It is scarcely surprising that in the real world of transport and other distance costs – including those arising from cultural differences, protectionism, etc. – businesses will look first to neighbouring countries for markets, labour, capital, or production sites. Hence higher levels of trade, capital flows, etc., will be found between adjacent territories such as Canada and the USA. In the colonial era, trade and capital flows were less geographically regional simply because the political systems of colonialism were designed to reduce those 'distance costs' for the merchants and financiers of the colonial power (and greatly increase them, of course, for those of other powers). Quite why the recent pattern of regionalisation should be considered as anything other than a concrete *form* of internationalisation is not clear. Interestingly, the Japanese debates on globalisation recognise that intra- and inter-regional trade and investment flows are intimately related (see e.g. Hasegawa and Hook, 1998, part I).

4. A 'triad' phenomenon?

It is undoubtedly the case that trade and investment flows are concentrated among the advanced industrial countries; again, this is hardly surprising, since they constitute the largest and richest markets in a world where most economic activity is now based on production for sale at a profit. At one level, this is a conclusion that only counts against the most extreme 'straw man' version of globalisation as a homogenising process, yielding equality of economic conditions between all nations. At another level, however, it is significantly misleading, in so far as it implies that globalisation (however exaggerated or mythical overall) is somehow more of a reality in the OECD countries. On the contrary, it is as a result of ever-deeper international integration that what used to be called the Third World has become ever more fragmented and differentiated in the last thirty years. Without, of course, challenging the 'triad' for industrial supremacy, the so-called NICs have built substantial industrial capacities and won significant shares of global industrial exports. At the same time, the most impoverished regions of the world are 'marginalised' precisely through exclusion from the global economy. Finally, the financial crises that have struck so many non-OECD countries in the last twenty years, and indeed some 'weaker' OECD members such as Mexico (1994) and South Korea (1997-8), have their origins and their resolutions in the subordination of national financial systems to world capital and money markets.

5. Embeddedness – 'holding down the global'

Sceptics argue that the globalisation myth centres on an image of hypermobile capital, or better, *vulture capital*, circulating high in the ethereal realm of global money, and descending to feast on the state treasuries and pay-packets of immobile governments and workers. They rightly point out that while this might apply to short-term or explicitly speculative capital movements – holdings of cash or short-dated bonds – the more significant and transformative capital movements involve putting down economic, social and political roots. Direct investments typically lead to the purchase and installation of fixed plant and equipment, the training and retraining of staff whose productivity depends on length of service and mutual loyalty, and the long-term nurturing of essential supporting relations with suppliers, customers and above all national and local governments and officials[2]. Such arguments can draw effectively both on transaction-costs economics, and on the 'embeddedness' literature, which usually refers back to Polányi (1944) and lies at the heart of the modern comparative sociology of economic systems.

However, while the sceptics are right to reject a naive 'vulture capital' model, they tend to exaggerate the extent to which capital can be 'held down'. First, many of the investments that have most concerned analysts of globalisation are precisely ones which empirically require little in the way of sunk costs: not only the labour-intensive manufacturing, assembly and service work that forms the 'new international division of labour' (Frobel et al 1980, Nash and Fernandez-Kelly 1983), but also some of the most highly-skilled activities in R&D and finance, where human resources are highly mobile. Secondly, when investors do 'tie up' capital and thereby put it at risk, they demand 'incentives' which have the effect of off-loading that risk onto local taxpayers and workers: in a world where there is intense competition for inward investments, these demands are usually met[3]. Thirdly, 'embeddedness' is by no means exclusively a local or national phenomenon. A dense network of international institutions, both private and public, also 'embed' businesses operating across borders, while business practices, norms, standards and cultures are increasingly shaped and reproduced at a global level[4].

6. The powers of national governments

In the ongoing debate in IPE, this is the critical issue. There is little doubt that deeper international economic integration, and especially the globalisation of finance, has reduced significantly the 'traditional' post-1945 capacity of national governments to manage 'their' economies by means of fiscal and monetary policies, labour and welfare legislation, and a variegated regulatory regime for business which included extensive public ownership. Thus for Robert Gilpin, by the 1980s, 'the fundamental question initially posed by late nineteenth-century Marxists and subsequently by Keynes regarding the ultimate compatibility of domestic welfare capitalism with a liberal international order once again came to the fore' (Gilpin 1987 p. 389).

However, the sceptics, from Warren (1971) to Gordon (1988) to Weiss (1998), nonetheless argue about the extent and the reversibility of this loss of 'state capacity'.

Broadly, there are three themes in this strand of scepticism. The first is related closely to the empirical arguments already reviewed on the extent of globalisation: for example, Weiss (1998, pp. 190-2) surveys evidence that governments do have the power to sustain differences in fiscal and monetary policies, while Helleiner (1996) argues that financial liberalisation is in fact reversible. A common theme is that policy changes which have been presented as the result of inexorable globalisation have in fact been chosen, more or less freely, by governments, perhaps in response to special *domestic* interests, and these governments can equally well choose to restore the *status quo ante.*[5] Secondly, particular varieties of state, or of 'state-societal arrangements' (Hart 1992), may be better equipped to resist the erosion of state capacity, or to refashion it around new zones of autonomy: thus Weiss (1998) cites the 'governed interdependence' between state and business in Japan as permitting the evolution of industrial policy rather than its abandonment. Thirdly, it may be argued that in the context of supranational regionalisation, traditional capacities could be recovered at a regional level, for example in the European Union (e.g. Chorney 1996), although this would require a major advance in the degree of political integration (Hirst & Thompson, 1996, pp. 163-7).

Many other writers, however, from Murray (1971) to Gill and Law (1988) to Drache (1996) continue to insist that there has been a real loss in the policy autonomy of national governments which cannot easily be recovered. Empirically this view rests mainly on two points. Firstly, the changes from broadly Keynesian-welfare-statist policies to broadly neoliberal policies have been so consistent through the past twenty years and all around the world that it is hard to see them as either contingent or the result of independent policy choices by national governments. If there are certain exceptions, or variations, this is scarcely surprising given the enormous and indeed growing inequalities of wealth and power, both private and public, in the world today; in any case, many of the exceptions cited by the sceptics are contested[6]. Secondly, the transformation of the IMF, the World

Bank and the GATT/WTO from benign intergovernmental regulators to the global policemen of the free market represents a deep institutionalisation of this trend; one which is buttressed by the proliferation of other forms of transnational regulation, both regional (NAFTA, EU) and global (OECD, BIS), whose institutions by and large sing to the same tune. Again, the fact that, for example, the OECD has been unable as yet to bring to fruition the Multilateral Agreement on Investment (MAI) merely indicates that in a highly differentiated world capitalism the establishment of uniform norms is bound to be a difficult matter: twenty years ago, even the drafting of the MAI would have been unthinkable.

Within the conventional IPE framework, the debate on the continued existence of state capacities will continue to centre on the accretion of empirical evidence.[7] It certainly remains feasible to press for the restoration of regulatory public powers over private interests, both nationally and transnationally, if only because, as Hirst and Thompson (1996) in particular emphasise, the nation-state remains the primacy locus of political legitimation.[8] However, the real need is to address the question of what it is that 'the state' is trying to do, and why (Panitch 1994).

7. Globalisation, capitalism and the 'Anglo-Saxon' model

An apparent implication of globalisation is that it not only is intimately associated with neoliberal policies, but also is leading to the dominance of liberal or 'Anglo-Saxon' capitalism, and the gradual erosion or (as in the Soviet case) abrupt disappearance of all alternative economic systems. Proponents of globalisation on the political right and in much of the business press make no secret of their objective: a universal 'free market' capitalism in which the state is 'rolled back' to the limited functions supposedly sanctioned by Adam Smith. In the 1990s, the 'Anglo-Saxons' have been on a roll: they can point to the collapse of the Soviet model, the 'sclerosis' of continental Europe and Japan, the renewed dynamism of liberalised Latin America, and most recently the 'East Asian crisis', as convincing evidence for their case. This is particularly galling for globalisation sceptics, since many of them have either contributed to or drawn upon literatures which champion alternative models on the basis of their superior performance in earlier decades.

One line of response in the face of globalist triumphalism is to continue to argue, empirically or theoretically, the merits of more organised or 'trust-based' forms of capitalism. Thus for Carlin and

Soskice (1997), it is precisely because of its distinctive institutional structures that Germany has been able to weather the unprecedented strains of absorbing the former East Germany; while Berggren and Nomura (1997) argue that despite some changes in Japanese business behaviour in the 1990s, its system too demonstrates remarkable resilience. In more theoretical vein, both Chang (1994) and Lo (1997) convincingly draw on heterodox economics to press the case for forms of state intervention in industry; while in the field of labour studies and human resource management, the debate on skill formation and productivity growth still goes against the neoliberals (Ashton and Green 1996). Secondly, if, as appears to be the case, Anglo-Saxon liberalism is closely associated with regressive tax and welfare policies, and a redistribution of income and wealth from rich to poor, this can be presented as an unacceptable price to be paid. Similar arguments, rooted in the traditional claim about the market's failure to deal with economic externalities and social costs, are advanced from an environmental standpoint. Thirdly, growing instability in the world economy can be blamed not on too much regulation, but rather on too little. Thus, Wade and Veneroso (1998) attribute responsibility for the East Asian financial crisis on both the deregulation of national financial systems, as in South Korea in the 1990s, and the absence of regulation which generated excessive lending to the region by American and European banks.

On the face of it, the empirical evidence from the 1990s does on balance suggest a strengthening of the Anglo-Saxon model.[9] On the other hand, the fashion for identifying and contrasting competing models of capitalism, which was given a strong fillip by the collapse of the Soviet system, conceals important methodological weaknesses, many of them inherited from the Cold War comparisons of models of 'industrialism' or 'post-industrialism': notably a tendency to lapse into crude functionalism. In addition, if we examine in more detail some of the key institutional components of the models, there is enormous variability within particular countries, both through time[10] and across sectors, which tends to undermine the emphasis in the comparative literature on the 'path-dependence' of national systems. Finally, it is not clear whether superior performance should be attributed to institutional differences, or whether the persistence of particular institutional patterns should be attributed to superior economic dynamism, or to the possession of specific military, political or economic advantages that have no particular institutional shape.[11]

8. Building alternatives to neo-liberal globalisation

Whatever the long-term prospects for the Anglo-Saxon model of capitalism, the current political dominance of neo-liberalism is only too apparent. But the sceptics argue that this can be challenged by mobilising those interests that have suffered from this dominance, essentially around the reconstruction of a regulatory, interventionist state. If globalisation, deregulation, privatisation, etc., directly benefit particular groups of capitalists[12] or bureaucrats, then this can be reversed in the political arena by offering an alternative that is more attractive. Generally, the sceptics seek to update social democracy: what they offer is not a simple return to the postwar recipe of state intervention, welfarism, etc. – nowadays routinely caricatured even by supposed progressives as 'tax-and-spend' policies – but a 'modernised' social democracy which accepts the basic economic and political structures of capitalism, but seeks to ameliorate the outcome for the disadvantaged. The main political goal to which this capacity is to be directed is the traditional social democratic one of improving living standards, defined now in ways that take on board the concerns of 'new social movements'. Crucially, the state can and should focus on improving human resources: on increasing workforce skills, the stock of productive knowledge, and the efficiency of both private and public management. In the context of more competitive world markets and the grudgingly-admitted greater openness to trade and capital movements, these improvements in human resources are viewed as the necessary foundation of international competitiveness (Reich 1992). The apparent failure of public ownership, central planning and other 'old' forms of state intervention makes imperative the adoption of a new form of 'mixed economy', in which the proven incentive systems of the private sector are harnessed to the altruistic goals established by the political process.

The sceptics remain convinced, as already noted, that the state has the capacity to tame the forces of globalisation. A measured reregulation of global trade and finance can be achieved by a mix of national, regional and global initiatives: these can be constructed by convincing financiers and markets that these measures will safeguard the benefits of liberalisation, and reduce the risk of costly major crises (see e.g. Hirst and Thompson 1996, ch. 9; Wade and Veneroso 1998).[13] Furthermore, a recasting of industrial, education and employment policies by a 'developmental' (Amsden 1989, Wade 1990) or 'catalytic' (Weiss 1998) state can allow a country to respond effectively to the challenge of global markets and avoid being caught in a low-skill, low-wage, low-investment vicious circle. Since for the sceptics transnational corporations remain bound to their country of origin, they can be harnessed as the flagships of national regeneration.

Reviewing the actual pattern of events over the past thirty years, it is very hard to see much evidence for the feasibility of this political strategy. Initiatives to reregulate global trade and finance, from the 'New International Economic Order' of the 1970s to the Tobin tax, have made no headway whatsoever. Within Europe, the Maastricht Treaty has enshrined the monetarist, free-market core of the EU; despite the existence of a 'social chapter' in the treaty, there is a clear trend towards levelling-down of welfare, and the 'flexible' labour markets championed as much by 'New Labour' in Britain as by the bosses in Germany, France and Italy (Radice 1999). Equally telling is the case of Eastern Europe. Here, Amsden's attempt (Amsden et al, 1994) to apply the lessons of South Korea to the restoration of capitalism in the region failed totally to connect with political realities: far from the market 'meeting its match' as she predicted, a pragmatically-moderated neoliberal programme has been remarkably successful in ensuring economic and political stability, in large measure due to the pervasive role of Western capital (Radice 1998b). As for East Asia, it is far too soon to judge how well the benchmark exemplars of state activism, South Korea and Japan, will weather the storm. Can the South Korean débacle be blamed on the liberalisation and opening of its financial sector, and on the weakening of the state's powers of economic direction, in the last ten years? Or did these developments simply indicate that the state-business arrangements were now 'catalysing' the breakneck expansion of South Korean capital abroad, rather than the development of the national economy?

In the end, however, the globalisation debate yields such unsatisfying political conclusions because its conceptual apparatus is so impoverished. The sceptics *assume* the degree of state autonomy that is necessary for their political prescriptions to have credibility. Clearly, if the state is (a) powerful, and (b) dominated by the democratic will, then globalisation and its discontents can be readily thrown aside in favour of a more acceptable agenda of national economic and social progress; what is more, there is then no need to contemplate the messy and thus far unproductive strategy of building an international movement. However, there are strong arguments against this Panglossian position.

III. A CRITIQUE: BRINGING CAPITALISM BACK IN

As I have already indicated, the root problem with the sceptical critique of globalisation is its view of the state, and in particular the autonomy of the state. Although this is a view shared across a number of intellectual traditions in the social sciences, it has been articulated most explicitly in modern international political economy. The 1985 collection of essays edited by Peter Evans, Dietrich Rueschemeyer and Theda Skocpol under the title *Bringing the State Back In* (Evans et al. 1985) epitomises this view. The editors aimed to go beyond what they saw as overgeneralised neo-Marxist and neo-Weberian views, on state autonomy and on state strength respectively, through detailed case studies which could reveal the more significant structures and processes at work within states and between states and social groups. Although they frequently stressed the open-ended nature of these explorations, the ultimate aim was to develop 'state-centered explanations' (op.cit, p. 7) which would in turn help to develop effective state policies: for example, Rueschemeyer and Evans (ch. 2) explicitly tried to identify the conditions for 'effective state intervention' (p. 44 and *passim*) in economic and industrial development.

Cammack (1989,1990) has argued strongly that this volume was part of a project designed to break with the Marxist or neo-Marxist approach to the state in the Third World, which in turn had developed in the 1960s and 1970s out of the theories of imperialism and under-development. Marxist debates on the state in the 1970s had moved beyond the limitations of traditional structuralist and instrumental views, and explored a wide range of cases and issues using more flexible concepts, for example that of 'relative autonomy', that could handle the contingent and variable aspects of capitalist state institutions and practices. One result of this was a considerable overlap in research agendas and debates between neo-Marxists and more orthodox social scientists in many fields. In the 'final analysis', however, all varieties of Marxism see the state through the prism of the class nature of capitalism. While those who adopted the neo-Marxist approach and sought to change the state from within quickly found themselves marginalised or ejected,[14] most mainstream social scientists found it easier to distance themselves from a class approach.

The collapse of the Soviet Union and its satellite states in Eastern Europe made this task much easier. In the short term, this was readily accepted as prima facie evidence of the failure of Marxism, which had remained the official ideology of the Soviet bloc: the attempts, by

Western anti-Stalinist Marxists and by East European 'third way' advocates alike, to establish a bridgehead for democratic socialism were quickly routed by the triumphant march eastwards of the 'free market'. The most that socialists could hope for, apparently, was to work for an amelioration of capitalism, without even the long-term perspective of revolutionary transformation that earlier generations of reformists, from Bernstein to Crosland, had explicitly retained.

However, the neoliberal triumph has been short lived. The demise of the Soviet model led first to expressions of the need for an alternative bogeyman with which to scare the citizens of the 'free world': radical Islam, eco-terrorism, drugs, economic migration, all variants on the theme of 'the barbarian at the gates'. But it was soon apparent that capitalism itself retained all its historical capacity to wreak destruction upon humanity, whether in its birth-pangs in the rubble of communism, in the industrialisation of China, in the persistence of mass unemployment in Western Europe, or in the financial crises that engulfed Britain in 1992, Mexico in 1994 and now East Asia in 1997-8.

From this standpoint, what is abundantly clear is that globalisation is intrinsically a *capitalist* process. In the context of globalisation, it makes no sense to analyse the state in abstraction from capitalism, because the concrete conditions and events that confront states at present arise from economic and social processes organised along capitalist lines. This is not to say that all, or indeed any, such events can be reduced to the inevitable outcome of some sort of mechanical unfolding of history. But in the face of widespread and repeated phenomena such as high levels of cyclical and structural unemployment; financial crises caused by over-lending and inadequate regulation; the subordination of education and culture to commercial forces; the dismantling of public systems of social security in favour of private pension rackets; the ever-widening gap between rich and poor; bitter struggles over trade union rights; environmental threats arising from uncontrolled commercial exploitation of nature; – need I go on? Can *any* of these be adequately understood as the outcome of 'autonomous' state actions and processes? Of course not; which is why in *practice* the theorists of 'stateness' have to bring in through the back door the factors that they dismiss at the front door as smacking of 'economic determinism' or 'class reductionism'. This is brought out very clearly in a recent essay by Peter Evans (1997), which is subtitled 'reflections on stateness in an era of globalisation'.

Twelve years after *Bringing the State Back In*, Evans reviews the challenge that globalisation in its neoliberal form poses to the state, but he continues to claim from the East Asian cases '...the possibility of a positive connection between high stateness ... and success in a globalising economy' (Evans 1997, p. 70). Like other sceptics, Evans emphasises the ideological dimension of globalisation, which is carried through into formal injunctions to individual states through Anglo-American dominance in the intergovernmental organisations of the IMF, WTO, etc. However, an 'economically stateless world' cannot provide the stability and order that transnational investors require, and the complexities and risks of global finance impress this need ever more firmly upon them: 'While globalisation does make it harder for states to exercise economic initiative, it also increases both the potential returns from effective state action and the costs of incompetence' (p. 74). In addition, the 'new institutional economics' of the information age means that attacks on the state as 'rent-seeking' are blunted by the increased economic importance of public goods, whose availability depends on public enforcement of property rights and/or on public provision. Even a revived role for 'civil society', Evans argues, does not mean a correspondingly reduced role for the state, because of evidence for 'state-society synergy': civic associations require a capable and involved state if they are to act effectively in society. Thus, for both 'external' and 'internal' reasons, a 'return of the pendulum' back towards 'stateness' seems likely.

But what is the *content* of this stateness? This is where capitalism suddenly enters as a concept, slipping in through the back door, for as a result of the economic dominance of transnational business, it seems to Evans that the state can only be restored to a positive role if that role is restricted to '...activities essential for sustaining the profitability of transnational markets' (p. 85). The welfare state remains diminished, and indeed delivering services and security to business 'means devoting more resources to the repression of the more desperate and reckless among the excluded, both domestic and international' (p. 86). In other words, the state is being restructured around a specifically *capitalist* project of 'development', in which private profits are promoted at the expense of poor people and poor countries. Evans concludes by finding some hope that social interests other than business elites just might create 'state-society synergies' with 'beleaguered state managers and politicians disenchanted with leaner, meaner stateness' (p. 86); indeed he finds this 'no less implausible than the alliances that were actually forged between labour organisations and the state during the early decades of the twentieth century'.

Thus the trajectory of Evans' work leads back from an abstract emphasis on the developmental role of the state, to an acknowledgement that the actual thrust of state activities is determined at present by the power of the business elite, in other words the capitalist class; and that a real alternative to the dominance of neoliberalism depends on the political mobilisation of 'citizens and communities'. What remains, however, is the need to link this more systematically to an analysis of whether and how the economics of capitalism have changed.

If we start from the capitalist nature of globalisation, the first task is to characterize briefly the main features of global capitalism today, abstracting from its divisions into nations. Precisely because of the global integration of production, markets and finance, the common dynamic of this system is more pervasive, and certain important features can therefore be seen to apply everywhere. Central to this common dynamic has been a shift of economic and political power towards capitalists across much of the world. In the developed capitalist countries, the century or so up to the 1970s saw significant gains for workers, in the context of persistent national rivalries, world wars and the secession of the Soviet bloc from world capitalism. The latter decades of this period also saw an end to formal colonialism and the beginnings of a genuinely global and potentially democratic political order.[15] Since 1970, global integration has incorporated the former Second and Third Worlds firmly back into the capitalist fold, not merely by forcing open national markets and directing local production to the world market through debt peonage, liberalisation and privatisation, but also by incorporating local business and bureaucratic elites into the political, social and cultural world of the emerging global capitalist class. Above all, the greater mobility and penetrative capacity of capital has forged powerful weapons for rolling back the gains of workers in all countries. Pursuing this in more detail, I suggest eight features, the first four being 'microeconomic' features, while the remainder emerge at some more aggregate level:

1. Decline in labour's market power

Changes in technology and in patterns of demand have seriously affected the market power of labour. The concept of technological unemployment remains an ideological one, designed to scare workers into concessions: in the long run, accumulation in capitalist economies is based on employing labour, not on employing 'technology'. However, in advanced industrial societies, employment and production have shifted towards non-material 'service' activities, some of which are knowledge- and skill-intensive, and away from manual manufacturing tasks. The shift in demand has been magnified by the threat of job flight for manual workers in particular. The reality or threat of mass unemployment has enabled employers to weaken the organisations of labour either directly, or through legislative changes. None of this is gainsaid by the experience of certain countries such as South Korea or South Africa where at times industrial expansion has enabled significant increases in union membership and real wages. At the same time, the role of wages in normal cyclical rhythms of accumulation continues: thus in the U.S.A. at present, although the expansion has been unprecedentedly long, labour shortages are now (June 1998) starting to hit profits.

2. Reassertion of control over labour

There have been substantial changes in capitalist management, which has developed and refined both carrots and sticks, from the shopfloor to the boardroom, aimed at increasing the productivity and intensity of labour. Much – far too much – has been made of the idea of a new 'post-Fordist' era, of smaller-scale, flexible production systems in which workers have to be reskilled and reempowered in return for providing sophisticated, high-quality products: this bears as much relation to the realities of workplace domination and control as the ideology of the free market does to the real world of monopoly and *caveat emptor*. In substance, the changes in recent decades centre on the reassertion of management control over labour through a refined mix of the strategies of 'direct control' and 'responsible autonomy' (Friedman 1977). Nonetheless, despite the apparent sophistication of production and management systems, they still depend as always on the compliance of workers.

3. Corporate finance and control

The global tide of privatisation has opened up vast new markets for private capitalists, as well as handing over to them control over vital physical assets: not only in the transport, telecommunications and energy sectors, but in heavy industry, finance, tourism and increasingly now in health, education and social services. This has been accompanied by a dramatic extension of the corporate form of capitalist ownership and finance, in particular the shift from narrow ownership coupled with bank finance towards equity finance.[16] This shift is partly a response to the increased competitiveness and volatility of markets, since wider equity finance allows the 'insider' interests (including core banks) to offload risk onto outsiders. However, when taken in conjunction with well-orchestrated panics over public pension provision, it also mobilises at low cost the lifetime savings of workers, helping to tie the latter in to the practice and ideology of capitalist ownership.[17]

4. Capitalist competition reasserted

In the post-1945 'golden age', both conventional industrial economics and the heterodox traditions of institutionalism, Keynesianism and neo-Marxism argued, albeit with different terminologies, that competitive capitalism based on entrepreneurial small business had been progressively replaced by monopoly structures and practices. Scale economies and the high cost of innovation required market dominance, supernormal profits and price leadership, relegating the individual entrepreneur to marginal sectors or a strictly subordinate and dependent role. The last thirty years have provided ample grounds for restoring the classical view (of Smith, Marx or later Schumpeter) that competition is not about market equilibrium and prices, but about the search for sources of market power and profit. The giant corporations of today are not stagnant managerial bureaucracies, but dynamic and flexible profit-seekers – and transnational expansion has been a central concrete form of this competitive accumulation.

5. The economic role of the state

Although the neoliberal assault on the state has done little in most countries to reduce its absolute weight in the economy, as conventionally measured by ratios of public expenditure to national income, it has generated fundamental changes in the way the public sector is financed and managed. The key monetarist ideas, that 'bloated' public finances were inflationary and 'crowded out' private investment, reflected the growing realisation in capitalist circles that there was, otherwise, no logical limit to the enlargement of the public sector: ultimately, Keynesianism and the welfare/warfare state might turn out to be proto-socialist, rather than just a modified form of capitalism.[18] The enforcement of monetarist targets for public spending and debt, whether through the judgements of currency and financial markets or at the behest of lenders, has halted the ratchet-like trend of expansion in the public sector, with well-known consequences. Equally important is the shift in power within states towards finance ministries, central banks and cabinet offices, with spending departments obliged to realise 'efficiency gains', that is cuts, on a permanent year-by-year basis (Cox 1992). This has fed down through service providers in the form of financial and bureaucratic controls, applied in a way that strikingly resembles Soviet-style central planning, with all its familiar outcomes: a fixation on a limited range of quantitative targets at the expense of quality or content, the substitution of individual for collective incentives, relentless cost-cutting, demoralisation, corruption and waste.

6. States and markets in global capitalism

As already discussed in section II, this restructured economic role of the state has been generalised and enforced both through financial markets, and through inter-governmental bodies and processes. However, it also results from the process of economic integration itself. Competition for world markets ensures that, as long as states continue to exercise territorial jurisdiction in economic matters, they will continue to try to respond to the needs of 'their' national business sectors: hence the promotion of 'neo-mercantilist' policies, typically by industrial ministries (supported by the defense sector on security grounds). On the other hand, the more that accumulation by the national business sector is itself internationalised – through exporting, outward investment, technology imports, or whatever – the more it will need to relate also, directly or indirectly, to other states, and the more different states will need actively to manage resulting common interests and conflicting goals alike. This reality, of a multiplicity of competing states and capitals, is mostly analysed through bargaining models (e.g. Stopford and Strange 1991), but such an approach may conceal the extent to which states are so politically penetrated and dominated by business[19] that they cannot be seen as having independent objectives to be pursued by bargaining. Indeed, it is precisely in conforming to the agenda of business – transmitted through markets as well as political processes – that states have 'restructured' away from their Keynesian and welfarist goals. In the post-colonial underdeveloped countries and in the restored capitalisms in Eastern Europe, new comprador bourgeoisies emerge, as internationalisation forces national capitalists to link up (in a subordinate position) with powerful transnational interests: as McMichael (1996) argues, 'globalisation' has replaced 'modernisation' as the dominant ideology of development.

7. Transnational politics and regional groupings

Post-war Keynesian-welfare and postcolonial states, focused on national economic management and development, formed a transnational political order in which – in contrast to the interwar period – a range of multilateral intergovernmental organisations were developed with the purpose of structuring and regulating inter-state relations. This inter-state system in principle provided an economic and security environment which supported national capital accumulation. In particular, through the Bretton Woods institutions, adjustment mechanisms which could help all countries to avoid a return to the trade wars and depression of the interwar years. Despite apparent principles of equality among states, the system's installation and maintenance depended crucially on US hegemony. The mushrooming of global trade, investment and finance from the 1960s placed extra demands on this inter-state system at exactly the time when that hegemony was being challenged in the economic sphere by Western Europe and Japan. For some twenty-five years, calls for a fundamental redesign of the IGO structure have been resisted in favour of *ad hoc* changes of their agenda, supplemented by an updated form of traditional 'great power' diplomacy, of which the G5/7/8 'economic summits' are the most visible part. The existence and importance of these transnational political structures bears out the view of globalisation sceptics that the state has not withered away; on the other hand, repeated forecasts that trade and currency tensions would lead to the breakdown of inter-state cooperation and a return to interwar-style protectionism have proved wide of the mark. Regional groupings represent an attempt to create more durable and legitimate transnational political structures. Far from indicating an alternative to 'universal' global integration, they rest on exactly the same economic foundations: the greater intensity of economic integration between neighbouring countries generates greater pressure to find collective solutions.

8. The new imperialism

From around 1870, formal colonial empires and informal hegemonic powers formed an imperialist system, in which less developed and militarily weaker regions were politically and economically subordinated to one or other of the competing imperial powers. Formal political independence did not of itself change anything in countries locked into a traditional primary-producer role in the international division of labour, and in any case informal spheres of influence came to be exercised through bodies such as the British Commonwealth, the

Alliance for Progress in the Americas, and regional US-led security bodies like NATO. In the 1960s and 1970s, neo-Marxist and dependency writings broadly captured the continuance of imperialism, based on economic and political subordination, and generating still-increasing gaps in living standards between developed and underdeveloped regions. More or less radical policies of national development in those decades often challenged directly the power of foreign capital through nationalisations, forms of economic planning, and discriminatory monetary, fiscal and trade policy instruments, but with little success. In the 1970s, the growth of global capital markets appeared to offer a 'non-political' substitute for official aid flows, but did nothing in itself to change the chronic tendency towards balance of payments crises in LDCs.

The shift towards so-called export-oriented industrialisation accelerated as the problem of external debt spread to engulf most of the non-oil-producing Third World: in the 1980s, this provided the right circumstances for a major economic, political and ideological offensive aimed at 'opening up' the markets and resources of the Third World again to foreign capital. As the annual reports of the UNCTAD's Division on Transnational Corporations and Investment have charted (e.g. UNCTAD 1996), there have been almost universal moves to liberalise controls on trade and FDI, including controls on foreign ownership of banks and other financial institutions, and of minerals, energy, transport and communications companies. It is these foreign investments that form the core of the new imperialism. As Sunkel (1973) argued long ago, once these investments become central to development strategy, they serve to tie local capitalists, managers, politicians and bureaucrats to the economic interests of parent TNCs and other foreign investors. This is supported by the extensive role of the IMF and the World Bank in designing and enforcing 'structural adjustment' policies; the regular participation of the elites in transnational political forums both official (IMF, etc.) and unofficial (e.g. the annual Davos conferences); by the continued education of these elites in the leading business and other graduate schools of the USA and Western Europe; and by routine corruption and kleptocracy, as notoriously in Indonesia.

IV. CONCLUSION: RESPONDING TO GLOBALISATION

What conclusions, then, does the 'globalisation debate' lead to when recast in this light? First, in the last thirty years or so national economies have become significantly more internationally integrated, and as a result national governments have lost much of the autonomy that they enjoyed in economic policy-making. This has restored the salience of world market forces in shaping economic outcomes, and encouraged a halting and *ad hoc* multiplication of intergovernmental institutions and processes. Secondly, the vast majority of the largest privately-owned firms, in all sectors and countries of origin, operate transnational networks of production, and in turn generate lower-level networks of trade and production that engage a significant proportion of formal-sector workers everywhere. Thirdly, notwithstanding the continued differences in national legal and regulatory systems, a growing proportion of workers find themselves entering labour markets that are *de facto* global. Fourthly, nation-states are an integral part of the process: they have accommodated and even accelerated this global integration with policy changes that have shifted the balance of economic and political power towards employers and owners, and away from the majority of workers and their dependents.

For a century, despite a lot of lip-service to internationalism, socialist and progressive movements of all kinds have functioned primarily at the national level and below: this has been true as much of trade unions and other organisations of 'civil society' as of political parties. Given the resulting legacy of institutions, practices and political cultures, and the gains in economic justice and political democracy realised through national struggles during that century, it is hardly surprising that the immediate reaction to the perceived threat of globalisation is framed at the national level. Accustomed as most of us are to the formal structures and processes of electoral democracy, we seek to bring the issue on the agenda of our organisations, and we look to national government to orchestrate a response. We look for single-issue alliances to build support for such responses, for example linking trade unions, environmental groups, and consumer organisations in challenging excessively pro-business measures of privatisation and deregulation.

The problem is that, when we get to the national level, we find that the state has become increasingly structured around an agenda that intrinsincally excludes or subordinates our concerns. On the national terrain, for example, a weakened labour movement may, as in the UK, find itself excluded, as tripartite structures are abandoned as part of a general assault on labour. On global trade and investment issues, crucial debates and decisions have moved to little-known and relatively inaccessible intergovernmental bureaucracies, allowing 'our' governments to say that their hands are tied: indeed, in heavily-indebted countries these unelected bureaucracies take over key governmental policy functions.

In these circumstances we have two choices, if a straighforward reactive resistance along customary lines fails (which is clearly not always the case). First, we can accept the limitations of national politics and seek to identify new and effective policy aims and instruments. This is what is offered, in very different ways, by the reconstituted social-democratic parties of the left, and the conservative-nationalist parties of the right. For the latter, globalisation has cruelly undermined their vision of a nation united against its enemies, because big business insists on being free to operate on a world stage. The revival of conservative-nationalism in Europe and elsewhere is built on a populist response to this, and traditional big-business parties alternate between resistance and concessions as they seek to limit the appeal of the renewed far right.[20] But social-democratic parties, including the ex-communist parties of Eastern Europe, have recovered electorally after the long onslaught of neoliberalism, essentially by accommodating to it. As well as accepting fiscal and monetary constraints and rejecting protectionism, they now offer a 'new New Deal' that enshrines the world market as the ultimate arbiter over what is and is not produced, and incorporates the political ideology of individualism into everyday life at work and at home. Amid all the talk of joint private/public ventures, of new ways of regulating the private sector and of 'supplementing' public welfare provision, in the end this amounts to a political sea-change, in which the fundamental interests of business – a cheap and appropriately-trained workforce, gullible consumers and 'responsive' regulators – form a protected core in the political agenda, while everything else depends on 'what we can afford'. Above all, 'we' have to accept the real world by pursuing the common national goal of world market competitiveness, through improving the productivity of labour: the main consequence of this being an inexorable pressure to 'level down' wages and conditions, whatever is said about the virtues of 'reskilling', 'increasing value added' and so on.

Alternatively, we can seek to develop a transnational collective response. This is still often enough rejected as a desirable but hopelessly unrealistic aim. Yet if we believe that effective social movements arise when the activities of participants create shared circumstances and immediate interests, as well as beliefs, then deeper global integration is precisely creating the basis for transnational social movements. This is certainly the case for labour movements today.[21]

Quite apart from the more spectacular demonstrations of solidarity, such as over the Renault-Vilvoorde closure, and in support of dockers in Liverpool and Australia, to an increasing extent routine collective bargaining is undertaken in a global context. The threat of transfer of jobs to overseas affiliates hangs over local and national negotiators in all the more mobile industries,[22] while public sector workers are told that the world's financial markets will not tolerate the increase in public spending that would result from higher pay increases. Most recently, the campaign against the OECD's Multilateral Agreement on Investment has brought together international NGOs concerned with environmental protection and poverty, trade unionists seeking to maintain labour standards, and protection-minded national business sectors. Although it can be argued that the crucial factor in temporarily halting the MAI was the unwillingness of President Clinton to risk splitting the bizarre coalition of interests that make up the Democratic Party in a mid-term election year, the campaign began with, and is being continued by, a grass-roots transnational alliance rooted in shared interests.

None of this is to deny that the development of alternatives to present-day global capitalism requires an enormous political effort at the local and national levels. If capital is to be tamed, let alone supplanted as the main organising concept in our political economy, we obvously have to craft alternative forms of economic and social organisation in each state as well as across states (Albo 1997, Panitch 1996). But a transnational dimension to this work is both necessary and feasible.

NOTES

1 Indirectly in cases where an intranational transaction is induced by or contingent upon an international transaction.

2 Similar arguments were advanced some years ago, for example by Moran (1974) in his concept of the 'obsolescing bargain': fixed investments (in this case in the copper industry) would give host governments the leverage needed to strike a better deal with investors.

3 Thus *Business Central Europe*, June 1998, blames the low level of FDI in Estonia on its lack of government incentives (p. 10), and praises the announcement of "long-awaited" new incentives in the Czech Republic (p. 25).

4 On the internationalisation of state structures see Picciotto 1991.

5 This point is taken up again in the next section.

6 For example, contrast the rosy view of Germany's current prospects in Weiss (1998, ch. 5) with that of Streeck (1997) as well as the essay by Mahnkopf in this *Register*.

7 Interestingly, Rodrik argued in a recent study, published by the prestigious and mainstream Institute for International Economics in Washington, that globalisation had 'gone too far', and could not be guaranteed to give rise to unequivocal welfare benefits either within or between nations (Rodrik 1997) .

8 Except of course when global or regional 'powers' choose to override this principle and 'intervene'.

9 This proposition is developed more fully in general terms in Radice (1998a), and in the case of Europe in Radice (1999).

10 For example, Japan's industrial finance was largely stock-market-based before World War II, while the USA's was significantly bank-based prior to the Great Depression.

11 For example, both Japan and Germany were banned from military research after the Axis defeat. This may be more important in explaining their subsequent industrial dynamism than certain institutional features of their 'innovation systems' which only emerged later on.

12 For an extreme example, see Wade and Veneroso's reference to 'anecdotal evidence' that the bribery of key officials by Japanese and Western financial institutions played a part in South Korean financial deregulation (1998 p. 9).

13 For Helleiner (1996), the governments that *chose* to liberalise can now choose to rein in global finance – although it may take a 'major global financial crisis' (p. 206) to bring them to make this 'choice'.

14 To quote the title of a British neo-Marxist study of state institutions and policies (London-Edinburgh Weekend Return Group 1980).

15 It seems hard to recall now that in the mid-1970s the so-called Cold War blazed hotly across large parts of sub-Saharan Africa as Washington and London propped up the tottering regime of apartheid in a desperate and finally successful attempt to stave off communism in the region.

16 On the dramatic growth of stock market flotations in Europe, see *Business Week* (1998).

17 Needless to say, the *active* functions of ownership – trading and voting stock – are appropriated by the investment intermediaries; although where the prospect of profit is minimal, worker buy-outs (ESOPs in the US) are permitted.

18 The clearest example of this realisation came in Sweden (see e.g. Wilks 1996).

19 As suggested by Evans (1997).

20 In Britain the struggle remains within the Conservative Party.

21 See Herod 1995, Breitenfellner 1997 and Ramsay 1997 for recent assessments of the present state of international trade unionism.

22 Thus unionised workers in the City, Britain's financial centre, are routinely threatened with the loss of business to other European financial sectors.

REFERENCES

Albo, G. (1994), '"Competitive austerity" and the impasse of capitalist employment policy', in R. Miliband and L. Panitch (eds), *Socialist Register 1994: Between Globalism and Nationalism*, London: Merlin.

Albo, G. (1997), 'A world market of opportunities? Capitalist obstacles and left economic policy', in L. Panitch (ed), *Socialist Register 1997: Ruthless Criticism of All*

That Exists, London: Merlin.

Amsden, A. (1989), *Asia's Next Giant*, New York: Oxford UP.

Amsden, A., Kochanowicz, J. and Taylor, L. (1994), *The Market Meets its Match*, Cambridge, Mass.: Harvard UP.

Ashton, D. and Green F. (1996), *Education, Training and the Global Economy*, Aldershot: Edward Elgar.

Berggren, C. and Nomura, M. (1997), *The Resilience of Corporate Japan*, London: Paul Chapman.

Boyer, R. and Drache, D. (eds) (1996), *States Against Markets: the Limits of Globalisation*, London: Routledge.

Breitenfellner, A. (1997), 'Global unionism: a potential player', *International Labour Review* 136 (4), pp. 531-55.

Business Central Europe (1998), 6(51), June.

Business Week (1998), 'The Euro's warm-up act: IPOs', June 22nd pp. 24-5.

Cammack, P. (1989), 'Review article: bringing the state back in?', *British Journal of Political Science* 19, pp. 261-90.

Cammack, P. (1990), 'Statism, new institutionalism and Marxism', *Socialist Register* 1990, pp. 147-170.

Carlin, W. and Soskice, D. (1997), 'Shocks to the system: the German political economy under stress', *National Institute Economic Review* 159, pp. 57-96.

Chang, H-J. (1994), *The Political Economy of Industrial Policy*, Basingstoke: Macmillan.

Chorney, H. (1996), 'Debts, deficits and full employment', ch 16 in Boyer and Drache (1996).

Cox, R. (1992), 'Global *perestroika*', in R. Miliband and L. Panitch (eds), *Socialist Register 1992: New World Order*, London: Merlin.

Drache, D. (1996), 'From Keynes to K-Mart: competitiveness in a corporate age', ch. 1 in Boyer & Drache (1996).

Evans, P.B. (1979), *Dependent Development: the Alliance of Multinational, State and Local Capital in Brazil*, Princeton: Princeton UP.

Evans, P.B. (1997), 'The eclipse of the state? Reflections on stateness in an era of globalisation', *World Politics* 50 (1), pp. 62-87.

Evans, P.B., Rueschmeyer, D. and Skocpol, T. (eds) (1985), *Bringing the State Back In*, Cambridge: Cambridge UP.

Fröbel, F., Heinrichs, J. and Kreye, O. (1980), *The New International Division of Labour*, Cambridge: Cambridge UP.

Gill, S. and Law, D. (1988), *The Global Political Economy: Perspectives, Problems and Policies*, London: Harvester Wheatsheaf.

Gilpin, R. (1987), *The Political Economy of International Relations*, Princeton: Princeton UP.

Gordon, D. (1988), 'The global economy: new edifice or crumbling foundations?', *New Left Review* 168, pp. 24-64.

Hart, J.A. (1992), *Rival Capitalists: International Competitiveness in the US, Japan and Western Europe*, Ithaca: Cornell UP.

Hasegawa, H. and Hook, G. (eds) (1998), *Japanese Business Management: Restructuring for Low Growth and Globalisation*, London: Routledge.

Helleiner, E. (1996), 'Post-globalisation: in the financial liberalisation trend likely to be reversed?', in Boyer & Drache (1996).

Herod, A. (1995), 'The practice of international labour solidarity and the geography of the global economy', *Economic Geography* 71(4), pp. 341-63.

Hirst, P. and Thompson, G. (1996), *Globalisation in Question*, London: Polity.

Kindleberger, C.P. (ed) (1970), *The International Corporation*, Cambridge, Mass.: MIT Press.

Levinson, C. (1971), *Capital, Inflation and the Multinationals*, London: Allen & Unwin.

Lo, D. (1997), *Market and Institutional Regulation in Chinese Industrialization*, Basingstoke: Macmillan.

London-Edinburgh Weekend Return Group (1980), *In and Against the State*, London: Pluto.

Magdoff , H. (1969), *The Age of Imperialism*, New York: Monthly Review Press.

McMichael, P. (1996), 'Globalisation: myths and realities', *Rural Sociology* 61(1), pp. 25-55.

Moran, T.H. (1974), *Multinational Corporations and the Politics of Dependence: Copper in Chile, Princeton: Princeton UP.*

Murray, R. (1971), 'The internationalisation of capital and the nation state', *New Left Review* 67, pp. 84-109.

Murray, R. (1972), 'Underdevelopment, international firms and the international division of labour', in Society for International Development, *Towards a New World Economy*, Rotterdam: Rotterdam UP.

Nash, J. and Fernandez-Kelly, M.P. (eds) (1983), *Women, Men and the International Division of Labour*, Albany: SUNY Press.

Panitch, L. (1994), 'Globalisation and the state', in R. Miliband and L. Panitch (eds), *Socialist Register 1994: Between Globalism and Nationalism*, London: Merlin.

Panitch, L. (1996), 'Rethinking the role of the state in an era of globalization', in J.Mittelman (ed), *Globalization: Critical Reflections. International Political Economy Yearbook*, vol.9, Boulder, CO: Lynne Riener.

Perraton, J., Goldblatt, D., Held, D. and McGrew, A. (1997), 'The globalisation of economic activity', *New Political Economy* 2(2), pp. 257-77.

Picciotto, S. (1991), 'The internationalisation of the state', *Capital & Class* 43, Spring, pp. 43-63

Polányi, K. (1944), *The Great Transformation*, Beacon Hill: Beacon Press.

Radice, H. (ed) (1975), *International Firms and Modern Imperialism*, London: Penguin.

Radice, H. (1998a), '"Globalisation" and national differences', *Competition and Change* 3(4), forthcoming.

Radice, H. (1998b), 'Capitalism restored: East-Central Europe in the light of globalisation', in T.Krausz (ed), *The Change of Regime and the Left in Eastern Europe*, Budapest: Akadémiái Kiadó (forthcoming).

Radice, H. (1999), 'Britain under "New Labour": a model for European restructuring?', in R.Bellofiore (ed), *Which Labour Next? Global Money, Capitalist Restructuring and Changing Patterns of Production*, London: Edward Elgar (forthcoming).

Ramsay, H. (1997), 'Solidarity at last? International trade unionism approaching the millenium', *Economic and Industrial Democracy*, 18(4), pp. 503-37.

Reich, R.B. (1992), *The Work of Nations*, New York: Vintage.

Rodrik, D. (1997), *Has Globalisation Gone Too Far?*, Washington: Institute for International Economics.

Rueschemeyer, D. and Evans, P.B. (1985), 'The state and economic transformation:

towards an analysis of the conditions underlying effective intervention', ch. 2 in Evans et al. (1985).

Ruigrok, W. and van Tulder, R. (1995), *The Logic of International Restructuring*, London: Routledge.

Servan-Schreiber, J-J. (1968), *The American Challenge*, New York: Athenaeum.

Stopford, J. and Strange, S., with Henley, J. (1991), *Rival States, Rival Firms: Competition for World Market Shares*, Cambridge: Cambridge UP.

Streeck, W. (1997), 'German capitalism: does it exist? Can it survive?', *New Political Economy* 2(2) pp. 237-56.

Sunkel, O. (1973), 'Transnational capitalism and national disintegration in Latin America', *Social and Economic Studies*, 22(1), pp.132-76.

Tugendhat, C. (1971), *The Multinationals*, London: Eyre and Spottiswoode.

UNCTAD (1996), *World Investment Report 1996: Investment, Trade and International Policy Arrangements*, Geneva: UN.

Vernon, R. (1971), *Sovereignty at Bay*, New York: Basic Books.

Wade, R. (1990), *Governing the Market*, Princeton: Princeton UP.

Wade, R. (1996), 'Globalisation and its limits: reports of the death of the national economy are greatly exaggerated', ch.2 in S.Berger and R.Dore (eds), *National Diversity and Global Capitalism*, Ithaca, NY: Cornell University Press.

Wade, R. and Veneroso, F. (1998), 'The Asian crisis: the high-debt model versus the Wall Street-Treasury-IMF complex', *New Left Review* 228, pp. 3-23.

Warren, B. (1971), 'The internationalisation of capital and the nation state: a comment', *New Left Review* 68, pp. 83-8.

Waters, M. (1995), *Globalization*, London: Routledge.

Weiss, L. (1998), *The Myth of the Powerless State*, London: Polity.

Wilks, S. (1996), 'Class compromise and the international economy: the rise and fall of Swedish social democracy', *Capital and Class* 58, pp. 89-111.

Zysman, J. (1996), 'The myth of a 'global' economy: enduring national foundations and emerging regional realities', *New Political Economy* 1(2), pp. 157-84.

MATERIAL WORLD: THE MYTH OF THE 'WEIGHTLESS ECONOMY'

Ursula Huws

'The Death of Distance',[1] 'Weightless World',[2] the 'Connected Economy',[3] the 'Digital Economy',[4] the 'Knowledge-Based Economy',[5] the 'Virtual Organization'.[6] All these phrases were culled from the titles of books published in the six months prior to writing this essay, in spring, 1998. They could have been multiplied many times: 'virtual', 'cyber', 'tele-', 'networked' or even just 'e-' can, it seems, be prefixed interchangeably to an almost infinite range of abstract nouns. Without even straying from the field of economics, you can try 'enterprise', 'work', 'banking', 'trade', 'commerce', or 'business' (although the device works equally well in other areas: for instance 'culture', 'politics', 'sex', 'democracy', 'relationship', 'drama', 'community', 'art', 'society', 'shopping' or 'crime').

A consensus seems to be emerging – in economics as in other fields – that something entirely new is happening: that the world as we know it is becoming quite dematerialised (or, as Marx put it, 'all that is solid melts into air') and that this somehow throws into question all the conceptual models which have been developed to make sense of the old material world. We are offered a paradoxical universe: geography without distance, history without time, value without weight, transactions without cash. This is an economics which sits comfortably in a Baudrillardian philosophical framework, in which all reality has become a simulacrum and human agency, to the extent that it can be said to exist at all, is reduced to the manipulation of abstractions. But these books have not been designed as contributions to postmodernist cultural theory; far from it. Frances Cairncross's *Death of Distance* comes with a glowing testimonial from Rupert Murdoch on the front of its shiny blue dust-jacket, while Diane Coyle's *Weightless World,* not to be outdone, carries an endorsement from Mervyn King, executive director of the Bank of England, on its back cover. These are not academic inquiries into the nature of the universe; they are practical manuals for managers and policy-makers. A new orthodoxy is in the making, an orthodoxy in which it becomes taken for granted that 'knowledge' is the only source of value, that work is contingent and delocalisable, that globalisation is an inexorable and inevitable process and that, by implication, resistance is futile and any assertion of the physical claims of the human body in the here-and-now is hopelessly old-fashioned. The implications of this emerging 'common sense' are immense. Capable of shaping issues as diverse as taxation, employment legislation, levels of welfare spending, privacy rights and environmental policy, these notions serve to legitimise a new political agenda and set the scene for a new phase of capital accumulation.

The task I have set myself in this essay is to re-embody cyberspace: to try to make visible the material components of this virtual world. In this, I find myself rather oddly positioned. Having been arguing for over two decades for greater importance to be given in economic and social analysis to white-collar employment, and to the ways in which information and communications technologies have facilitated its relocation, it seems perverse, to say the least, to respond to this sudden new interest in the subject by saying, in effect, 'Well, hang on a minute. Are things really changing all that much? How 'dematerialised' are most developed economies? To what extent is service employment really expanding? What contribution does 'knowledge' make to economic growth? And how global are most economies anyway?'.

In addressing such questions a delicate path has to be picked. On the one hand it is necessary to subject the claims of the proponents of the 'new economics' to some empirical tests. Before throwing out the bathwater, in other words, it is wise to check it for babies. On the other, it is necessary to avoid the opposite danger of assuming that nothing has changed: that because something cannot be measured accurately with existing instruments it does not exist at all. I cannot claim to have walked this path to its conclusion. However I hope here to have flagged some of the more important landmines to be avoided along the way. If I have not found solutions, I hope I have at least identified some problems.[7]

At the risk of appearing pretentious, it does seem necessary to set the problem in its epistemological context. The current hegemonic position of postmodernism in most university departments (with the partial exception of the 'hard' sciences) has created a number of obstacles to addressing such questions.[8]

First, and most obviously, postmodernism throws into question the very scientific project itself. Even to admit to trying to discover the 'truth' about what is happening is to run the risk of being accused of vulgar positivism. If one accepts that all facts are contingent and socially constructed there is no rational basis even for selecting the data with which to test an argument, let alone for claiming any special validity for one's own discoveries. This is not the place for a detailed discussion of how – or indeed whether – it is possible for a scholar to find a third route, which avoids both the hard rocks of crude positivism and the swampy morass of relativism to which such an approach inevitably leads.[9]

Second, by insisting that all science is socially constructed, postmodernism makes it very difficult to produce a stable concept of the body – the flesh-and-blood body which gets on with the business of circulating its blood, digesting, perspiring, shedding old cells, lactating, producing semen, menstruating and a myriad other functions (including, no doubt many that a positivist might describe as 'yet to be discovered') regardless of what its inhabitant is thinking. The problem is urgent: how to resolve the crude dualism which is set up when 'the biological' is counterposed to 'the social' (or 'nature' to 'culture', 'body' to 'mind', 'manual work' to 'mental work', 'the material' to the 'ideological', that which is studied to the scientist, and so on). But postmodernism has yet to produce a definitive resolution to this difficulty. Baudrillard's solution is to regard the human body itself as just another culturally constructed simulacrum.[10] An alternative model, proposed by Donna Haraway, is to acknowledge the ways in which science and technology have penetrated the natural by proposing that the body cannot be viewed independently from its cultural surroundings but has, in effect, become a cyborg.[11] In both of these approaches the body is reduced to a cultural construct, which has the effect of rendering its materiality difficult to grasp and analyse. This is relevant in this context because without a concept of the body as something distinct and separate from capital (or any other abstraction) any theorising about the weightless economy will be circular: one is, in effect, trying to see the place of labour in the capital accumulation process having already written out the possibility of being able to define (and measure) that labour.

The post-modernist approach has also led to a third problem which is pertinent in this context: the conception of 'culture' as series of discourses, endlessly renegotiated and reproduced by all those who participate in them. This, combined with the focus on semiotic analysis to analyse these discourses, makes invisible the fact that cultural products such as books, films, 'science' or advertisements – and the 'ideas' they contain (at least to the extent that these are a conscious result of mental effort) are also the products of human intellectual and physical labour. Without some means of modelling, and measuring, this labour (whether waged or not), it is extremely difficult to make analytical sense of the 'weightless economy'.

Having outlined some of the difficulties, let us go on to examine the main tenets of the 'weightless economy' school. Three quite distinct themes emerge in this literature: dematerialisation; the 'productivity paradox' and globalisation. Although these are capable of being separated from each other conceptually, they tend in practice to be discussed together.

One of the leading proponents of the dematerialisation thesis is Danny Quah,[12] a Harvard-trained econometrician who is a professor at the London School of Economics. His central argument is that the economy is becoming increasingly dematerialised with intangible services increasingly replacing physical goods as the main sources of value. He distinguishes two aspects of dematerialisation which he regards as having macroeconomic importance: 'The first is simply increased weightlessness deriving from the growth of services – as opposed to, say, manufacturing in particular, or industry in general. The second is dematerialisation deriving from the increased importance of IT'.[13]

Let us look first at the growth in services. It has been an article of faith in most of the literature, at least since Daniel Bell first coined the term 'post-industrial society' in the early 1970s, that a, if not the, major trend of the 20th Century has been the rise of services at the expense of agriculture and manufacturing.[14] The most usual measure of this rise is service employment, and it is readily illustrated by graphs (usually derived from census data) showing employment in services soaring heavenwards as the century progresses, whilst employment in agriculture and manufacturing falls dramatically. Before going on to a more detailed discussion of service employment, it is worth noting several difficulties with this representation.

First, the standard industrial classification system, which is used as a basis for assigning workers to sectors, fails to take account of the major changes in the division of labour which accompany technological change and the restructuring of economic activity, both in terms of ownership and of organisation. Thus, for instance, the 'decline' of agricultural employment, which is visible in terms of the numbers of people actually working on the land, can only be demonstrated by leaving the mechanisation of farming and the commodification of food production out of the picture. If you were to include, for example, all the people employed in making tractors, fertilisers and pesticides, and all the people engaged in packing and preparing food, and those involved in its distribution to supermarkets as part of the agricultural workforce, the graph would slope much less steeply. Similarly, the decline in manufacturing employment is usually demonstrated within a particular national context, or that of a group of nations (for instance the OECD nations, NAFTA or the EU). This fails to take account of the manufacturing employment which has simply been relocated to another part of the globe (although it may still be carried out by the same companies, based in the same countries and retaining their service employment there). Finally the growth in service employment over the course of the century can only be demonstrated convincingly by leaving out domestic servants, whose numbers have declined steadily as employment in other forms of service work has risen.[15] In Great Britain, for instance, domestic service accounted for 40% of all female employment in 1901, but had fallen to 5.2% by 1971.[16]

These qualifications aside, there are deeper difficulties involved. Any analysis which uses as its raw material aggregated data on 'service activities', whether these are derived from employment statistics, output data or other sources, is in effect collapsing together several quite different types of economic activity, involving contrasting and contradictory tendencies. While it may be possible to make out a case that dematerialisation is taking place in some of these, it is my contention that in others precisely the opposite tendency is occurring, and that in the long run this tendency of commodification, or the transformation of services into material products, is the dominant one in capitalism.

The aggregated category 'services', which Quah and others use as the basis for their calculations, can be broken down into three distinct types of activity. The first of these consists essentially of a socialisation of the kinds of work which are also carried out unpaid in the home or neighbourhood. It includes health care, child care, social work, cleaning, catering and a range of personal services like hairdressing. It also includes what one might call 'public housekeeping' such as the provision of leisure services, street cleaning, refuse collection or parkkeeping. Even 'live' entertainment – and the sex industry – can plausibly be included in this category. (Under the standard industrial classification scheme (SIC) it is mostly classified under 'hotels, catering, retail and wholesale distribution', 'miscellaneous services' or in the public sector, although it is not coterminous with these categories.)

Whether or not outputs from these activities or employment in these sectors are visible in the economic statistics varies according to a number of factors including demographic structure, the degree of political commitment to providing public services, cultural variations, the extent of female participation in the workforce and what Gøsta Esping-Andersen has described as 'de-commodification', defined as 'the degree to which individuals or families can uphold a socially acceptable standard of living independently of market participation'.[17] These activities become visible in the public accounts when they are first socialised and enter the money economy: when, for instance, it becomes possible to attend a public concert instead of singing around the piano at home, to take an ailing baby to a clinic or to get one's legs waxed at a beauty salon. Conversely, they revert to invisibility if they are not available in the market. If, for instance, a political decision were made to abandon the state provision of school meals, employment of school meals staff would decline, but this would not necessarily mean that the labour of preparing such meals had disappeared; it would in all likelihood simply have re-entered the sphere of unpaid domestic work.

I have argued elsewhere that it is not simply the boundary between paid and unpaid labour which is permeable and shifting here; this kind of 'service' activity is also in an active process of commodification.[18] The general tendency is for new technologies to be used, not to dematerialise these activities but to materialise them (albeit in some cases with more and more 'knowledge' embedded in the new commodities). Thus we have a historical progression from washing clothes in the home as an activity either carried out unpaid or by the labour of paid domestic servants, via the provision of public laundries (staffed by 'service' workers) back into the home where it is now once again generally carried out as unpaid work but using an ever-burgeoning variety of new commodities such as washing machines, detergents, tumble dryers, fabric conditioners and steam irons. These undeniably material goods are made in factories and transported physically from these factories by various means to a growing proportion of homes throughout the world. The need to purchase them serves as one of the many ties pulling the 'underdeveloped' portions of that world ever more tightly into the cash nexus.

Washing, of course, is not the only activity which has been commodified in this way. One could point with equal justification to the processed food industry or the drugs industry as examples of commodified domestic labour. A random perusal of the advertisements in the room as I write this article throws up 'lunch-box-sized individual fruit-flavoured portions of fromage frais' (packaged in foil tubes!), 'panty-liners with flexible wings', 'under-eye moisturiser' and a 'universal remote control'. Not only can all of these commodities be traced readily back to their origins in unsocialised activity it would also be fair to say that none of them, with the possible exception of the moisturiser, would have been conceivable a generation ago; the ability of capitalism to generate new commodities can seem almost magical, as though they are being conjured out of the air in a perfect reversal of the 'dematerialisation' hypothesis. We must remind ourselves, however, that their raw materials come from the earth and that the only magic involved is human inventiveness and labour.

A few statistics on the consumption of these raw materials underline the point: in the UK, iron consumption has increased twenty-fold since 1900; the global production of aluminium has risen from 1.5 million tonnes in 1950 to 20 million tonnes today.[19] In the decade 1984-1995 (during a period in which we should have seen the 'weightless' effect becoming visible, if the theorists are to be believed) aluminium consumption in the UK rose from 497,000 tonnes to 636,000; steel consumption increased from 14,330,000 to 15,090,000 and wood and paper consumption more than doubled, from 41 million to 93 million tonnes.[20]

This inexorable drive towards the creation of new commodities is perhaps the central drive in the history of capitalism; the physical production of material goods being the simplest way of deriving value from living labour. It is not, of course, the only way. There are profits to be made, for instance, from running private nursing homes, or contract cleaning agencies, from servicing computers, arranging conferences or organising rock concerts. However – partly because of the limitations on the extent to which human productivity in these areas can be enhanced by automation and the consequent dependence on a geographically fixed and skill-specific workforce – it is easier and in the long run more profitable to be in the business of manufacturing and/or distributing endlessly reproducible material commodities. Thus while most of the major opera houses in the world require a public subsidy to stay open, selling Pavarotti's Greatest Hits on CD is hugely lucrative. Similarly, commodified medicine, in the form of mass sales of patented drugs, seems likely to remain much more profitable than employing doctors and nurses. These products do, of course, 'contain' knowledge (in the first case in the form of the composer's score, the performance of the conductor, orchestra and singer, the skills of the producer and studio engineers, the intellectual labour of the scientists and technicians who developed recording technology in general and CD technology in particular, and so on; in the second case *inter alia* in the form of inputs from doctors, scientific researchers and laboratory technicians). Except where this knowledge is paid for on a royalty basis, however, this can be regarded as 'dead' labour, whose cost is amortised in the early stages of production, producing a steadily increasing profit margin which grows with the size of the production run.

We can see, therefore, that in at least some parts of the service sector, the trend is one of materialisation, rather than dematerialisation. What of the others?

A second category of service activity could be classified as the development of human capital – the reproduction of the knowledge workforce itself. Into this category come education and training and some kinds of research and development. This sector is not immune from commodification – witness the standardisation of courses and the development of products such as interactive CD-ROM to deliver instruction. David Noble has argued that the introduction of intranets (a combination of computers linked together on an internal telecommunications network) into universities is ushering in a new era of commodification in higher education. In his words,

> The major change to befall the universities over the last two decades has been the identification of the campus as a significant site of capital accumulation, a change in social perception which has resulted in the systematic conversion of intellectual activity into intellectual capital and, hence, intellectual property. There have been two general phases of this transformation. The first, which began twenty years ago and is still underway, entailed the commoditization of the research function of the university, transforming scientific and engineering knowledge into commercially viable proprietary products that could be owned and bought and sold in the market. The second, which we are now witnessing, entails the commoditization of the educational function of the university, transforming courses into courseware, the activity of instruction itself into commercially viable proprietary products that can be owned and bought and sold in the market.[21]

The content of these new commodities is abstract, in the sense that it has been abstracted from the lecturers, researchers and graduate students employed in this sector. Unlike past forms of commodified scholarship, such as text-books, these newer means of abstraction rarely acknowledge the authors' ownership by means of royalties. Nevertheless, they do not differ fundamentally from the process whereby the design of a carpet is abstracted from a skilled weaver and embedded in the programming instructions for an automated loom. What it is important to keep sight of here is that the workforce has not disappeared. Even if the more original and creative (and perhaps hence the most troublesome) workers could somehow be emptied of all the knowledge that their employers find useful and got rid of, a workforce – including original and creative people – would still be required, however deskilled and intensified the rest of the work process had become, to replenish the stock of intellectual capital, produce new educational commodities and administer the new standardised courses, in standardised doses, to the next generation of students.

The systematisation of education which has taken place in recent years bears a close resemblance to the systematisation of other forms of non-manual work. For instance, the way in which the assessment of students' work may be transformed from a mystified and subjective process of exercising individual professional judgement to the ticking of boxes on a standard marking scheme is not unlike the way a bank manager's assessment of a client's eligibility for a loan or mortgage increasingly turns on the administration of a standard questionnaire, with standard built-in criteria, in which the decision is effectively made by the software programme.

This sector, then, is one where enormous changes are taking place in the labour process (and, with it, the capital accumulation process) in association with the introduction of the new information technologies. It does not, however, appear to raise any new problems which are not soluble within the framework of the 'old' economics.

The third category of service activity is the one which most concerns Quah and the other economists of the 'weightless' school. This is the 'knowledge work' which is either directly involved in the production of physical commodities, or involved in the production of new commodities which are entirely weightless. In the former category, an oft-cited example is that of the fashion shoe, only a fraction of the price of which is attributable to the raw materials and the cost of physical manufacture and transport. The main value, it is argued, comes from the 'weightless' attributes of the shoe, derived from its design, its brand image, the way in which it is marketed and so on. As Diane Coyle puts it, the 'buyer is paying for what they do for her image rather than something to protect her feet'.[22] Notwithstanding the extra money a purchaser is prepared to pay for a high-status product, it is still, at the end of a day, a material object which is being purchased, and from which the manufacturers derive their profit. The snob value of a Nike running shoe in the 1990s is not different *in kind* from that of a sought-after Paris bonnet in the 19th century;[23] the main difference lies in the fact that the former is mass-produced while the latter was individually made. In the former case, the 'knowledge' has been abstracted from a specialist knowledge-worker in a reproducible form; in the second it lay embedded in the skill of the milliner whose bodily presence was thus required to produce each new bonnet.

The emergence of the specialist knowledge worker is thus a product of the increasingly specialised division of labour in manufacturing.[24] In this process, as the physical business of production becomes more and more capital-intensive, through automation, the manual processes of assembly become progressively deskilled, enabling the work to be done ever more cheaply. In the case of sports shoes, this is often by the use of extremely low-paid labour in developing countries. In 1995, for instance, it was reported that twelve thousand women were employed in Indonesia making Nike shoes, working sixty hours a week and many earning less than the government's minimum wage of US $1.80 a day. It was estimated that raising their wages to US $3.50 per day would still bring the labour cost component of a pair of shoes to less than US $1 a pair. In 1993, by contrast, Michael Jordan alone received over US $20 million from Nike for allowing his name and image (and by implication his sporting achievements) to be associated with their product – equivalent to more than the total labour cost for all the 19 million pairs of Nike shoes made in Indonesia.[25] Traditional economics allows us to understand the very small proportion of the cost of the final shoe attributable to the labour involved in its manufacture as the super-exploitation of a vulnerable group of workers; the 'new' economics simply renders them invisible. Yet it is difficult to see the division of labour in the production process as anything intrinsically new; rather it can be seen as the continuation of a process which has been evolving for at least the past century and a half.[26] Michael Jordan may be earning considerably more, but his contribution to the value of the final product is not different *in kind* from that of the little girls who posed for the Pears Soap advertisements at the turn of the century[27] or the members of the royal family who give their official blessing and the use of their coats of arms to pots of marmalade.

What is perhaps new is the large-scale introduction of new technologies not just into the process of *production* of commodities but also into their *distribution*. The creation of global markets for mass-produced commodities has generated imperatives to increase the efficiency of this distribution workforce and, indeed, to introduce entirely new ways of reaching potential customers and persuade them to buy. In some cases this has produced the rather paradoxical effect of recreating the illusion of a return to the customisation of products associated with the era before mass production. Thus, for instance, there are now web-sites into which you can input your measurements to enable you to order a pair of blue-jeans tailored to your own precise individual dimensions (provided, of course, you are prepared to select from a menu of standard styles from a single manufacturer). The computerisation of parts of the production process has been combined with the use of the new communications technologies to create a direct interactive link between customer and producer. This also has the effect of cutting out various intermediaries (such as the wholesaler and the retailer) and of reducing the manufacturer's risk of over-producing, or producing the wrong product, almost to zero: only that which has already been ordered by the customer need ever be produced. In this case, however, there is still a material commodity which has to be manufactured, packed, and delivered over real physical distances to its customer.

In other cases, the commodity being distributed is less easy to pin down in its material form. An example of this might be the use of a call centre for activities like selling airline tickets, providing directory enquiry information, arranging financial transactions, providing assistance on software problems or dealing with insurance claims. Again, the sophisticated use of new technology makes it possible to personalise these services, however remote the site from which they are delivered. Software can, for instance, be programmed to use the area code from which a call is originated to direct the caller to an operator who will reply in the right language or even the appropriate regional accent, thus creating an illusion of local response whatever the actual location or time zone. The same digital trigger (the caller's telephone number) can also be used to ensure that the caller's personal file is visible on the screen to the operator before the first 'hello' has even been uttered, making it possible to generate a highly personalised response and, indeed, an illusion of intimacy, as well as maximising the operator's productivity by avoiding any waste of time in taking down unnecessary details.

The use of computer-generated scripts which pop up on the screen to be read verbatim by the operator can reduce the skill requirements to a minimum. This sort of work is also amenable to a high degree of remote monitoring and control. Studies of call centre workers in the UK – already an estimated 1.1% of the workforce[28] in a market estimated to be growing at the rate of 32% per annum across Europe[29]-

have found that the work is highly controlled, relatively low-paid, frequently involves round-the-clock shift-working and produces a very rapid rate of staff turnover, with 'burn-out' typically occurring after 12 to 20 months on the job.[30] The evidence suggests that, far from constituting some new kind of knowledge worker, formerly unknown to economics, these are the Taylorised, deskilled descendants of earlier forms of office worker (such as bank tellers, insurance salespeople, booking clerks and telephone operators) even though the work may be taking place at different locations and under different conditions of employment. There seems to be no good reason why the value which they add to the products or services being delivered (which may, or may not, be of a tangible nature) cannot also be measured by the traditional means.

This brings us to the other kind of knowledge work in this category discussed in the 'weightless economy' literature – the kind which produces no material end-product whatsoever. This may take the form of algorithms (such as a software program), intangible financial products (such as a life insurance policy), creative works (such as a film script) or speculations (such as an investment in futures). Again, none of these is new in itself: a musical score, the perforated roll of paper which contains the 'instructions' for a pianola, a chemical formula, the blueprint for a machine or indeed a recipe book, represent essentially the same kind of algorithm as a computer program, for example. And various forms of gambling, usury and insurance seem to have been around for as long as money. In the seventeenth century, one of the earliest uses of official statistics (in this case the *London Bills of Mortality*, from which the merchant John Graunt constructed life expectancy tables) was for the calculation of annuities.[31] And writers, poets, dramatists, visual artists, scientists, inventors and musicians have been producing 'intangible products' for centuries. When we read of rock musicians borrowing money on the world's stock markets against their future royalty earnings this may seem like some new semi-magical way of generating income out of thin air, but is it really very different from the way in which impecunious young aristocrats in the 18th century settled their gambling debts by the use of IOUs drawn against their future inheritance? Danny Quah argues that weightless products defy the traditional laws of economics because they are simultaneously infinitely expandable, indivisible and inappropriable. In other words a new idea can only be discovered once; once discovered it can not only be used over and over again without being 'used up', and even if there are formal restrictions, in the form of patents or copyright, on so doing it can in practice be freely reproduced.[32] While it is certainly true that the new communications and reproductive technologies have made the rapid dissemination of ideas easier than ever before, this again does not appear to be a new phenomenon. Surely these features have always been present when new discoveries have been made (such as the use of penicillin to heal infection, or the theory of gravity, or the discovery of electricity)? And the copying of ideas is as old as the history of fashion.

It is possible to argue about the exact relationship of these abstract products to material reality. In some cases they may act as proxies for material goods (as in the case, for instance, of a mortgage, which can be exchanged for a house, or an insurance policy which can be exchanged for a new car or indeed a credit card transaction which can be exchanged for goods or cash). In other cases (for instance in the case of a piece of music or a poem) it is more useful to envisage them in relation to the human desires they satisfy.

If we are to avoid constructing a purely abstract universe, constituted entirely of 'knowledge' (in which disembodied entities inhabit a virtual space, are sustained by virtual inputs, and produce virtual outputs – a universe without birth or death, a universe where infinite consumption is possible without the generation of waste), it is useful to retain an awareness of this underlying materiality. From an economic perspective, I would argue, it is important to retain a more specific awareness of the materiality of the worker and his or her labour process. It is only by examining this process in some detail that it becomes possible to tease out the specific contributions made at each stage to the 'value' of the final commodity. Such an analysis can also illuminate the process which Marx identified whereby labour is progressively abstracted and incorporated into capital in its specific relation to 'knowledge' work in an economy increasingly dependent on the use of information and communications technologies.

In brief, we could say that in the 1990s the division of labour has evolved to a point where a substantial part of the labour force is engaged in 'non-manual' work; is, in other words, engaged in the generation or processing of 'information' (even though this work nevertheless involves the body in a series of physical activities, such as pounding a keyboard, which have implications for its physiological well-being). The development of computing technology has made it possible for this information (or 'codified knowledge', as it has been conceptualised by David and Foray[33]) to be digitised and for some aspects of its processing to be automated, and the development of telecommunications technology has enabled this digital information to be transmitted from one place to another with great rapidity and at very low cost. These technologies in combination have made it possible for many of these processes to be standardised, as a result of which it has become possible for the workers to be monitored by results, and for the task to be relocated to any point on the globe where the right infrastructure is available together with a workforce with the appropriate skills.

We must now ask ourselves what, precisely, is the relationship of this workforce to capital? How is the value of the final commodity constituted? In relation to its material content, Marx has already given us the answer: there is the dead labour of past workers embodied in the machinery used to make it, and in the extraction of the raw materials and the capital used to set the enterprise up, and the appropriated living labour of the workers who process it. In relation to the intangible content, there is also the dead labour of the people whose past work made the idea possible; but there is also living labour in two quite distinct forms.[34] The first of these is the routine labour of deskilled workers who are essentially following instructions. We might call these 'process' knowledge workers. These may be involved either in the production process (for instance coders working on the development of software, graphic designers laying out web pages, copy-typists inputting data, managers supervising the purchasing of raw materials or the organisation of the production process, quality controllers checking the final output) or in the distribution process (such as call centre staff or invoice clerks). Although when it is casualised some form of payment by results (or piece-rate) may be applied, it is normally paid by time, as is the case with manual work. Even if the activity is outsourced, the wage or salary bill is verifiable and it is thus a relatively straightforward task to relate these labour costs to the output in order to calculate the value added.

Then there is also another kind of knowledge work, which we might call 'creative' or 'originating' labour (some of which may be contributed, with or without acknowledgement, by the 'process' workers) which generates new intellectual capital, in the form of ideas, designs, programs or more definable (if not tangible) intellectual products such as words, music or images. The contribution made by this work is harder to calculate. The ideas may be appropriated from a waged workforce (in most countries, ownership of intellectual property produced by employees is automatically assigned to the employer). However they may be produced by freelances or other independent individuals or organisations under agreements which assign all or part of the ownership of rights to the creator. In such cases, the right to use the intellectual product may involve the payment of fees or royalties or the negotiation of complex licensing agreements. Alternatively the ideas may simply be stolen. Intellectual property rights can be legally asserted not just in the outputs of workers who are conscious of their roles as generators of valuable ideas, for instance as writers, artists or inventors. They also apply to the tacit knowledge of people who have no awareness of the alienable nature of what they own. The music of tribal peoples, for instance, may be appropriated to be used on CDs or film soundtracks; their visual art may be photographed and printed on tee-shirts or wrapping paper, or scanned in to give an 'ethnic' feel to the design of a web page; their sacred artefacts may be used as 'inspiration' for a new range of designer clothes or jewellery. It does not stop there: supermarkets developing 'own range' 'ethnic' convenience foods will generally insist that the subcontractors who prepare the food for them give them an exclusive right to use the recipe; the handed-down knowledge of the family or community thus becomes appropriated as privately-owned intellectual capital.[35] Even more extreme is the patenting of human genetic codes for research purposes, a development of the practice of patenting the DNA of various plants and animals (with a slight tweak to ensure its uniqueness) for use in new drugs and genetic engineering products.[36]

It is no accident that the ownership of intellectual property is currently one of the most hotly contended issues both at the level of international trade agreements and at the level of workplace negotiation. In the UK, for instance, the National Union of Journalists has found itself in recent years in a series of disputes with large employers over the right of freelance journalists and photographers to retain ownership of copyright in their own work. Many employers, including the supposedly left-of-centre *Guardian* newspaper, now make it a condition of employment that all rights, electronic or otherwise, become the property of the newspaper.[37] On one level, this can be regarded as a simple dispute between labour and capital, with workers fighting for a larger share of the products of their labour. However the concept of ownership is rather different from that which pertains in a typical factory. It is now over two centuries since workers effectively gave up their right to a share in the ownership of the product of their labour in return for a wage. The knowledge worker who insists on a royalty, or on the right to re-use what s/he has produced, is not behaving like a member of the proletariat; s/he is refusing alienation.

Nevertheless, the worker's right to ownership of the 'idea' (as opposed to the right to be paid for the time put in on the processing of that idea) is profoundly ambiguous. The knowledge worker usually occupies an intermediate position in what might be seen as the knowledge food chain. Ideas do not come from nowhere: they may be copied, consciously or unconsciously, from others; they may draw on what has been learned from teachers, or from books, or from observations of people who do not regard themselves as creative; or they may have arisen from the interactions of a group of people working together as a team. A journalist or television researcher generally obtains inputs from interviews with 'experts' (who may or may not be salaried academics or writers with an interest in plugging their books); there is no rational basis for deciding whether the end result should 'belong' to the journalist's employer, the journalist, the 'expert', or someone further down the chain, for instance the 'expert's' research assistant, or a person interviewed by the research assistant in the course of carrying out the research, or indeed the parents of the person interviewed by the research assistant who inculcated the views expressed in the interview. An analogous intermediary position could be said to be occupied by the scientist doing research on disease resistance in rice who obtains information from South-East Asian peasants as part of the process which eventually leads to his or her employer registering a claim to ownership of the new strain which is developed; or by Neil Simon incorporating tribal music into 'his' work; or by the photographer who records the face of an elderly Jamaican fisherman to use to advertise a canned drink.

In the final analysis it is market strength which determines who can claim what share of the cake, but the analysis of how the 'value' is formed is complicated by these considerations. The fact that it is complicated to model does not render the task impossible. In order to do so, it is necessary to take account of the fact that real people with real bodies have contributed real time to the development of these 'weightless' commodities.

This brings me to the second issue which occupies such a large place in the weightless economy literature: the so-called 'productivity paradox'. The starting point for this discussion is the belief that growth rates, measured in GDP (gross domestic product) and TFP (total factor productivity) have in most developed countries remained obstinately low since 1973 – well below their post-war levels up to that date. This year is chosen as the watershed partly because it was in 1973 that the oil crisis generated a number of dramatic hiccups in the economic statistics, and partly because it more or less coincided with the beginnings of what has been various described as the 'knowledge economy', the 'information economy', the 'second industrial revolution' or the 'computer revolution'. If, as is widely argued on both the left and the right of the political spectrum, the introduction of these new technologies can unleash human potential, making workers more productive and creating a host of new products and services, then this ought to have led to a surge in economic growth. The apparent evidence that it has not done so is one of the main factors leading to the belief that a new economics is required. However the paradox may not be as surprising as it first appears.

First, the evidence itself: productivity is normally measured by the relationship between the value of outputs and that of the inputs of labour and capital. As Danny Quah has pointed out, if we are to judge by the statistics alone, the most productive group of workers in the world are French farmers.[38] The implication is that apparently high productivity can simply be an effect of artificially high prices of final outputs. This suggests that part of the explanation for the 'productivity paradox' may lie in the very sharp reduction in prices which has accompanied the process of computerisation.

But do the empirical data support this definition of the problem? In this connection, Neuburger has convincingly shown that although there was a sharp drop in *output*, labour productivity did not exhibit a correspondingly sharp fall, and in some OECD countries did not fall significantly at all.[39] Moreover for the UK he has also shown that the present system of public accounts would only reveal the kind of productivity gains delivered by information technology in about ten percent of the sectors comprising the total economy.[40] Nonetheless a paradox does seem to exist, even if not in nearly as extreme a form as generally supposed. So what might be the explanation for it? Is political economy really incapable of providing one?

Here, I can only indicate some of the main possible solutions to the puzzle out of the many which have been proposed. One has to do with the effects of globalisation. It is very difficult for nationally-based systems of accounting to deal accurately with the transactions taking place in a globalised economy. Where high levels of output are recorded in one country, but some of the inputs may have been in the form of very cheap labour in another, and complex adjustments have to be made to allow for such factors as fluctuating exchange rates and transfer pricing practices within large transnational companies, then some slippage may take place which affects the GDP figures positively or negatively.

There are also many ways in which the extra productivity produced by information technology may not reveal itself in output figures. It may increase the efficiency of *unpaid* rather than paid labour, for example by making it much quicker and easier for a library user to identify a book, or a customer to withdraw cash from a bank. To the extent that information technology encourages the development of self-service this will not be reflected in the figures. It could be argued that a firm which improves its service to customers will thereby gain market share and that this will ultimately feed through into increased output figures, but this does not take account of the generalised effect which takes place when the whole sector has adopted this new technology; customer expectations will have risen but no single firm has a competitive advantage. Jeff Madrick has, in addition, raised a number of other technical issues, including a possible oversupply of services, that may have affected the statistics in the USA.[41]

There are also very specific problems here associated with the public sector: improvements in efficiency and quality of service resulting from the introduction of new technologies into public administration or the delivery of public services may well lead to a better quality of life but this will not be reflected in the output figures, since national accounts do not at present capture in any direct way things like cleaner air, healthier children, happier cyclists or less confused form-fillers. It is sometimes argued that the nature of Britain's publicly-funded National Health Service creates a consistent bias in the national accounts leading to an underestimation of GDP.

A study of the public sector also raises some more fundamental questions relating to the socialisation of domestic labour (discussed above in the context of service employment). Part of the apparent fall in productivity from the 1970s onward might be a direct effect of the greater labour force participation of women during that period, and hence an increase in the need for a market supply of childcare and other services previously provided in the home.[42] A group of Norwegian researchers used a social accounting framework to decompose GDP growth into productivity gains and 'reallocation' gains resulting from the transition from unpaid household production to the labour market. They concluded that 'about one-fourth of the growth in GDP in Norway over the period 1971-90 can be attributed to the transition of household services from unpaid to paid work'.[43]

Neuburger's own explanation for the 'productivity paradox', insofar as it exists, is an interesting one. He hypothesises that during the 1970s there was a qualitative improvement in working conditions across most of the OECD countries and that the increased cost of inputs (reflected in lower productivity growth figures) represented a real gain for labour, in the form of improved health and safety at work, a better working environment, longer holidays and other achievements. In most developed countries, 1970-76 was, after all, as well as being a time of considerable trade union militancy, the period in which equal pay, protection against discrimination, maternity rights, protection against unfair dismissal, the right to a safe working environment and a number of other rights were, at least formally, enshrined in employment protection or anti-discrimination legislation. Although much of the legislation was difficult to implement and many workers fell through the net it did, according to Neuburger, lead to some measurable redistribution from capital to labour, and the productivity figures provide the evidence for it.

These issues of productivity and growth are, then, evidently complex; but we can at least conclude that they cannot be understood in relation to technology alone, but must be analysed in their full social and historical context.

A third strand in the discussions about the weightless economy concerns globalisation. Perhaps one of the most dangerous illusions fostered here is the notion that the new information technologies mean that anything can now be done by anyone, anywhere: that the entire population of the globe has become a potential virtual workforce. The issue of globalisation is crucial because it raises very directly the question of how the virtual economy, insofar as it exists, maps on to the physical surface of the globe we inhabit.

Although it is full of euphemistic descriptions of the 'death of distance' or the 'end of geography', the literature on the subject is surprisingly short on empirical evidence.[44] At one extreme, sceptics such as Paul Hirst and Grahame Thompson go so far as to assert that a global economy cannot be said to exist in any meaningful sense, and even maintain that the world economy is somewhat *less* global now than it was before the first world war.[45] At the other extreme is a large literature, much of it by postmodernist geographers, which takes the presumption that globalisation is taking place as its starting point, and is concerned to develop an understanding of the social, cultural and economic implications of this. The empirical evidence on which it draws is, however, slight, rarely going beyond the anecdote or case-study writ large.[46] Few systematic attempts have been made to establish the scale of relocation of information-processing work across national boundaries.[47]

It is in fact extraordinarily difficult to obtain a statistical picture of the changing international division of labour. Apart from the difficulty of distinguishing between final outputs and intermediate ones, the traffic in jobs will not necessarily even appear in an easily identifiable form in the trade statistics, because of the range of different contractual arrangements which might apply, each of which is visible in a different way in the national accounts. Material goods must be transported in a physical form across national boundaries, and are therefore generally recorded in import and export statistics; but information sent over the internet leaves no such trace and there is no easy way to assess the value of such traffic. It is, of course, possible to measure its *volume* but, despite the arguments of Luc Soete and others who propose a 'bit tax',[48] this is not a good indicator of value: a computer program which has taken thousands of skilled person-hours to write will typically be much smaller in volume (measured in bits) than a video clip or scanned-in photograph in whose generation only a few moments of unpaid time have been invested.

The fact that something is difficult to measure does not, of course, mean that it does not exist, and it is clear that the widespread use of computers for processing information, and of telecommunications for transmitting it, *has* introduced an enormous new range of choices in the location of information-processing work.

However it would not be correct to infer from this that these choices are entirely untethered from the material. First, and most obviously, they depend on a physical infrastructure. The process which was formalised in the liberalisation of the telecommunications market following the ratification of the World Trade Organisation pact of 15 February 1997 by 68 countries has opened up most of the world as a market for the major telecommunications multinationals and involved a rapid spread of infrastructure and a sharp fall in telecommunications costs. But this process has been highly selective; it certainly cannot be said to have given all the world's population access to the 'information society'. In many developing countries whole communities are effectively without any telephone access whatsoever and even those lines which exist are of poor quality. The optical fibre cable which is required to transmit high volumes of information quickly, and which provides a vital underpinning for many 'weightless' activities, is so far only available in selected parts of the globe, mainly in large cities, such as Singapore, where high usage, and hence profitability, is anticipated.

Even 'wireless' communications are dependent on material goods, like satellites, to continue functioning. On May 20th, 1998,

Americans were reminded sharply of this when there was a malfunction in the onboard control system and a backup switch of the Galaxy IV satellite, owned by PanAmSat. The satellite reportedly provided pager service to more than 80% of US pager users, and also carried NPR, several television networks, and Reuters news feeds. Whilst CBS services were quickly switched to Galaxy 7, pager users, including many hospitals, were left without any service.[49]

Telecommunications infrastructure is not the only material prerequisite for participation in the global weightless economy. There is also a need, continuously renewed because of its rapid obsolescence, for hardware: for personal computers, mobile telephones, modems, scanners, printers, switches and the many components and accessories involved in their manufacture and use. Not only do the costs of these differ in absolute terms from country to country, but so does their cost relative to basic income and subsistence. Mike Holderness has pointed out that 'a reasonable computer costs about one year's unemployment benefit in the UK or about the annual income of three schoolteachers in Calcutta' and that the annual subscription to Ghana's only internet host is about the same as the entire annual income of a Ghanaian journalist.[50]

The notion that anyone can do anything anywhere is therefore in practice constrained by a number of spatial factors. It is also, of course, constrained by the fact that not all human activities are delocalisable in this way. The majority of jobs are, and seem likely to remain, firmly anchored to a given spot, or series of spots, on the world's surface because they involve the extraction of the earth's raw materials, their processing, the manufacture of material commodities (which is delocalisable, but within limits), transport, construction, or the delivery of physical services (ranging from health care to garbage collection).

That said, it is undeniably the case that more and more work *is* delocalisable. The reasons for this are many. First, there are the changes in the division of labour which have increased the proportion of jobs which simply involve processing information. Second, the digitisation of that information has vastly increased the extent to which it can be accessed remotely, removing the need for physical proximity to sources and eliminating transport costs. Third, the standardisation of tasks associated with computerisation has enabled a growing proportion of activities to be monitored remotely (replacing management of the work process with management by results) which in turn allows them to be outsourced or located at a distance from the manager. Fourth –

partly because of the hegemonic power of companies like IBM and Microsoft – there has been a convergence of skill requirements across occupations and industries, with a few generic skills (such as a knowledge of Word or Excel) replacing a large number of machine-specific, firm-specific or occupation-specific skills which have in the past both constrained the mobility of workers and created a dependence on their skills among employers, effectively anchoring them to the places where those skills were available. Fifth, as already noted, there has been both a rapid diffusion of the infrastructure and technology and a sharp fall in its cost.[51]

This should, in principle, have enabled any region in which the right combination of infrastructure and skills is present to diversify its local economy and enter the global market in information-processing work on an equal basis with any other region. By removing the strategic advantages of some regions (created by such things as economies of scale or proximity to markets) it should have levelled the playing field. It is this idea which underlies much of the optimistic rhetoric about the ability of new information and communications technologies to regenerate remote regions. However the results of empirical research reveal that things are not so simple. The very fact that employers now have a huge range of alternative locations to choose from appears, paradoxically, to have increased, rather than decreased, the degree of geographical segregation in the global division of labour. Although its specific components may have changed, comparative competitive advantage is more, rather than less important, with each location having to compete separately for each type of activity. No longer constrained to have most of their information processing activities on one site, corporations are now free to seek out the best location on an activity by activity basis, with the whole world to choose from. Thus a company might decide to get its manufacturing done in Mexico, its research and development in California, its data entry in the Philippines, its software development in India and establish two call centres, one in New Brunswick, Canada, and one in the Netherlands. In each case, the site would be selected on the basis of the availability of skills and the advantageousness of other local labour market conditions, tax regime, etc. If the market became more competitive, or local workers started demanding higher wages or better conditions, or the local tax regime changed, it might switch: it might, for instance, go to Indonesia for manufacturing, to the Dominican Republic for data entry, to Russia for programming or start using homeworkers for some of the more routine call centre functions. Even within countries, this increasing geographical specialisation (generally accompanied by polarisation in incomes and standards of living) can be observed. Some recent research I carried out in the UK revealed a steadily growing gap between those regions which were successful in attracting high-skilled 'creative' knowledge work (mostly concentrated in an affluent 'green' corridor to the west of London) and those which had succeeded only in attracting routine back-office functions and call centres (almost exclusively in declining industrial areas).[52] Remote rural areas with poor infrastructure had failed to attract either type of employment.

Such findings cast serious doubt over many of the claims made by economists of the 'death of distance' school. They suggest that location has actually become *more* rather than less important. Some places seem likely to be able to build on their comparative advantages to increase the gap between themselves and the rest of the world; others seem likely to be able to find niches for themselves in the new global division of labour, by exploiting things like language skills, time zone advantages, cheap labour, specialist skills, or good infrastructure; still others will be left entirely out in the cold. The dream of a fully diversified local economy in any given area seems likely to remain unrealisable except for a few privileged pockets.

And what of the future of knowledge work? It seems likely that two existing tendencies will intensify. On the one hand, there is likely to be a continuing erosion of the traditional bureaucracy (as first anatomised by Max Weber at the beginning of the century) with its stable hierarchies, rigid rules, orderly – if implicitly discriminatory – promotion patterns, 'jobs for life', process management and unity of time and space, in favour of an increasingly atomised and dispersed workforce, managed by results, insecure and expected to work from any location. If they are not actually formally self-employed, this group of workers, which will include a high proportion of the 'creative' knowledge workforce, will increasingly be expected to behave as if they are. On the other hand, there is likely to be the creation of what is in effect a new white-collar proletariat engaged in the more routine 'process' knowledge work, closely monitored with Taylorised work processes and stressful working conditions. Geographical segregation will make it difficult for members of the second group to progress to the first.

The geographical distribution of intellectual labour (the movement of jobs to people) is only one aspect of globalisation, of course. In analysing the forms of capital accumulation which prevail as the century draws to a close it is also important to look at the global division of labour in terms of the physical movements of migrant workers (the movement of people to jobs) and in terms of the development of mass global markets.

In order to do so, however, it is not necessary to develop a new economics of weightlessness. On the contrary, we must reinsert human beings, in all their rounded, messy, vulnerable materiality – and the complexity of their antagonistic social relations – at the very centre of our analysis.

NOTES

1 Frances Cairncross, *The Death of Distance: How the Communications Revolution will Change our Lives*, Harvard Business School Press, Boston, 1997.

2 Diane Coyle, *Weightless World: Strategies for Managing the Digital Economy*, Capstone Publishing, Oxford, 1997.

3 Christopher Meyer and Stan Davis, *Blur: the Speed of Change in the Connected Economy*, Addison-Wesley, South Port, 1998.

4 Don Tapscott (ed) *Blueprint to the Digital Economy: Wealth Creation in the Era of E-business*', 1998; Don Tapscott, *The Digital Economy: Promise and Peril in the Age of Networked Intelligence*, McGraw Hill, New York, 1995.

5 Dale Neef (ed) *The Economic Impact of Knowledge (Resources for the Knowledge-based Economy)*, Butterworth-Heinemann, Boston, 1998.

6 Bob Norton and Cathy Smith, *Understanding the Virtual Organization*, Barrons Educational, Hauppage, N.Y., 1998.

7 In doing so, I have been helped immeasurably by discussions with the economist Henry Neuburger who has brought more sceptical rigour to these questions than anyone else I know. He is not responsible, of course, for any inadequacies in my arguments, for which I take full blame.

8 There is some encouraging evidence that this may have peaked, and that the old modernisms are beginning to reassert themselves. Nevertheless, we now have several generations of students already in or about to enter the intellectual labour market who have been taught to view the world through postmodernist lenses, and whose practices will be influenced by these views.

9 The critical realism of Roy Bhaskar seems to offer the most promising way forward currently on offer – see Roy Bhaskar's own *A Realist Theory of Science*, 1975, republished by Verso Books in 1997 (Verso Classics 9) and *Dialectic: The Pulse of Freedom*, Verso Books, London, 1997; Andrew Collier, *Critical Realism: An Introduction to Roy Bhaskar's Philosophy*, Verso Books, London, 1994; and the interesting discussion of Bhaskar's work in Meera Nanda, 'Restoring the Real: Rethinking Social Constructivist Theories of Science' in Leo Panitch (ed.), *Socialist Register, 1997*, Merlin Press, Rendlesham, 1997.

10 Jean Baudrillard, *Simulacra and Simulation (The Body, in Theory: Histories of Cultural Materialism)* translated by Sheila Faria Glaser, University of Michigan Press, Chicago, 1995.

11 Donna J. Haraway, *Simians, Cyborgs, and Women : The Reinvention of Nature*, Routledge, London and New York, 1991.

12 Email address: weightlesseconomy.com.

13 Danny T. Quah, 'Increasingly Weightless Economies' in *Bank of England*

Quarterly Bulletin, February, 1997, p. 49.

14 Daniel Bell, *The Coming of Post-Industrial Society*, Basic Books, New York, 1973.

15 I do not have the resources while writing this article to demonstrate this conclusively on a national scale. However in 1979-80, with the invaluable help and guidance of Quentin Outram, I carried out a detailed study based on data from the decennial Censuses of Employment supplemented in more recent years by data from Census of Employment, of service employment by occupation and industry (i.e. including those 'service' workers whose employers were categorised in 'manufacturing' or other non-service sectors) in one part of Britain – West Yorkshire. While doing this work – which focused particularly on women's employment – we were greatly struck by the almost exact parallel between the decline of domestic service and the expansion of other forms of service employment between 1901 and 1971. The report, which was published under the title *The Impact of New Technology on Women's Employment in West Yorkshire,* by Leeds Trade Union and Community Resource and Information Centre, 1980, did not, unfortunately, draw attention to this finding.

16 C.H. Lee, *British Regional Employment Statistics, 1841-1971*, Cambridge University Press, Cambridge, 1979.

17 Gøsta Esping-Andersen, *The Three Worlds of Welfare Capitalism*, Polity Press, Cambridge, 1990.

18 First in Ursula Huws, 'Domestic Technology: liberator or enslaver?' in *Scarlet Women,* No 14, January 1982, reprinted in *Sweeping Statements: Writings from the Women's Liberation Movement* 1981-1983, eds Kanter, Lefanu, Shah and Spedding, The Women's Press, London, 1984; then in Ursula Huws, 'Challenging Commodification', in *Very Nice Work If You Can Get It: The Socially Useful Production Debate,* Spokesman, Nottingham, 1985. The argument is summarised in Ursula Huws, 'Consuming Fashions', *New Statesman & Society,* August 1988 and, most recently, in Ursula Huws, 'What is a Green-Red Economics?: the Future of Work' *Z*, September, 1991.

19 Tim Jackson, *Material Concerns : Pollution, Profit and Quality of Life*, Routledge, London, 1996.

20 Department of the Environment *Digest of Environmental Statistics,* information supplied by Friends of the Earth.

21 David Noble, 'Digital Diploma Mills: The Automation of Higher Education', article distributed on the internet with the author's permission by the Red Rock Eater News Service (pagre@weber.ucsd.edu), October, 1997.

22 Diane Coyle, 'Why knowledge is the new engine of economic growth', *Independent,* 23 April 1998.

23 I am indebted to James Woudhuysen for this comparison.

24 Harry Braverman's *Labour and Monopoly Capital: the Degradation of Work in the Twentieth Century,* Monthly Review Press, New York, 1974 remains the classic account of this process.

25 'There is No Finish Line – Running Shoes: the Follow-Up', *News from Irene,* Issue No 22, March, 1995, pp. 33-36.

26 The publication of Charles Babbage's *On the Economy of Machinery and Manufactures* in London in 1832 is as convenient a starting point as any to select for the systematic and conscious introduction of processes designed to reduce labour costs in manufacturing to a minimum.

27 Selected annually in a 'Miss Pears' beauty contest which continued certainly up

to the 1950s, when I was a child, and quite possibly for many years afterwards.

28 Sue Fernie and David Metcalf, 'Hanging on the Telephone', in *Centrepiece: the Magazine of Economic Performance*, Vol 3, Issue 1, Spring, 1998, p. 7.

29 Research by Datamonitor, quoted in Una McLoughlin, 'Call centre staff development' in *T*, October, 1997 pp. 18-21.

30 Incomes Data, *Pay and Conditions in Call Centre,* IDS Report 739, June, 1997, Geraldine Reardon, G. 'Externalising Information Processing Work: Breaking the Logic of Spatial and Work Organisation', United Nations University Institute for New Technologies Conference on *Globalised Information Society: Employment Implications*, Maastricht, October 17-19, 1996, and Sue Fernie and David Metcalf, 'Hanging on the Telephone', in *Centrepiece: the Magazine of Economic Performance*, Vol 3, Issue 1, Spring, 1998.

31 Martin Shaw and Ian Miles, 'The Social Roots of Statistical Knowledge' in John Irvine, Ian Miles and Jeff Evans (eds) *Demystifying Social Statistics*, Pluto Press, London, 1981, p. 30.

32 Danny Quah, 'Policies for the Weightless Economy', Lecture to the Social Market Foundation, London, April 21, 1998.

33 David and Foray, 1995, incompletely referenced citation in Luc Soete, 'The Challenges of Innovation' in *IPTS Report 7*, Institute for Prospective Technological Studies, Seville, September, 1996, pp. 7-13.

34 Luc Soete distinguishes three forms in which knowledge becomes embedded in a commodity (or, in his language 'contributes to growth') These are 'easily transferable codifiable knowledge', 'non-codifiable knowledge, also known as tacit knowledge (skills)' and 'codified knowledge'. See Luc Soete, 'The Challenges of Innovation' in *IPTS Report 7*, Institute for Prospective Technological Studies, Seville, September, 1996, pp. 7-13. This typology is extremely useful for analysing the components of value added but less so for keeping the labour process in focus.

35 This is certainly the practice in the West London district of Southall, which houses a large population from the Indian subcontinent and one of whose major industries is the preparation of curries and other Indian foods for British supermarket chains. See Ursula Huws, *Changes in the West London Economy,* West London Training and Enterprise Council, 1992.

36 The excellent bi-monthly *GenEthics News: Genetic Engineering, Ethics and the Environment,* chronicles new instances of this in every issue.

37 This is documented in the National Union of Journalists' monthly magazine, *The Journalist.*

38 Danny Quah, 'As Productive as a French Farmer', *Asian Wall Street Journal,* September 29th, 1997.

39 Henry Neuburger, 'Thoughts on the Productivity Paradox', unpublished paper, undated, p. 1. Arguing that measurement of total factor productivity is circular, he selected labour productivity as providing a more robust indicator.

40 Henry Neuburger, loc. cit., p. 9.

41 Jeff Madrick, 'Computers: Waiting for the Revolution' *The New York Review of Books,* March 26th, 1998.

42 Sue Himmelweit, discussion of ONS Households satellite accounts, Royal Statistical Society, November, 1997, quoted in Henry Neuburger, 'Thoughts on the Productivity Paradox', loc. cit.

43 Iulie Askalen, Olav Bjerkholt, Charlotte Koren and Stig-Olof Olsson, 'Care work

in household and market: Productivity, economic growth and welfare', paper submitted to the IAFFE-sponsored session at the ASSA meeting, Chicago, 3-5 January, 1998. I am indebted to Sue Himmelweit for bringing this important research to my attention. Henry Neuburger has partially tested this hypothesis in the UK by modelling – in the form of household satellite accounts – two areas of activity, childcare and catering, using both input and output measures. He concluded that 'conventional GDP by omitting unpaid child care understated growth in the 1960s and overstated it in the 1970s'. See Henry Neuburger, 'Modifying GDP', unpublished paper, undated, p. 2. For an interesting discussion of the development of satellite accounts and social accounting matrices, see Neuburger, 'Measuring Economic Activity', unpublished paper, undated. The evidence is clearly complex and contradictory, but such studies do point up the incomplete picture gained from the conventional accounting procedures.

44 I have discussed this literature at some length in Ursula Huws, *Teleworking: an Overview of the Research,* Joint publication of the Department of Transport, Department of Trade and Industry, Department of the Environment, Department for Education and Employment and Employment Service, London, July, 1996; and Ursula Huws 'Beyond Anecdotes: On Quantifying the Globalisation of Information Processing Work', United Nations University Institute for New Technologies Conference on *Globalised Information Society: Employment Implications,* Maastricht, October 17-19, 1996.

45 Paul Hirst and Grahame Thompson, *Globalization in Question,* Polity Press, Oxford, 1996, p. 27.

46 I have discussed this problem in 'Beyond Anecdotes: on Quantifying the Globalisation of Information Processing Work', in *Globalised Information Society: Employment Implications,* United Nations University Institute for New Technologies Conference, Maastricht, October 17-19, 1996.

47 I am currently engaged, along with the United Nations University Institute of Technology, in the design and implementation of a study which will, for the first time, provide reliable empirical evidence of the extent of teleworking and teletrade in services in Malaysia, with a sister study in Bombay.

48 Luc Soete and Karin Kamp, *The "BIT TAX": the case for further research,* MERIT, University of Maastricht, 12 August, 1996.

49 Richard I. Cook, MD, Cognitive Technologies Lab., Dept of Anaesthesia and Critical Care, University of Chicago, quoted in RISKS-FORUM Digest 19.75, forwarded by Red Rock Eater News Service (pagre@weber.ucsd.edu), May, 1998.

50 Mike Holderness, 'The Internet: enabling whom?, when? and where?', *The Information Revolution and Economic and Social Exclusion in the Developing Countries,* UNU/INTECH Workshop, Maastricht, 23-25 October, 1996.

51 I have summarised these, and other related factors, in a number of publications including, Ursula Huws, *Follow-Up to the White Paper – Teleworking,* European Commission Directorate General V, September, 1994, also published as *Social Europe, Supplement 3,* European Commission DGV, 1995; Ursula Huws, *Teleworking: an Overview of the Research,* Joint publication of the Department of Transport, Department of Trade and Industry, Department of the Environment, Department for Education and Employment and Employment Service, July, 1996; and Ursula Huws, 'Telework: projections', in *Futures,* January, 1991.

52 Ursula Huws, Sheila Honey and Stephen Morris, *Teleworking and Rural Development,* Rural Development Commission, Swindon, 1996.

GLOBALISATION AND 'THE EXECUTIVE COMMITTEE': REFLECTIONS ON THE CONTEMPORARY CAPITALIST STATE

Konstantinos Tsoukalas

Introduction

The old Marxian question is still unanswered and unanswerable: how can it be that an increasing majority of non-owners continue to lie under the democratic dominance of a shrinking minority of property owners? Why should the many accept the continuing domination of the few? More specifically, how does an increasingly inegalitarian democracy remain viable? The mechanisms that secure the continuity of the system thus appear as the most crucial of political issues. The fundamental role of the state in ensuring the reproduction and political cohesion of capitalist class societies remains the most important question of political theory.

The most critical issue is the articulation between class domination and political power. One must consequently continue to ask the same old questions even as one tries to understand what is distinctively new about the current period. In what sense is the problem of the relations between the state apparatus and capital different than it was in the 1970s? And to what extent has the relative autonomy of the state been modified? Can one observe new specific forms of reproduction of social relations within, both dependent social formations, and those belonging to the capitalist 'core'? And how is the new situation reflected on the level of social practices and class struggles?

These questions are, I believe, of enduring significance. It is my contention that some tentative answers to them can be offered by drawing on Nicos Poulantzas' analysis of what he identified as the new phase of imperialism.[1] In this period, inter-imperialist antagonisms are present not only in 'interstate' political confrontations but also, and I would add mainly, *within* all countries concerned, dependent or not. The phenomenon of 'induced reproduction' of imperialist antagonisms is crucial in this connection. No longer can one speak, in Lenin's terms, of a geographical partition of the globe into more or less defined zones of imperialist influence and dominance. The growing mobility of capital and new productive and information technologies have led to a concomitant mobility and fluidity of the economic bases of accumulation and exploitation. Direct exploitation of labour can potentially be pursued by capital in various social formations simultaneously but under very different conditions.

This tendential 'de-territorialisation' and destabilisation of exploitative forms, already anticipated in the 1970s but considerably accentuated since, has been accompanied by a universal rise of the rate of exploitation which has been countering the tendency of the rate of profit to fall. At the same time, the period of national Keynesian welfare states and differentiated norms of redistribution has come to a close, in the face of a new orthodoxy intent on reversing all welfarist trends on a universal scale. In all developed countries, including the metropoles, and even more so in dependent formations, economic inequality is rising rapidly, and simultaneously socially accepted 'tolerance levels' of unemployment, poverty and misery have been rising everywhere. When, in countries like Spain, a quarter of the active population is registered as unemployed, one may well ask at what point the 'acceptable' or inevitable begins and ends, and whether there are 'normatively determined' limits to exploitation and misery. What seemed to be socially unthinkable some years ago is now accepted as a matter of course. On the level of political representation, internalised 'social equilibria' are being rapidly supplanted by what are now seen as 'socio-technological equilibria'. Ethical controversies and policy considerations are being recast in terms of, and in some cases supplanted by, purely functional, performative standards of judgement.

In what follows, I touch very briefly on four specific points. First, the question of the precipitous decline, or even structural impossibility, of a 'national bourgeoisie' capable of retaining a relatively autonomous basis of capital accumulation, and of the new resulting internal equilibria in the dominant power blocks. Second, the growing fragmentation of the labouring population into numerous, mobile, differentiated and largely antagonistic fractions, with all that this implies for the process of dislocation and disorganisation of traditional forms of class struggle. Third, the new functions of the capitalist state which, in its increasingly authoritarian form, assumes overall reproductive responsibility by means of a growing regulation of the deregulation process. This is generating an unprecedented fusion, or confusion, of the state's economic and ideological functions. Fourth, the new developing forms of articulation between the various state apparatuses and the professional political personnel occupying their summits, on the one hand, and the representatives of big capital on the other.

The national bourgeoisie

All these issues are linked to the traditional territorial fragmentation of the world into relatively coherent 'national' social formations in the specific context of which capitalist social relations are materialised and reproduced. Obviously, territoriality itself has not evaporated. Indeed, the internationalisation of relations of production can by no means be understood to imply that economic activities take place in a trans-territorial class vacuum. Exploitation must always take place somewhere: in other words, within the territories of specific societies organised as sovereign states. Whatever the organisational forms taken by accumulation, their concrete operationalisation must remain, by definition, 'domestic'.

Thus, irrespective of the processes and mechanisms employed by capitalists in their search for profit, the main question to ask must concern the various forms of social activity of the bourgeoisie, or fractions thereof within the given domestic socioeconomic environments. If the constitution of domestic power blocks and their internal antinomies and political antagonisms can only be properly understood in conjunction with their trans-territorial entrepreneurial capacities, they must nonetheless also always operate within definite borders, however loose their dependence on internal markets may be. Even if capital may be controlled in the ether, it must be accumulated on earth.

In this respect, Poulantzas proves to have been quite prophetic. The pertinent question is in what sense can the 'nationally' operating capitalist forces be 'national' at all? Conversely, we are obliged to ask ourselves about the limits of accumulative autonomy of the dominant fractions of capital within national formations. Poulantzas underlined the gradual decline of traditionally autonomous national fractions of the capitalist class. Against the prevalent positions of the left in the early 1970s, not only did he pin down the decline and historic supersession of the accumulative autonomy of national bourgeoisies, but he also insisted on the necessity of a new concept, the 'interior bourgeoisie'. In contrast both to the 'national' bourgeoisie and the 'comprador' bourgeoisie, the new concept served to denote the emerging and thereafter dominant fraction of a domestically operating capital which was already permeated by, and was thus reproducing, 'external' inter-imperialist contradictions. In other words, it was becoming obvious already in Poulantzas' time that there could no longer be a dominant fraction of the domestic ruling classes which might continue the accumulation process within the narrow horizon of the domestic market.

Indeed, it is by now clear that with the partial exception of the US, Japan, and to a lesser extent some European countries, there can be less and less question of autonomous national bourgeoisies. Globalisation has brought about a further restriction of the accumulative autonomy of immobile domestic capital. This is evident in the proliferation of new developments that are undermining the traditional organisation, technologies and strategies by national firms. The spread of horizontal and vertical joint supranational ventures, the prevalence of trans-territorial technological and information networks, and the total liberation of trade and capital movements have transformed the competitive horizon of domestic capitalists. In this changing environment, the contradictions and antagonisms of international capital are now directly present within national socioeconomic formations. Transnational concentration has reached previously unheard of levels. At the end of the 1960s the 200 largest 'multinational' firms controlled 17% of the Gross World Product. By now, their activities are estimated to be of the aggregate order of 8 trillion dollars annually, almost one third of the planet's revenue.

Nevertheless, a major problem remains unresolved. The dominant discourse on 'globalisation' tends to neglect the fact that the process is neither unambiguous nor conceptually clear. On the one hand, it refers to forms of trans-territorial mobility, to the vertical or horizontal integration of productive activities and to mechanisms of international capital circulation. On the other hand, globalisation refers to new joint forms of control and to new strategies of capital accumulation. The two facets are certainly interrelated, but not identical. Organisational trans-territorialisation does not necessarily bring about any kind of supranational trans-territorial control. Metropolitan imperialist centres that remain ideologically, politically and economically bound to their national contexts compete for world hegemony. Even if accumulation tactics are de-localised, power strategies are still organised on the basis of definable inter-imperialist antagonisms, all the more so as long-term advantages seem contingent upon a relative military, economic, political and symbolic strength that can be represented and made use of only on the level of organised national territories. In this sense, deterritorialisation is by no means incompatible with intensified inter-imperialist struggle.

Indeed, to the extent that national states are not abolished, there can be no deterritorialised imperialism. If the fragmentation of organised political systems can be instrumental in permitting and encouraging mobile and de-localised forms of accumulation, at the same time these organised state entities provide the framework for the universal pursuit of collective power. In this context, new contradictions have given birth to new and complex capitalist strategies. On the organisational level, growing mobility has brought about a world-wide free market, which is preproduced by means of a conjunction of purely economic flows and the interplay of hegemonic interventions of national territorial interests. It may well be that the dominant capitalist mode of production is gradually putting in place a new original political superstructure that more perfectly corresponds to the perceived long-term interests of the competing metropolitan nations. If the relative autonomy of small and dependent states has traditionally been challenged by direct diplomatic, political or military interventions, by now utter dependence vis-à-vis the core countries is being enhanced and strengthened through the intermediation of what is conceived as a universally globalised capital which is free to impose its allegedly transnational will. Together with exploitation, imperialism is hiding behind the 'neutral' logic of a supposedly uncontrolled transnational market logic. This may well be one of the most important overall ideological effects of the globalisation discourse.

Once more following Poulantzas, it is now even more true that the contradictions between fractions of capital within national states are 'internationalised'. As a consequence, the disarticulation and heterogeneity of national bourgeoisies is further accentuated. Indeed, it may be doubtful whether the very term corresponds to a specific social reality. All dominant domestic forms are by now tendentially internal in Poulantzas' sense. The recent dismantling of national plants by Renault, a public and therefore by definition national firm, is a striking sign of the new era. Poulantzas' interior bourgeoisie may well prove to have been only a transitional form of organisation in a period when the internationalisation of capital was not yet completed. It is clear that the last remnants of these autonomous national bourgeoisies have been almost totally infeodated to mobile and potentially delocalised 'international' capital. Even if ultimate control remains in the hands of firms and cartels maintaining strong national affiliations, and this is obviously the case in the strongest metropolitan capitals, both investments and profits are potentially increasingly de-localised.

A manifestation of this new situation is the total repudiation of policies advocating import substitution. 'National' capital cannot be protected any more, for the simple reason that there is no material domestic structure that must be protected. Domestic deregulation is only an induced effect of international deregulation. Characteristically, the further liberalisation of international trade institutionalised by the Uruguay round – and, incidentally the complete collapse of protectionist 'anti-imperialist' third world solidarities in the UN and elsewhere – was imposed against residual protectionist tendencies both in the US and in Europe. Within the intercapitalist front, national bourgeoisies are being increasingly marginalised and defeated both economically and politically.

A word of caution is called for, however. It would, of course, be totally unwarranted to maintain that new supranational agencies directly reflecting the interests of world capital like the International Monetary Fund or the Group of Seven have supplanted territorial state sovereignty, directly imposing the concrete terms of national economic interventions. Far from constituting themselves independently as new sources of autonomous political and economic power to which states are forced to submit, these agencies reflect state-sponsored processes of globalization. In this sense, the nation-state remains as always the central terrain of class struggle.

The case of Europe is instructive on this point. Despite the rhetoric of integration, European member states are far from having fused into a single ideological and organisational structure giving birth to a coherent and relatively homogeneous system of class relations. There still is no European working class nor a European national bourgeoisie. If the treaty of Maastricht imposed a certain number of common fiscal and economic policies, it carefully refrained from anticipating the eventuality of common social policies. The overall responsibility for reproducing internal class relations and equilibria resides with national states. The Maastricht 'criteria' only refer to quantitative macroeconomic standards of economic, monetary and fiscal 'performance'. Despite the rhetoric on the dangers of social exclusion, the European Union does not demand that its members succeed in reducing unemployment, restricting poverty or minimizing social exclusion. In no sense does the impending emergence of a monetary union imply the construction of a 'social Europe'. Social coherence, systems of exploitation and class conflicts remain purely internal affairs. There still can be only one kind of political sovereignty: state sovereignty. And this is precisely the reason why the most pertinent political question today remains that of the relative autonomy of the *national* state.

Nevertheless, there can be no doubt that the internal forms of sovereign domestic political decision-making have been substantially modified. More than anything else, the free trade, austere public budgets and tight monetary policies called for by the Maastricht treaty reflect the new limits of the autonomy of responsible bourgeois states and the power blocks they are called upon to represent. They also reflect an incapacity, self-induced or otherwise, to imagine autonomous forms of domestic planning and economic intervention. But they also express a continuing antagonism between ideologised crystallisations of power.

Indeed, the potential mobility of capital is so overwhelming that all locally-bound investment decisions are increasingly dependent on the adequacy of domestically-secured rates of profit. Domestic productivity and exploitation rates can in practice not be raised other than by further squeezing 'social costs'. If they are to survive the growing competition the dominant fractions of internal capital (in alliance or not with fractions of mobile world capital) must always be able to disinvest and de-localise their activities, if need be. A territorially restricted capital can no longer compete with its mobile counterpart. And this is the reason why all capital is now capable of blackmailing the domestic system within which it chooses to pursue the accumulation process. Any substantial increase in the 'social costs' of redistribution will result in the threat of capital flight.

The political responsibility of states is consequently geared mainly towards maximising domestic productivity and exploitation rates on the terms of mobile capital. Once more with the partial, but significant, exceptions of the great American metropolis and Japan, investment forms adopted by big capital evoke the particular independence of the historically de-localised shipping industry. By dint of the fact that 'flags of convenience', which permit exploitation rates that are not burdened with any but minimal social costs, are eminently present and available, wages and labour security will tend to be restricted everywhere. Free inter-territorial mobility brings about a 'free market' of labour power which is indirectly reflected in the general fall in the relative remuneration of labour. All the more so with the collapse of 'existing socialism', now that the 'political risks' of subversion – risks which impeded free universal mobility – have been effectively minimised on a world scale.

The fragmentation of the labouring population

Transformations in the labour process and working class organisations have accompanied these processes of capitalist restructuring. Scientific developments in cybernetics, automation and computer science since the 1970s have contributed to an enormous increase in the productivity of labour and have rendered a growing fraction of the working population functionally redundant. By now, 'primary' labour markets are hardly distinguishable from 'secondary' ones. Structural unemployment and deregulation have afflicted all branches, even those most central and technically advanced. In parallel fashion, the continuous rise in life expectancies and longer periods of education have increased the percentage of people technically and structurally excluded from the production process. The absolute and relative cost of social welfare, including education, was constantly rising as a result; a development which was rationalised in terms of a 'fiscal crisis of the state'. Thus, the combination of the overaccumulation of capital, growing intercapitalist competition and soaring social costs led to a universal trend towards a 'renegotiation' of the overall terms of labour contracts and for a concomitant reorganisation of the exploitation patterns in the world economy.

The combined effect of a global reduction in growth rates and the deterritorialisation of productive activities acted to disarticulate and disorient working-class organisations everywhere. 'De-proceduralisation' of labour conflicts undermined solidarities and further disorganised class affiliations, threatened as they were by the adverse socio-psychological effects of the new technologies which transformed the subjective representations of organised productive units. Even more to the point, the gradual but uncontainable increase of unemployed and unemployable masses led to a further fragmentation of the working class. Consequently, technical and economic progress has been internalised in increasingly non-political terms: working class organisations which had been previously led to believe that they would actively and permanently participate in the decision making process, and thus negotiate the overall terms of income distribution, were once more pushed to the sidelines. While still nourishing hopes for uninterrupted progress towards petty consumer paradises, they suddenly found themselves to be more or less ousted from the power game. Internal political systems were subsequently pressured to accept and regulate redistribution norms according to the dictates of the free market. However, this was only one of the aspects signalling the spectacular retreat of responsible public initiatives into new forms of regulative inertia. States have been progressively unburdening themselves of the task of shaping both the present and the future. The responsible 'pastor-state' is being rapidly dismantled.

The working class faces a genuine dilemma in its struggle to defend what is left of its postwar gains in the real and social wage. In the best case, organised labour may succeed in clinging to some gains from the previous era, such as free education and medicare. In the worst case, labour seems obliged to accept, however reluctantly, that with further redistributional demands considered an impediment to 'competitiveness', the gloomy present must be permanently traded off against the doubtful hope of a sunnier future, or at least the doubtful security of the status quo. The uncertain temporal dimension of labour struggles is absolutely novel both in its strategic implications for, and in its tactical effects on, the ideology of the Left. Flexible representations of time, flexible labour forms, flexible individual strategies and the flexible internalisation of social roles necessitate a flexible class consciousness and equally flexible forms of mobilisation.

Thus, anomic and recurrent labour pressure seems to be perfectly compatible with what is left of redistributional and reformist demands which are now ostensibly tied to domestic capital accumulation. Disorganised and uncoordinated activities have tended towards a further political and social fragmentation of the labouring class. Indirectly, the long-term strategy of the bourgeoisie, which has always aimed at dividing the working class into fractions, has thus met with a good deal of success. As a side effect, post-fordist organisational realities have led to a growing and cumulative political segmentation and fragmentation of workers and dispossessed alike. Meanwhile growing numbers of desperate and largely unemployable masses are pushed towards adopting unorganised individual survival strategies. Predictably, the new forms of informal survival are closely tied to 'postmodern delinquency' practices. New 'illegalisms' are being constantly promulgated within societies where increasing police controls and extending penitentiary systems are becoming more and more crucial mechanisms not only of social control, but also of class regulation.

It is obvious that the political and ideological 'retreat' of working class struggles since the 1980s is a 'pertinent effect' of the new phase in the process of reproduction of class relations. It is an effect which is not isolated within the strictly economic sphere, but is also determined by the remarkable ideological and political forms of the overall victory of the bourgeoisie. If nothing else, the new political direction indicates not only that prevailing global relations of production are accepted as portrayed by the discourse of globalization, but also, significantly, that the unilaterally imposed norms of income distribution within concrete social formations may extend to a temporal horizon that seems to be indefinitely receding into a distant future.

The new functions of the capitalist state

Within this context, the tendencies described by Poulantzas in the early 1970s have been largely consolidated. The economic functions of the state are being progressively amalgamated with its repressive and ideological functions. In this respect, the rise of technocratic 'developmental' authoritarianism may precisely be understood in light of the fact that the 'interior' field in which it is called upon to operate is already circumscribed by the contradictions of the dominance of mobile international capital. More and more, the main economic functions of the state must therefore be geared towards ensuring the institutional and ideological conditions of the internationally-imposed deregulation of economic and labour relations, as well as to contributing to the general acceptance of the alignment of public policies to the norms of international competitiveness. As already mentioned, above and beyond the project of developing of the national economy, the demand for unregulated competitiveness must reign supreme. In this sense, the most pressing ideological task of the state is to convince everyone of the need to de-institutionalise and 'de-substantialise' all previous forms of consensual negotiation – i.e. to *dis*-incorporate social classes.

It is thus no accident that, irrespective of the ideological and political 'colours' of the government in power, it is only within the strongest core countries (e.g. Germany, France, Sweden, Canada) that the new authoritarian techno-orthodoxy may still be somewhat resisted in order to maintain existing equilibria. Weaker links in the imperialist chain, even if formally run by social democrats (e.g. Italy, Spain, Greece), are obliged to accept induced forms of labour division and deregulation much more unconditionally. As things stand, it is only in the few countries that constitute the hard imperialist core that domestic class contradictions can still be politically negotiated. Wherever 'national economies' are weak, states feel obliged to deflect or simply neutralise redistributive demands.

In this respect, the ideological functions of the state are of crucial importance. Never before has the ideological notion of the 'international competitiveness of the national economy' been more compulsively central. Under the auspices of the state, all ideological apparatuses (schools, media, parties, mainstream intellectuals, trade unions, etc.) are systematically geared towards the dominant developmental tenets, characteristically modified to suit the new imperatives. If long-term development is synonymous with deregulated competitiveness, the very terms in which the socially desirable is defined are fundamentally modified. In lieu of an 'autonomous', 'sustained' and 'autocentred' national development – the overriding myth of the 1960s and 1970s – international 'productivity' and 'competition' now appear as the new objectivised gods.

The first preoccupation of state intervention is thus to 'convince' people of the developmental ineluctability of 'modernisation' via technocratic deregulation. The restitution of the inherent 'sovereign rights' of the market lurks behind all public rationalisations. It is no accident that in contrast to the social-democratic period, which relied on social, political and ideological arguments, the burning issue of 'nationalising' or 'de-nationalising' industries and utilities is now seen uniquely in terms of its repercussions on quantitative economic 'performance'. Deregulation is the new dominant theme, and unlimited performative deregulation is not only a specific form of active intervention but also the main ideological tenet that must prevail. Intervention in the deregulating process is, however, an internally contradictory process. The constant public attention needed to bring about appropriate institutional and legal deregulatory reforms calls for increasingly authoritarian forms. The state is present to ensure that the 'national economy' is organised so as to compete with the other 'national economies' under the best possible terms. Furthermore, this general assertion is made acceptable precisely because of its alleged technical validity. The obvious Hobbesian metaphor may be expressed in military terms: states are at 'war', each to protect its national economy; the true enemy being, however, not other states, but each state's domestic subjects (i.e. its working class).

In this context, the concrete effects of competitiveness on the forms of class struggle, and even the question of who gains and who loses, may appear as irrelevant and 'ideological'. Regardless of the 'nationality' of the bourgeoisie which is to profit from market deregulation, it should be encouraged to make full use of its class prerogatives. The main agents of class struggle are a deterritorialized and integrated bourgeoisie versus a territorially tied and fragmented working class. This 'geo-social' imbalance is only the latest expression of the structural power asymmetry between capital and labour. And the exacerbation of these asymmetrical terms seems to impose new structural limits on the 'accepted' forms of class conflict, as they must be secured, imposed and legitimated by the state.

In this sense, as Poulantzas was the first to note, the internationalisation of capital 'neither suppresses nor by-passes nation states, either in the direction of a peaceful integration of capitals 'above' the state level (since every process of internationalization is effected under the dominance of the capital of a definite country), or in the direction of their extinction by the American super-state'. On the contrary, national states provide the necessary mechanisms and 'take charge of the interest of the dominant imperialist capital in its development within the 'national' social formation'.[2] Indeed on the material level, deregulation, labour fragmentation, productivity and profit maximisation can only be ensured within a juridically-given territorial context. In this sense, far from dispensing with national states' functions and services, the extended reproduction of the accumulation of international capital is totally dependent on their constant intervention.

Thus, the institutional and economic prerequisites of capital accumulation rest on the national states' capacity to guarantee the new forms of accumulation internally. It is precisely in this sense that the political and ideological cohesion of social formations, still materialised only by and through states, provides the basis for reproducing the (interchangeable) coherent socioeconomic and legal environments necessary for any productive organisation. The jurisdictional fragmentation of sovereign political formations can consequently be seen to correspond ideally to the interests of de-localised capital. Whereas the organised state remains a necessary mechanism for securing the external conditions of production and reproduction, these conditions are far better served if all states are separately induced to reproduce their internal institutional and ideological order on the universal deregulatory model. On the contrary, the eventual appearance of a universal democratic 'Super-State' could lead to the resurgence of political autonomies liable to curtail unlimited capitalist power.

The fragmentation of relatively autonomous sovereign territorial political jurisdictions thus corresponds to the interests of deterritorialised capital. If nothing else, this justifies Poulantzas' assertion that one should not *stricto senso* speak of 'state power': the 'post-modern', 'post-industrial' and 'post-fordist' 'national state-system' provides a perfectly suitable institutional and ideological setting for ensuring the reproduction of trans-territorial forms of accumulation.

Relations between the personnel of the state and capital

Finally, the state of affairs described above has some further important implications for the objective forms of articulation between political personnel and big capital. This is one point at which the question of relative autonomy may be concretised and empirically substantiated. One of the central objects of discussion between Miliband and Poulantzas in the 1970s referred to the theoretical relevance of relations between the personnel occupying the 'summits' of the state and big capital respectively. While Miliband insisted on the importance of demonstrating the bourgeois class origin of political personnel and their special class links to the management of big firms, Poulantzas completely disregarded class origin and underlined the objective character of relations between the ruling class and the state apparatus. Poulantzas was mainly preoccupied with the structural determination of state interventions; he considered that whatever motivations, behavioural tendencies and personal links there might be between political personnel and big capital, the operation of these objective relations was a simple effect of the objective cohesion of public apparatuses, necessitated by their overall function.

On the epistemological level I would tend to side with Poulantzas. Recent developments, however, may suggest new objective reasons why the 'personal links' between capital and political personnel are henceforth not only empirically ascertainable, but in another way, structurally determined, if not inevitable. Regardless of their class origin, and independently of whatever class allegiances they might feel, those at the summits of state bureaucracies are increasingly tied to the private sector. The objective cohesion of the state apparatus, including that of political parties, calls for new 'particularistic' forms of structural articulation between high public office holders and private capital. Indeed, it is my contention that, in a convoluted and indirect way, the new internalised functions of the capitalist state described above have contributed towards a growing political and economic dependence of political personnel on capital.

Very briefly, this emerging tendency may be suggested in the form of a number of points.

(i) The universal domination of competitive instrumental rationality has led to a restriction of the economic policy options of most states. The growing disillusionment and depoliticisation of the population at large is an immediate consequence. Most developed countries seem to be advancing in the steps of the US where the crystallisation of political antagonisms do not immediately correspond to clear class alternatives.

(ii) An important result of this new conjuncture is the dwindling 'internal' basis for financing political parties. Less and less are labour and professional organisations capable of mobilising their members in collective actions aimed at intervention and struggle on the political level. Hence the prevalence of fragmented and individualistic free-rider attitudes – described as 'natural' by liberal organisational theorists – in growing sectors of social life. Inevitably, contributions of funds and energy by individual militants are being drastically curtailed.

(iii) In a related development, political conflict is concentrated on secondary debates and cannot directly reflect well-established and internalised class issues. To the extent that earlier collective images animating political struggle have been rapidly eroding, political discourse is suffering an increasing loss of substance. The social alternatives opened up by democratic political antagonisms must be constantly reiterated on the level of collective representations. In this sense, one may legitimately speak of a growing 'theatricality' of internal political conflict, still organised in parties. Political competition, in which parties constantly struggle to increase electoral and ideological influence, is developing into a subsystem ever more detached from any social and class foundations.

(iv) However, desubstantialised controversies are becoming more and more expensive, in both absolute and relative terms. On the one hand, organisation costs have soared far beyond available organisational resources. On the other hand, the very fact that the issues separating the main contenders for political power are becoming far less visible increases the importance of what is now termed 'political communication'. The everyday political game of propaganda and public image-making is now an integral part of political life. Elections increasingly are won or lost not according to the relevance of issues that are increasingly beyond the grasp of the population at large, but as a result of the success or failure of pervasive public relations activities. Persons and parties are thus forced to rely on expensive media coverage and on the services of highly-paid professionals. On all fronts, the costs of democratic competition are accumulating.

(v) If direct contributions are dwindling and costs are soaring, the democratic political-electoral game must be suffering an increasing deficit. To the extent that the 'political costs' necessary for the reproduction of the political system cannot be covered by the voluntary micro-contributions of individual party members, and external financing becomes a functional necessity, the question of new sources of 'political money' must inevitably be raised.

(vi) At the same time, an increasing amount of public-decision making consists of making contracts with big business. Privatisation, military expenses, public works, and all kinds of political choices, translating into contracts with the private sector, represent a growing fraction of public budgets. Obviously, deregulation refers to the capital-labour relation and not to the importance of public contracts which, if anything, have been growing in inverse proportion to the restriction of economic activities directly organised under the auspices of the state. It is no accident that inter-territorial 'bribes' are now not only widely acceptable but also accorded tacit official approval: in most European countries, 'unsuccessful' bribes are considered to be a legitimate business cost to be taken account of in domestic tax exemptions. Even if it is 'internally' frowned upon, transnational corruption is officially legitimated as part of the game. Inevitably, the articulation between 'domestic' public decisions and 'deterritorialised' private profits is thus more structured and continuous than ever before.

(vii) Like all forms of capital, state-linked big business reproduces on the domestic scale all the contradictions and antagonisms of de-localised international capital. Competition for particularistic state favours and contracts is becoming wider and deeper. The 'interior' bourgeoisies, together with their international linkages, are engaged in constant (oligopolistically organised) struggles in the expanding international market for public works, contracts, licences and interests.

(viii) Against this background, bids from national and international firms tend to be accompanied by more or less open offers of pay-offs. The question of '*functional corruptibility*', endemic in dependent countries, has rapidly become an objective structural feature of most, if not all, state structures. Indeed, the gravity of the problem is reflected in the fact that, like the USA, most European countries have recently implemented severe restrictions on electoral costs. Public financing of parties and elections is only one of the solutions that has been proposed. However, numerous studies have demonstrated that official public funds can account for only a fraction of soaring political costs. Political costs are virtually unlimited and uncontrollable. Whether this implies a growing structural corruption of political personnel – a fact which not only seems obvious but is amply corroborated by empirical studies – or whether this constant input of resources from the private sector to public and party decision-making is used exclusively to promote the organisational interests of parties and collective public entities, is irrelevant to my argument. The main point to underline is that, objectively, political personnel and parties seem obliged to solicit and 'accept' large private 'contributions' in order to reproduce themselves as communicationally viable candidates for public office. Apart from the question of 'corruption' and all the normative issues associated with it, it is a fact that new systemic factors are pushing the political structure towards an increased dependence on unofficial and usually hidden forms of financing. 'Personal links' are in this way structurally determined.

This development, in turn, exacerbates the general disillusionment with democratic forms. If general depoliticisation results in a growing dependence of political organisations on an uninterrupted flow of resources originating in the private sector, and to the extent that this new objective link between politicians of all shades and their respective (or common) economic 'sponsors' becomes public knowledge, the depoliticisation process will become cumulatively more pronounced. 'Lobbies' and 'sponsorships' are both functionally and organisationally integrated. By dint of their very success, the new forms of articulation between capital and top state personnel thus seem to be undermining general political credibility and further exacerbating both the financial deficit of the political game and its resulting financial dependence on capital.

Conclusions

What may be inferred from the above is that what has changed is the specific *form* of articulation of a particular branch of the state – indeed the most important and powerful of them, the elected political summit – and not the *principle* of the relation of articulation itself. The new dominant forms of capital accumulation on a world scale are precisely reflected in the new forms of relative autonomy of national states. The international tendency towards restricting the external regulation of capitalist competition has called for a concomitant circumscription of public decision-making processes within new limits. The symbolic and functional presence of national states is more necessary than ever for the cohesion of social formations at the same time that their economic and ideological interventions are far more 'deregulating' than before. This poses new dilemmas for the successful reproduction of the state.

It may well be that one of the growing contradictions within the contemporary capitalist state resides in the novel discrepancy between the professed aims of the political personnel responsible for the regulation of deregulation, on the one hand, and the established state bureaucracy entrusted with the symbolical, juridical and ideological cohesion of national social formations on the other. Antagonistic relations between government and traditional public organisations – such as schools, local administrations, and health and welfare institutions – seem to be emerging on a scale that transcends the predictable response to threats to public services. Privatisation and rationalisation touch the core of what was the main institutional and political manifestation of the overall relative autonomy of a state apparatus guaranteeing social cohesion. The new obsessive doctrine of a quantifiable 'productivity' applied to all organised state functions – from the judicial to administrative and from the military to educational – introduce a universal technical-economic measure of assessment to functions that were traditionally legitimised though their autonomous value. In a convoluted way this may be seen to effectively diminish the relative autonomy of the state. Obviously, to the extent that market logic is introduced directly into the evaluation of public functions, not only is the internal system of organisation tendentially transformed, but more to the point, public services and functions are becoming detached from their original functions. Whereas the desirability of free urban public transportation was still an open issue in the 1970s, by now the debate is centred uniquely around the question of the possibility of running public transportation in 'efficient' ways. The very principle of redistribution serving the needs of social reproduction is blurred by the notion that all services and mechanisms, private or public, must 'naturally' bow to the technical prescriptions of profitability and competitiveness.

This development suggests another potential contradiction between the elected summits of the state personnel, who must direct the regulation of deregulation, and the rest of the state apparatus which remains responsible for the day-to-day social and symbolic cohesion of society. On the level of representations, this contradiction may be summed up in the ostensible incompatibility between public 'neutrality' and particularistic 'preferentiality'. These incommensurable principles must be actively reinterpreted by the state to open up new possibilities for a resolution. The state must be capable of taking preferential deregulatory decisions while simultaneously preserving the mask of bourgeois respectability. This is precisely what happens when the state summits and the organised political subsystem form direct financial links with capitalists in ways that uphold their assumed autonomy, while the principal normative 'separation' between private and public still reigns supreme. The ideological consistency of the system must confront the growing discrepancy between the 'neutrality' of the state and the functional dependence of its summits. Techno-authoritarian discourse provides a way out. But the price to be paid is the growing delegitimation of democracy. More than ever before, the social contract is reduced to an increasingly unconvincing procedural legality.

For all intents and purposes, it is capital itself that assumes the soaring costs of reproduction of the entire political subsystem in the narrow sense of the word: a new kind of 'faux frais', or false political cost, is thus emerging as a structural prerequisite for the smooth functioning of the state system. This fact largely explains why, as a matter of course, big capital offers direct and simultaneous financial support to all serious contenders for elected political power, regardless of ideological shade. For the representatives of the internal bourgeoisies – divided as they are among themselves – the issue is not so much one of maintaining political personnel on their direct payroll, but rather, one of sustaining a system of political representation that is dependent on direct inflows of uninterrupted capital 'subventions'.

One may conclude that while relative state autonomy still remains important, this autonomy is more and more structurally 'selective'. In the contemporary international setting, the overall function of national states is being rapidly reconfigured by 'pseudo-autonomous' forms of articulation between the political and the economic. But this 'pseudo-autonomy' is not reflected in the same way throughout the various branches of the state apparatus in all their growing interrelation and complexity. Henceforth, if the mass of the state apparatus, including the judiciary, is still governed by the overall class contradictions, and thus continues to intervene in the interests of overall social reproduction, state 'summits' must assume the ambivalent but now essential role of imposing the required forms of deregulation.

Under these circumstances, one might well speak of a 'differentiated' relative autonomy, reflected in the internal contradictions between the various 'branches' of the state apparatus. It is precisely these contradictions which mark the character of the present phase. Indeed, if state summits function in ways that bring to mind the most schematic of marxist formulations – one is more and more tempted to return to instrumentalist conceptions – its overall role must still consist in securing a minimum of social cohesion under the hegemony of the dominant class, a cohesion the costs of which are by now mainly 'political'. In addition, one might add, the political and ideological dangers emanating from the political personnel's incapacity to reproduce itself in a visibly autonomous way is counterbalanced by the further fetishisation of the professed technical and ideological neutrality of other branches of the state apparatus. The more obvious it becomes that the specific objective forms of articulation between the state summits and the bourgeoisie are increasingly ambiguous and suspect, the more it is ideologically fundamental to cling to the illusions of public meritocracy and technocratic neutrality. If possible, these internal contradictions between branches of the state, in respect of the forms of their 'relative autonomy', must be masked behind a wider techno-authoritarian discourse covering the entire function of what is still considered to be the public sphere.

I hope to have shown here that the newly crystallised forms of articulation between the political and the economic must be re-examined in view of the global effects of a growing non-correspondence between the 'national' scale of political-ideological organisations and struggles on the one hand, and the 'inter-nationalised' and deterritorialised scale of capital accumulation on the other. In this respect, the national state, still the fundamental instance ensuring the reproduction of social cohesion, has been led to modify spectacularly the form of its specific interventions as well as its functional role in neutralising the dominant forms of class struggles, both on the economic and on the political-ideological level. In this context, new contradictions between the various components and functions of the state apparatus have appeared, endangering its internal cohesion. As a consequence, the ideological and political prevalence of the new dominant 'techno-authoritarianism' assumes a paramount importance.

One of the main political side-effects of the present conjuncture is that it has become clear that working-class struggles have entered a new phase and face unprecedented challenges. The contradiction between the national and international loci of class struggles has led to a growing disorganisation and demoralisation of the victims of exploitation. Obviously, I cannot suggest the ways in which these new trends may be overcome. But it seems to me beyond doubt that it is impossible for the various fragments of the working class to advance towards new strategies and tactics if the political implications of complex new forms of state intervention, and the concomitant question of the modes of its relative autonomy, are once again given the highest priority.

NOTES

This is an abbreviated and revised version of a paper prepared for the symposium on 'Miliband and Poulantzas in Retrospect and Prospect,' City University of New York Graduate Centre, April 24–25, 1997.

1. Nicos Poulantzas, *Classes in Contemporary Capitalism*, London 1974.
2. Ibid., p. 73.

CONTRADICTIONS OF SHAREHOLDER CAPITALISM: DOWNSIZING JOBS, ENLISTING SAVINGS, DESTABILIZING FAMILIES

Wally Seccombe

W.R. Timken Jr, fourth in a venerable family line of industrialists, heads a bearing and steel company in Canton Ohio. The city's biggest employer, the Timken company is very advanced technologically with an excellent reputation for high quality products; yet in another sense it is an old-fashioned firm. As they *New York Times* reports, Mr. Timken is a paternalistic boss.[1] Born and raised in Canton, he worked for the firm for two decades under his father's tutelage before taking it over, and he has no intention of moving the company anywhere. Proudly, he shows the *Times* reporter a letter his grandfather sent to his sister in 1922 stating:

> Money should be conscientiously used to some extent right here in Canton where all of it came from. I recognize our bounden duty to do something for Canton and the thousands of men and women here who have toiled and made the many millions each of us have.

Here is a frank acknowledgment that capital's wealth derives from labour, plus a firm commitment to the company's workers and their home town – both antiquated sentiments in today's world of free-floating 'shareholder value' and jet-setting CEOs with several residences but no fixed address.

Wall Street brokers don't look at modern capitalism in the way Mr. Timken does. He is a representative of fixed, productive capital rooted in Canton for four generations; they head up circulating capital, zipping around the world in cyberspace, seeking places to park some notional cash today in order to take off with much more of it tomorrow. The Street doesn't like Mr. Timken's company very much. The *Times* reporter explains:

> The rap on the Timken Company from Wall Street analysts is that it could be even

> more profitable if it would only be more aggressive about downsizing its work force of 18,000, if it were not so preoccupied with striving to produce the top quality bearing and steel products in the world and if it was less worried about its responsibility to the people of Canton. 'The company is so focused on quality and its reputation and pleasing its customers,' said Tobias Levkovich, an analyst at Smith Barney, 'to some degree it hurts the profit margins.

The money managers contrast Timken with another firm headquartered in Canton, the Diebold Company. Diebold is North America's leading maker of automated teller machines, so there is an obvious affinity with Wall Street's business. The ATM extends the computerization of financial transactions, displaces more labour from the circulation of wealth, and enlists the savings of the masses in the business of capital accumulation in a much more direct way than the traditional savings account ever did. It's a marvellous instrument for asserting the dominance of circulating over fixed capital, part of a much larger process that is installing money managers at the head of the banquet table in the new digital economy. But the main reason Wall Street analysts love Diebold is that the company has cut costs and made a bundle in the last decade, opening several lower-paying factories in the South, moving hundreds of decent-paying manufacturing jobs out of Canton.[2] If Diebold awards its top executives with stock options, as four in five large U.S. corporations do today, then the company's soaring stock-price will have personally enriched them in a multi-million dollar way for shedding employees in Canton.

When the bull market began its record-setting run in 1982, the Dow Jones Industrial Average stood at 776; sixteen years later, it has just broken through 9000 as I write. Hoping to moderate the market's steep ascent and thus avert a crash, Federal Reserve Chairman Alan Greenspan warned in December of 1996 that American investors had fallen prey to 'irrational exuberance'. Since then, the Dow has risen 65%. No-one knows how long this will last or whether the market's frothy bubble can be gently deflated. When the Crash of October 19th 1987 knocked 22.6% off the Dow in a single day (the largest one-day drop in its history), most money managers agreed, with the chastened wisdom of hindsight, that the market was overvalued and due for a major correction. So what are these sages saying today, with the Dow in orbit at three and a half times the peak it reached prior to Black Monday? Not much. Most are too busy raking in the loot to fret about the minority of nay-sayers in their ranks who warn that the market is seriously overvalued.

The persistent rise of equity markets is a euphoric bet by investors on the stellar future of 'shareholder capitalism' and its capacity to keep driving up profit margins. Psychologically, the willingness to bet is related to many factors, above all the free-market elation that swept across the Western world with the collapse of Communism. And conversely – the doubts lurking beneath this giddiness – there is a nagging feeling that the deregulated future is shaping up as a very scary place. Millions of middle-aged baby boomers (the author included) fear that by the time we lose our jobs, retire, or require extensive hospital care, the supports provided by the welfare state won't be there in a reliable form. We'll be left, with our families, to fend for ourselves. This ominous prospect makes it prudent to start investing our personal savings in a retirement fund during our peak earning years while we are still in a position to do so.

The meteoric rise of stock markets has been spurred by the computerization of long-distance financial transactions and the deregulation of cross-border capital flows. In the past decade, trade has expanded at twice the rate of GDP, foreign direct investment at three times, and cross-border share-transactions at ten times.[3] In 1970, transactions in bonds and equities across U.S. borders represented 3% of the nation's GDP; by 1996, 164%.[4] In the post-war era of fixed-rates (before the U.S. went off the gold standard in 1971), the vast bulk of foreign exchange was directly related to trade, tourism and foreign direct investment. Today, these activities account for a small fraction of the flow; nine-tenths of it is orchestrated by fund managers speculating on currency swings, or by firms and investors trying to defend themselves against such swings through the use of derivatives and hedging strategies. Money is changed between currencies today at the mind-boggling rate of $1.5 trillion on an average business day, double the volume of five years ago. Daily turnover on the world's foreign exchange markets often exceeds the total reserves of the major central banks.[5] The resulting currency gyrations have made it much more difficult for governments to coordinate their macro-economic policies and almost impossible to predict or control the terms-of-trade between countries – two essential conditions of international financial stability. When things go horribly wrong – as they have most recently in East Asia – the global money traders shun countries and denounce governments that they had embraced just yesterday, diverting attention from the ways their own speculative machinations precipitate financial chaos. This exculpatory exercise follows predictably from the first article of neo-liberal faith – that 'the markets' are never wrong.

Freed from substantial government restraint, the anonymous power of circulating capital has 'turbo-charged' Anglo-American capitalism and spread its neo-liberal currents around the world.[6] Working in concert with other forces, the tidal wave of near-money sloshing around in cyberspace is shifting the balance of power:

- altering the prevailing patterns of capital accumulation, the pecking order among the agents of capital, and the organizational form of large corporations;
- turning the balance of class power against labour by intensifying job insecurity on the one hand, while luring the family nest-eggs of fully employed workers into a compensatory bet on the continued appreciation of financial assets on the other, thus confounding their class interests.

The paper examines these changes in turn.[7]

Fund Managers and the Triumph of Shareholder Capitalism

As the hired guns of circulating capital, money managers champion 'shareholder capitalism'. They snap up the shares of companies whose top executives aggressively slash the payroll, shut-down unprofitable plants, sell off sideline businesses and use the profits extracted by ruthless cost-cutting to boost dividend pay-outs and repurchase company shares. In most cases, radical pruning 'works' – at least in the short term: profit margins rise and the net gain is passed through to shareholders. But what if CEOs have longer-term, fixed-capital priorities – such as offering employees job security and training opportunities, signing multi-year contracts with local suppliers, and retaining earnings for longer-range R&D investments? This is 'stakeholder capitalism' (a term of derision on Wall Street) wherein executives eschew the immediate advantages of layoffs, outsourcing and spot-markets in favour of deepening the firm's relationships with its employees, suppliers and local communities in the belief that these *in situ* commitments will benefit the company and its shareholders in the long-run. The *modus operandi* of the major Japanese corporations has been more reflective of stakeholder priorities, and we know what a reversal of fortune has occurred between American and Japanese capital in the past decade. Following Wall Street's lead, the world's money managers are increasingly inclined to shun companies that insist on preserving the stakeholder model.

Initially, incumbent executives and board-insiders rebuffed the demands of the brokers and fund managers, resenting the latter's intrusion on *their* turf. During the 1980s, they fought back with poison pills, golden parachutes, staggered board terms, and a raft of other measures designed to make managers harder to dump and companies unappealing targets for hostile takeover bids. By 1990, about half of America's largest companies had adopted such measures.[8] But even as corporate executives tried to defend their traditional prerogatives, money managers increased their leverage through a judicious combination of carrot and stick – if a company's share-price outperformed the market average, its top executives would reap millions through performance bonuses and stock options; but if it lagged behind its competitors for long, they might be shown the door.

The directors of publicly-traded companies whose stock 'underperforms' are no longer prepared to be patient with CEO's who seem shy about 'making the tough decisions' to cut costs and streamline operations. And if they won't pull the trigger, institutional investors with big blocks of shares will press for changes at the top, or failing that, ally with the firm's competitors to oust entrenched managers. The waves of mergers and acquisitions that have fuelled the escalation of North American stock-markets since the early 1980s have been based upon identifying companies that are *not* aggressively maximizing shareholder value, taking them over, turfing out the old managers and bringing in executives prepared to do whatever is necessary to restore the company's profit margins.

Slimming Corporations and Fattening Shareholders

Under intense pressure from fund managers to boost shareholder value, corporate executives have embarked upon a crash-course in divestment and re-engineering – spinning off sideline businesses, shutting down losing divisions and shifting production to regions with lower labour costs. They've become so keen to cut costs that radical pruning is undertaken by thriving firms as well as those who are floundering. A 1992 survey of 530 large firms in the U.S. found that three-quarters had downsized in the past year, and one in four had divested, merged or acquired businesses. The great majority were making money.[9]

When drastic cuts are made by desperate corporations awash in red ink, the workers and communities hurt by job losses regret management's decisions but generally find them understandable. When, however, downsizing is undertaken by the managers of prosperous firms with flush balance sheets, their actions are more likely to provoke disbelief and outrage. Slashing the payroll of profitable companies breaks with past practice and violates an implicit understanding that most workers felt they had with their employers. Robert Reich, former Secretary of Labor in the Clinton Administration, comments:

> The norm had been, until relatively recent years, that if a company was highly profitable, workers could be assumed to have steady employment. Indeed, if company profits increased, workers' benefits and wages would increase with them. . . . That is no longer the case . . . Highly profitable companies now shed thousands, if not tens of thousands, of workers. In doing so, companies are in certain cases doing nothing more than redistributing income from employees to shareholders.[10]

Successive waves of corporate streamlining in the eighties and nineties have reversed the post-war trend towards vertical integration and horizontal conglomeration. Capital markets today impose a 'conglomerate discount' on the parent company's stock, exerting enormous pressure on firms to eliminate intertwined ownership structures and 'fix, sell or close' money-losing subsidiaries.[11] Wall Street's new mantra is: 'Back to basics, refocus on the core business'.[12] After two decades of such 're-engineering', most major North American corporations are leaner than they were in the 1970s. Slimmer, but not smaller. Despite the glib talk by futurists and management gurus about the virtues of nimble 'networking' corporations, downsizing does not normally entail shrinking the corporation. What gets shrunk is the number of employees in relation to company revenues. From 1971 to 1991, the world's 500 largest multinationals increased their revenues by seven times without increasing the number of workers they employed globally.[13]

Neo-classical economists argue that in most cases downsizing raises the efficiency of firms and boosts their profit margins, with the gains being passed through to shareholders. While ostensibly refraining from moral judgment, the implication is that whatever makes private corporations more efficient must be good for almost everyone. The normative premiss lurking in the mainstream paradigm is revealed when the social devastation that results from corporate culling is referred to as an 'externality'; this is tantamount to telling laid-off workers, their families and by-passed communities: 'gee, we're sorry you got in the way, but Progress stops for no-one these days'. Marxists view corporate downsizing from the dynamic standpoint of 'many capitals' in competition with one another, not from the microeconomic standpoint of the (ideal) firm. From this perspective, corporate purging is an essential corrective to capitalism's recurrent 'tendency to over-production'.[14] In the competitive quest to increase market-share, firms rush to expand their productive capacity. Sooner or later, entire industries becomes glutted with more product than can be sold at a profit. In the face of brutal price competition, the only way firms can restore sagging profit margins is to discharge surplus capacity by laying off workers, shutting down older production facilities and driving less efficient firms out of business. Short of wars and depressions, financial markets are vital to the Darwinian process of revitalizing the economy by culling laggards from the flock. While investment floods new business ventures and 'leading edge' technologies, it abandons the fixed capital embodied in older plants and less efficient enterprises, compelling uncompetitive firms to renovate, sell out, or die. Marxists would therefore agree with neoclassical economists that destroying surplus productive capacity by means of aggressive downsizing is perfectly rational from the standpoint of firms. Yet we would explain capitalism's tendency to devastate the lives of those it expels and leaves behind not as an incidental by-product of rising efficiency, but as the *systematic* result of firms treating labour-power as an expendable commodity while maximizing returns to shareholders under rigorously competitive conditions.

The Holy Terror and IBM's Born-Again Experience

The recent history of IBM provides a textbook case of the process at work with the stock market riding herd. As its mainframe business sagged and IBM stumbled badly in the PC and server markets, the company's stock got mauled, falling from an all-time high of $175 per share in August of 1987 to an eighteen-year low of $41 just six years later – a loss of 77% in the midst of a rising market. IBM's board finally 'got the message': the only way to regain the market's confidence and save the proud behemoth from slow death-by-disinvestment was to dump John Akers, the CEO, and parachute in a turnaround specialist, breaking with the company's longstanding tradition of promoting top executives from within.

After hiring an executive search firm to shop the top job round the upper echelons of corporate America, the recruiters approached Louis Gerstner, a free-agent with a fierce reputation after brief stints as the top boss at American Express and RJR Nabisco. Some IBM board members were worried that the candidate knew almost nothing about the computer industry, but the chief-recruiter prevailed: 'Lou was tougher than nails. Hard things needed to be done. I knew he could do them.' The candidate turned down an initial offer, but the recruiting team persisted. In a breathless *Fortune* magazine cover-story on the devout Christian (entitled 'The Holy Terror Who's Saving IBM'), Betsy Morris explains how Gerstner was persuaded.

> The recruiters told Gerstner that he had a moral imperative to take the job. He must do it for the good of the country. That worked. Said one individual involved: 'It appealed to his ego, his larger self – this concept of serving society as well as making money and being successful.'

Emboldened by higher purpose, Gerstner negotiated his terms. The main sticking point was that the board offered him a stock-option on a measly 500,000 shares and the candidate felt he was worth a million. With the promise of 'future considerations', he accepted the job.

When Gerstner took over Big Blue in April 1993, he arrived with his retinue of loyal disciples in tow, executives who had moved with him from company to company in his tours of duty. In a firm with an old-fashioned reputation for lifetime employment and corporate loyalty, tough-as-nails 'Lou and crew' finished off a massive downsizing that slashed IBM's payroll almost in half, from a high of 406,000 employees in 1986 to 219,000 by 1994. Predictably, they turned the stock-price around in the process.

> Heedless of criticism inside and outside the company, Gerstner began to cut costs, restructure and weed out disbelievers. He jolted the culture with shock therapy.... He slashed long-term debt from $14.6 to $9.9 billion, managed nonetheless to buy back $10.7 billion in stock, and goosed IBM's share price to $168, $6.75 below its all-time high.[15]

The company's PR department claims that under Mr. Gerstner's leadership IBM is going all-out to regain its dominant position on the 'cutting edge' of information technologies. A glance at the balance sheet tells a different story. From the end of 1994 to March 31, 1997, IBM shelled out $13.2 billion buying back its shares, while spending only $9.9 billion on research and development. In April 1997, Gerstner raised IBM's dividend a further 14% and announced that the company would repurchase another $3.5 billion shares.[16] The stock rose $8 on the news, and went on to reach an all-time high in May 1997. These spending priorities have already shrunk the company's net worth by 15% and do not bode well for its global competitiveness in the long-term. But IBM shareholders are not complaining. These fair-weather friends have made a bundle as Big Blue's share-price has risen five-fold under Gerstner's leadership; they will continue to hold the stock only as long as the company appears set to make them more in the near future.

For his part, Mr. Gerstner's book-value profit on the company's stock recovery was a tidy $69 million, and the board has granted him an option on another 300,000 shares. While he proclaims the public benefits of private greed, some IBM executives are more reticent.

> At a dinner with top executives and their spouses... Gerstner rubbed some people the wrong way by blatantly talking about how much they'd all reap as a result of the dramatic runup in IBM's stock.[17]

Perhaps they were reminded of the biblical story of their boss's Lord-and-Savior driving the moneychangers from the temple.[18]

The Bull Market in Stock Options and Share Buy-Backs

Exempting executive suites from the cost-cutting frenzy, corporate boards have jacked up the compensation of their top managers at a dizzying pace – 500% from 1980 to 1995. A study of 365 of the largest American corporations revealed that the average compensation of CEO's had bounded 30% in 1995 and another 54% in 1996. While lecturing their employees about the need for 'team-work and shared sacrifice', these hypocrites made 209 times that of an average American factory worker in 1996, up from 44 times in 1965.[19] Money managers are quite prepared to bestow their blessings upon the seven and eight-figure incomes top CEOs rake in annually, as long as the company's share-price is rising in line with its competitors. (The incomes of top fund managers, after all, are roughly comparable.) However, when a firm's profits sag and its share-price languishes, today's fund managers do not hesitate to publicly question the worth of its CEO. This generates bad press, pointed questions from shareholders at annual meetings, and attracts the unwanted attention of takeover sharks who smell blood in the water – all of which may shorten the tenure of bosses who fail to keep their company's share-price competitive.

The leap in executive pay has been driven by a shift in remuneration from basic salary to stock options. Ever since Berle and Means' classic study of the joint-stock company highlighted the separation of managers from owners, mainstream economists have fretted about the firm's 'agency problem' – how to ensure that managers consistently place the shareholders' interests above all other considerations. The stock option is designed to address this issue by providing managers' with a direct incentive to act in ways that will benefit shareholders; the 'virtuous circle' is closed when investors snap up the firm's stock, lift its share-price and enrich the option-laden executives whose priorities have pleased them.[20] In the past decade, this inducement has become a very sweet carrot indeed. The senior executives of publicly-traded American companies now receive about 40% of their pay in stock options, and in the largest corporations, the proportion is much greater. While the average salary of the twenty highest-paid U.S. executives in 1996 was a paltry $9.1 million, their stock-option gains averaged $72.8 million.[21]

In floating the huge stock options they offer their top executives, corporate boards usually prefer to repurchase stock in the market rather than issue new shares; in this way, they avoid adding to the outstanding shares in circulation and 'diluting shareholder value'. In effect, boards send the company's cash on a farewell tour through the stock-market (usually to rapturous applause) rather than handing it over directly in the form of salary hikes or bonuses. In 1996, the firms listed in the S&P 500 index announced repurchase schemes worth $145 billion; this represented an 87% leap over the prior year, which is especially remarkable in light of the sky-high prices the bull market placed upon them.[22]

It is easy to understand why top executives loaded with stock options would push repurchase schemes; but why have company directors gone along for the ride?[23] Under what circumstances does it make sense for directors to drain the operating capital of companies in order to boost their stock-prices? The answer seems to be: when firms have more cash on hand than they can productively invest and fear disgruntled shareholders.[24] There is no doubt that company coffers are now brimming with cash; since the recession of the early 1990s, profit margins have rebounded sharply. But high profit-rates in earlier periods did not trigger a buy-back binge of this magnitude. What is different now? Managements used to feel that it was prudent to retain the bulk of corporate earnings to fund major investments in future years or simply to cushion the firm's passage through the next recession. Nowadays, they act more like worried store-owners who empty out the cash register when they close up shop at night, leaving the till standing open in plain view of the street. To be seen hoarding earnings is asking for trouble from dissatisfied fund managers demanding higher dividend pay-outs, or worse, from corporate raiders vowing to 'unlock shareholder value' through a takeover bid. Far better to use the money to appease shareholders and inoculate them against takeover fever.

The wave of share buy-backs reflects an unusual conjunction of factors – exceptionally high returns to capital coupled with persistent constraints on expanding productive capacity. The source of the latter impediment is sluggish consumer demand, directly related to capital's success in cutting payroll costs and intensifying workers' insecurity. Since the mid 1970s, real wages have stagnated and workers have become increasingly worried about losing their jobs. With saving-rates at an all-time low, people are concentrating on paying down mountains of personal debt and are no longer spending with reckless abandon. The upshot is that many product-markets have become glutted. In this economic climate, major investments in new plant are too risky; so companies have opted instead to spend the surplus reacquiring their shares, boosting stock dividends and shopping for other companies. During the past fifteen years, U.S. non-financial corporations (in aggregate) have financed their investments *entirely* from retained earnings, while pouring additional billions into the market in the form of dividends, buy-outs and share-retirements, well in excess of new-share issuance and initial public offerings.[25] One recent study estimates that capital expenditure has dipped beneath 70% of cash-flow, a near-record low.[26] This shifts capital-value massively from the sphere of production into the sphere of exchange. As share-prices go into orbit and the average daily trading volumes on North American stock exchanges escalate, the total number of shares in circulation is actually contracting. Since households have also been injecting their savings at a record pace (more on this below), wealth is not flowing through North American capital markets in either direction; it is accumulating in the sphere of exchange as a vast swirl of speculative liquidity seeking higher returns.

Mergers and Acquisitions: Shopping for a Mate

When corporations have more cash on hand than they know what to do with, they can always go shopping. From 1981 to 1995, U.S. non-financial firms laid down 34% of their total capital expenditures buying one another. The 'M&A' binge which helped to drive the stock markets skyward shows no sign of abating. The 1980s were billed as the decade of 'merger mania'; yet in 1997, the fourth year in a row of record highs, the value of U.S. deals reached $957 billion, 12% of GDP. This is almost three times the volume of 1988, the peak year of the prior decade.[27] The merger waves of the 1980's were typified by hostile takeover bids sprung on ambushed companies by corporate raiders – notorious outsiders such as T. Boone Pickens, Carl Icahn and Ronald Perelman – who pursued their objectives by means of proxy fights and leveraged buyouts funded by junk bonds. While shotgun marriages still occur, the asset-strippers of the previous decade have been replaced by more respectable suitors, such as the CEOs of Johnson & Johnson, Hilton Hotels, Citicorp, and the Royal Bank of Canada. They are more inclined to sit down with their prospective partners behind closed doors and work out 'a good fit'. Executives often see an opportunity for strategic mergers when seeking to make their companies major players in rapidly evolving markets that neither firm has the capacity to fully exploit on its own.

As soon as companies announce deals, they are assessed by financial analysts from the top brokerage houses who broadcast their views instantaneously. The widely-publicized verdicts of the more prominent analysts are vital to the rapid formation of a consensus in capital markets, where windfalls are reaped by making the same move as everyone else but doing so just ahead of the pack. If the leading analysts declare that a proposed merger 'makes sense' – has a realistic chance to make money for shareholders in the not-too-distant future – the executives who cooked up the deal are rewarded by sharp jumps in their companies' stock prices.

While the typical merger deal is hailed from the office towers as 'a match made in heaven', down below on the shop floor, the company announcement reads much more like the weather advisory of an approaching tornado, threatening to suck up earth-bound creatures and spit them out onto the street. After watching other firms go through mergers and takeovers, workers anticipate that the consummation of their company's deal will provide top executives with a one-time chance to jettison contractual obligations, suspend the seniority principle, cull redundant staff in overlapping departments, and sell-off subsidiaries that bosses now view as peripheral to the amalgamated company's core business. From the vantage point of employees, today's 'civilized' mergers do not look very different from the asset-stripping shoot-outs of a decade ago.

Pouring Personal Savings Into Financial Markets

We shift our attention now from firms to households on the other side of capital markets. As real interest rates slowly descended through the 1990s, vast numbers of baby boomers concluded that they were no longer making enough money on their savings in the standard safe-havens of bank accounts, guaranteed investment certificates and Treasury Bills. So they opted to take greater risk in the pursuit of higher returns by shifting funds into equities and bonds, mainly via mutual funds. If investors are willing to ignore the broader social fallout and calculate their interests narrowly, this appears to be a good bet. Historically, the world's major stock markets have risen much more than they have fallen. The chances of coming away from the table with more money than one bet in the first place is vastly better here than in any casino. And since the odds are in the investors' favour, the longer they play, the more money they are likely to make – the exact opposite of gambling in a casino. It stands to reason, then, that people with savings and a mounting anxiety about the future of public provision would be willing to 'put their money down' on private capital. The only surprise is the sheer number and size of the bets being made. Once we take that into account, the stock market's blast-off is explicable in terms of the prosaic laws of supply and demand – a torrent of cash chasing relatively few investable assets. Since the start of 1995, the total value of shares owned by American households has surged by almost $5 trillion.[28]

Does the deluge of cash pouring into financial markets mean that households are spending less and saving more? Not at all. From the mid 1970s, when the real incomes of wage-earners stopped rising, most families dipped into their savings and went into debt in order to sustain their living standards. American households now save 3.8% of their disposable income, the lowest level in 58 years.[29] The share of disposable income they must pay to service their debts has reached the unprecedented level of 18%.[30] The indebtedness of Canadian households is only slightly less onerous. By 1996, the household savings rate of Canadians hit a 50 year low at 4.6% of disposable income.[31] In short, the tidal wave of new investment reflects a major *reallocation* of savings and not an increasing propensity to save. This is what economists call 'disintermediation'. Middle and working-class savers used to let the banks put their money to profitable use; now they are much more inclined to invest their own savings. The trend is transforming finance capital and hitching the fortunes of Main Street to Wall Street as never before.

The great bulk of the new money flooding into capital markets has been channelled through collective instruments such as mutual funds, pensions, insurance portfolios and trusts. This is a new trend. Wealthy Americans have always preferred to hire brokers, place their own bets, and hold shares individually. In 1985, individual investors held 57% of the shares of America's largest corporations and 'institutional investors' the remaining 43%. Nine years later, these proportions were reversed as vast numbers of middle- and working class households poured their savings into the capital markets. Mutual funds in particular are growing at a torrid pace. In the past seven years, the asset-value of U.S. mutual funds has quadrupled and now stands at $4.6 trillion.[32] 66 million U.S. citizens now have mutual fund accounts and for the first time ever, Americans have more value tied up in mutual funds than they hold on deposit in the nation's banks (at $4.2 trillion). Pension funds have also grown rapidly and are presently valued at $3.5 trillion.[33] The same trends are occurring north of the border. In 1986, Canadian mutual fund assets stood at C$20 billion; by April 1998, they totalled C$329 billion. Mutual funds and pension plans combined now hold a majority of the country's publicly-traded shares.[34] On both sides of the border, most of the new investment is going into equities. In 1990, U.S. stock funds accounted for less than a quarter of mutual fund assets; seven years later, over half. In Canada, the portion climbed from 37% in 1992 to 52% by 1996.[35]

When dispersed investors pool their savings in mutual and pension funds, they concentrate formidable power in the hands of fund managers. By and large, the latter exercise this power 'passively', simply playing the markets. There is no legal barrier to fund managers becoming active shareholders. A minority of pension managers have led the campaign for 'shareholder activism' and taken seats on corporate boards; a few have even become embroiled in takeover battles. But most money managers have too many stocks in their portfolios to get involved with specific companies; they prefer to sit at computer terminals and place their bets anonymously.

While money managers are capitalism's new magnates, wielding tremendous power *in* financial markets, they must submit to the discipline *of* those markets, held hostage by the same 'numbers game' they run on corporations. The price-performance of mutual funds is listed every day in the papers. Comparative historical data are readily available, and there is a rapid proliferation of guide-books by free-lance analysts who specialize in rating mutual funds for prospective investors. The latter are free to redeem their units at a day's notice and shop their savings around. Many unit-holders are impatient for results and mirror the restless attitude that money managers display towards companies. In fact, the short-term dispositions of both are linked, for when investors rush to withdraw their money from a fund, they force the manager to sell holdings to pay them off. Fund companies put their managers under intense pressure to deliver results and attract more money to their funds. The ones who lag behind their competitors may find themselves ousted and replaced by newer hot-shots on a roll – just like the underperforming CEOs they pressure.

In an era of resurgent 'shareholder power', mutual funds make the link between investors and companies more tenuous than ever. The unit-holders of a mutual fund do not actually own shares in the companies in the fund's portfolio; legally, the fund's trustee holds them (in segregated accounts) on behalf of the unit-holders. The decision to invest one's savings in financial markets is thus divorced from ongoing decisions as to where to invest it; this is a significant change in the history of capitalism.[36] Mutual fund investors are like money-travellers who decide which region of the world they would like to visit and pick a tour-operator who offers an attractive package-deal in the area. When they arrive at the airport, the operator takes over, planning the itinerary and hiring someone to drive the electronic tour-bus, deciding which sites to visit along the way. At this point the analogy breaks down, because at least the travellers on a real tour-bus take an interest in the sites they visit. In the case of most pension contributors and mutual-fund investors, ignorance is bliss. They have no idea what companies the fund currently holds in their name; that's what they hired the manager to worry about. The fund manager executes the trades that drive their imaginary bus through cyberspace, whistling cheerful tunes (in the form of quarterly fund reports) designed to persuade the paying customers not to rush for the exits when the road gets bumpy.

Labour's Capital Goes to Market

Corporate assets are held much more widely now than they have ever been. At the time of the 1929 Crash, only 3% of American households held shares; before the October 1987 crash, 25% did; now roughly 45% do.[37] Pensions have grown very substantially. In 1975, 45 million U.S. workers were enrolled in private pension plans with $259 billion in assets; by 1998, almost twice as many workers were included in pension plans with assets of $3.5 trillion, roughly 60% of the country's GDP. In 1957, 818,000 workers across Canada were enrolled in pensions worth C$2.3 billion; by 1996, 5.1 million workers (42% of the paid labour force) were registered in plans worth C$ 485 billion, equal to 62% of the country's GDP.[38]

While the base of the financial pyramid has been spreading out and down, the richest households still hold a disproportionate share. In the U.S., the wealthiest 10% of households claim 81% of stocks and 88% of bonds that are individually held (with pooled investments being much more broadly spread).[39] The property foundations of the capitalist class remain firmly in place. Since the overall distribution of wealth and income has become even more unequal in the past two decades, the Right's claim that we have entered an era of 'people's capitalism' is risible. Yet it would be equally foolish, from the Left, to conclude that nothing much has changed from a class perspective. Deferred labour income has become a *major* source of new money flowing into capital markets and the traditional dividing line between wage-income and capital accumulation has been blurred.

The new money flooding into financial markets shows up in data on household wealth, where financial assets are growing rapidly even in relative terms. In 1980, Canadian households held 20% of their assets in financial investments; a decade later, 30%. I have no current figure, but it is undoubtedly much higher now, perhaps 40%. In the U.S., financial assets now represent 43% of total household wealth. This is a 50 year high, and may well be an all-time record. The shift from physical to paper assets is related to the sag in the real estate market. Millions of working people have chosen to invest their savings in mutual funds rather than paying down the mortgage; thus far, it's been a profitable choice. American households today have more equity tied up in the stock market than they do in their own homes.[40]

Precisely because they are not rich, small investors tend to worry about how their investments perform. The more insecure they feel concerning their jobs and the public provisions of the welfare state, the more they count on private investments to help fund the future expenses associated with aging, retirement and their children's post-secondary education. People invest hope in capital markets together with their hard-earned cash. Will the finance minister's new budget be tough enough to please the bond market? Will the economy's growth slow down a bit so that the central bank doesn't raise short-term interest rates? Will the share-price of company X perk up when the CEO announces plans to restore profitability by shutting down several plants? These prospects may sound ominous to workers, but they please investors. Wage-earning investors have a foot in both camps. The main financial concern of younger employees is to take home enough pay at the end of the week to cover current expenses; as they reach middle-age, workers become increasingly concerned with the future. They wonder when they can afford to retire and worry that their families will sink into poverty when the paychecks suddenly stop. Acting prudently, many middle-aged workers save and invest so that they will have an additional source of income to supplement pension benefits and social security payments when they retire.

Pension Plans and Workers' Binary Class Interests

Twenty years ago, the management consultant Peter Drucker wrote a book entitled *The Unseen Revolution: How Pension Fund Socialism Came to America.* He saw the rise of employee pensions as having major implications:

> The shift to an economy in which the 'worker' and the 'capitalist' are one and the same person, and in which the 'wage fund' and the 'capital fund' are both expressed in and through 'labor income' is a radical innovation and at odds with all received theory. That the 'capital fund' is created out of labour income – and payments into a pension fund, whether made by employer, employee, or both, are 'deferred wages' and 'labor costs' – is perfectly sound Marxism. But it is totally incompatible with both classic economic theory and Keynesian neoclassicism. That this 'capital fund' is in turn channelled back through 'labour income' – which is what pension payments are – is again perfectly sound classical theory. But it is totally incompatible with Marxism, even at its most revisionist.

The worker and the capitalist have not become 'one and the same person' and the U.S. is today more thoroughly capitalist than ever. But Drucker was nonetheless prescient in drawing attention to an important structural change in the American economy that neither neo-classical economists nor marxists could readily acknowledge. The ensuing two decades have deepened the intermingling of class incomes across the life-course that he highlighted in the 1970s.

The changeling of labour savings into capital markets is a two-edged sword. Conceivably, unions could seize control of their own pension funds and put them to co-operative use. Concerted strategies along these lines are certainly possible. Several bold and exemplary attempts have been made; they deserve to be more broadly studied and discussed by the Left.[41] But let us also be clear that there are formidable obstacles in venturing down this road; the resistance to capital redeployment is not confined to the rich. Millions of working people are counting on these funds to provide retirement income, and they have reason to fear the harsh verdict of the financial markets on non-maximizing capital investment.

Consider the Ontario Teachers Pension Plan. With $54 billion aboard, the OTPP directs one of the largest pools of capital in Canada; the Plan owns 3% of the TSE 300, the Toronto Stock Exchange's top three hundred companies. As with most pension funds, its managers are prohibited by the Plan's constitution from having any investment objective other than risk-adjusted maximization. As the OTPP's President insisted in his 1993 Annual Report:

> A number of teachers have suggested that corporate governance be extended to social investment. The purpose would be to prohibit investment in companies that, in some people's perception, produce 'socially unacceptable' products or behave unacceptably in terms of environmental conduct, labour relations, human rights, and other political and social matters. The teacher's pension plan is not, in our view, a political pool of capital . . . The plan exists solely to provide members with retirement income and related benefits . . . Fiduciary duty requires us to resist suggestions to alter the plan's investment policy to advance the social and political ideology of some people at the expense of all plan members.[42]

'Social and political ideology', in this context, means any policy that is potentially at odds with the Plan's duty to accumulate capital as quickly as possible on a risk-adjusted basis – any strategy, in other words, that runs counter to the reigning neo-liberal orthodoxies of our day. For teachers who are relying on the Plan, and very little else, to furnish them with income upon their retirement for the rest of their lives, the President's warning to beware of 'social investment' sounds ominous.

The OTPP's money managers are renowned as 'shareholder rights' advocates. Asked about the wave of corporate downsizing, the Plan's chief investment officer says:

> Companies aren't put together to create jobs. The number-one priority is creating shareholder wealth . . . When we buy shares in a company, we treat it as if we're owners of the company. We believe the board of directors . . . has a duty to maximize the share value for us. If its not going to be looking after our interests first and foremost, then we will invest elsewhere.[43]

Holding a huge portfolio of Ontario bonds, OTPP's managers are also hard-line fiscal conservatives. Their stance contrasts sharply with the teachers' unions who were major organizers of the Days of Action, a series of city-wide strikes and demonstrations against the Ontario government's deep cuts to social services. At the 1996 demonstration in Hamilton, teachers' comprised more than half the turnout which police estimated at 100,000. The follow-up demonstration in Toronto was even larger, and the province's teachers once again turned out in massive numbers. They then led the charge against an odious Bill 160 (removing power from local school boards and vesting it with the

Minister of Education) with an all-out province-wide political strike for two weeks which sustained widespread public support and shook the government. In the meantime, the OTTP's managers – to judge by their previous statements – probably commended the Harris government behind the scenes for it's drastic spending cuts on the grounds that they were 'investor-friendly'.

This 'mixed message' cannot be plausibly ascribed to the divergent ideologies of union leaders and money managers; both are representing teachers and can reasonably claim to be acting on their behalf. The truth is that teachers have conflicted class interests, as have other workers with substantial pension funds circulating through financial markets. How would we estimate the balance of teachers' interests across the labour-capital divide? A clear majority of the plan's 155,000 active teachers are entitled to retire with a full pension in the next fifteen years.[44] As retirement approaches, the financial health of the OTPP becomes much more important than modest changes in their present rates of pay. In the meantime, relatively few young teachers have been hired since 1975. For the first time in 1997, pension benefits paid out exceeded contributions from active teachers. As the Annual Report explains:

> The growth in pensioner population relative to the active teaching population means that we will have to depend more on investment income than is the case today. These demographics underscore the importance of implementing a diversified investment policy that maximizes long-term investment returns so that we can pay the pensions promised without increasing the contributions.[45]

'Maximizing returns' has entailed entering the equity markets in a big way. From 1990 to 1996, roughly three-quarters of the OTPP's asset-expansion has come from investment income and capital appreciation. The OTTP pattern is not unusual in this regard. In the past fifteen years, investment income has swelled Canadian pension funds at roughly *twice* the rate of contributions from employers and workers combined.[46]

If the dreaded bear market finally shows up in North America and sticks around for long, many pension funds that have struggled to remain viable will be threatened with depletion. Without a sustained boost from investment income, the retirement benefits of the baby-boom generation cannot possibly be funded by the contributions of the 'baby-bust' generation following in its wake. The younger cohort is much smaller to begin with, and its entry into the full-time labour-force has been delayed by chronically high levels of youth unemployment and prolonged schooling. Most have been unable to obtain regular employment on a year-round basis and to become steady contributors to pension plans until their mid to late twenties.

There is a widespread perception among the elderly today that they are now receiving in benefits simply what they paid in during their working lives, plus a modest investment income. In most cases, this is inaccurate. If they have contributed to pay-as-you go plans which favour early cohorts, and if they collect benefits for more than a decade, they will use up their own contributions; from then on, their pension benefits and social security checks will be paid for by active employees and taxpayers. As the ratio of beneficiaries to contributors increases, the 'medical breakthroughs' that have prolonged life will prove to be costly for the children of the elderly, both in terms of their responsibilities for direct-care and financial assistance. If the stock market holds up over the next two decades, investment income will probably fill the growing retirement gap for most members of the older generation and the situation will be alleviated. If it does not, North Americans seem bound to experience an inter-generational financial crunch as the boomers retire in droves. Under these deflated circumstances, the primary institution of inter-generational support and solidarity – the family – will come under increasing strain.

Deregulating Capital, Destabilizing Families

Conservatives are loath to admit it, but the 'shareholder capitalism' they herald is fast undermining the traditional family they hold sacred. While they prefer to blame the family's ills on sexual permissiveness, moral degeneracy and creeping welfare-socialism, the truth is that unregulated capitalism is hard on families, even small, nuclear and 'sub-nuclear' families. In shortening all forms of commercial contract, the free market militates against the long-term obligations to one's partner, parents and children that enable families – in whatever form – to endure and provide reliable support, binding three generations together over the life-course. The more atomized, turbulent and rootless economies become, the more difficult it is to justify costly childbearing, long-term monogamy, or taking time off work to care for one's elderly parents. In eroding the subsistence-base of the economy and commodifying every consumable, unfettered capitalism devalues the unpaid work done at home – overwhelmingly women's work – that provides for such elementary family pleasures as sitting down and eating a home-cooked meal together.

In a liberal-democratic state, the right to move around the country and compete for any job available is the foundation of free labour. But there is a vast difference between having the right to change jobs and being compelled to chase jobs all over the place simply in order to subsist. Quitting work and being sacked are not only very different experiences at the time, they have very different long-term consequences for people's lives and their capacity to keep families and communities together. Anything that renders employment more dislocated, temporary and irregular, anything that makes the future stream of labour income less reliable, destabilizes wage-earning families. The most obvious disruption is job loss, especially in conditions of mass unemployment where the competition for scarce jobs is intense. Across the OECD states (with the notable exception of the U.S.), the jobless rolls have grown enormously since the early 1970s. In Canada, the average rate of unemployment has risen for four straight decades. People who lose their jobs have a much harder time finding another. The average bout of unemployment was 14 weeks in 1974; by 1994, it had reached 24 weeks.[47] In the meantime, the contraction of the labour force in many industries has gone hand-in-hand with the scheduling of substantial overtime. Paying individuals in a shrunken workforce time-and-a-half is apparently cheaper than keeping more workers with benefits on the payroll. While the Right often blames this social perversity on high payroll taxes, it is worth noting that Marx observed the same combination 130 years ago:

> The overwork of the employed part of the working-class swells the ranks of the reserve, whilst conversely the greater pressure that the latter by its competition exerts on the former, forces these to submit to overwork and to subjugation to the dictates of capital.[48]

Recently, free-market advocates have been urging governments to make their labour markets 'more flexible'. This would be a blessing for working families if it meant that employees had more discretion in determining their working hours. But rather than flexibility *for* workers, more often it is a case of an obligatory flexibility *of* workers, bending to employers' demands in order to keep their jobs. What conservatives really mean by labour flexibility is that it ought to be easier *for employers* to:

- lay-off workers at any time;
- replace permanent staff with part-time workers who do not qualify for benefits;
- contract out corporate functions to specialized firms who hire

unorganized workers on short-term contracts and pay them much less;

- schedule more overtime to avoid recalling laid-off workers or hiring new ones; and
- transfer production to regions with fewer employment regulations and lower labour costs.

When companies are free to treat workers as dispensable commodities, they make the labour market *less* flexible for employees. Household routines are disturbed by changes in the way firms contract with labour and schedule shifts.[49] Just-in-time production schedules are organized to fill customer orders, tighten inventory levels, and secure technological efficiencies in batch processing. The result is that staffing plans must be finalized later – just-in-time – and workers are provided with less advance notice of their shift-schedules. In consequence, family events become that much harder to plan. Intensified competition in consumer markets fosters extended selling hours. As stores stay open later and Sunday shopping proliferates, retail employees must work more evening and weekend shifts. In Canada, nine-to-five days and the five-and-two week comprise a shrinking proportion of all employment. In 1976, 65% of Canadian workers put in a standard work-week; by 1995, only 54% did.[50]

Changes in the labour market are shaking up the life-course as well. As the pace of technological change accelerates, occupational skills become outmoded more quickly and career employment paths are more difficult to sustain; promotional ladders are disrupted by corporate downsizing, mergers, takeovers, and plant closures. As middle-aged workers who have worked for the same company for years lose their jobs, employers and politicians propose 'retraining' and 'life-long learning' as antidotes to a growing sense of insecurity. Young people in their late teens and early twenties find it increasingly difficult to enter the full-time labour force and become self-supporting adults; between 1990 and 1995, the average income of Canadians aged 15 to 24 fell 20%.[51] High levels of youth unemployment have forced many young adults to return to school when their job prospects appear dismal and to live with their parents far longer than either generation would have wished. The whole process of 'growing up and settling down' – finding a mate, living together, forming families and having kids – is delayed, disrupted, rendered uncertain and reversible.

The mass influx of married women into paid work – due in part to disruptions in male employment – has eased the financial pressure on households; but it has done so by adding considerably to women's work-loads and making the preservation of families more difficult in other ways. In multi-earner households, all members who are presently employed or are seeking jobs must be able to find suitable work close to home. The decision of one member to move to another location in order to accept a job offer there either splits the family or forces the rest to pull up stakes in order to stay together as a household, quitting their jobs and leaving schools and friends behind. 'Long-distance' families proliferate, where a breadwinner (usually male) migrates and leaves his family behind, often hoping to sponsor their eventual reunification at some point in the future.

The deregulation of the working day and the shift to a two-earner norm have complicated family time-management, exacerbating the trade-off between making money and 'making time'. The more hours the members of a household need to devote to paid work, the harder it is to set aside family-time together. When the work schedules of two or more members of the household cannot be synchronized, family meals together during the week are rare and sleep-times are disparate.[52] The domestic work that directly sustains family life is thus forced to adapt to the pre-determined timetables of work and school. Since women still do the great bulk of unpaid family work even when they work outside the home, it falls to them, much more than to men, to try to reassemble what the demands of the external world have pulled apart – making-do with disjointed meal-times, feeding the kids while preparing to eat later with husbands, caring for people who are coming and going at odd hours. As it becomes much more difficult to co-ordinate the family's life together, time-management issues become a major bone of contention between spouses.

Employers may recognize and quite genuinely care about their employees' need to safeguard family-time. But when their own profit-maximizing imperatives are competitively enforced and driven by the short-term interest of shareholders, they find it extremely difficult to accommodate the family needs of their workers. For their part, wage-earners realize that as individuals they can best compete in the labour market by being responsive and flexible, willing to pull up stakes on short notice to go wherever the best job opportunities present themselves. As committed family members, however, they strive to forge out of this unsettled landscape as much residential stability and community rootedness as they can. Employees who focus on making more money and climbing the corporate ladder tend to sacrifice involvement with their families; conversely, familial devotion inhibits the aggressive pursuit of market opportunities. Women have long been aware of this conflict; men who are trying to spend more time with their families now realize the magnitude of the problem.

At the core of the neo-liberal ideal of unfettered capital mobility and flexible labour markets lies an abstract individualism that makes it extremely difficult to keep families intact and communities pulling together. In the words of Edward Luttwak, 'turbo-charged capitalism . . . rewards acrobats at the expense of working stiffs who also happen to be fathers and stable members of the community'.[53] Listen to the voice of one working stiff, a steelworker in Hamilton, Ontario, on the way in which de-regulated capitalism is taking its toll on family life:

> You don't know if tomorrow you are going to have a job. . . . You don't know if your family is all of sudden just going to pack and leave on you because they are fed up with it. You know my kids will come home and I'll come home after like twelve hours of fighting and arguing with guys down there . . . and a kid looks at you and goes 'Dad'. You go nuts on him, eh. And you think 'Christ, if I don't get out of here I'm going to kill somebody . . . I'm going to beat up on the kids' . . . And that's why there is so much problems . . . because the parents can no longer cope.[54]

Conclusion

As corporate profits and household savings continue to flood into financial markets at an unprecedented pace, the global structure of capital becomes increasingly top-heavy and unstable. A vast sea of speculative liquidity is now sloshing around the world in cyberspace, swollen out of all rational proportion to the base of productive capital whose future earnings it presumably foreshadows. Driven by greed and fear (the ruling emotions of financial markets), this protean superstructure is increasingly prone to unpredictable booms and busts, as strong herding tendencies develop and the normal two-way flow of funds can easily turn into a one-way stampede overnight. In the boom phase, the tide rises and the sea expands; investment flows from the financial centers of New York, London and Tokyo into 'emerging markets' as money managers sing the praises of the newest 'economic miracles'. As soon as their glib prognostications are shattered by some unexpected piece of bad news, however, they rush for the exits, fleeing to the relative security of their own, better regulated, financial markets.

As the governments and peoples of East Asia have recently discovered, the mass exodus of anonymous investors can bankrupt a capital-poor country in a matter of days, depreciating its currency, ballooning its foreign debt, depressing its urban property markets and draining liquidity from its debt-ridden financial institutions. An avalanche of deflationary pressures soon force desperate governments into the arms of the World Bank and the I.M.F. whose officials typically insist – as a condition for lending them emergency funds – that governments push through fiscal austerity measures and 'structural reforms' designed to bring their economies into closer conformity with the preferred neo-liberal model. The resulting pain imposed on the broad mass of the population is declared to be unfortunate, but in the long run will do them a world of good, since 'tough medicine' is needed to 'restore the confidence of foreign investors' – the *sine qua non* of national prosperity in 'the new global economy'. In the meantime, the calamities that have suddenly befallen the country (whose virtues were widely touted until recently) are now discovered to stem from (take your pick) political corruption, 'entrenched cronyism', government mismanagement, or the nation's baffling cultural resistance to market incentives – anything but the international financial system.

Looking at the same destructive whirlwind from a very different vantage point, the readers of *Socialist Register* may be wondering why the deferred labour income of wage-earners from rich countries is fuelling finance capital's bonfire-of-the-vanities and burning the working people of poor countries – in Latin America yesterday, in East Asia today, and who-knows-where tomorrow. Seeking to explain working-class conservatism in rich countries, Lenin once argued that the upper strata of wage-earners had been bought off by the 'enormous superprofits' of imperialism, based upon the 'superexploitation' of the producers in poor countries. This enabled capitalists in the developed world:

> to bribe the labour leaders and the upper layers of the labour aristocracy . . . This stratum of workers-turned-bourgeois . . . who are quite philistine in their mode of life, in the size of their earnings and in their entire outlook . . . are the real agents of the bourgeoisie in the workers' movement.[55]

Shorn of its moralizing tone, this materialist analysis seems relevant in the current context. Ironically for Lenin – a fierce opponent of 'revisionism' – his argument subverts the strategic cornerstone of marxist orthodoxy: that the proletarians of *all* countries have a compelling interest in uniting to overthrow capitalism.

Marx did not foresee that the savings of wage-earners would one day become a major source of capital formation. He treated wages simply as a fund for 'individual consumption'. Most working-class families in his day were mired in a day-to-day struggle for existence and Marx largely ignored the inter-generational dimensions of working-class reproduction. Fixating narrowly on workplaces as the sole sites of wealth-creation and class-based power, he left households – with their intimate dependency-based forms of domestic power – out of account. But households are the incubators of labour-power and the ultimate source of society's future wealth; we can never adequately grasp the intricate value-flows back and forth between the sexes, between the generations, and, finally, between labour and capital if households are not present in the analysis.

The problem we face today is not so much Marx's blind-spot, but the failure of contemporary socialists – staring this demographic reality in the face – to come to grips with it. With all its shortcomings, Marx's analysis of capitalism contains profound insights that can assist us in this effort. Consider, for example, his subtle notion of 'the metamorphosis of the value form' as explicated in *Capital*, wherein the surplus value pumped out of 'living labour' in the sphere of production disguises its origins as it becomes money-capital and then shows up mysteriously in the sphere of exchange as an alien, unruly force that acts back upon workers to secure their submission to capital in the anonymous form of 'market discipline'. Marx sees the extraction of surplus value as a double-barrelled alienation – the separation of labour from its *wealth*, and the loss of working-class *power* over the disposition of money-capital in the process.

The potential strengths of this analysis are vitiated when we focus too narrowly on exploitation 'at the point of production' and gloss over the distinct circuits of capital. As I have tried to show, the labour-savings circuit is configured very differently than the more familiar corporate-profit loop. It is schematic and misleading to assume that the latter furnishes an adequate blueprint for apprehending the broader crisscrossed field of capital accumulation, especially when this terrain spans the globe (in space) and encompasses all three generations (in time).

The wealth that wage-earners hand over to money managers through pension and mutual funds derives from wages, not from profits; ultimately it returns to workers (their spouses and children) in the form of investment income. These funds join the general pool of investment-capital and for the most part are managed no differently than other investments. But legally they remain labour's capital; they can therefore be reclaimed by their 'rightful owners' and put to alternative uses much more readily than other forms of capital can. By contrast, the wealth that employers extract from labour which shows up as profit on the company's balance-sheet is more decisively alienated and much harder to reclaim. Might labour's collective access to 'its own' capital-pool open up a new front of anti-capitalist struggle and provide a powerful point of leverage for an alternative economic strategy? The potential gains of extricating labour's capital from the alienated orbits of circulating capital and placing these funds at the service of labour-friendly co-operative endeavours are considerable. So too are the difficulties in doing so. While the legal barriers do not seem formidable (wherever alternative investment objectives are democratically determined and fund managers are held accountable), the chief obstacle in my view is the perfectly understandable desire of most workers to maximize their investments in preparation for a retirement of unknown duration where the provisions of the welfare state look increasingly uncertain. Non-maximizing deployment threatens this interest. However, the consequences of unions failing to exert collective control over their pooled savings and simply leaving pension fund managers alone to 'to do what they do best' are also considerable. Under a profit-maximizing investment strategy, the beneficiaries are deeply implicated in the private accumulation process, since this part of their future income-stream derives from capital's success in raising the rate of exploitation and favouring shareholders over workers.

The politics of the next few decades will be incomprehensible without paying careful attention to demographic trends and intergenerational wealth-flows. A huge cohort of baby boomers are now contemplating their retirement in the not-too-distant future. How will they live out their senior years? With an inexorable decline in the ratio of working-age contributors to elderly beneficiaries in pension plans, there are serious doubts as to whether there will there be sufficient savings available in *any* form to prevent former wage-earners and their spouses from falling into abject poverty in their senior years.

Beyond the vexed issue of private pensions lurks the even thornier question of the public retirement funds promised by governments to their senior citizens upon reaching a specified age. In the face of projected shortfalls in these programs, the path of least resistance is to look for ways to raise the rate of return on their assets. In the U.S., for example, Republicans in Congress have been pushing for Wall Street's preferred 'solution' – to privatize Social Security by paying out the plan's accumulated assets to citizens who elect to opt out, so that they can invest their share as they see fit while releasing the government from its obligation to provide for them in old age. Predictably, those whose future retirements will be cushioned by other sources of wealth can afford to take this risk and might well gain personally from it, while the poor who are completely dependent upon public provision would almost certainly stand to lose, either by taking private risks that they could ill-afford, or by sticking with a shrunken government program that was no longer defended with any vigour by the affluent. How will the Left respond to this challenge? Clearly there are huge stakes involved in the struggle over the nature of society's publicly-funded retirement contract with its senior citizens.

In an aging society, the needs of the dependent elderly place increasing demands on families and the welfare state. This raises unavoidable questions about the proper distribution of responsibilities for direct care and financial support between next-of-kin and public agencies on the one hand, and within families on the other (between daughters and sons, cohabiting members and kin living elsewhere, childhood families and in-laws, close friends of the sick and their own kin, etc.). The sinews of friendship and kin solidarity will be sorely tested in a money-driven society where market relations encourage a narrow calculus of personal interest and the sphere of interpersonal obligation has been steadily reduced, among most Westernized cultures, to the cohabiting members of the nuclear family. In sum, issues of class, gender and generation are all entangled on this terrain. How these issues get fought out, and the alliances that are forged to deal with them, will be critical to the prospects of reviving a broadly-based progressive politics in the early decades of the 21st century.

NOTES

1 Michael Winerip, 'He's Out of Step, but That's Fine with Canton's Biggest Employer,' *New York Times*, December 2, 1997, p. A1.

2 *New York Times*, December 2, 1997, p. A10

3 *The Economist*, October 18, 1997, p. 79.

4 *International Capital Markets, 1950-1995*, OECD publication, 1997, pp. 13-16; Joel Seligman, *The Transformation of Wall Street*, rev. ed., Northeastern University Press, 1995, p. 569; Stephany Griffith-Jones and Barbara Stallings, 'New global financial trends: implications for development,' in *Global Change, Regional Response*, Barbara Stallings, ed., Cambridge University Press, 1995, pp. 144-57. See also, Andrew Walter, *World Power and World Money*, rev. ed., Harvester Wheatsheaf, 1993; Jonathan Michie and John Grieve Smith, *Managing the Global Economy*, Oxford University Press, 1995.

5 William Greider, *One World, Ready Or Not, the Manic Logic of Global Capitalism*, Simon & Schuster, 1997, p. 234; *The Economist*, September 20th, 1997, p. 24.

6 'Turbo-charged' is Edward Luttwack's apt term. Cf. *Harper's Magazine*, May 1996, p. 38.

7 While these effects have been manifest far beyond the shores of North America, I shall confine myself here to the U.S. and Canada, and leave the global ramifications to be examined in a subsequent text.

8 Michael Useem, *Investor Capitalism, How Money Managers are Changing the Face of Corporate America*, Basic Books, 1996, p. 65. For a closely-grained review of this battle, see the second chapter, 'When Investors Challenge Company Performance'.

9 On these trends, see Michael Useem, *Executive Defense: Shareholder Power and Corporate Restructuring*, Harvard University Press, 1993; Michael Useem, *Investor Capitalism: How Money Managers Are Changing the Face of Corporate America*, Basic Books, 1996; Neil Fligstein and Peter Brantley, 'Bank Control, Owner Control or Organizational Dynamics: Who Controls the Large Corporation?', *American Journal of Sociology*, Vol. 98, 1992, pp. 280-307; Gerald F. Davis and Suzanne K. Stout, 'Organizational Theory and the Market for Corporate Control: A Dynamic Analysis of the Characteristics of Large Takeover Targets, 1980-1990,' *Administrative Science Quarterly*, Vol 37, 1992, pp.605-33; Mary Zey and Brande Camp, 'The Transformation from Multi-divisional Form to Corporate Groups of Subsidiaries in the 1980s,' *The Sociological Quarterly*, Vol. 37, #2, pp. 327-51.

10 Harper's Magazine, May 1996, p. 38.

11 In the words of Jack Welsh, the CEO of General Electric, one of the few North American conglomerates that investors still like.

12 David Sadtler, Andrew Campbell and Richard Kroch, estimate that the market value of companies spun off from their parents in Britain and the U.S. rose from $17.5 billion in 1993 to more than $100 billion in 1996. See *Break-Up! When Large Companies are Worth More Dead than Alive*. Capstone, 1997.

13 Michael Useem, *Investor Capitalism, How Money Managers are Changing the Face of Corporate America*, Basic Books, 1996, p. 164.

14 Cf. 'Excess Capital and Excess Population,' Marx, *Capital*, Vol 3, (Progress Publishers, 1971) pp. 250-9. Neo-classical economists have finally recognized this tendency – in their terms, the risk of firms overinvesting due to a surging cash flow in excess of potential investments with positive net present value. (See Michael Jensen, 'Agency Costs of Free Cash Flow, Corporate Finance, and Takeovers,' *American Economic Review*, Vol. 76, 1986, pp. 323-329.) But whereas marxists situate the contradiction of excess capital investment at the macro-level, as a destructive effect of the competitive scramble for market share, neo-classical economists remain wedded to the theology of market equilibrium, identifying the problem as an 'agency cost' of managers who fail to maximize shareholder value.

15 Betsy Morris, 'The Holy Terror Who's Saving IBM,' *Fortune*, Vol. 135, # 7, April 14, 1997, p. 71.

16 From 1995 to April 1998, IBM spent about $20 billion reacquiring its own shares. Despite revenues and profit margins that came in well below market expectations in 1998, the stock continues to set records because management continues to demonstrate its absolute devotion to shareholders by buying back more shares and raising dividends. See 'IBM plans steps to lift the share price,' in the *Globe & Mail*, April 29, 1998, p. B 11.

17 *Ibid*, p. 80.

18 Mark 11:15

19 'Executive Pay, It's Out of Control,' *Business Week*, April 21, 1997, pp. 58-66.

20 Adolf Berle and Gardiner Means, *The Modern Corporation and Private Property*, rev. ed. New York, Harcourt, Brace, 1932/1967. For a more recent rumination on the perennial issue of 'corporate governance', see Margaret Blair, *Ownership and Control: Rethinking Corporate Governance for the 21st Century*, Washington: Brookings Institute, 1995.

21 Calculated from the table on pages 58-9 of *Business Week*, April 21, 1997. Canadian trends lag behind, but are headed in the same direction. In a report on the 1997 annual incomes of the CEO's of Canada's largest firms, the top ten (in total compensation) averaged C$890,000 in basic salary, C$2.4 million in performance bonuses (mostly related to share-price appreciation), and C$9.5 million in stock-option gains. *Globe & Mail*, April 18, 1998, p. B6. Stock options permit managers to purchase shares from their companies at a bargain price. They must be exercised to generate the gains recorded in the compensation totals being cited here.

22 *The Economist*, June 28, 1997, p. 77.

23 The correlation between repurchase announcements and share appreciation has been noted in several studies. See Robert Comment and Gregg Jarrell, 'The Relative Signalling Power of Dutch-Auction and Fixed-Price Tender Offers and Open-Market Repurchases,' *Journal of Finance*, Vol. 46, 1991, pp. 1243-1271; David Yermack, 'Good Timing: CEO Stock Option Awards and Company News Announcements,' *Journal of Finance*, Vol. 52, 1997, pp. 449-476.

24 In the language of neo-classical economists, firms run the risk of overinvesting when they have a cash flow in excess of that required to fund all projects that have a positive net present value'. The buy-back disgorges the excess and mitigates the 'agency conflict' inherent in managers placing other objectives before the paramount one of maximizing shareholder value. For an empirically-based analysis of these trends, see George W. Fenn & Nellie Liang, 'Good News and Bad News About Share Repurchases,' a 1997 discussion paper distributed by the U.S. Federal Reserve, and available on the Fed's web-site.

25 Doug Henwood has shown that 'far from turning to Wall Street for outside finance, nonfinancial firms have been stuffing Wall Street's pockets with money.' (*Wall Street*, Verso, 1997, p. 73).

26 This estimate is based on the industrial companies in Standard and Poor's 500 index, as reported by Tom Galvin, chief equity strategist at *Donaldson Lufkin & Jenrette*: 'Stingy capital spending pays off in stock prices,' *Globe & Mail*, March 23, 1998, p. B6.

27 *Globe & Mail*, 'Mergers Hit Fever Pitch', Dec. 22, 1997, p. B1; Charles V. Bagli, A New Breed of Wolf at the Corporate Door,' *New York Times*, March 19, 1977, p. B1;, 'America Bubbles Over', *The Economist*, April 18, 1997, p. 67.

28 *The Economist*, March 28, 1998, p. 68.

29 'Last of the Big-Time Spenders', *Toronto Star*, August 5, 1997, p. D1. and Maria Ramirez, 'Americans at Debt's Door', *New York Times*, Oct. 14, 1997. See also, *New York Times*, Feb. 11, 1998, 'Share of Wealth in Stock Holding Hits 50 Year High', p. A1.

30 Maria Ramirez, 'Americans at Debt's Door', *New York Times*, Oct. 14, 1997.

31 The savings decline may well be halted or reversed in the next decade, as baby boomers save in earnest for their retirements; but thereafter, it seems destined to

resume its fall as the proportion of the population 65 years and older rises sharply. The prospect of an aging population draining the global pool of capital-savings in the next fifty years is clearly ominous, and has attracted the attention of the West's major research institutes. See, for example, Barry Bosworth, *Savings and Investment in a Global Economy*, The Brookings Institute, 1993; and the 1997 OECD report *Future Global Capital Shortages: Real Threat or Pure Fiction?*

32 As of March 1, 1998.

33 Michael Useem, *Investor Capitalism*, p. 26; *New York Times*, Sept. 25, 1997, p. C2.

34 *Globe & Mail*, January 3, 1997, p. B9; *Toronto Star*, January 16, 1997, p. E1.

35 *Globe & Mail*, March 18, 1977, p. B1.

36 See Robert Clark's 'The Four Stages of Capitalism: Reflections on Investment Management Treatises,' *Harvard Law Review*, 94, 1981, pp. 561-82.

37 This includes assets held by individuals, plus pooled investments such as mutual funds and pensions. *The Economist*, March 28, 1998, p. 18.

38 See *Pension Funds, Retirement-Income Security and Capital Markets, An International Perspective*, E. Philip Davis, Clarendon Press, 1995; *Pensions, Labor and Individual Choice*, David A. Wise, ed., University of Chicago Press, 1985; *Pension Plans in Canada 1996*, Statistics Canada, Cat. No. 74-401, 1997.

39 Doug Henwood, *Wall Street*, Verso, 1997, p. 67. Unlike the thousands of authors who write homages to Wall Street and supply hot tips that promise to make you a million, Henwood, the editor of the *Left Business Observer*, is a trenchant critic of the Street who proudly offers no advice on playing the market. I found *Wall Street* an illuminating read, particularly Henwood's analysis of the self-sufficiency of non-financial corporations who, far from sucking investment money in, have been paying it out, 'stuffing Wall Street's pockets'. My main objection is that he belittles the magnitude and importance of the flood of wage-earners' savings into the markets in the past decade via mutual funds and pensions. This permits him to preserve the comforting left-wing delusion that financial markets simply redistribute income among the wealthy and have not snagged a *rentier* interest among the ranks of the fully employed working-class.

40 *New York Times*, February 11, 1998, pp. A1, C4.

41 Some of the more promising ones are reviewed by Richard Minns in 'The Social Ownership of Capital,' *New Left Review*, # 219, September 1996.

42 Quoted from the President's Address, cited in the OTPP's mailing to members, *Highlights of the 1993 Annual Report*, p. 12.

43 *Globe & Mail*, March 23, 1996, p. B1.

44 Under the former agreement, about half of all active teachers were due to retire in 15 years. But just as this text was being finalized, the teachers' federations agreed to a new early-retirement deal with the government that will increase this proportion considerably.

45 *1996 Report to Members*, Ontario Teachers Pension Plan Board, p. 9.

46 See *Trusteed Pension Funds, Financial Statistics, 1994*, Statistics Canada, 1996, Cat. No. 74-201, p. 15.

47 Globe & Mail, January 3, 1997, p. A4.

48 *Capital*, (Progress, 1971), Vol. I, p. 595

49 See Manfred Garhammer, *Time and Society*, vol. 4, # 2.

50 From a *Statistics Canada* study by Mike Sheridan, Deborah Sunter and Brent Diverty, reported in the *Globe & Mail*, September 2,1996.

51 'Canadians got poorer in the 90s,' *Globe & Mail,* May 13, 1998, p. A 5.
52 The commodification of food and the devaluation of the home-cooked meal proceed apace. Over forty cents of every dollar Americans spend on food now goes to restaurant meals and take-out. Cited in Jane Brody, *New York Times*, June 16, 1998, p. B10.
53 *Harper's Magazine*, May 1996, p. 38.
54 'Down there' is Stelco's Hilton Works, and '12 hours' refers to the plant's new shift-schedule. This interview is from a study conducted by the author with Meg Luxton, June Corman and David Livingstone.
55 From the preface to 'Imperialism, the Highest Stage of Capitalism', *Lenin, Selected Works*, Volume 1. Moscow: Progress Publishers, 1963, p. 677.

LABOUR POWER AND INTERNATIONAL COMPETITIVENESS: A CRITIQUE OF RULING ORTHODOXIES

David Coates

> *'Though not in substance, yet in form, the struggle of the proletariat with the bourgeoisie is, at first, a national struggle. The proletariat of each country must, of course, settle matters with its own bourgeoisie'* (Marx and Engels, *The Communist Manifesto*, 1848)

When Keynes made his famous observation that 'the ideas of economists and political philosophers, both when they are right and when they are wrong, are more powerful than is commonly understood' and that 'madmen in authority, who hear voices in the air, are distilling their frenzy from some academic scribbler of a few years back', (Keynes, 1936, p. 383) he was thinking primarily of fascism and communism; but the relationship between political projects and intellectual positions to which he alluded is more widespread than that. Certainly in the corridors of power in Western Europe of late, projects and ideas have stood closely together, shaping the governing understandings of how (among other things) states in pursuit of economic success should relate to the labour movements that are central to its attainment. At least two related but distinguishable readings of the relationship of labour power to international competitiveness can be discerned in European governing circles over the last two decades: a neo-liberal reading, espoused with enthusiasm by political forces of the Right, and a more consensual and corporatist reading, espoused by parties and intellectuals of the Centre-Left. In the neo-liberal version, trade unions are the particular *bête noire.* There they stand condemned as institutions which price workers out of employment, block labour market flexibility, and (by their political influence) sustain excessive welfare provision. In the Centre-Left version, trade unions are seen more positively: as institutions whose pursuit of industrial rights and welfare provision can, under certain circumstances, trigger long term labour market flexibility and overall productive efficiency. In Western Europe generally, policy seems now to be drifting rapidly in a neo-liberal direction, as parties of both the Centre-Right and Centre-Left respond to sluggish growth and employment performances by cutting (with greater or lesser enthusiasm, depending on their political colour) welfare budgets and public provision. In the UK by contrast, after 20 years of such a project, a pale ('New Labour') version of the Centre-Left alternative is currently back in vogue. But in both instances, a common point of convergence is emerging: one built around the belief that successful competitiveness in a globalised economy requires – as Tony Blair told the British TUC in September 1997 – that 'we must be adaptable, flexible, open to change' (Blair, 1997, p. 6); and that the key to such flexibility lies in the resetting of the rights of workers and of their representatives.

From the standpoint of the Left it is quite clear that the policy consequences of the dominant neo-liberal orthodoxy are unacceptably severe. The creation of 'flexible labour markets' by parties of the Right have significantly reduced the rights and rewards of labour through the introduction of low wages, short contracts, unregulated working conditions and intensified managerial control of the work process. In Western Europe at least, such policies are now commonplace, and are legitimated (as a necessary response to globalisation) in the conventional language of neo-classical economics: which is why an effective rebuttal of neo-liberalism is currently so essential an element in the formulation of a coherent left-wing response to new global pressures. The widespread temptation on the Centre-Left, however, has been to make that rebuttal by canvassing varying versions of the consensual corporatist alternative: offering either modest industrial 'partnerships' or even full-blown 'class compacts' as a more civilised and effective route to the international competitiveness prioritised by neo-liberalism. The purpose of this paper is to argue that such a response is inadequate to the task, by indicating the weaknesses of *both* neo-liberal and centre-left understandings of how – in contemporary capitalism – labour power and international competitiveness interact.

I. THE DEBATE ON TRADE UNION POWER

The standard neo-liberal case against trade union power and worker rights is normally built around one or more of the following propositions:

1. Trade unions exploit their monopoly position within the labour market to increase the money wages of their members; but do so only at the immediate cost of other jobs (as employers substitute capital for labour), and at the longer-term cost of both output and employment (as inflated production costs erode competitiveness). Non-unionised firms and economies are, on this argument, much more likely than unionised ones to maintain long-term employment levels and market share.

2. Such long-term union pressure on wages then redistributes jobs and earnings between unionised and non-unionised employees, and so increases income inequality. It does so directly (as unions win settlements for their members alone) and indirectly (if by political pressure, unions persuade governments to overspend, when the resulting inflation further erodes the real incomes of workers excluded from union-negotiated wage deals). Heavily unionised labour forces, so the argument runs, are more vulnerable to inflation and wage inequality than are labour forces in which unionism is weak.

3. Trade unions are also said to distort the optimal distribution of productive resources by establishing blockages on the allocation of labour, on the extraction of high effort levels, and (via strike action) on the smooth organisation of production. Trade unions, that is, supposedly erode productivity and investment, and slow-down innovation and change, as well as contribute to inflation, unemployment, inequality and excessive welfare spending.

Centre-Left counter-arguments to this dominant view tend to focus on the third of those arguments: on unions as barriers to growth. The corporatist literature provides counter-arguments to the other two standard neo-liberal claims, as we will see; but the general Centre-Left defence of trade unionism and worker rights offers them as triggers for industrial dynamism, as follows.

1. According to the Harvard economists Freeman and Medoff (1984), 'unions have "two faces": in addition to the monopoly face, uniquely stressed by the orthodoxy, unions have a more positive face associated with "collective voice".' (Nolan, 1992, p. 9). Far from blocking adaptability, trade union strength facilitates more optimal distributions of resources by transmitting information and commitment between employees and their managerial superiors. Unions can be obstructive: but they can

also – if conditions allow – be a powerful advocate of efficiency.

2. Strong trade unions also contribute to the long-term dynamism of industrial capital by blocking off 'sweat shop' routes to competitiveness: making it more difficult/impossible for firms to compete on the basis of low wages and intensified labour processes, and obliging employers to compete by investing in new equipment and training. On this argument, since it is 'the advent of unionisation, with its associated labour costs, [that] *shocks* management into operating the firm more efficiently' (Booth, 1995, p. 183) it is not that strong trade unionism is a barrier to successful capital accumulation; but that weak trade unionism might be. As Mishel and Voos have it: 'the fundamental point is that high productivity, worker rights, flexibility, unionization and economic competitiveness are not incompatible. In actuality, they may be highly compatible components of a high performance business system' (Mishel and Voos, 1992, p. 10).
3. Finally, strong trade unionism and entrenched labour codes are said to aid competitiveness by creating the conditions (of security and trust) within which industrial change can be most effectively implemented; in this way meeting the needs of a supposedly post-Fordist universe in which 'the nature of work is fundamentally different from the way it is conceived in the free-market tradition' and in which – to be competitive – 'you have to win worker commitment' (Hutton, 1994, p. 254). There is, in other words, a 'trust/stakeholder' model of capitalism tucked away in many of the Centre-Left defences of trade unions and welfare, and a claim that the future lies with this model and not with unregulated labour markets (Lazonick, 1991: also Streeck, 1992).

So far from trade unionism being inextricably associated with poor economic performance, the Centre-Left counter-argument to the conventional orthodoxy expects exactly the reverse. It expects unions to be strong – and the industrial and social rights of workers to be at their greatest – in economies with high levels of investment in machinery and training, with rising labour productivity and wages, and with low levels of inflation and unemployment. And it expects trade unions to be valued as a key force for change: one that helps to trigger the replacement of old-fashioned productive methods by new and innovatory ones.

This clash of arguments has gone on at a number of different academic levels. It has been pursued at the level of micro-analysis, where there is now an extensive research literature on the impact (or otherwise) of trade unionism on the performance of individual companies. It has also gone on at the macro-level, in a debate about the relative performance of entire national economies. The micro debate is, in the end, an inconclusive one (Booth, 1995, p. 262). The research data produced within it is open to a variety of competing interpretations (see, for example, Mishel and Voos, 1992; Booth, 1995). It is also so overlaid by more general social processes that is difficult to specify with any certainty the direction of causality of any relationships posited there. The macro-debate has greater analytical and explanatory potential, however, not least because it contains two strategic national cases whose development offers particular insight into the relative claims and counter-claims laid out above. One such case is the UK before and after 1979: an economy whose labour relations were reset on neo-liberal lines, and whose experience therefore provides unrivalled insights into the ability of strong unions to erode competitiveness and of weak unions to permit its restoration. The other case is Sweden, whose post-war combination of strong trade unionism and sustained economic growth constitutes the Centre-Left's most powerful counter-evidence to neo-liberalism. We will use the UK and Sweden in turn, to test first one side of the argument and then the other.

II. THE EVIDENCE ON UNION POWER

(a) Neo-liberalism in the United Kingdom

The relationship between trade union power and international competitiveness in the UK has been used on many occasions to sustain the more general neo-liberal case. Indeed it is not too much to say that there now exists a sophisticated neo-liberal reading of post-war UK industrial relations which is rapidly gathering the status of received truth, a reading (or more properly, a *mis*reading) which is built around the following set of propositions.

1. UK economic under-performance prior to 1979 was largely the responsibility of the trade unions. Full employment in the post-war UK shifted industrial power from capital to labour, and produced 'the British disease': a mixture of union-inspired restrictive practices, industrial militancy and wage drift which

eroded UK price competitiveness and discouraged investment. The power of organised work groups in UK industry prior to 1979, and their systematic opposition to the introduction of new technology and the full utilisation of existing productive techniques, pushed UK-based manufacturing down the international league tables. And the political power of the trade unions to which those work groups belonged induced successive governments to compound that competitive weakness by providing special trade union legal rights, bloated public sector employment and over-generous welfare provision. The result was supposedly a wealth-destroying combination of high taxation and runaway inflation.

2. Fortunately for the UK the arrival of Margaret Thatcher in power reversed this union-inspired downward economic spiral. Under her leadership, Conservative governments broke the power of UK trade unions: closing down the corporatist decision-making institutions of Labour Britain; expelling union leaders from the corridors of power; incrementally re-codifying UK labour law; leading a series of public sector confrontations with militant unions; and privatising vast swathes of the former public sector. The result, so neo-liberals tell us, was reduced inflation, increased labour productivity, extensive job creation, renewed Foreign Direct Investment, and a qualitative improvement in the overall performance of the UK economy. Even among academic commentators sympathetic to New Labour, the belief has grown that, whatever else the Conservatives after 1979 did or did not achieve, at least they tamed the unions, and in so doing lifted the UK on to a higher growth path (on this, see Metcalf, 1990b, pp. 283–303; also Kitson and Michie, 1996b, p. 35).

Superficially this neo-liberal reading of the fall and rise of the UK economy is compelling; but here, as elsewhere, first appearances mislead.

1. The UK before 1979

Many of the general neo-liberal claims about trade union legal privileges and excessive militancy are intrinscally comparative. They compare the UK before 1979 with even earlier UK experience, and they compare the UK over time with other advanced capitalist economies. Yet they do not do so accurately. Trade union legal 'privileges' in the UK (which were never commensurate with the legal protection provided to shareholders through limited liability legislation) peaked in 1975; but that peak (Labour's 1975 Industrial Relations Act) arrived too late to explain patterns of UK economic under-performance that stretched back to at least the 1950s, if not the 1890s. Nor did the terms of Labour's legislation in the 1970s do more than leave the UK at a mid-way point on the continuum of legal codes available to leading labour movements: positioned somewhere between economies which were more successful in the post-war period than the UK and yet had more generous labour codes (like West Germany and Scandinavia) and economies (like that of the USA) which had been no more successful than the UK but which possessed labour codes which were even less generous to workers and unions than those prevalent in the UK prior to 1975.

Nor does the claim of excessive industrial militancy in the UK in the 1970s easily stand international comparison. It is true that the UK experienced an explosion of industrial disputes between 1969 and 1973; but then so did the vast majority of major industrial economies. What is striking about the first four years of Labour government in the 1970s is not the level of industrial disputes, but rather how effectively and with what speed Labour politicians and trade union leaders contained them; and how the brief (and subsequently much mentioned) strike wave of the 'winter of discontent' which followed reflected a straining of the relationship between government and unions caused by that containment. Critics of trade unionism in the UK in the 1970s can hardly have it both ways: either the trade unions had the Labour Government in their grip throughout (and hence had no need of industrial action); or they did not (in which case any return to industrial militancy must be read as an index of their powerlessness, not of their potency).

In fact there is little doubt that the trade unions in the UK did enjoy a very brief period of unprecedented political influence over the incoming Labour Government. The Labour Party in opposition had forged a social contract with the unions, trading wage restraint for government policies on industry and welfare. The explicit nature of that agreement was unprecedented in UK terms – though not in Scandinavian ones – and because of its existence, the subsequent balance between inflation and unemployment in the UK in the 1970s *was* struck somewhat differently from that struck elsewhere in non-Scandinavian Europe: with inflation higher and unemployment lower than the general European norm. But it is one thing to note trade union influence on the way in which a Labour Government managed the general crisis of Keynesian economics in the 1970s; it is quite another to say, or to imply, that union influence was the cause of that crisis. It was not. In all the major industrial economies in the 1970s – whether heavily unionised or not – governments had to trade off inflation and unemployment at levels unanticipated in capitalism's post-war 'golden age'. The need for that choice arrived in the UK earlier than elsewhere in Northern Europe because of the UK economy's already emerging weakness (on this, Coates, 1980, pp. 180–201), but it came to them all eventually, in a generalised retreat from Keynesian demand management for which European trade unionism cannot, and should not, be allocated prime responsibility.

To claim or to imply that the UK trade unions 'abused' their relationship with the Labour Party in the 1970s for narrow sectional ends is to mis-read the actual sequence of events. What actually happened to the relationship between UK trade unions and the Labour Government in the 1970s was that it quickly fell back into a quite standard social democratic form: with the unions 'delivering' their side of the social accord while progressively failing to oblige the Government to deliver its. Between 1974 and 1979 UK trade unions repeatedly called for investment initiatives, for planning agreements and for public ownership, while superintending four years of falling real wages for their members. But as usual they experienced the standard 'cycle of union influence' (Minkin, 1991, p. 639): with ministers first responsive and then not, as stronger industrial and financial forces pushed the Labour Government towards an early form of monetarism. Far from trade union political power being a potent cause of UK economic under-performance in the 1970s, it seems safer to argue that, if there was a causal process at work here, it was one triggered by trade union political *weakness*. The UK trade unions failed to stop the Labour Government's drift into deflation and non-interventionism, and so failed to prevent a Labour Government bequeathing to its Conservative successor an economy scarred by high levels of inflation *and* unemployment and by low levels of investment. No other social or industrial force seemed capable of (or interested in) preventing such a retreat from economic management by the UK state. The unions certainly wanted an active and radical industrial policy from Labour; but they lacked the political resources to impose one, when more conservative voices began to prevail.

The vulnerability of the UK economy to stagflation was rooted then (as now) in under-investment in manufacturing plant and equipment and in human capital. All the main commentaries on the present UK economy agree on this much at least (Kitson and Michie, 1996b, p. 35). What is more contentious between them is the extent to which that under-investment was a product in the 1970s of trade union and work group resistance to the introduction and full utilisation of new technology. The most widely cited research literature says (or implies) that union power did erode productivity: both the literature on the 1970s itself (Pratten 1976; Caves, 1980), and that on the 1980s (such as the work of Crafts and Metcalf, which suggest that industrial relations reform after 1979 removed a powerful blockage to change). But on closer inspection, the 1970s research literature on the determinants of UK productivity proves to be partial in coverage and inadequate in design; and the literature on the Thatcherite 'supply side miracle', as we will see later, is hardly more convincing. The 1970s findings were misleadingly selective in their coverage of what to research. They effectively wrote out of the story of under-performance the persistent TUC calls for policies to stimulate industrial investment, and for programmes of industrial retraining and power sharing which alone might have eased the introduction of new technologies for the workers directly involved. More significant still, the core 1970s research literature on work groups and industrial productivity was flawed by quite staggering inadequacies of design and measurement. These weaknesses have been documented elsewhere (see Nichols, 1986; Coates, 1994, pp. 110–114) but their effect remains. Their existence makes it illegitimate to treat as uncontentious the claim that, in general, trade unions and work groups in the UK in the 1970s acted as major barriers to the strengthening of the economy's competitive base. Trade unions may have acted in that way: but the research evidence on unions and productivity is too flawed to permit us to say one way or the other.

Yet we do need to be clear on what did, and what did not, happen in UK industry in the 1970s. The more general research evidence certainly indicates a limited but real shift in power – at shop floor level – from line management to shop stewards and work groups in core UK manufacturing industries. The research evidence also shows that labour productivity in UK-based manufacturing firms in the 1970s was lower than that achieved in competitor economies like West Germany and Sweden. What the research evidence does not show, however, is that the first of these stylised facts *caused* the second. The timing of the two processes is too out of step to allow an easy move from correlation to cause here. Relative levels of labour productivity began to fall in the 1950s. Shop steward power, always limited and uneven in coverage, did not fully crystallize until the 1960s when, at most, it could only play a secondary and supporting role to other causal forces (see Coates, 1994, pp. 108–9). And even then, its impact on competitiveness, profits, investment and growth was softened by another feature of UK industrial relations in the 1970s which is not much mentioned by the critics of trade union power: namely the extent to which, by then, UK labour costs were 25% lower than the European average (Ray, 1987, p. 2). Cheap labour is hardly a barrier to competitiveness in most neo-liberal theories of growth: and yet labour was cheap in the UK, relative to that in the rest of Northern Europe, throughout the 1970s. So it seems churlish to point the finger at UK labour when striving to explain the remarkable decline of competitiveness by UK manufacturing industry in that critical decade.

2. The UK after 1979

The neo-liberal case against trade unionism in the UK after 1979 is no stronger than the case made against trade unionism prior to 1979. There can be no doubt that the Conservative Government after 1979 did significantly reduce the power of both trade unions and organised work groups, and did roll back both the size of the public sector and the scale of its welfare provision. Nor is there any doubt that the gap in labour productivity between the UK and its main European competitors did narrow at the same time. What is in doubt is whether these enormous changes were in any way causally related.

To take the productivity issue first: both the level and growth rate of labour productivity in the UK did rise after 1979; but they did not do so on the back of either large increases in the output of the manufacturing sector or in the level of investment in machinery and skills. Instead, the UK economy after 1979 experienced periods of growth intermingled with first deep (1980–82) and then prolonged (1989–92) recession, which kept levels of manufacturing output and investment *below* 1979 levels until the end of the 1980s. Indeed as late as 1992, the volume of manufacturing output in the UK had only crept to a level one per cent higher than it had been in 1973, as against a 27% growth in manufacturing volume in France over the same period, 25% in Germany, 85% in Italy and 119% in Japan (Select Committee 1994). The increase in labour productivity in the UK in the 1980s was not the result of extensive industrial modernisation. It was predominantly triggered by an intensification in the rate and length of work in the context of large-scale unemployment and the widespread closure of the least efficient plants. It was the product less of new investment than of 'piecemeal change in work organisation and production techniques' and 'more intensive work regimes which may or may not prove sustainable' (Nolan, 1994, pp. 67–8). If the productivity gap between the UK economy and its major European competitors then narrowed in the 1990s, latest research suggests that it did so primarily because of the growing under-performance of economies elsewhere in Europe (Wolf, 1996; Crafts, 1997): and in any case, the productivity gap between the UK and the rest still remains – and with it, the UK's persistent deficit on its balance of trade. Indeed, the *fall* in union power in the 1980s coincided with a *rise* in the UK's underlying trade deficit, quite contrary to the expectations of competitiveness raised by standard neo-liberal accounts of the relationship of trade unionism to economic growth.

Nor are the employment figures particularly supportive of the neo-liberal case against trade unionism. The 1980s witnessed a culling of more than trade union power. It also witnessed a culling of full-time jobs. 1.7 million such jobs were lost in the recession of 1980–82. A further 1.9 million full-time jobs went in the recession of the early 1990s. Of course there has been job creation: but the vast majority of the new jobs created in the UK since 1979 have been part-time ones. In 1993 there were just under six million part-time workers in a total UK labour force of some twenty one million; and of those six million part-time workers, at least 70% worked for less than sixteen hours a week, and did so for very low wages and with very little training. Then, as more new jobs came on stream between 1993 and 1996, only 38% of them offered full-time and permanent employment. An equal number were full-time and temporary, with the rest part-time of various sorts: to give the UK 'the worse of two possible worlds: the massive wage inequality of the decentralised US labour market together with high and lengthy spells of unemployment, European style' (Barrell, 1994, p. 5). From a neo-liberal point of view, it is *strong* trade unionism that is supposed to generate wage inequality and prolonged unemployment; but in the 1980s in the UK at least, wage inequality and unemployment intensified as trade union power *declined*.

Nor did this diminution in trade union power then trigger a renaissance in price stability and investment. It is true that inflation in the UK is now much lower than it was in the 'union dominated' 1970s; but so it is elsewhere in Western Europe (and the UK's relative inflation performance remains unchanged). It is also true that the UK has attracted large quantities of particularly Japanese Foreign Direct Investment. But Foreign Direct Investment is not the full story of the UK's investment experience since 1979. Overall in the UK, 'manufacturing net investment (as a share of manufacturing output) has been declining since the early 1960s, with negative figures for the early 1980s and 1990s' (Kitson and Michie, 1996b, p. 35; see also Kitson and Michie, 1996a, pp. 201–2). FDI alone could not, and did not, reverse that trend. In fact the scale of FDI (and its impact on employment) was tiny throughout the Conservative years, when set against the total movement of capital and employment in and out of the UK. Between 1979 and 1992 the overall flows of capital out of the UK *exceeded* those coming in for each year except 1987 (Radice 1995); and the employment effects of Japanese implants in particular (with 25,000 new manufacturing jobs created in the 1980s) were drowned by the destruction of 200,000 equivalent jobs by the top 25 British-owned transnationals (Williams et al, 1990). Nor was the flow of FDI into the UK of itself evidence of the general applicability of neo-liberal arguments on trade union power. Just the reverse: for Thatcherism as a model for international competitiveness was essentially *parasitic* on the corporatist models it would replace. It only worked in the UK because it had not yet spread across Northern Europe. Foreign Direct Investment was attracted to the UK primarily because of the UK's position on the edge of a European market sustained by higher wages and levels of social provision than the UK provides. If Germany ever reduces its wages and levels of labour market regulation to UK levels, it is inconceivable that Japanese investment would still flow to a UK short of skilled labour and scarred by regional under-development, when it could then redeploy to a Germany in which skill levels are high and the social infrastructure is bountiful. And indeed by the end of the Conservatives' period of office, the latest research data was showing France, and not the UK, as the major European recipient of Foreign Direct Investment, and indicating low wages as only one factor explaining capital redeployment, and a minor one at that (Quilley et al, 1996: Barrell and Pain, 1997). So the impact of the Conservatives' industrial relations 'reforms' even on FDI has proved neither as permanent or as far-reaching as their architects like to claim.

Overall indeed, the original neo-liberal case looks less secure than it first appeared, when its claims are exposed systematically to the complexity of the full UK experience. The rise and fall of trade union power in the UK has not correlated accurately with the UK record on overall investment flows, output levels and the balance of payments. In comparative terms, reductions in trade union power have not improved the UK inflation performance, or the capacity of the UK economy to provide full-time permanent employment; and because of the persistent shortfall in investment, nor have reductions in trade union powers effected a permanent productivity revolution. What the years of Thatcherism actually suggest is that the relationship between trade union power and international competitiveness is not one set in stone, as neo-liberalism would have it. The compatibility or otherwise of worker rights with capital accumulation and international competitiveness is fixed by a prior decision on *the dominant growth strategy* to be pursued in the quest for profitability. If growth and competitiveness are to be won on the basis of low wages and intensified work routines, then trade union power in whatever form *is* a barrier to growth. The Conservative Government in the UK after 1979 opted for this low wage strategy; and in so doing increasingly positioned the UK in the emerging international division of labour as a warehouse and assembly economy on the edge of more affluent European markets (while, through de-regulation, expanding the City's role in international finance). Trade union power did not initiate or pre-determine that positioning, except in so far as union *weakness* prevented its emergence. But to the degree that UK manufacturing capital is now settled into this particular international niche, any revival of trade unionism must threaten its long-term viability; which is presumably one reason why business groups in the UK, having weakened trade unionism so effectively, are now striving with such determination to keep that weakness in place.

(b) Corporatism and the Swedish case

When we enter the literature on corporatism in general, and on Swedish social democracy in particular, the whole tenor of the argument shifts. Then, and quite contrary to the general focus of the UK debate, the claims *for* trade unionism become the dominant motif, and the enthusiasts for market systems suddenly become the minority voice.

1. The general case for corporatism

Much of the research literature concerned with corporatism and economic competitiveness focuses on the relative performance of different advanced economies after 1973. The general thrust of this literature is that corporatist economies coped with the strains of intensified competition after 1973 *better* than non-corporatist economies. Quite what the data appears to show depends in part on how corporatism is defined and which economies are therefore labelled as corporatist, which time periods and performance indicators are chosen, and which sets of countries are included in the survey; but it is certainly not uncommon in the corporatist-focused research literature to meet versions of the claim that 'where the Left was politically strong, and the trade union movement was centralized and unified, [economies] performed somewhat better than where those conditions were less prevalent' (Garrett and Lange, 1986, p. 517; see also Cameron, 1984; Lange 1984; Lange and Garrett, 1985; Katzenstein, 1985; Martin, 1986). The claim is normally sustained by the use of one or both of two linked clusters of argument: one on the impact of strong ('encompassing') trade unions on wage levels; the other on the impact of generalised welfare provision on labour market flexibility and investment in human capital.

1. One general argument widely deployed in much of this literature is that high levels of economic performance can be expected from political systems at both ends of the capitalist spectrum: from fully marketised economies and from strongly corporatist ones, but not from economies caught half-way between these polar alternatives (see in particular Calmfors and Driffill 1988: also Kendix and Olson, 1990; Paloheimo, 1990). The reason for this, so the argument runs, is that the protection and enhancement of national competitiveness after 1973 required substantial structural adjustments which *either* untrammelled markets *or* strongly regulated ones were able to deliver: the first because of the impact of unemployment on wage rates; the second because 'strongly co-ordinated union movements are prone to wage moderation rather than militancy' (Kenworthy, 1995, p. 127) and/or because 'a high degree of social solidarity on the part of those with secure jobs' (Glyn 1992, p. 133) allowed state employment and reductions in working time to soften the impact of private sector restructuring on general levels of unemployment. Garrett and Lange's claim is particularly pertinent here: that 'countries with symmetrical or coherent political structures – in which labour was strong both organisationally and politically (corporatist cases), or in which labour was very weak on both dimensions (approximating market economies) – were able to adjust to the post 1974 international

crisis better than the mixed cases in which the political economies were less coherent (politically strong and organizationally weak, or vice versa)' (1986, pp. 531–2).

2. A second and related line of argument on corporatism is that, contrary to neo-liberal expectations and policy proposals, the welfare states sustained by strong trade unionism can and do compete with economies carrying fewer and lower social overheads. At its most modest, the claim is simply that – when the welfare state is under attack as a burden on competitiveness and growth – the case for the prosecution remains unproven (Korpi, 1985; Gough, 1996, p. 219; Corry and Glyn, 1994, p. 212) and that for the defence remains 'plausible' (Atkinson, 1995, p. 730). Slightly more self-confidently, there is also the claim that the record of welfare capitalisms on competitiveness and growth is mixed rather than uniformly poor, and that the negative impact of welfare expenditure is minor and exaggerated. This defence of welfare expenditure – in the hands of Pfaller, Therborn and Gough, is then turned into a nuanced advocacy of welfare systems: firstly by emphasising the persistence of Swedish 'exceptionalism', and then by re-asserting the positive impact of strong welfare rights on investment in human capital and the orientation of national economies to 'high productivity and high quality production' (Pfaller et al, 1991, p. 296). The balance of weakness and strength is tipped even more in corporatism's favour by a series of writers keen to establish the importance of trust relationships in the workings of modern capitalism. Here the defence/advocacy of corporatism (with its strong publicly-created trust relationships between capital and labour) often merges with, or is discussed alongside, a defence/advocacy of the Japanese form of trust capitalism, where the emphasis is on cooperative relations between sections of capital, and on private, corporately-provided, welfare underpinnings to secure cooperation between labour and capital (Hutton, 1994, pp. 262–8; Kenworthy, 1995, p. 196; even Katzenstein, 1985; Marsden, 1994). And by this stage in the literature, it is the *superiority* of welfare-based capitalisms over market-based capitalisms which emerges as the argument's central motif. Far from unions being a barrier to economic competitiveness, they emerge as a vital prerequisite to economic success. To quote Hicks, another enthusiast for welfare-based capitalisms, 'organisationally and govern-

mentally, strong labour movements may emerge as major societal benefactors, as purveyors of relatively rapid income growth, and also of somewhat more equal distribution of income' (Hicks, 1988, p. 700).

But may they? It would be good to think that the matter was that simple. However it is not; as a fuller reading of the relevant research literature makes only too clear. For over the full range of economic and social performance indicators, the performance of economies labelled as corporatist is too uneven to sustain the claims for general and permanent superiority. In fact, the performance of individual corporatist economies on any one set of indicators is too uneven to allow easy generalisation of any kind; and the individual studies of economies and performance just vary too greatly in the content and reliability of their findings to permit much certainty at all. Rather, what the research data indicates is a definite *variety* of relationship between corporatism and competitiveness, which in its turn suggests that factors other than trade union strength and centralised collective bargaining are over-determining the results (positive/negative) that both advocates and critics of corporatism mobilise on their own behalf.

The 'unevenness' and 'indeterminacy' of the corporatist-competitiveness relationship cannot really be avoided when the full range of available comparative studies in examined in detail. From what is now an enormous literature a few examples will suffice to make the point. Therborn used a 1973–85 OECD data set to examine the impact of two kinds of corporatism – interest intermediation and concerted public policy-making – on cross-national variations in economic performance; and found little evidence that either form played a significant explanatory role (Therborn, 1987). Crepaz examined the impact of corporatism on macro-economic performance in 18 industrialised countries between 1960 and 1988; and found a strong and positive impact on unemployment and inflation but not on economic growth (Crepaz, 1992). Henley and Tsakalotos – using OECD data for the same period and criticising Crepaz for the methodology underpinning his survey – were equally cautious on growth, but were impressed by the positive impact of corporatist institutional arrangements on investment, inequality and unemployment (Henley and Tsakalotos, 1993). Golden, noting the different degrees of wage restraint achieved recently in Sweden and Germany, tentatively argued that it was the degree of monopoly of representation achieved by trade unions, and not their involvement in formal corporatist structures, that was decisive in each case (Golden, 1993, p. 451). And finally Pekkarinen and colleagues, judging economic performance in comparative terms since the 1970s, found that 'the corporatist countries display considerable variety', Sweden doing broadly very well during their period of research, Austria generally less well, with Denmark bad on unemployment but good on wage equality, and so on (Pekkarinen et al, 1992, p. 6).

This variation in research findings has been enough to persuade the more sophisticated of the research teams active in this field to differentiate *types* of corporatist system. Pekkarinen, Pohjala and Rowthorn, for example, distinguish those with inclusive tendencies from those without, and posit a different dynamic at work in each (Pekkarinen et al, 1992, pp. 2–3, 14–15). Gough follows a similar line, as did Esping-Andersen before him, speculating that different types of corporatist system pose different problems for those pursuing national economic competitiveness, and are differently threatened by that pursuit (Gough, 1996, pp. 227–8; Esping-Andersen, 1990). All this seems eminently sensible. What seems less adequate is the line of analysis developed by Garrett and Lange which, for all its ostensibly progressive nature, actually offers powerful hostages to fortune in the debate with neo-liberalism. For their argument about the need for institutional symmetries not only protects corporatist arrangements where the Left is strong; it also gives Thatcherism a retrospective justification where the Left is weak. If strong trade unionism and right-wing governments are incompatible as growth partners, then neo-liberals are absolutely right to make anti-trade union legislation the centre-piece of their project. Moreover, a defence of corporatism that asserts its superiority to market liberalism as a mechanism for protecting profits in booms and sharing austerity in recessions is ultimately no defence of corporatism at all. For if corporatism is to be of any value to the contemporary Left, the claim for its superiority over market-led solutions to competitiveness and growth has to be one that asserts its ability to generate *qualitatively superior outcomes*, and not one – as with Garrett and Lange – that rests essentially on corporatism's ability to arrive in a more civilised manner at *qualitatively the same outcomes* as those imposed by unregulated market processes. The general literature on corporatism hints at such a defence when it compares patterns of unemployment and income inequality between types of economic system; but it does not conclusively establish the superiority of corporatism on growth and competitiveness, not least because the general record of corporatist economies on these indicators is both mixed and (in comparative terms) unremarkable. So if such a defence is to be mounted – if the potential (if not always the reality) of the Centre-Left's project is to be demonstrated as inherently superior to that of neo-liberalism – that defence has to be based on more specific evidence derived from corporatism's strongest case: which is why the performance of the Swedish model is so important an issue here.

2 The rise and fall of the Swedish model

The Swedish achievement – in combining generous levels of equalitarian welfare provision with high living standards based on sustained economic growth – has been (and remains) a powerful model and inspiration for the European Centre-Left and a serious challenge to many of the conventional understandings of mainstream economics. Welfare provision expanded rapidly in Sweden only from the 1960s (Ginsburg, 1993, p. 174); but once under way it left Sweden by 1980 at the 'top of the equality league in terms of employment (per head of population), female as compared to male wages, progressiveness of tax system, generosity of public pensions, public provision of health, education and welfare services, relative absence of poverty and overall income equality' (Glyn, 1995, p. 50). Sweden was also by then second only to Switzerland in Europe in its record on employment and to Norway in income per head. Sweden was (and still is) in comparative terms a high wage and very high tax economy, with the largest public sector of any OECD country and with very high levels of union membership: union density peaked in 1986 at the quite remarkable figure of 86% (Kjellberg, 1992, p. 119). For all these reasons, and with the brief exception of the period immediately following the devaluation of 1982, 'Swedish industry has constantly operated with higher labour costs than those of its major export competitors' except the USA (Pfaller et al, 1991, p. 235); and from the 1970s has been subject to extensive labour codes (including the 1976 Co-determination Law) which have no UK parallel. Yet at the same time, Sweden possesses a large, internationally-competitive and export-oriented industrial sector: one currently capable of exporting 30% of its GDP when the unweighted average for exports as a share of GDP in the OECD as a whole is a mere 19% (Henrekson et al, 1996, p. 247). Sweden, that is, quite against the grain of conventional expectations, has managed until very recently to combine West German scales of international competitive performance with unparalleled levels of welfare provision, employment security and wage equality.

The post-war Swedish combination of successful private capital accumulation and generous public welfare provision was based on a quite unique class accommodation: a historic compromise initiated in the 1930s and presided over thereafter by Swedish social democracy in a long period of virtually unbroken political rule (1932–76, 1982–91, 1994–). 'The formal part of the Swedish Historical Compromise was the so-called Main Agreement between the unions and the employers, negotiated between 1936 and 1938': (the Saltsjobaden Agreement) 'The most important part, however, was an informal agreement or understanding between labour and capital to cooperate to generate economic growth' (Korpi, 1992, p. 104). In Sweden the Left *was* dominant both industrially and politically for a very long period; and because it was, the post-war Swedish labour movement was free to pursue what has become known as the Rehn-Meidner model (for details, Pontusson, 1992, pp. 312–4; Meidner, 1992, pp. 160–61). It was free, that is, to pursue both a solidaristic wages policy and the creation of a universalistic/encompassing welfare state. It was also free to break the tendency of full employment to trigger inflation by trading wage restraint (and opposition to spreading wage differentials) for active and selective labour market policies.

The Swedish experience is certainly evidence that it was possible – in the years after 1945 – successfully to combine strong trade unionism, generous welfare provision and economic growth. Indeed it is also evidence that, in the right conditions, such a combination could enable particular national economies to out-compete economies which were equipped with weaker trade unions and more limited welfare provision. Taken alone, therefore, the Swedish experience seems entirely to reverse the conventionally understood relationship of union power to international competitiveness. However it is not entirely wise to treat the Swedish experience in isolation, not least because the performance of the Swedish economy of late has proved less robust in the face of international competition than hitherto, and less remarkable in comparative terms. In particular, the 'exceptional' performance of the Swedish economy on unemployment since 1973 has not been matched by any commensurately outstanding performance on growth and productivity. On the contrary, Swedish growth rates have settled at 'roughly one percentage point *below* the OECD average over the last quarter century' (Henrekson et al, 1996, p. 280); and by the same token, after an outstanding productivity record in the first half of the century (Gordon et al, 1994, p. 148), the productivity performance of the Swedish economy as a whole now lags behind all the major OECD economies (see also Lindbeck, 1994, pp. 8–9). Even unemployment has recently soared: from 1.5% in 1990 to 14.2% in August 1994 (Wilks, 1996, p. 93), as 'Swedish GDP fell by 5.1% between 1990 and 1993 (as compared to a rise of 2.6% in Europe)' (Glyn, 1995, p. 51) and as Sweden's standing in the international league tables of per capita income slipped from 3rd in 1970 to 14th in 1991 (Lindbeck, 1994, p. 10). By 1993 indeed, and for the first time since the 1950s, less than half those out of work in Sweden had found places in active labour market schemes. In the 1950s the standard percentage of the unemployed in such schemes had regularly been 80% (Clement, 1994, p. 115). Clearly something has gone seriously awry with the workings of the Swedish model in the 1990s, and had begun to do so even before EC entry and Maastricht conversion criteria made their own serious dent in the space for Swedish exceptionalism.

In part the current crisis of the Swedish model is a product of emerging *internal* tensions, and of resulting corrosions of essential internal pre-requisites for its success. The Rehn-Meidner model was built upon the wage restraint/solidaristic wage policies of unions representing predominantly manual workers in the manufacturing sector; but its solution to the needs for high productivity growth there (namely the toleration of industrial restructuring to move workers from low productivity industry to high productivity industry) eventually gave way to a structural shift of employment from manufacturing in general to the public sector, as state employment 'came to take over the labour-absorbing role of the high productivity manufacturing enterprise in the active labour market policy model of the LO economists' (Strath, 1996, pp. 104–5). This shift quickly created a major and destabilising imbalance between the Swedish economy's marketed and protected/public sectors, increasing the tax-take on the wages of manufacturing workers, without resolving the problem of low productivity in labour-intensive public service provision: and in consequence eventually eroded the tolerance of high levels of taxation by key groups of Swedish workers (Lundberg, 1985, p. 29) and undermined the enthusiasm of unions in the marketed sector (especially the key Metalworkers Union) for solidaristic wage policies. One consequence, that is, of the 'success' of the Swedish model was the eventual fragmentation – now into four federations representing blue and white collar workers in the public and private sectors – of a united labour movement whose high degree of centralization had initially made the model possible.

There is a key relationship between productivity growth and the timing of Sweden's contemporary crisis tucked away in this fragmentation of union solidarity. The high productivity of manufacturing industry encouraged by the Rehn-Meidner model enabled Sweden to hold at bay through the 1970s the tensions between sections of organised labour that, in weaker economies like the UK, was already evident before the onset of Thatcherism, and which (in the UK case) paved the way for the Thatcherite capture of the votes of skilled workers in private manufacturing industry. For as Glyn correctly observed, 'the overwhelming proportion of the cost of egalitarian redistribution' in Sweden was a cost which 'was met out of wages – redistribution within the working class, broadly defined. The crucial point' however, for the viability of the model in the 1950s and 1960s, was that 'the dynamism of the private sector allowed this redistribution to occur within the context of growing consumption per worker' (Glyn, 1995, p. 45). But after 1973, that dynamism was harder to guarantee. The 1970s was a lean decade for Swedish investment; and though investment levels then recovered, even in the 1980s total gross investment as a percentage of GDP in Sweden settled 5 percentage points lower than the levels achieved in the 1960s (Henrekson et al, 1996, p. 262). So as productivity eventually dipped in Swedish manufacturing, the standard contradiction of interests between workers in different sectors emerged in Sweden too, and pulled away at the unity of purpose and policy which had hitherto sustained so remarkable a period of industrial peace. Swedish labour still remains more willing than do other European labour movements to tolerate the redistribution of resources away from productive workers in manufacturing to less productive public service provision. The social wage is still more tolerated/valued by the workers whose taxes finance it in Sweden than elsewhere (Mishra, 1990, pp. 63–4); but that tolerance has lessened in Sweden of late, as the Swedish economy has failed to deliver the rapid economic growth which – in the model's heyday in the 1950s and 1960s – enabled private consumption and public provision to rise together. That just did not happen with the same regularity and ease after 1973 as before: indeed, between 1973 and 1985 'consumption out of the average worker's earnings *fell* by nearly 2% per year or some 20% in total' (Glyn, 1995, p. 51).

Moreover, as even one the model's architects, the economist Rudolf Meidner, has conceded, one problem with the original model was that 'firms with high profitability [made] 'excess profits' since their capacity to pay high wages [was] not fully used' (Meidner, 1992, p. 167; also Meidner, 1993, p. 218). This failure had at least two consequences. It reinforced the concentration of capital in Swedish industry into a remarkably limited number of hands/families – 'fifteen families clustered around two banks' (Gordon et al, 1994, p. 146) – and so reinforced the strategic significance of the higher industrial bourgeoisie as underwriters of the Swedish historic compromise. It also left incomplete the final stage of Swedish social democracy's original radical project – namely the socialisation of investment flows themselves. By 1976 – under Meidner's leadership – the Swedish Left was ready to embark on that final stage, through the initiation of collective wage earner funds that would absorb surplus profits and slowly transfer ownership or control from capital to the unions. But this proposal, far more than any other initiated by Swedish Social Democracy since the 1930s, challenged the fundamental class compromise at the heart of the Swedish model – and in particular antagonised the very group of large-scale export-oriented capitalists with whose predecessors the original compromise had been made (Swenson, 1991, p. 514; Pontusson, 1992, p. 319). Swedish capital – through its employers organisation, the SAF – then responded by a series of moves against centralised wage bargaining, welfare provision and trade union rights. The SAF began actively to campaign in the 1970s 'against growing public expenditure, against the welfare state, against collectivism in general' (Fulcher, 1987, p. 245); and to urge on successive Swedish governments a steady stream of conventional neo-liberal policies. Sections of Swedish capital also systematically withdrew from centralised collective bargaining amid a series of industrial disputes/lockouts which they triggered: effectively by 1990 killing off this key element of the Swedish model. And most important of all, in the 1980s major Swedish companies began to export capital on a large scale for the first time (Kurzer, 1991, p. 5): taking Swedish capital exports from 1% of GDP in 1980 to about 6% by 1990 – from a level in the early 1980s that was normal among capitalist economies to one in the 1990s that was higher than elsewhere (Wilks, 1996, p. 103: also Albo, 1997, p. 9).

It is the increasingly global nature of large-scale Swedish capital which now poses the major threat to the viability of Swedish exceptionalism. To work properly, the Rehn-Meidner model required low levels of internationalisation among high productivity Swedish companies, since it 'rested on the premise that the "excess profits" generated by solidaristic wage restraint would translate into increased production and employment by firms or sectors with above-average productivity' (Pontusson, 1992, p. 322) *within Sweden itself.* But the model worked less well when (and to the degree that) Swedish firms moved percentages of their production/employment abroad: which they did progressively after 1960 and at a quickening rate after capital controls were eased in 1985. This corrosion of one vital element in the post-war Swedish equation tells us much about the determinants of international competitiveness and the role of trade unions in its enhancement. It makes very clear that the unions are not the only – or ultimately even the decisive – determinants of the persistence and effectiveness of 'historic compromises' between major social classes. The Swedish model is now in difficulties not primarily because of divisions on the side of labour, but because dominant groups within the Swedish capitalist class are no longer willing to participate in its central institutions (Wilks, 1996, p. 94). That unwillingness is in part a product of the intrusion into their interests, resources and freedom of action created by the rules and institutions of Swedish corporatism, and by the revitalised radicalism of the Wage Earner Fund initiative. The unwillingness is also in part the product of a major revival of neo-liberal ideas (and confidence) in Swedish governing circles. But it is also a product of the changing nature of capitalism as a global system: a product of the intensification of international competition – and the changing modes of work organisation being developed by successful international competitors – to which Swedish manufacturing industry is now subject; and of the greater facility now available to holders of capital (including Swedish holders of capital) to shift both their portfolio and their productive investment off-shore. With the benefit of hindsight it is becoming clearer that the success of the Swedish historic compromise – as a growth model for Swedish capital and as a source of rising living standards and social justice for Swedish labour – was intimately associated with the productive conditions prevailing in capitalism's post-war 'golden age': an age of Fordist regimes of accumulation and high levels of national economic autonomy. And by association, the fall, deterioration or challenge to the model (depending on how pessimistic your reading of the future is) is a product of the extent to which those conditions have been eroded by changes in forms of production and by processes of global economic integration.

III. CONCLUSION

This link between 'class compromises' and wider social structures of accumulation is the point of vulnerability in the whole Centre-Left argument on trade unions and competitiveness; and it is one that neo-liberal critics have been quick to exploit as the Swedish success story has soured (Lindbeck, 1985, 1994). But as the empirical record on the post-war UK indicates, neo-liberal theses on trade unionism and competitiveness have their own deep problems, of which three general ones stand out.

1. One is the inability of such arguments (however much their advocates genuflect in this direction) to grasp/allow for the full significance of the *qualitative* difference between a labour market and any other form of commodity market in capitalist societies. Labour is not just any other commodity, to be analysed in abstracted models of labour market performance. On the contrary: it is a very special commodity which, because it is both highly perishable ('it cannot be stored, and if it is not used continuously it is wasted' (Rothstein, 1990, p. 325); and highly active (with workers needing to be present at its delivery), requires managing in a very particular kind of way. This is especially the case in a capitalist mode of production, where there is a perpetual wage-effort bargain to be struck between managers and workers within a context of highly differentiated patterns of reward. Labour markets are inherently complex social systems, and have to be understood and studied with a sensitivity to the wider social universes in which they are inserted (Rubery, 1994, p. 341). At the very least this means that the definitions, goals, motivations and stocks of knowledge that individual labourers bring to the production process inevitably shape productive outcomes. It also means that the workings of labour markets are shaped by sets of social forces (institutions, histories, cultures and practices) which lie beyond the immediate control of any one individual labour market actor (labour markets are quintessentially *not* the appropriate territory for forms of analysis based on the interaction of socially-abstracted rational individuals). And most important of all, it means that the settlements arrived at inside labour markets have outcomes and significances that stretch far beyond the boundaries of the labour market itself, such that nothing going on within the market can safely be treated in isolation from wider questions of status and power.

2. The second limitation of neo-liberal analyses of trade unionism is this: that it is just not the case that labour markets will 'clear' at socially/economically optimal levels but for trade union intervention, or that what we face, without trade unionism, is a level playing field between capital and labour which trade unionism

then distorts. We do not. Labour markets in a capitalist economy are stacked heavily against labour. There is a basic asymmetry of power between the individual worker and his/her employer that trade unionism attempts to *redress*. There is a gradient of power running against labour in capitalist societies unless unions act to pull it back (Coates, 1983, pp. 58–62; 1984, pp. 88–91). That retrenchment/redressing has never been more than partial; though it has been at its greatest, historically, in the corporatist labour codes of the Western European welfare states. In those societies, trade unions have pulled the gradient down a little in favour of workers: giving them rights in the workplace, welfare rights beyond it, and higher wages. If neo-liberals now want to reduce those rights and make the gradient steeper once again, what they are actually saying is that rapid capital accumulation currently requires an intensification of inequality, and a reduction in the degree of redress previously achieved. And in truth, that is the core of the right-wing critique of UK trade unionism in the 1970s – that capital accumulation, UK-style, required a significant imbalance of power and reward between capital and labour, an imbalance which the modest pro-labour reforms of the mid-1970s then threatened and challenged. But put that way, it throws an entirely different light on the role of unions and their members in post-war UK economic under-performance than that characteristically generated by neo-liberal critics: namely that trade unions and their members were more sinned against than sinning, the victims of deeper processes and stronger social forces, before which the unions' main crime was to be, not too strong, but too weak.

3. So to claim, as neo-liberals often do, that trade unions are a (or the) source of income inequality in a capitalist labour market is quite ludicrous, and invariably deliberately disingenuous. Capitalist labour markets only work by entrenching inequalities of power and income between whole social classes. They are machines for the manufacture of social hierarchies, not of individual equality. To criticise trade unions for allowing wage inequalities within one social class both ignores the important Swedish counter-case (of solidaristic wage policies) and masks the extent to which income inequality as a whole is likely to intensify as trade unionism is weakened. That was certainly the UK experience after 1979. Even in Sweden, for all the wage

> solidarity achieved *within* the working class, income inequality *between* classes was the price even Swedish labour was obliged to pay for the sustenance of its 40 year long exploration of the limits of class collaboration within corporatist institutions. Inequality, that is, is not a product of trade unions. It is a product of *unregulated* labour markets, and of the untrammelled workings of the privately-owned market institutions with whose interests the neo-liberal advocates of trade union restraint invariably identify. Neo-liberalism is quite wrong to market its own policy proposals as the only viable ones available. The issue is not a lack of alternatives now facing privileged and non-privileged classes alike, but an unwillingness on the part of the privileged to pay the cost of radical policies for employment and growth. Neo-liberalism is in that sense a class project, as well as a theoretical argument, and needs to be recognised as such.

With this in mind, we can go back to the arguments of Garrett and Lange. Their defence of corporatism as a viable growth strategy is also best understood in class terms – as advocating a strategy of collaboration between classes for strategic international advantage, in its Swedish manifestation as an alliance between organised labour and large-scale Swedish industrial capital. Now it is very hard to argue, as much neo-liberal theorising implicitly does, that in social terms – for the labour forces caught up in it – the experience of life under Swedish corporatism was *inferior* to that under Thatcherite neo-liberalism. On the contrary, and on virtually any morally-defensible performance indicator you care to name – industrial and social rights, living standards, gender equality, job security, human dignity – corporatism was (and is) superior. That is why the issue for us, in examining the theory and practice of Centre-Left arguments on unionism and competitiveness, is not whether the Centre-Left model is *better*: it clearly is. The question is rather whether it remains a *viable* one; and against that question there are a number of troubling things to say (for a general critique, see Albo, 1997).

1. One point of caution concerns the relationship of productivity growth to the maintenance of class alliances. The significant ghost in the machine throughout the Swedish story is the question of the productivity of labour in Sweden's manufacturing sectors. As productivity there rose, and as its rise was encouraged by the Rehn-Meidner model, the collaboration between classes at the heart of the Swedish model held – profits and wages rising

together for a prolonged period. But in the end they did not. Overall productivity in the economy slowed, as the weight of public sector employment failed to be compensated by commensurate increases in labour productivity elsewhere. In the end, that is, the Swedish model hit the same contradiction between sectors as had the UK economy a decade earlier. In Sweden, as in the UK, the rise in public sector employment was a *response* to the falling capacity of the manufacturing sector to sustain rising labour productivity and output. It was not, as neo-liberalism has it, the *cause* of that fall; but once underway, dwindling manufacturing productivity was then accentuated by levels of public spending whose financing took the sorts of toll that neo-liberalism so often emphasises – and in the process did, internally as it were, erode the space within which corporatist class-compacts could be sustained.

2. Such a rise and fall of industrial productivity – and the associated opening and closing of a space for a certain kind of class politics – brings the issue of *time* back into our understanding of the relationship of unions to competitiveness, and raises the possibility that such a relationship may itself be *contingent* on the presence and character of a wider set of economic and social institutions and processes. Neo-liberal critics of trade unionism implicitly discount dimensions of time and contingency: for them, trade unions are *always* an impediment to output, production and costs. In their stridency, they have invited and stimulated an equally universal counter-claim from the Centre-Left: one that asserts the compatibility of trade unionism with high performance on neo-liberalism's chosen economic indicators, and also with high performance on indicators (like employment and equality) to which neo-liberalism pays less attention. But when we look at the evidence which is deployed in support of that counter-claim, we find that much of it derives from the functionality of welfare regimes, government spending and high wages to the realisation of profits in the accumulation regimes established in western Europe in capitalism's post-war 'golden age'. Class compacts of a corporatist kind did function satisfactorily for both labour and capital in a number of leading European economies in the hey-day of Fordism; and in doing so, did provide powerful counter-factual evidence to neo-liberalism's general anti-union case. But the question we have to ask is

whether the special conditions permitting such class compacts are not now beginning to erode, whether we are not, in some fundamental sense, now at/approaching 'the end of Fordism'?

3. Fordism may or may not be going – that is a much discussed issue – but at the very least it is changing: as a new international division of labour and the emergence of more globally mobile forms of capital reduce the degree of national autonomy available to policy-makers keen to reconstitute compacts between locally-based social classes. Labour is still available for those compacts. Capital increasingly is not. Which brings us back once more to the Garrett and Lange argument that we currently face *two* viable growth packages: one corporatist, one neo-liberal. For behind such a view lies an unexplored assumption about the character, not of labour and trade unionism, but of capital and of capitalism. If strong trade unionism was compatible with high levels of investment in local manufacturing industry in Sweden, but was not in the UK, then, since both economies contained for most of the post-war period highly organised labour movements, it suggests that variables other than labour were at play, and that in particular *the character of local employing classes*, and their role in the world economy, may in fact have had a far more potent impact on patterns of economic performance than trade unions *per se*. And if that is so, it is not the symmetries of institutional arrangements that hold the key to why unionism has different economic effects in different advanced capitalisms, but the nature of the integration of different national capitalisms into the overall world system. In the 1960s and 1970s the UK capitalist class was already internationally-oriented and globally mobile. The Swedish was not; that was the key difference. Then the question becomes – which capitalist class is now representative of the situation of capital as a whole: and if it is the UK's – if capital in general is becoming internationally mobile and globally oriented (as it surely is) – then it is the Swedish case which has been 'exceptional' and the UK case which is a better guide to the norm. In other words, the argument of Garrett and Lange, when explored more deeply, is as vulnerable as is corporatism itself to a critique based on the globalisation of capital.

Academics of a neo-liberal persuasion are making that critique right now, with great enthusiasm, claiming ideological victory after years of under-representation in the Scandinavian case. But they should not gloat. If corporatist class compacts are now to be criticised for their diminished record on investment, living standards and job security, there is just no evidence that a return to unregulated markets will produce a more impressive set of outcomes. On the contrary, the future neo-liberalism offers is one of continued uneven economic development, as growth trajectories diverge through processes of cumulative causation (Albo, 1997). What has always been at stake in corporatist class compacts is the balance of class forces. A particular balance was critical to the consolidation of the Fordist social structure of accumulation. Now, in the world system as a whole, that balance is shifting again: ostensibly because capital is more globally mobile, actually because of the steady proletarianisation of the Asian peasantries. In that shift, one particular historical option is being foreclosed – that of nationally-based class compacts which allow wages and profits to rise together in core capitalist economies. But that foreclosing does not oblige the Left to surrender territory, ideologically or politically, to neo-liberalism. It simply obliges the Left to meet that ideological and political challenge without reproducing the illusion that national class compacts remain a viable option for progressive forces. They do not.

NOTES

Albo, G. (1997), 'A world market of opportunities? Capitalist obstacles and Left economic policy', in L. Panitch (ed), *The Socialist Register 1997*, Merlin, pp. 1–43

Atkinson, A.B.(1995), 'Is the welfare state necessarily an obstacle to economic growth', *European Economic Review*, vol. 39, pp. 723–730

Barrell, R. (ed) (1994), *The UK Labour Market: Comparative Aspects and Institutional Developments*, Cambridge University Press

Barrell, R. and Pain, N. (1997), 'The growth of Foreign Direct Investment in Europe', *National Institute Economic Review* no. 160, April, pp. 63–75

Blair, T. (1997), *Speech at the Trades Union Congress*, 9th September, BBC

Booth, A. (1995), *The Economics of the Trade Union*, Cambridge University Press

Calmfors, L. and Driffill, J. (1988), 'Bargaining structure, corporatism and macroeconomic performance', *Economic Policy* 6(1), pp. 14–61

Cameron, D. (1984), 'Social democracy, corporatism, labour quiescence and the representation of economic interest in advanced capitalist society', in J. Goldthorpe (ed), *Order and Conflict in Contemporary Capitalism*, Oxford University Press, pp. 143–178

Caves, R.E. (1980), 'Productivity differences among industries', in R. E. Caves and L.B. Krause (eds), *Britain's Economic Performance*, Brookings Institute, pp. 125–98

Clement, W. (1994), 'Social Democracy unhinged', *Studies in Political Economy*, vol. 44, Summer, pp. 95–123

Coates, D. (1980), *Labour in Power? A study of the Labour Government 1974–79*, Longman

Coates, D. (1983), 'The political power of trade unions', in D. Coates and G.Johnston (eds), *Socialist Arguments*, Martin Robertson, pp. 32–63

Coates, D. (1984), *The Context of British Politics*, Hutchinson

Coates, D. (1994), *The Question of UK Decline*, Harvester

Corry, D. and Glyn, A. (1994), 'The macro-economics of equality, stability and growth', in A. Glyn and D. Miliband (eds), *Paying for Inequality: the economic costs of social injustice*, IPPR/Rivers Oram Press, pp. 205–216

Crafts, N. (1991), 'Reversing relative economic decline: the 1980s in historical perspective', *Oxford Review of Economic Policy*, vol. 7(3), pp. 81–98

Crafts, N. (1997), *Britain's Relative Economic Decline 1870–1995: A Quantitative Perspective*, Social Market Foundation

Crepaz, M.M.L. (1992), 'Corporatism in Decline? An empirical analysis of the impact of corporatism on macro-economic performance and industrial disputes in 18 industrialised countries', *Comparative Political Studies*, vol. 25(2), pp. 139–168

Esping-Andersen, G. (1990), *The Three Worlds of Welfare Capitalism*, Princeton University Press

Freeman, R.B. and Medoff, J.L. (1984), *What Do Unions Do?* Basic Books

Fulcher, J. (1987), 'Labour movement theory versus corporatism: social democracy in Sweden', *Sociology*, vol. 21(2), pp. 232–252

Garrett, G. and Lange, P. (1986), 'Performance in a hostile world: economic growth in capitalist democracies 1974–1982', *World Politics* vol xxxviii, July, pp. 517–545

Ginsburg, N. (1993), 'Sweden: the Social Democratic Case', in A. Cochrane and J. Clarke (eds), *Comparing Welfare States: Britain in international context*, Sage, pp. 173–204

Glyn, A. (1992), 'Corporatism, patterns of employment and access to consumption', in J. Pekkarinen et al (eds), *Social Corporatism: a superior economic system*, Oxford University Press, pp. 132–177

Glyn, A. (1995), 'Social Democracy and Full Employment', *New Left Review*, 211, May/June, pp. 33–55

Golden, M. (1993), 'The dynamics of trade unionism and national economic performance', *American Political Science Review*, vol. 87(2), pp. 439–454

Gordon, W. et al, (1994), 'Equality and the Swedish work environment', *Employee Responsibilities and Rights*, vol. 7(2), pp. 141–160

Gough, I. (1996), 'Social Welfare and Competitiveness', *New Political Economy*, vol. 1(2), pp. 209–232

Henrekson, M, Jonung, L. and Stymme, J. (1996), 'Economic growth and the Swedish model', in N. Crafts and G. Toniolo (eds), *Economic Growth in Europe since 1945*, Cambridge University Press, pp. 240–289

Henley, A. and Tsakalotos, E. (1993), *Corporatism and Economic Performance*, Edward Elgar

Hicks, A. (1988), 'Social democratic corporatism and growth', *The Journal of Politics*, vol. 50(4), pp. 677–704

Hutton, W. (1994), *The State We're In*, Cape

Katzenstein, P. (1985), *Small States in World Markets*, Cornell University Press

Kendix, M. and Olson, M. (1990), 'Changing unemployment rates in Europe and the USA: institutional structure and regional variation', in R. Brunetta and C. Dell'Arringa (eds), *Labour Relations and Economic Performance*, Macmillan, pp. 40–67

Kenworthy, L. (1995), *In Search of National Economic Success: balancing competition and co-operation*, Sage

Kitson, M. and Michie, J. (1996a), 'Britain's industrial performance since 1960: under-investment and relative decline', *The Economic Journal*, vol. 106 (no. 434), pp. 196–213

Kitson, M. and Michie, J. (1996b), 'Manufacturing Capacity, Investment and Employment', in J. Michie and J. Grieve Smith (eds), *Creating Industrial Capacity: Towards full employment*, Oxford University Press, pp. 24–51

Kjellberg, A. (1992), 'Sweden: can the model survive?', in A. Ferner and R. Hyman (eds), *Industrial Relations in the New Europe*, Blackwell, pp. 88–142

Korpi, W. (1985), 'Economic growth and the welfare state: a comparative study of 18 OECD countries', *Industrial and Labor Relations Review*, vol. 38(2), pp. 195–209

Korpi, W. (1992), 'Strategies of reformist socialist parties in a mixed economy: the Swedish model', *Socialism of the Future*, vol. 1(1), pp. 101–109

Kurzer, P. (1991), 'Unemployment in open economies: the impact of trade, finance and European integration', *Comparative Political Studies* vol. 24(1), pp. 3–30

Lange, P., (1984), 'Unions, workers and wage regulation: the rational bases of consent', in J. Goldthorpe (ed), *Order and Conflict in Contemporary Capitalism*, Oxford University Press, pp. 98–123

Lange, P. and Garrett, G. (1985), 'The politics of growth: strategic interaction and economic performance in the advanced industrial democracies, 1974–1980', *Journal of Politics* vol. 47(s), pp. 792–827

Lazonick, W. (1991), *Business Organisation and the Myth of the Market Economy*, Cambride University Press

Lindbeck, A. (1985), 'What is wrong with the West European economies', *The World Economy*, vol. 8(2), pp. 153–170

Lindbeck, A. et al, (1994), *Turning Sweden Round*, MIT Press

Lundberg, E. (1985), 'The rise and fall of the Swedish model', *Journal of Economic Literature*, vol. xxiii, pp. 1–36

Marsden, D. (1994), 'Regulation versus de-regulation: which route for Europe's labour markets', *Employment Policy Institute: Economic Report*, vol. 8(8), November, pp. 1–5

Martin, A, (1986), 'The politics of employment and welfare', in K. Banting (ed), *The State and Economic Interests*, University of Toronto Press, p.p.

Martin, P. (1997), 'Manufacturers must try harder: an OECD study of productivity', *Financial Times*, 17 April, p. 12.

Meidner, R. (1992), 'The rise and fall of the Swedish model', *Studies in Political Economy*, vol. 39, pp. 159–171

Meidner, R. (1993), 'Why did the Swedish model fail?', in R. Miliband and L. Panitch (eds), *The Socialist Register 1993*, pp. 211–228

Metcalf, D. (1989), 'Water Notes Dry Up: the impact of the Donovan reform proposals and Thatcherism at work on labour productivity in British manufacturing industry', *British Journal of Industrial Relations*, vol. 27, pp. 1–31

Metcalf, D. (1990a), 'Union presence and labour productivity in British manufacturing industry: a reply to Nolan and Marginson', *British Journal of Industrial Relations*, vol. 28(2), pp. 249–266

Metcalf, D. (1990b), 'Trade unions and economic performance: the British evidence', in R. Brunetta and C. Dell'Arringa (eds), *Labour Relations and Economic Performance*, Macmillan, pp. 283–303

Metcalf, D. (1993), 'Industrial relations and economic performance', *British Journal of Industrial Relations*, vol. 31(2), pp. 255–283

Metcalf, D. (1994), 'Transformation of British industrial relations? Institutions, conduct and outcomes, 1980–1990', in R. Barrell (ed), *The UK Labour Market*, Cambridge University Press, pp. 126–157

Minkin, L. (1991), *The Contentious Alliance: Trade unions and the Labour Party*, Edinburgh University Press

Mishel, L. and Voos, P.B. (editors), (1992), *Unions and Economic Competitiveness*, M.E.Sharpe.

Mishra, R. (1990), *The Welfare State in Capitalist Society*, Harvester Wheatsheaf

Nickell, S., Wadhwani, S and Wall, M. (1989), *Union and Productivity Growth in Britain 1974–1986*, Centre for Labour Economics Discussion Paper 353, London School of Economics

Nichols, T, (1986), *The British Worker Question: a new look at workers and productivity in manufacturing*, Routledge and Kegan Paul

Nolan, P. (1992), 'Trade Unions and Productivity: Issues, Evidence and Prospects', in *Employee Relations.*, vol. 16(2), pp. 3–19..

Nolan, P. (1994), 'Labour market institutions, industrial restructuring and unemployment in Europe', in J. Michie and J. Grieve Smith (eds), *Unemployment in Europe*, Academic Press, pp. 61–71

Paloheimo, H. (1990), 'Between Liberalism and Corporatism: the effect of trade unions and governments on economic performance in eighteen OECD countries', in R. Brunetta and C. Dell'Arringa (eds), *Labour Relations and Economic Performance*, Macmillan, pp. 40–67

Pekkarinen, J., Pohjala M. and Rowthorn, B. (eds) (1992), *Social Corporatism: a superior economic system?*, Oxford University Press

Pfaller, A., Gough, I and Therborn, G. (1991), *Can the Welfare State Compete? A comparative study of five advanced capitalist countries*, Macmillan

Pontusson, J. (1992), 'At the end of the third road: Swedish social democracy in crisis', *Politics and Society*, vol. 20(3), pp. 305–322

Pratten, C. (1976), *Labour Productivity Differentials within international companies*, Cambridge University Press

Quilley, S., Tickell, A and Coates, D., (1996), *Corporate Relocation in the European Union*, European Parliament Directorate-General for Research, Working Paper Series, Social Affairs series

Radice, H. (1995), 'Britain in the world economy: national decline, capitalist success?', in D. Coates and J. Hillard (eds), *UK Economic Decline: Key Texts*, Harvester, pp. 233–49

Ray, G.F., (1987), 'Labour Costs in Manufacturing', *National Institute Economic Review*, May, pp. 71–4

Rothstein, B. (1990), 'Marxism, institutional analysis and working class power: the Swedish case', *Politics and Society*, vol. 18(3), pp. 317–346

Rubery, J. (1994), 'The British production regime: a societal specific system?', *Economy and Society*, 23(3), pp. 334–354

Select Committee on Trade and Industry (1994), *Competitiveness of UK Manufacturing: Second Report*, HMSO

Strath, B. (1996), *The Organisation of Labour Markets: modernity, culture and governance in Germany, Sweden, Britain and Japan*, Routledge

Streeck, W. (1992), *Social Institutions and Economic Performance: studies of industrial relations in advanced capitalist economies*, Sage

Swenson, P. (1991), 'Bringing Capital back in, or social democracy reconsidered', *World Politics* vol. 43 (July), pp. 513–544

Therborn, G. (1986), *Why some peoples are more unemployed than others*, Verso

Therborn, G. (1987), 'Does corporatism really matter: the economic crisis and issues of political theory', *Journal of Public Policy* vol. 7, pp. 259–284

Wilks, S. (1996), 'Class compromise and the international economy:: the rise and fall of Swedish social democracy', *Capital and Class*, no. 58, pp. 89–111

Williams, K. et al. (1990), 'The hollowing out of British manufacturing', *Economy and Society*, vol. 19, pp. 456–90

Wolf, M. (1996), 'End of Relative Decline', *Financial Times* June 12

BETWEEN THE DEVIL AND THE DEEP BLUE SEA: THE 'GERMAN MODEL' UNDER THE PRESSURE OF GLOBALISATION

Birgit Mahnkopf

At the end of what Hobsbawm calls the 'Short Twentieth Century', Europe is no longer haunted by the 'spectre of Communism': the 'spectre of globalisation' now stalks the earth in its place. From the viewpoint of many economists, globalisation is the 'leitmotif of the twenty-first century' as Paul Kennedy puts it, and for many sociologists a 'world society' already appears to be a statement of fact. In everyday political debate, on the other hand, it is becoming increasingly common to hear that 'globalisation' is a mere 'fetish', a 'phantom', or even a 'myth', the ideological contents of which remain a well-kept secret but essentially amount to an argument deployed to legitimise the absence of any political input into the shaping of economic and social processes.

Those who take this latter position claim that economic globalisation processes are actually nothing new, and the proof of this is usually said to lie in quantitative data on the development of world trade, world production, the mobility of capital and the international migration of labour. From the evidence provided by this data, it is readily demonstrated that the degree of world economic integration experienced today is roughly equivalent to that seen during the period of *Pax Britannica* before the First World War. The level of world economic integration at that time was, however, much lower than today and many economies that were then excluded from world trade and the system of international institutions are now integrated into the world economy. By relying on macroeconomic data based on long-range time series, the new character of globalisation is not easily discernible; this character is not just a result of the magnitude of today's economic processes – as manifested in higher levels of productivity, income, capital stocks and, above all, natural resource consumption – compared to those in place at the end of the nineteenth century. We are better equipped to explain this situation if we go beyond references to the quantitative extent of global economic integration and take up the qualitative developments which have forced themselves into our consciousness at the end of the twentieth century. These developments will form the focus of the first section of this analysis.

I. WHAT'S NEW ABOUT GLOBALISATION AT THE END OF THE TWENTIETH CENTURY?

The development of a world market has proved to be a long-term process which began with the great discoveries of the sixteenth century and the subsequent colonisation of regions beyond Europe. However, the specifically capitalist dynamic of this process only came with the industrial revolution (see, for example, Amin, 1996). In the course of this 'Great Transformation', money, along with nature and labour, was converted into commodities and capital; this principle of 'commodification' was described by Karl Polanyi (1944) as 'disembedding' from social bonds and local commitments. With the revolution in energy systems in the course of the 'fossil-fuel' revolution that accompanied the industrial revolution, the social form of profit was released from the narrow confines of traditional biotic sources of energy and thus also from the corresponding space and time regimes.

At the end of the twentieth century we are experiencing a further stage of 'disembedding' (cf. Altvater/Mahnkopf, 1996, p. 109–136; Altvater/Mahnkopf, 1997): the emergence of 'synthetic indicators' (as furnished by the sub-balances of the balance of payments) with which societies are comparatively evaluated in the abstract functional space of the global market. Such evaluations would be harmless if they were only about the judgements in the national economy by interested politicians or scientists. But they define the comparative position of a currency area within the global economy and thus the context of a nation's currency area within global currency competition. Just as sovereignty in nineteenth- and early twentieth-century thought remained bound to the territoriality of states, so now it defines itself in a world of money through a currency area whose borders are defended at the counters of the foreign exchanges or within the global 'swift-network' of internationally operating banks. Once delivered into the hands of market mechanisms, subordinated to global time and space regimes and dependent upon the price of money (interest and exchange rates), societies must accommodate themselves to the disembedded economic mechanism. The world market with its time and space regimes, with the global monetary and credit system that is maintained through the fossil fuel sources and their associated material and energy conversion systems, is the frame of reference for socialisation.

This is the primary aspect of globalisation in our own time. A second stage of 'disembedding' is now money's acquisition of a life of its own in relation to the 'real economy'; the decoupling of monetary from real accumulation; and the crystallization of a globally operating financial system which is subordinated to neither social norms nor political direction. Money is defined in terms of credit and debt, i.e. as money that no longer functions only as a medium of circulation within the commodity cycle. It is 'money as money'. This 'autonomization' as money transforms the 'global society' into a society of 'wealth owners' (J. M. Keynes). Disembedded powers therefore feed back onto social relationships and system of political institutions as external constraints. This finds expression in the 'hierarchy of markets' already described by Keynes: the money market steers the market in commodities with prices, and this in turn is relevant for demand on the labour market. In terms of the life practices of dependent employees, disembedding means therefore that their chances on the labour market are directed by processes on the global market which they cannot influence at all. For the political system this same process is responsible for the loss of sovereignty in economic policy.

What has proved crucial for political action in the context of globalised markets is the extraordinary dynamism which has driven the extensive world economic integration of the post-war era. This is due not least to the numerous tariff negotiations which have taken place within the framework of GATT and which have led to the widespread removal of trading obstacles. As a result of the technical and logistical 'revolution' in the communication and transport sectors and the reduction in the real cost of fossil fuels since the oil crisis in the mid-1970s, the geographical boundaries which had determined the movement of money and capital, goods, services and (to a lesser extent) labour have been removed. Since then, transport costs are no longer an impediment to crossing national frontiers. Territorial or 'natural' borders of competition between production locations become less important. Producers in these locations are now forced to behave as 'price takers' and must try to lower costs and/or meet global standards.

The tendency towards globalisation brings with it an enormous acceleration of all processes of monetary, real economic and social transformation. The 'globalisation of time' is manifested most clearly in the financial markets, where modern communications, information technology and complex computer programmes eliminate the time differences between the various capital markets, allowing money and capital to circulate practically in 'real time'. Globalisation along the 'time-axis' is also taking shape in cross-border production networks. Under the conditions of deregulated, liberalised markets and drastically shortened product life cycles, 'time competition' is becoming a critical factor in global market success. Periods of production standstill are proving to be decisive cost factors, which means that such periods must effectively be eliminated. Compared to the financial burden of production stoppages, labour costs incurred during the actual course of production are less significant. The overarching aim is the acceleration of capital circulation: all capital bound to materials and machinery should be 'set free' for renewed deployment.

The most important characteristic of economic globalisation at the end of this millennium is that an abstract global 'space and time regime' has come to prevail over the conflicting space and time commitments of societies and individuals; the latter must conform to rapidly changing standards and the quicker this conformity is achieved, the quicker the pace of the resulting transformation processes. Today it is credit schedules which determine the rhythm of global time regimes. It is no longer the harvest cycle, as in agrarian societies, nor the rate of circulation, as in large-scale industry, but the maturing of debts which defines the horizon of action and the periodization of cycles within a globalised finance capitalism. In this way money's logic dominates a 'global society'. It is not difficult to see that the sheer speed of change is inextricably linked to certain social and ecological costs; these can be seen in the rapid devaluation of qualifications and in the accelerated consumption of resources.

Another novelty of economic globalisation lies in the fact that the process of marketisation has largely penetrated all societies world-wide. There are no more 'patches of white' on the map, no more significant areas where people's lives are not dependent on the market. It is above all financial markets which have achieved a truly global status, and localised human relations have become subject to their dynamic. Global financial markets control the goods and service markets through pricing money (interest) and currency (exchange rates) and these, in turn, affect the level of demand in labour markets.[1]

Moreover, tendencies towards globalisation show that after the collapse of the planned economies in Central and Eastern Europe, there have been *no alternatives* to the path of capitalist modernisation and national economic and societal rationalisation, nor to the normative power of world markets and world money. After the disappearance of the 'white patches' on the map, the 'red patches' also suffered the same fate. Since 1989, the principle of the capitalist market economy has been uncontested; it therefore no longer needs to prove its superiority in the 'competition of the systems' in terms of its social performance. The socialist planned state had at least one thing in common with the Keynesian, interventionist and welfare state in the industrialised countries, and with the 'developmental State' in the Third World: following the experience of world economic collapse in the thirties, the conclusion was drawn that social and economic processes could not be left to market forces alone. Like the strategy of 'import substituting industrialisation' in the South, Socialist planning in the East, and Keynesian interventionism in the West were attempts to counter the practical constraints of the world market through national control.

However, this particular strategy has become problematic under the changed conditions outlined above. To an ever greater extent, states are proving too weak to impose rules which regulate the affairs of a particular territory. Today, the rules of the nationalisation processes are less than ever the product of autonomous economic policy: they result from the effects of a world market no longer constituted by a collection of national economies, but one which itself constitutes a single 'geo-economy'. The world market is extending its irresistible power to control the price of money and currencies on the one hand, and on the other hand to set technical standards and generate as well a common production- and consumption-model characterised by efficient technology, high levels of output in manufacturing, urbanisation, and a high degree of mobility and individualisation.

Governments throughout the world today see themselves bound to the unavoidable logic of 'structural adjustment': like the countries of the former 'Second World' and the Newly Industrializing Countries (NICs), the governments of the modern welfare states are coming under pressure to give priority to facilitating the necessary adjustment to the monetary standards of global financial markets and the international competitiveness of business. The countries of the South and East are forced by the World Bank and the IMF to implement structural adjustment programmes on a permanent basis, while the industrialised countries are doing this 'voluntarily'. The result is nevertheless identical in both cases: deregulation (of labour markets in particular), the liberalisation of prices and exchange rates, de-nationalisation (of public utilities), the stabilisation of national currencies, restrictive budgetary policies and political protection for making profits on productive investment which are above world market interest rates (including a risk surcharge).

It is above all monetary globalisation, and in particular the competition of currencies, which sets the standards in those areas seen as appropriate for intervention: wages, incidental wage costs, the regulation of the work and employee protection. Local reactions to global forces must be generated locally. The pressure thus increases on individual states to offer 'global players' the best conditions in the 'location competition'. In what Paul Krugman calls the 'race of the obsessed' the state is losing a significant degree of its sovereignty, yet its economic duties are increasing. In an area where it has been the traditional responsibility of government to provide for 'law and order', it now has to raise the competitiveness of businesses in the global market. In doing so, the state is changing its role: formerly a 'buffer' between the demands of international markets and the social interests of citizens, it is becoming an 'adapter' of these interests to the demands of borderless markets (see Sakamoto, 1994).

Two final peculiarities also characterise globalisation at the end of the twentieth century. Inside and across the borders of national economic areas, new (invisible) borders are being erected around productive 'microregions' such as Baden-Württhemberg in Germany, Silicon Valley in the USA, Lombardia in Northern Italy or Southern Ontario in Canada. Networks built up between business, politics and academia ensure that competitiveness is achieved in the global sphere by 'productivity and innovation pacts' based on a qualified workforce, technical efficiency, a modern infrastructure and social consensus. Moreover, supranational (regional) economic blocks are being created in many areas of the world; these include, for example, free trade areas such as NAFTA in Northern and Central America and the single market in Europe. Their goal is to erect new borders against the pressures of globalisation in the form of custom duties, regulations and possibly even the introduction of a common currency (as in the case of the EU) – and, if possible, to set globally binding standards in the course of 'macroregional' innovation.

In the EU, the highly unsettling outcome of globalisation and the associated deregulation of the market is twofold. *First*, regional variations arise in labour costs, and hence in incomes and living standards, despite progress towards political unity. *Second,* the obverse of monetary deregulation is protectionism in the real economy of the product markets, which may become a broadly supported strategy because it seems the only way to protect workers' interests. At present protectionism finds its way onto the international agenda only in the context of relations between large economic blocs (the EU, the USA or Japan) and of North-South or East-West relations. Nonetheless, protectionist tendencies could well become rife within Europe, even at a regional level, acting as an emergency brake to counter the excessive economic and social demands of the deregulated market – at least if competitive modernisation should falter and wage flexibility fail to lower cost.

To summarise the phenomena outlined above, the term globalisation can be said to refer to a *megatrend* which also embraces social, cultural and, above all, ecological dimensions, aside from the monetary, economic and technological aspects which are our primary concern here. When we direct our attention to these secondary factors, we can see that the social and ecological limits of globalisation are already being drawn. In contrast to the rhetoric of free trade, the thesis will be put forward here that the 'achievements of adaptation' which are required as the price for securing international competitiveness are, in fact, overloading the social system. The continuous reference to the seemingly overmighty 'systemic constraints' of the market can indeed bring people to heel and make them ready for sacrifice. Because decisions are removed from political responsibility and submitted to private forces – and therefore de-politicised – governments do not even have to fear severe losses in legitimisation. However, it is a 'squaring of the circle' (R. Dahrendorf) to manage competitiveness on the world market, democratic participation on the national level, and (welfare state) systems for social security all at once. Since every cut in the social security net means damaging the material foundation of people's identity as self-confident political citizens, they can hardly be expected to trust parties and other institutions of civic participation to represent their interests (cf. Mahnkopf, 1998).

In the industrialised countries, this development is best seen in the institutions regulating the labour market – of which the following analysis of the 'German model' should provide an example. In north-south relations this same development finds expression in increasing inequality, impoverishment and 'de-civilisation'. Linked to this is a second thesis which asserts that no 'world society' can come out of economic globalisation – precisely because under the sign of 'global hyperliberalism' (see Albo, 1994; Panitch, 1996) a convergence of economic-political answers to the new conditions of globalised competition is evident in all countries, south, east and north.

Apart from the social brakes on economic globalisation, ecological barriers to the realisation of globalisation must also be reckoned with. These barriers mean that the mobility of global finances, world trade, information technology and foreign direct investments from industrial and service businesses cannot bring about a just global society, that the promise of 'prosperity for all' cannot be fulfilled. At the high levels of natural resource consumption already reached, many goods which belong to the industrial model are becoming 'positional goods' (Hirsch, 1976), i.e. goods which cannot be used by everyone without destroying the entire framework of consumption. The ecological limits of globalisation must be be kept in mind when a strategy of 'progressive competitiveness' is considered by the political Left as an *alternative* rather than merely a 'subsidiary element in the process of neoliberal capitalist restructuring and globalisation' (Panitch, 1996: p. 106). In the German globalisation debate, such a strategy is propagated under the slogan 'innovation competition' instead of 'cost-cutting competition' – and this by a cross-party majority which includes large elements of the political Left as well as prominent representatives of the conservative camp.

II. GERMAN PECULIARITIES: CONTESTING GLOBALISATION WHILE DEFENDING THE 'STANDORT'

Global competition makes 'Rhineland Capitalism' (Albert, 1994) appear 'too expensive', although it is an economic model which has proved very successful to date. The robust 'German model' has entered an existential crisis. Many employers, politicians and associated academics and journalists in the economic field have claimed that high labour costs are responsible for the fact that some businesses have relocated parts of their operation abroad in areas where wages and welfare costs are considerably lower. Social institutions which had 'embedded' the (West) German labour market[2] in a system of protective and redistribution agreements are considered today to be the archaic remains of conservatism and collective agreements; they appear to impede rapid adjustment to the demands of global markets. Even social scientists, who until recently were convinced that the 'German Model' would provide an answer to the social and political crisis in exemplary fashion, now fear that Michel Albert's pessimistic predictions could be realised that the less effective Anglo-American model of capitalism might prevail over the high-performance 'Rhineland capitalism', simply because the former shows a closer structural compatibility with the deregulative forces of globalisation (see Streeck, 1995).

Members of the Bonn coalition government, company directors and representatives of influential economic research institutes have been demanding for some time that production be increased, without wage increases, that companies be relieved from social welfare contributions, and that increasing wage disparities should be established. In addition, a reduction in the top tax rate is demanded along with a further shifting of the tax burden onto labour, the 'less flexible production factor'. According to the internally consistent logic of the neoliberal project of 'deregulation' and 'denationalisation', this policy is the necessary result of the international battle of the systems for 'taxable incomes' (see Jungnickel/Keller, 1997). This strategy is countered by the Social Democratic Party (SPD) and the Greens opposition, who propose two essentially connected positions: on the one hand, they protest against the damaging social consequences of cutting public spending, and on the other they propose a milder version of the same policy.

At first sight, this appears somewhat contradictory. Closer consideration of the situation, however, reveals a particular trait of the German economic globalisation debate. Even politicians, academics and journalists of social-democratic Keynesian (or indeed of a Green-alternative) persuasion follow those in the neoliberal mainstream in conducting the globalisation debate almost exclusively in terms of the competitiveness of '*Standort Deutschland*' (Germany as an economic location). A cross-party consensus gives political priority to ensuring the competitiveness of the German economy: President Herzog is in the company of most high-ranking trade union officials, broad sections of the Social Democrats and influential *Realpolitiker* from Bündnis90/the Greens in drifting along with the political mainstream. Debate is conducted principally about *how* the competitiveness of the German industrial *Standort* can be best secured: either through a reduction in costs and/or through radical product and process innovation.

Pointing to the practical constraints of global competition, some on the Right are advocating a reduction in costs at all levels. That would include a reduction in social security contributions as well as an undermining of collective agreements, increasing the flexibility of employment conditions and tax cuts for property owners and industrialists. At the other end of the political spectrum, a large number of opposition politicians, trade unionists and academics view the 'threat of globalisation' as a pretext generated by politicians interested in distracting attention from domestic difficulties. From their point of view, the pressure currently exerted on the 'German model' of 'Rhineland capitalism' is not the result of economic globalisation but a result of a misguided unification policy financed by credit and not taxation, the rigid monetary policy of the Bundesbank and the temporary overvaluation of the Deutschmark (until 1995). In order to fend off neoliberal attacks against important industrial-social institutions, the supporters of these institutions question the statistical relevance of the globalisation thesis for the German economy. This is achieved by citing macroeceonomic data on international trade, foreign direct investment and wage costs per unit of output compared with other countries. The point of the exercise is firstly to show the qualities of Germany as an economic location, and secondly to refute the thesis that national politics has lost all meaning.[3]

In order to exorcise the 'spectre of globalisation' and to retain the fiction of the large, unchanged scope of national politics in the economic and social-political sphere, the supporters of *Standort Deutschland* never tire of emphasising Germany's strengths in international competition. On the one hand, the export surplus achieved in foreign trade is quoted as an argument against Germany's putative competitive weakness. More important, however, is the demonstration that *Standort Deutschland* in no way suffers from overly burdensome (West German) wage costs because these costs correspond to high levels of productivity: if compared internationally, real wage costs per unit of output (in West Germany), are not overly high, nor have they increased significantly since the 1980s.[4] At the same time, competitive advantages due to low increases in unit labour costs were counteracted by the effects of the Deutschmark revaluation, particularly from 1992–95. With taxes representing 23.6% and social security contributions 15.4% of GDP, Germany is actually in the last third of European countries with regard to tax burden. Since 1982 the average tax burden on businesses has fallen, and in international terms, with the real tax burden taken as a basis for comparison, it is very low (see Schäfer, 1996). Even the balance of direct investments hardly proves the weakness of the *Standort*. The flow of German capital out of the country cannot be explained by the pressure of costs, but has other causes such as market development and protection, or – in the case of German direct investments in the USA – efforts to avoid currency risks. It is an undisputed fact that only a small portion of German direct investment has flowed into countries outside Europe and East European low-wage economies.

Within the framework of the German *Standort* debate, the contention has rapidly surfaced that the increase in cross-border economic activity is effecting a form of regionialisation, rather than a form of globalisation; or to be more precise, a Europeanisation of economic relations. Because Germany is a driving force and not a passenger within the EU, it is doubtful that the escalating competition of economic locations for the finance and investment capital of 'stateless' market forces necessarily means that national systems of governance – by which Germany is always meant – are becoming less important. On the contrary, many social democratic and Green politicians put their money on the 'German model' to provide a European answer to the constraints of globalisation.[5] The fact that many left-wing social scientists are concerned almost exclusively with the strong German economy also explains why many lend their support to the view (expressed until recently only by neo-classical economists) that globalisation can result in a win-win situation for all those involved.

Not differing from those politicians and business representatives who use globalisation as a threat to force renunciation of any further demands, representatives of the 'head-in-the-sand' position, who wish to take the wind out of the sails of globalisation by calling it a 'phantom' or a 'myth', also call for a need to adjust to the global pressures. The argument is the following: Germany has been successful for some time in the rather traditional technology-intensive fields such as car manufacturing, mechanical engineering and the electrical (but not electronic) and chemical industries. Faced with the advantages of the low-wage 'late-comer' economies, Germany is losing the advantage it had as a result of its specialisation. The German production model relied until now on the medium-tech sector, which still claims its share of world trade. The German economy has nevertheless missed out on the opportunity to build a strong position in the high-tech areas of growth in the global economy; clear weaknesses in its technological competitiveness are apparent in the high technology sectors, such as information technology and communications, the aero-space and biotechnology industries. German research and development is thus deemed 'too conservative'. Only in environmental technology can German firms claim a leading position; the number of patents registered for chemical and pharmaceutical products has even dropped (see, for example, Priewe, 1996; Matraves, 1996; Audretsch, 1996; Potratz/Widmaier, 1996). According to the 'innovation gap' thesis, a fatal error is being made in 'remaining largely content with a good European position and shunning global benchmarking' (Priewe, 1996: p. 88). The basic institutional conditions at the centre of the national system of innovation, which supported the gradual modernisation in the medium-tech field in the past, are today considered to be an obstacle to the promotion of radical innovation in the high-tech sector (see Soskice, 1996).[6]

From their diagnosis of a growth-stifling 'innovation deficit'[7] in the German economy, the supporters of the 'German model' conclude that the competitiveness of *Standort Deutschland* should not be protected by lowering wages and welfare payments. Instead, they advocate a policy of innovation and productivity competition within an exclusive circle of developed market economies. In the last section of this essay I will return to the question of the supposed mutual exclusivity of innovation competition and cost reduction competition as possible reactions to world market constraints. The primary question will be whether the innovation competition propagated by a cross-party group of 'modernisers' allows for a regulation of the social and ecological limits which confront the process of financial and real economic globalisation at the end of the twentieth century. But in order to assess the 'path dependency' of the proposed structural transformation, I would like first of all to recall the characteristics and strengths of the 'German model'. After this, some of its most important structural weaknesses will be listed.

III. THE 'GERMAN MODEL' UNDER DISCUSSION

Let us recall, first, the characteristics of 'Rhineland capitalism' and later the 'German model', which have been admired periodically over the last twenty years. The 'German model' was a Social Democrat election slogan from the 1970s which became a synonym for the consensual incorporation of corporatist interest groups into a process that Fritz W. Scharpf and Volker Hauff have called a global market-oriented 'national economy modernisation' strategy. Since then, the words 'German model' have come to mean a form of 'organised capitalism' in which state intervention in the workings of market forces serves to increase economic efficiency (see Wever/Allen, 1992).[8] At the same time, the state has the constitutional obligation to assist in reducing, within limits, social inequalities, and thus creating a more just social order. In other words, it is a catch-word which stands for an economically based 'productivity pact' of labour and capital supported by state social policy – particularly in terms of pensions, health and 'human relations' in the workplace – and which (at least in the beginning of the 1970s) has been accompanied by educational reform. In post-war (West) German society, it has thus been synonymous with the fusion of international economic competitiveness, on the one hand, and a high degree of social cohesion and low levels of wage inequality and labour conflict, on the other. The Social Democratic model of moderate class compromise could admittedly rely on 'pre-Fordist' political structures and social institutions which reach far back into German history.

The backbone of this model was formed without doubt by the dual system of employer-employee relations, which instituted a very clear legally-defined division of tasks between trade unions and the representatives of business interests; the priority accorded to industry-wide wage agreements between employers' associations and trade unions over the arrangements of individual companies; the comprehensive legal regulation of company employment relations; and a complex system of employee participation in company decision-making. In the past, a wide-ranging standardisation of the rights of employers and the obligations of employees was in the interests of both parties. For the trade unions it was particularly important that standardised pay agreements allowed the centralisation of wages policy and a resulting evening-out of differences between occupations, levels of qualification and the regions. Those educated to different levels, those working in differing economic sectors, those in different regions and employees in companies of varying size were therefore subject to less wage inequality in Germany than in other industrialised countries (although it is important to add that wage inequality between the sexes has to this day barely been addressed).

The standardisation of employer-employee relations by way of pay agreements has been in the interests of employers because it has reduced competition between companies in Germany, kept disagreements with trade unions manageable and allowed a certain degree of forward planning. Also considered central to the German success story over the last decades are the institutions which form the dual system of specialist training, in which both the state and the economy share responsibility for on-the-job training and vocational instruction in schools. The high degree of centralisation and uniformity within the employers' associations and the trade unions permitted the development of cross-industrial institutional regulations for vocational and additional training. As a result the degree of Taylorist division of labour could be kept to a minimum. However, it included only the skilled male labour element in the high-productive 'efficiency wage' sector of the German economy.

In addition to this, the system of banking has encouraged a long-term commitment to large, small and medium-sized businesses from home-grown banks. This has created a greater degree of financial stability for German companies than has been experienced by businesses in other countries.[9] Together with the active state promotion of research and technology, which has fostered innovation within a wide spectrum of businesses, but particularly within medium-sized businesses, these institutions have formed the long-term foundation for an internationally competitive and crisis-resistant variant of what Robert Boyer calls 'flexible Fordism', or what Wolfgang Streeck calls 'diversified quality production'. Predominantly male, highly qualified employers of German nationality have manufactured quality products in the medium-tech industries which have made large profits in the export markets. Within the framework of German co-determination and a business culture imbued with the spirit of this framework, workers' representatives have found it relatively easy to shoulder a certain degree of responsibility for the economic efficiency of businesses. In return for this, they have been able to exact wage increases in the past, and have achieved improved working conditions and a considerable reduction in working hours.

However, this 'Fordist productivity pact', inclusive of government and the various levels of parliament, must be seen as a coalition at the expense of nature. Considerable growth rates in labour productivity, and thus in prosperity, are inextricably linked with a high input of energy (and mineral and agrarian) resources. This process of non-renewable resource consumption appears to be productive rather than destructive because the amount of labour required to sustain it is actually sinking.[10] 'Expensive' human labour (or the biological energy of the labour force) is being substituted by 'cheap' machine labour (or by fossil energy and, no less problematically, by atomic energy) and thus by the massive consumption of natural resources effectively taken free of charge.[11] The 'fossil-fuel basis of Fordism' (Altvater, 1992) is the reason why the destruction of nature – made possible by the rapid increase in the deployment of technology – has also brought job losses with it. This is because productivity increases are impossible without an increase in the consumption of energy and raw materials, and in times of stagnation or moderate economic growth, this entails, first and foremost, a process of labour-saving rationalisation, i.e. the replacement of 'expensive' human labour by the increased use of 'cheap' energy.

In the heyday of the 'German model', those who found themselves on the fringes of the labour market or who were forced temporarily into unemployment when the 'productivity whip' was cracked, could at least rely on the social security net to prevent them falling into long-term unemployment or social marginalisation (these people were mostly women, the low skilled and foreign workers). The corporative consensus which aimed to secure the international competitiveness of German businesses thus had a functional equivalent: welfare state institutions which were tied to gainful employment. This relationship between the production of quality goods by qualified and skilled male labour, the perception of joint interests and the corporatist welfare state is what Hans-Olaf Henkel, the President of the Federal Association of German Industry (BDI), has in mind today when he categorically demands the end of 'this consensus nonsense'. He is certainly not the only one to question the relationship between the increase in productivity and economic prosperity, social welfare and democratic order which was at the heart of the 'German model'. Voices from economic and academic circles are calling ever more openly for the state to become an entrepreneurial actor. Instead of demanding solidarity with the *Standort* from businesses, the 'national competition state' (Cerney, 1990) should create the conditions for a structural transformation in line with the global market. This means accepting the reduction of the macroeconomic room for manoeuvre and the loss of the capacity to protect uncompetitive production factors. Germany, according to the view of most economists, politicians and journalists, must be freed from the burden of a costly consensus culture. 'Consensus tends to etch in stone what already exists and fails to create new challenges for itself' (President of the Deutsche Bundesbank, Hans Tietmeyer, quoted by Buhl, 1997).

In his much vaunted 'Berlin Speech' of April 1997, the President of the Federal Republic, Roman Herzog, made it patently obvious why a socially bound capitalism is no longer a timely ideal: the global challenge requires the rapid transformation of all established structures, but in Germany, an irrational resistance to innovation and a reform inertia are delaying the necessary changes. 'Fruitless debate rituals' should therefore be consigned to the past, 'fears' about the dangerous effects of growth-orientated innovation must be dispelled, doubts about nuclear energy, biotechnology or digitalisation must be banished and 'excessive regulation' of the labour market in particular must be stopped (cf. Herzog, 1997). The message is clear: social conflicts no longer have to be dealt with or smoothed out democratically by the representatives of political or social interests – i.e. by parties, unions or employers' associations. The different interests of the unemployed, welfare recipients, pensioners, employees and employers have been designated as mere 'special interests'. In the current controversies surrounding pension security and tax reforms, organised interests are asked to subordinate their goals to a supposed 'common goal' and a supposed 'community'. Like many public statements made recently by the Social Democrat Minister of Lower Saxony and candidate for the Chancellorship, Gerhard Schröder, Roman Herzog's 'Berlin Speech' also takes up elements of the authoritarian state tradition ('*Obrigkeitsstaat*'): under the pressure of globalisation, an appeal is being made to an anti-party and anti-association sentiment which has hindered the progress of democracy more than once in German history.

The anti-democratic temptation is given clearest expression today, however, by representatives of the neo-liberal camp, and in unusually provocative terms. In the 'competition of the nations' to attract investors, even the constitution of the Federal Republic has recently come under fire. In the opinion of Rüdiger Pohl (President of the Institute for Economic Research in Halle), the globalisation of the economic sphere presents us with an urgent need to revise the German constitution, which allows an excessive fragmentation of governmental power among the Republic, the *Länder* and established interest groups (including the trade unions). The Honorary President of the FDP, Otto Graf Lambsdorf, is also urging reform to alter the division of power between the Republic and the Länder. His motives correspond to those of the head of the BDI, Hans-Olaf Henkel, who is calling for 'political reengineering': by 'correcting' the federal structure so that it would comprise fewer *Länder*, and by cutting the veto power of the *Bundesrat* (the upper chamber of the German parliament), the government would be able to put its policies through more quickly because there would be no constitutional constraint to contend with. Even an electoral arrangement based on Britain's first-past-the-post system is being suggested because it creates unambiguous majorities in parliament. The German constitution instituted a three-tier system of checks: associations, political opposition groups and the *Länder* can act as blocks against the political decisions of the government within the system. Within the framework of the neo-liberal projects, it makes sense to rationalise the constitution too: if the speed of adaptation to new globalised conditions is a determining factor in assessing the viability of the *Standort*, a constitution which slows everything down can no longer be allowed.

Democratic participation, negotiating processes and checks on decisions are considered to be extra baggage in the quest to modernise along global lines. They are time-consuming – i.e. because they are a way of resisting capital dumping social costs on labour. Yet, democracy can only develop at a minimum level of prosperity; below this level, the chances of authoritarian patterns of direct repression increase and/or societies may degenerate into apathy. In this political moment of 'weariness', fundamentalists gain influence. Many people afraid of social declassification find simplistic solutions such as nationalist or regional separatism, closing markets against 'cheap imports' or closing borders against 'foreigners' an attractive alternative to unlimited globalisation. Attempting to establish new boundaries against 'others' holds for many the promise of restoring a security that has been undermined by the process of permanent innovation[12]. This dimension of economic globalisation has remained virtually untouched by the German *Standort* debate. Nevertheless, the German consensus model, and particularly the system of industrial relations, is thought to be responsible for hindering the programme of 'structural adaptation' to the demands of the global market.

IV. THE 'GERMAN MODEL' UNDER PRESSURE

But quite apart from these debates, the 'German model' is in any case not going to function in the future as it has in the past. This expresses itself, initially, in a growing injustice in the distribution of wealth, in the erosion of the industrial relations system, and also in a clear change in the 'politics in production' (Burawoy, 1979). Let us take each of these in turn.

1. Increasing differences in wealth distribution

The increase in mass unemployment, the dismantling of social services and increasing wage differentials since unification have led to a clear increase in the number of people classified as poor, in both the *Länder* of the former East Germany, and those of the old Federal Republic. In 1995 almost 12% of the population earned less than half the average net income of a West German; according to EU standards these people qualify as poor. Regional disparities have also clearly increased since unification. When compared with other countries within the EU, Germany is the country with the largest regional disparities in economic wealth: while the region of Hamburg has a GNP per person that is 196% of the EU average, the region of Thuringia reaches only 38% (see EUROSTAT quoted by Krätke, 1997).

For the past decade and a half, wage rates have been sinking virtually continuously: in 1997 gross wages as a proportion of gross national income are expected to be only 67.7% (BMAS, 1996: Tab. 9.7), i.e. the level of the immediate post war period. The improvements in the conditions of distribution that employees were able to achieve after 1970 were lost in the 1980s and 1990s; in fact, the situation worsened, and they sank below the level of the 1970s. When inflation is taken into account, between 1980 and 1995 the average income of employees increased by just 3.1%; this means an increase of a mere 0.2% per year. Since 1992, increases in real wages have remained continuously below increases in worker productivity and it is through this, above all, that employers have been able to increase profits so considerably; between 1980 and 1993, company profits rose by 185% gross, and by 251% net. As a result of changes in taxation laws during this period, the tax burden on incomes from capital and entrepreneurial activities has dropped from 19.9% of gross income to 9.7%, while the burden of income tax and social welfare contributions on the income of employees (in the old Federal Republic) rose to 36.6% (Schäfer, 1996). In spite of the considerable reduction in costs, however, the new jobs predicted by supply side theory have not been created. Quite the opposite in fact: since 1992, the rate of unemployment has accelerated considerably. No question: the 'German model' has not been dragged into crisis by virtue of the alleged technological deficiencies in German (export) industry, but rather because of the extent of Germany's mass unemployment. By mid-1997, 12% of all people with German citizenship were unemployed; in the eastern German *Länder*, the percentage of unemployed was almost 20%, whilst in 1998 the DIW (*Deutsches Institut fur Wirschaftforschung*) is expecting the number of the officially registered jobless to break the five million barrier (DIW-Wochenbericht 27/28, 1997).

Actors in the *territorial* 'work society' (*Arbeitsgesellschaft*),[13] particularly the trade unions, severely weakened by sustained mass unemployment, are becoming ever less successful in ensuring the participation of those holding financial assets in financing the institutions of the 'work society' (see Altvater/Mahnkopf, 1996: chapter 16). In Germany too the interests of those belonging to a *global* 'society of wealth owners' (*Gesellschaft der Geldvermögensbesitzer*), and the interests of the local society whose members are limited in their mobility and are more than ever dependent on the redistribution benefits of the (now, as ever) nationally-based welfare state, are diverging. This dependency increases the more employment growth and (according to all predictions only moderate, medium term) economic growth diverge. In contrast, the holders of financial assets as members of a global 'club-society' have an effective 'exit' option: they vote with their money by 'fleeing' from one currency and investing in another 'safer' one. They exercise their rights with the dollar or German mark accounts they own. They do not need the votes of the voters. They only use the mechanism of democracy to fend off the demands of the 'work society'. For the owners of financial assets, interested mainly in a stable currency and high interest rates, the nation is primarily a currency space. Anything not associated with serving short-term monetary and currency stability (such as social benefits) is not in their interest. They can do without contributing to the common welfare state, since their safety, property, education, health and mobility can also be bought privately. It is not surprising, therefore, that the wealthy leave the community of tax-payers and refuse to pay their share to maintain the public welfare and support those who are often regarded as 'superfluous' members of the territorial 'work society'.

The owners of wealth are the ones drawing currencies into global competition. In this currency competition, central banks are forced to attempt to maintain the value of their respective national currencies to prevent the flight of capital. They do this by enforcing a restrictive monetary policy supported by restrictive fiscal policies (i.e., reduction in social expenditures). If the welfare state is under siege due to structural mass unemployment, both in terms of raising revenues and meeting expenditures, the state is forced to respond with deficit financing. Such a strategy benefits the owners of wealth, since the interest paid on the debt accrues as private income to the private lenders. At the same time, the owners of wealth fear that stability is jeopardized if taxes are raised or expenditures increased to finance the social security net. Inflation could not only diminish the external value of their money but also lead to exchange losses, if the central bank reacts by increasing base rates. To attract international mobile capital into a country, it is necessary, according to the market fundamentalist recommendation of *mainstream* economics, to ensure that the internationally less mobile factors, especially labour, bear the cost. A decreasing proportion of the adult population which is gainfully employed, and the businesses that employ them, have to support an increasing section of the population that has no direct acces to market-income. In Germany this is termed 'socialism in one class' (Scharpf, 1987 following Panitch, 1976).

2. The erosion of the industrial relations system

The crisis of the 'German model' is, at its core, a crisis of the established system of industrial relations. In the past this system was understood as a promoter of growth and democracy, making the specific asymmetrical power relations between capital and labour inherent in the capitalist order acceptable to wage earners. Today, the representatives of employers associations are shifting the once highly regarded 'social partnership' of autonomous collective bargaining nearer to premodern traditions. Free collective bargaining and flat rates of pay are regarded as relics of the corporate state, or merely as an instrument by means of which trade unions retain power; they are considered to be the equivalent of talks between particularly insidious cartels.

The once robust German system of industrial relations is seen as 'fossilised', inflexible and not open to innovations. Still able to rely on a large number of legal regulations, trade unions with wide experience of negotiation and employee representatives at firm level are able to put a spanner in the works of companies under pressure to reach quick decisions. Participation in company decision-making costs time; it does not square with the increasing dynamism of economic globalisation. Even if the discussions today between labour and capital in Germany still reach joint solutions – and this distinguishes relations in Germany from those in France, for example – negotiations still require far too much time. In Germany, as in other countries, employee rights, once regulated by law or by pay agreements, are now being brought into question. It is hardly surprising that the Anglo-American model is being pursued by many German employers: it is founded on the principle of worker insecurity and therefore reassures employers who fear an ('excessive') desire for security amongst their employees, a desire which can easily put the brakes on rapid change.

This conflict, which is not merely about material factors, but also involves political sensibilities, could prove to be a symbolic turning point in industrial relations. In September 1996 a majority in the *Bundestag* agreed – alongside other measures – to a reduction in the continued payment of sickness benefits from 100% to 80% of pay. Workers had achieved the 100% level as result of prolonged strike action in the Schleswig Holstein metal industry in the 1950s, and it remained a very important issue for the unions. In most economic sectors there were regulations governing the payment of sickness benefits, and therefore it was equivalent to a 'declaration of war' on both workers and their unions when the employers association *Gesamtmetall* and a number of well-known large companies demanded that the new ruling be adopted promptly; they imagined themselves strong enough to be able to push through their interests even if they were in breach of the law. However, when Daimler Benz chairman Jürgen Schrempp took the initiative in attempts to breach the tariff agreement in early October 1996 by announcing that sickness benefit levels would be reduced to 20%, 20,000 workers in the factory at Untertürkheim failed to turn up for their additional weekend shifts. This action cost the company 200DM million worth of production and as a result of the conflict *IG Metall* took in almost 30,000 new members.

The managing director of Daimler-Benz, supported by other employers, had contravened established rights and long-held norms of equality with little reflection, and shown the sacrosanct principle of a 'social partnership' in Germany to be a lie. In the end, employers traded sickness payments against concessions on wages. Meanwhile it began to dawn upon German workers and their trade unions that their opponents were no longer the German companies of the 'reconstruction generation', but a new generation of managers schooled in American universities under the dominance of an all-pervasive economic liberalism.

It should not be forgotten that German unification has acted as a catalyst for labour market developments which were already much more advanced in other European countries (cf. Mahnkopf, 1992 and 1994). These developments include more flexibility within the pay agreement system and a decentralisation of the wage and working hours policies at company level, i.e. areas which in Germany had been highly regulated hitherto.[14] According to official statistics, roughly 90% of West German employees still benefit from pay agreements. However, industry-wide collective agreements have already lost much of their binding power in the reality of business practice. Many collective bargaining agreements are circumvented by concession bargaining at plant level. Innumerable company-level agreements on cost-lowering and productivity increases authorised by works councils in eastern and western Germany in the last few years effectively contravene the law: reductions in wages and salaries of up to 30%, unpaid overtime and days off, the extension of regular working hours without salary and the abandonment of previously agreed reductions in working time. More than this, many employers today openly demand the reintroduction of the 40 hour week without any increase in wages. This process can be seen as a socially backward step *through* the mechanism of collective agreements, as a specifically German variant of 'concession bargaining'. Instead of social improvements, future concessions to employers will be negotiated. This will be done through centralised industry-wide collective agreements and not through plant-level agreements or individual contracts, as has been the case for some time in other European countries (for example Great Britain and France).[15] With the onset of the practical decentralisation of interest representation, the DGB trade union confederation has adopted a new (highly controversial) political programme, which actually approves the 'adaptation of collective agreements to plant-level conditions'. This programme indicates that the 'modern' forces within the trade union movement have come to the fore, forces that for a long time have demanded 'the real erosion of flat pay rates as a starting point from which to conduct their own policies', instead of demanding the retention of the collective bargaining arrangements previously held up as a model (Schröder/Ruppert, 1996: p. 615).

The employers' desire to change the rules of the game extends far beyond this, however. At least this is the case for those elements in the employers' associations which have been particularly vocal in the last three years. They will not be satisfied with a mere regulated flexibilisation of the general collective bargaining agreements. These groups strive for a general reform of the shorter working hours agreement formulated in the 1980s, and demand a *legal* right to undermine standards, or, better still, a general decentralisation of collective bargaining policies. As the works constitution law effectively rules this out, employers are seeking some sort of change to this law.[16] Lawmakers and economists concur that competition in the markets should be promoted; legally required levels of redundancy payments or the right of employees to participate in company decisions are detrimental to this. One particular speaker for an employers' group, backed by the findings of conservative labour law experts, argues for further changes in the law governing strikes, or to be more precise: for the replacement of strikes with a peaceful arbitration procedure which sees strikes as 'damaging' to both companies and jobs. Social welfare benefits in all forms and legal measures protecting workers are viewed as obvious competitive disadvantages.

Ideological arguments over labour laws, for example, which have substantial and far-reaching implications for 'civil liberties' in T.H. Marshall's sense of the term, cast light on the regulatory ability of those intermediate organisations previously concerned to maintain the social cohesion of the 'German model'. Trade unions, employment associations, even trade and industry chambers of commerce, membership of which was compulsory – all these suffer as a result of having fewer members and less discipline. The sixteen DGB trade unions have lost almost a fifth of their entire membership in the last five years through rationalisation and the wave of redundancies in the traditional industrial sectors.[17] Added to this, the conjunction of persistent mass unemployment, the increasing economic dominance of tertiary sectors, the decentralisation of the internal organisation of companies (in the form of in- and out-sourcing company functions) and labour migration throughout Europe have led to an 'informalisation' of certain sectors of the labour market. The increase in casual work, subcontracting, part time work, fixed term working, the dependent self-employed and new TV and home-working practices mean fewer workers with worker status.[18] The number of potential trade union recruits has consequently fallen too.

The depletion in members and the problem of dwindling ability to integrate can actually be highlighted even more dramatically by the case of the employers' associations than it can by that of the trade unions.[19] Many of the newly established companies that have emerged from company splits are not prepared to enter an employers' association. More significant, however, is the fact that many companies leave associations as they are proving more and more unsuccessful in reconciling economic differences of interest between suppliers and producers, between capital- and personnel-intensive industries, between those who are export and national market-oriented, as well as between profit-making and loss-making industries. In more than two-thirds of the metal companies which have left employer associations over the last few years, the workforce of the company is unionised at an above average level. Therefore the company management consider themselves able to resolve matters without the assistance of an employers' association, even in those companies where unions are strongly represented (see Schröder/Ruppert, 1996: p. 42). In this sense, the erosion of German employer associations can be understood as a reflex response to the weakness of the unions.

From this development, one can see why, in the winter of 1995, IG Metall failed in its attempt to induce employers and the Federal government to enter into an 'alliance for work': there are no employers' associations capable of forming deals, willing to seek consensus or able to control their membership effectively enough to sustain such a neo-corporatist arrangement.[20] This is not to say that the ability of unions to reach agreements under the pressure of such conditions is a thing of the past. At least the unions' internal membership and organisational crises have not yet reduced their mobilisational capabilities in increasingly tough distributional conflicts, and they have shown their willingness to compromise in other (wage) conflicts. However, the ability of the trade unions to reach binding agreements is increasingly open to question. They no longer enjoy unquestionable recognition as intermediary organisations compelled to take part in the regulation of work-related matters, but rather struggle to be recognised as wage negotiators in what can more or less be seen as a desperate war of attrition.

3. The changing model of 'politics in production'

A 'model change' is thus called for in Germany, and not just on the level of collective bargaining. The German system of dual occupational training, still seen as an international model for long-term 'human resource management', is also seriously under threat – principally from the reduced willingness of industry and business to offer enough apprenticeships. In *Standort Deutschland* the pool of skilled workers is becoming scarce: labour market researchers and many leading figures in the German economy agree that Germany will experience a grave shortage of suitably qualified industrial workers by the year 2005. However, companies are not making enough trainee vacancies available; they train just enough people to suit their own very limited needs. According to the findings of a business panel from the Institute for Labour Market and Job Research (*Institut für Arbeitsmarkt und Berufsforschung*), the number of trainee positions available since 1992–93 has gone down, despite an increased number of applications; as in previous years, the number of applicants for such positions in 1997 has exceeded the number of positions available.[21] In the last few years, it has been primarily the large businesses which have reduced their quota of trainees positions; their restrictive personnel policies have been most brutal in regulating the number of trainees taken on. In the next few years it is believed that a further increase in the demand for apprentices will simultaneously coincide with a further decrease in the number of positions available (see Pfeiffer, 1997).

The reaction of politicians to this dire situation amounts to nothing more than helpless appeals to create more training places. In addition, the Federal Government continues to place demands on employers' associations to reduce funding for training, and has reduced the scope and duration of the technical college day and introduced shorter, two-year apprenticeships leading to a lower level of qualification than the normal apprenticeship. To firms it appears that the once proclaimed 'export success' of the 'German model' of dual training is now too 'rigid' and too complex. In reality, companies are revoking the 'social contract' which has governed the training of apprentices until now. A long German tradition is thereby brought into question which had hitherto ensured that individual companies, characterised by a self-interest engendered by competition, did not have sole jurisdiction over training. Rather a joint chamber, under the auspices of the state, regulated which occupations required what form of training, when this should take place, what level of remuneration was required, and what should be included in the curriculum of state-organised technical schools.

A fundamental shift in values has also occurred with reference to forms of technology and labour within German companies. Certain industrial sociologists have recently observed an 'Americanisation of thought' which could bring down 'the labour policy pillar which has supported the German production model', if carried to its logical conclusion (Kern/Schumann, 1996: p. 720). In the technical field, it is expected that a certain degree of automation will be abandoned and with it, the ergonomic benefits gained in the 1980s. The idea is no longer dismissed that the German car industry, at least, could see a renaissance of classic production-line work and the employment of an only averagely qualified workforce. If the 'path-specific' industrialisation policies promoting the cultivation and remuneration of 'human resources' are changed in favour of short-term planning strategies restricted to easily operationalised dimensions, many well-known industrial sociologists fear that 'consensus rationalisation' in German industry could suffer. As a result, an appeal is being made to the enlightened self-interest of companies not to jeopardise the innovation consensus vital for future increases in productivity by favouring a short-term cost-cutting programme. The weak point in the German production model – the innovation deficit in the high-tech industries – should, these voices argue, be overcome by administering a targeted, but indeed substantial dose of 'insecurity' to some workers and their representatives (see Kern, 1995). Accordingly, an obsession with the 'professional nature of work', bolstered by the German system of vocational training, would be abandoned, along with the traditional idea of companies as a place of worker participation and as the central organisational focus of the trade unions.

The recommendation to the trade unions is that they conclude an 'innovation pact' with reform-friendly managements in order to boost productivity. The 'German model' would thereby make a decisive move towards an agreement that would maintain the financing of productivity increases where possible. This is the answer formulated by the left in response to the demands of globalisation. However, it is not a measured response to the foreseeable social and economic parameters of globalisation: this problem is the subject of the last section of this essay.

V. IS INNOVATION REALLY THE BETTER ANSWER TO GLOBALISATION?

Processes of innovation are, firstly, processes of what Schumpeter called 'creative destruction'. They dispose of the 'old' and replace it with the 'new' – by abstracting from their contents. However, from the point of view of the individual satisfaction of needs and social development, technological advances have frequently proven to be counter-productive. The 'new' is not necessarily better than the old. This is especially clear when 'competitive innovation' is considered in the light of its effects on ecology and employment.

In Germany, however, an almost *unconditional* 'productivity and innovation policy' stretches across all political parties. This is a highly risky strategy even with regard to job creation policy. The hopeful message is that innovation increases productivity and competitiveness. By means of increasing output the effects of rationalisation might be overcompensated, i.e. a net increase in jobs might occur. This said, no one has yet been able to show how an accelerated restructuring process could succeed in creating more jobs. Basically, the idea is to achieve higher growth rates through innovation at the expense of labour intensive low-tech sectors and in favour of product groups which are research- and development-intensive. Following this path, Germany would continue its export drive and thus export unemployment to other countries. The innovation debate (inherently critical of the government's policies) calls for the increased spending on education as a necessary condition to ensure the leading position of the German economy in the next century. With advances in the tertiary sector and the globalisation of economic activity, however, the benefits of allocating public resources to research, science and education do not automatically flow into the national economy. Today one must not be concerned solely with using nationally generated knowledge, but rather with the coming together over national borders of different forms of knowledge and information. The *absorption* of knowledge generated worldwide is just as important as the national promotion of knowledge (see Gerybadze et al., 1997).

However, it is not just currently in Germany, but also in other industrialised countries and the emerging markets of the so-called 'first generation', that efforts are being made to improve the 'systematic competitiveness' of (micro) regional economies through 'upgrading' strategies. Alongside the promotion of regional networks, within which the flow of knowledge is organised efficiently and regional spillover effects can take place, more investments in research and development, in education, training and further education, in software, in the improvement of management, information and organisation also contribute to this upgrading process. By virtue of the implementation of information and communication technologies, it is easier to codify at least parts of the technical knowledge now available and to work with it outside national boundaries. Forces of innovation and qualification-oriented competition would therefore only produce success if product and process innovations are accompanied by a lowering of costs. There is no alternative which offers either competition-based innovation *or* a lowering of costs. The one makes no sense at all without the other. Those who enter into global competition have to accept the rules of competition: only global comparisons can establish the acceptable returns on capital from (innovative) productive investments or how low wages (for highly qualified workers) must be. Productivity alone does not influence decisions on the location of production sites (near to their markets and to research and development sites). In this respect, it is just wishful thinking to assume that innovations at German locations will permit much higher wages and social standards than in firms operating under Anglo-American or Asian conditions.

Added to this is another problem: as a rule, those who advocate 'radical innovation' do not demand innovations that are more labour- and less capital-intensive. On the contrary, if whole regions, industries and certain types of workers in the world economy – above all women, foreign workers and less well qualified workers – end up as losers in the process of 'structural adjustment', this is understood as a price which has to be paid. It is clear that non neo-corporatist industrial and structural policies will succeed in creating optimal conditions for all potential investors in industry and the service sector. Research and capital-intensive industries demand incentive structures, resources, and non-material infrastructures which are different from those needed by industries and companies at home in certain advanced, but not high-tech, segments of the economy (cf. M. Krätke, 1997). Thus the plea for innovation rather than cost-cutting competition means that labour-intensive production and the production of services which demand middle or lower level qualifications (and this is more frequently the case than ever before) will be transferred abroad. Domestically this will sharpen social divisions and marginalisation in the labour market.

The current debate over 'ways towards greater employment' thus does not centre on the catch-up development of the Swedish model, which involves an expansion of the public service sector. Rather it focuses on a socially bearable but 'Americanised' labour market policy. Because, according to Fritz Scharpf (1997), political opposition to the raising of taxes in Germany has 'already become too strong', the American way of expanding employment in the area of private services will proceed, as will the adoption of a low wage employment market for simple activities that require lower rates of productivity. For reasons of constitutional law, and for those of political acceptance, no one in Germany is fully prepared to advance the position that workers could be employed – as in the USA – in low-paid jobs where their net earnings keep them below accepted poverty levels. From this stem the calls to combine low-level incomes with an additional welfare income (or a negative income tax).

There already exists a 'grand coalition' in Germany supporting a growth-oriented path of innovation, approved even by sections of the Green Party, and a similar cross-party consensus is evident on the 'social question'. Basically, the idea is that if the aim of building an internationally competitive German economy is not realistic without causing a split between its formal and informal sectors, then ways and means have to be found to stem the rise of expectations of disadvantaged groups that has continued to take place over the last half century. In the opinion of the 'Future Commission' (1997), the reasons that point towards the causes of Germany's high unemployment are: the rapidly increasing tendency for women to work and the (high) expectations of German employees, including aspirations to individual development and self-fulfilment as well as material security. Therefore, wage reductions are a prerequisite for the creation of new 'alliances for work' in Germany.

Yet it is above all in the economic sphere, and not just the social one, that the *sustainability* of this path of development is questionable. What people systematically ignore is that global competition within the field of innovation leads to an acceleration in technical advancement and, correspondingly, to more rapid use of resources and of energy. An 'innovation pact' intensifies the *acceleration* of socio-economic change, whereas, from both a social and ecological viewpoint, it is necessary to slow down the speed of productivity increases, to diminish rates of development and to lessen the scale and scope of spatial mobility.

It is not just in companies, but rather in society as a whole, that an acceleration of change intensifies synchronisation problems. On the one hand, ever larger quantities of knowledge and information must be processed in a given period, while on the other hand a growth in knowledge will lead to older forms of knowledge and information becoming obsolete more quickly. The growing intensity of worldwide competition increases the pressure on all existing social and economic structures, and consequently the pressure on social and economic actors to respond to this rapid change. In turn, this response gives the acceleration of change renewed impetus, so that unions must rapidly adapt, thus reducing the time available to develop alternative policies and hence reducing the range of available options. The rapid innovation of technical advancements has many additional negative side effects, not least the defensive reactions in the labour market that are provoked in response to the repeated necessity to adapt to changing conditions. Examples include reactions against the 'unreasonable' demand for 'life long learning' because life long learning also means a certain inability to plan one's life, or to be sure of one's job; because a new mobilisation of all personnel resources is always demanded; because everything – the ability to communicate, social graces, personal attributes or moral standards – are made into 'market factors' which have to be flexible enough to be compatible with the changing market environment.

In the German debate, the option of developing new spheres of growth through radical grass roots innovations is always tied up with the predominant objectives of ensuring international competitiveness for businesses and of maintaining the production base at home. As a rule there is no classification that could make new products and technologies 'viable in the future'. In the last analysis it is the market, with its 'ingenious ability for invention', that fosters innovation. Of course the plea for the creation of an 'innovation regime' in Germany, with modern products and technologies, comes with the rhetorical proviso that only what is 'ecologically sound' should be promoted: namely products that use fewer resources and produce fewer damaging chemicals. However, in view of the urgent need to reduce consumption of almost all resources by up to 90% (in highly industrialised, rich countries like Germany, according to the calculations by the Wuppertal Institute, 1996), the concept of achieving 'sustainable *growth*' can itself no longer be sustained. What is necessary for the economy is a strategy of directed growth, selection and contraction. 'Sustainable *development*' will not be achieved merely by the adoption of ecologically high-tech industries: it demands a different economy, different laws and different consumer behaviour.[22]

In principle we do not have to worry about the development of new products for new markets, but rather about new techniques – including risky ones like biological and genetic technology – that will transfer even more resources into even more activities, functions, services and products and use technical advancement as an additive. Even if the aim of a competition in innovation ensures that products, goods and services can be produced with fewer and fewer resources and energy, causing less harm to the environment (and this is highly questionable), the so-called 'rebound effect' will have to be reckoned with at least in the future, so that all previous increases in efficiency and the savings made per unit of performance do not lead to complacency. Savings that may perhaps result from technical advances will almost certainly be transferred immediately into increased human activity; this leads to more consumption, more mobility, progressive urbanisation, to individualisation and above all to the efficient deployment of new technologies, leading to yet further increases in worker productivity. It follows, moveover that under *ceteris paribus* conditions, the effects on employment will be negligible, even in a process of comprehensive economic modernisation towards ecological goals.[23]

So long as innovation is understood to be mainly technical, so long as progress is seen as an increase in productivity per person and so long as the safeguarding of social welfare and democratic relationships is only conceivable in the context of industrial growth, the 'innovation battle' is really only a case of replacing one evil with another, or *a choice between the devil and the deep blue sea.* Through enforced modernisation of production methods and processes, globalisation is supposed to have its threatening element removed. If this path is taken, however, a just economic order will not emerge, nor will an answer to the ecological crisis be found.

NOTES

1 Because globalisation can no longer be carried out in the form of spatial-territorial expansion, today's economic and financial dynamic is directed ever increasingly inwards – at people's 'lifeworld' (*Lebenswelt*) (cf. Habermas, 1987: p. 332ff. especially) which is important for individual and social identity, and at the nanostructures of life (gene science and biotechonolgy). It can also be directed outwards, into space or down to the ocean bed, i.e. those areas yet to be opened up by the market.

2 I am unable here to enter into detailed discussion of the specific characteristics of the East German economy and its labour market.

3 See Simons/Westermann 1997, Küchle 1996, Krätke 1997, Dolata 1996 and Zinn 1997, who, amongst many others, put forward a similar argument. A disconcerting peculiarity of the German globalisation debate is that its participants constantly 'discover' the same (long-range) sets of figures and pass them off as original discoveries which are then used to 'enlighten' the lay person ignorant of economics about the 'myth of globalisation'. Somewhat irritating for the lay person is not just the litanical argumentation which has convinced neither the 'global players' nor those who are effected negatively by their decisions (employees, for example), but also the questionable academic manners evident in the unwillingness of many authors to quote others who have pursued a similar line of thought. Behind the reluctance to take globalising tendencies seriously it is not hard to see that an attempt to salvage a theoretical paradigm is being made: i.e. a specifically national perspective on economic processes, which is at the heart of the discipline which in Germany is still called '*Volks* wirtschaftslehre', generally translated as 'national economy', but also carries the sense in German of the 'people's economy'. For further discussion of the adequacy of this perspective, which takes the global economy to be the mere aggregation of domestic economies and cannot conceive of a new global quality, see Altvater 1997a.

4 Between 1973 and 1994, wage costs per unit output in Germany (calculated in national currency) rose by 94%, whilst its most important national competitors saw an average rise of 270%. Within the last four years, wage costs per unit output in West Germany fell by 1%, whilst in the European Union as a whole they rose by 4.5% between 1994 and 1997 and by 10% in the USA (DIW, 1997: p. 473).

5 See Junne 1996, Boyer/Drache 1996 and Streeck 1996, who all express scepticism, although from differing perspectives, about this vision of the preservation and further development of 'Rhineland capitalism' throughout the European macroregion.

6 Admittedly, the 'innovation gap' in the German national economy discovered by critical social scientists, politicians and trade unionists is not an original idea. Since the beginning of the nineties, representatives of the political class have conjured up a 'Japanese-American Challenge' (Seitz, 1992) to Europe and maintain that the necessary structural reorientation towards key technologies is being hindered by institutional rigidities in Germany.

7 The most important indicator of technological competitiveness is the level of industrial expenditure on research and development. In state-of-the-art technologies, the ratio of expenditure on research and development to turnover is estimated at 8.5%, but only 3.5–4% in the higher revenue technologies. Since the

end of the 1980s, the entire research and development expenditure in Germany – as in the USA since the mid '80s – has in fact been in decline; however, in terms of per capita investment in research and development, Germany is still in second place behind the USA and followed by Japan (DIW – Wochenbericht 22/1997). For this reason, the German Institute for Economic Policy (DIW – Deutsches Institut für Wirtschaftspolitik) cannot identify any innovation deficit, in contrast to announcements from the Federal Research Ministry and circles of left-wing social scientists.

8 It is not possible to discuss here whether 'the German model', with its corporatist and concerted 'social market economy', would ever have arisen or had a chance of survival without the continual reminder and challenge of state socialism (a reminder then exploited under the conditions of the cold war) and the 'competition between the systems' (Offe, 1996: p. 195).

9 On the other hand, 'newcomers' who base their existence as independent business people primarily on the resource of 'knowledge' find it relatively difficult in Germany to gain access to capital (see Vitols, 1995).

10 In the case of the Federal Republic of Germany, it can be shown that the national product is devalued by more than half as a result of the damage done to nature, health and future prospects, and that net prosperity is actually no longer increasing (see Scherhorn, 1996).

11 Butterweck (1995) maintains that the economic advantage of higher productivity is achieved on the basis of a 'subsidy' of the economic rationalisation process provided by the coming generations. These future generations will not be able to rely on 'stocks' of non-renewable resources. We are leaving them not only a poisoned environment and a planet with a reduced capacity to absorb radiation of heat, but also depleted and hardly accessible mineral deposits which can only be reached by resorting to a higher consumption of energy and other resources which are themselves becoming ever more 'ecologically dear'.

12 A backwards development of modern mass democracies to authoritarian patterns becomes more probable as environmental destruction increases and the linkage of mass democracies to the promised 'prosperity for all' proves to be chimerical for ecological reasons. A new authoritarianism would probably not oppose free trade or the tendencies of globalisation, individualisation and denationalisation, but complement and complete these following the motto: politics and society have to submit to global economy. However, this means that the participative citizen of civil society has less and less to say in face of market forces.

13 In German parlance the term 'Arbeitsgesellschaft' is constructed in relation to the Fordist 'standard model' of work and employment. Although this model of employment has changed, work and employment remain the most important determinants of 'life-chances' for the majority of the population.

14 Certainly the hopeless situation of many eastern German firms and the catastrophic situation evident in the eastern German labour market have come just at the right moment to soften the 'institutional rigidities' in western Germany.

15 An example of this concerns IG Chemie, an industrial trade union which represents workers from the chemical, paper, ceramic, coal mining, energy and leather industries. A short time ago, IG Chemie agreed to an 'opening clause' in a collective bargaining agreement allowing individual companies to cut wages in the name of improving their own competitive standing.

16 This concerns §77, abstract 3, of the works constitution law which forbids

companies to set their own levels of working hours and wages and protects the priority of standard setting by general collective bargaining agreements.

17 The losses were most dramatic in eastern Germany; of the 9 million workers who were organised in the FDGB in 1989, only 2.4 million are now members of a (DGB) union.

18 According to a study by the Future Commission of the *Freistaaten* of Bavaria and Saxony' (*Kommission für Zukunftsfragen der Freistaaten Bayern und Sachsen*) (1997), the proportion in western Germany of those employed in 'standard employment' who are thus liable to pay welfare contributions has declined from 84% in 1970 to 68%. Therefore, by the beginning of next decade it is possible that every second employee in western Germany (as is already the case in eastern Germany) may have a job in an area of precarious employment.

19 In the 20 years from 1964 to 1984, the degree of organisation across employers' associations in the metal and electrical industries dropped, on average, by 11%; while over the last few years this downward trend further accelerated. 43% of metal working companies in western Germany today are still members of an employers association; in the eastern German metal and electrical industries, this number has not yet reached 30%. Even in Baden Württemberg, where these industries have traditionally been widely dispersed, only 36% of companies organise themselves in an employers' association (see Schröder/Ruppert, 1996).

20 Debates conducted among political scientists, on the other hand, refer to the deep historical roots of (German) corporatism and its resistance to short-term changes in the economic and political environment.

21 Even in the federal states where spectacularly corporatist 'Bündnisse für Ausbildung' have been agreed upon, the number of apprenticeships available has not stabilised, and in the eastern German states the market for apprentices is an unmitigated disaster.

22 Of course this is not the opinion of federal 'modernisers' across the political spectrum. Wolfgang Clement, Social Democratic economics minister in the highly populated state of Nordrhein Westphalia, argues, for example, against an 'ecologisation of lifestyles'. Like his colleague in the SPD, Gerhard Schröder, Prime Minister of Lower Saxony, or Federal President Roman Herzog, he is against this 'horribly pessimistic picture of the world' and the 'technophobia' that has manifested itself in the German environmental movement, and advocates instead a form of technocratic nature management (see *Handelsblatt*, 27/28.6.97).

23 At best sections of the car manufacturing industry, which is no longer cost-effective in Germany, could be replaced by the export of more environmentally friendly cars and products of other less resource-intensive technologies. Even this modest prospect of creating a few hundred thousand jobs in Germany is inextricably linked with the assumption that the growth of new markets is more important than the desired increase in productivity. Otherwise the loss of old jobs would not be counterbalanced by the creation of new ones.

REFERENCES

Albert, M. (1994): *Capitalism vs. Capitalism*, New York (Four Walls Eight Windows).

Albo, G. (1994): 'Competitive Austerity' and the Impasse of Capitalist Employment Policy, in: R. Miliband/L. Panitch (eds.), *Between Globalism and Nationalism: The*

Socialist Register 1994, London (Merlin Press)/New York (Monthly Review).

Altvater, E. (1992): *Der Preis des Wohlstands oder Umweltplünderung und neue Welt(un)-ordnung*, Münster (Verlag Westfälisches Dampfboot).

Altvater, E. (1997): Financial Crisis on the Threshold of the 21th Century, in: L. Panitch (ed.), *Ruthless Criticism of All that Exists: The Socialist Register 1997*, London (Merlin Press)/New York (Monthly Review)/Halifax (Fernwood Publishing): 48–74.

Altvater, E. (1997a): Ort und Zeit des Politischen unter Bedingungen ökonomischer Globalisierung, in: D. Messner (ed.), *Die Zukunft des Staates und der Politik. Möglichkeiten und Grenzen politischer Steuerung in der Weltmarktwirtschaft und gesellschaft*, Bonn (Dietz)(im Erscheinen).

Altvater, E./Mahnkopf, B. (1996): *Grenzen der Globalisierung. Ökonomie, Ökologie und Politik in der Weltgesellschaft*, Münster (Verlag Westfälisches Dampfboot).

Amin, S. (1996): *Les Défits de la Mondalisation*, Paris/Montréal (Éditions L'Harmattan).

Audretsch, D. B. (1995): The Innovation, Unemployment and Competitiveness Challenge in Germany, Discussion paper FS IV 95–6, Wissenschaftszentrum für Sozialforschung, Berlin.

BMAS (Bundesministerium für Arbeit und Sozialordnung)(ed.)(1996): *Statistisches Taschenbuch* 1996, Bonn.

Boyer, R./Drache, D. (1996): Introduction, in: R. Boyer/D. Drache, *States against the Market*, London/New York.

Buhl, D. (1997): Schluß mit der Harmonie? in: *DIE ZEIT* vom 7.2.1997.

Burrawoy, M. (1979): *Manufacturing Consent: Changes in the Labour Process under Monopoly Capitalism*, Chicago/London (University of Chicago Press).

Butterweck, H. (1995): Arbeit ohne Wachstumszwang – Essay über Ressourcen, Umwelt, *Kapital und Arbeit*, Frankfurt/M./New York (Campus).

Cerney, P. G. (1990): *The Changing Architecture of Politics: Structure, Agency, and the Future of the State*, London (Sage).

DIW (Deutsches Institut für Wirtschaftsforschung): *Wochenbericht* 22/97 (Wissensintensivierung der Wirtschaft: Wie gut ist Deutschland darauf vorbereitet?).

DIW: *Wochenbericht* 27–28/97 (Tendenzen der Wirtschaftsentwicklung 1997/98).

Dolata, U. (1997): Das Phantom der Globalisierung, in: *Blätter für deutsche und internationale Politik*, No.1 (1997): 100–104.

Future Commission (Kommission für Zukunftsfragen der Freistaaten Bayern und Sachsen) (1996): *Entwicklung von Erwerbstätigkeit und Arbeitslosigkeit in Deutschland. Entwicklung, Ursachen und Maßnahmen, Teil III: Maßnahmen zur Verbesserung der Beschäftigungslage*, Bonn, November 1997.

Gerybadze, A./Meyer-Krahmer, F./Reger, G. (1997): *Globales Management von Forschung und Innovation*, Stuttgart (Schäffer-Poeschel).

Habermas, J. (1987): *The Theory of Communicative Action*, Vol. 2: *The Critique of Functionalist Reason*, Cambridge (Polity Press).

Herzog, R. (1997): Durch Deutschland muß ein Ruck gehen, Abdruck der 'Berliner Rede' vom 26 April 1997 in: *Frankfurter Rundschau* vom 28.4.1997.

Hirsch, F. (1976): *Social Limits to Growth*, Cambridge/Mass. (Harvard University Press).

Jungnickel, R./Keller, D. (1997): Standort Deutschland im Abseits, in: *Wirtschaftsdienst*, Vol.77, No. 2 (1997): 81–86.

Junne, G. (1996): Integration unter den Bedingungen von Globalisierung und

Lokalisierung, in: M. Jachtenfuchs/B. Kohler-Koch (eds.), *Europäische Integration*, Opladen (Leske + Buderich): 513–530.

Kern, H. (1995): Soziale Sicherheit durch Prozeßnormen. Thesen zur Rolle der Gewerkschaften in der Innovationskrise. In: *Gewerkschaftliche Monatshefte*, Vol. 46, No. 10 (1995): 610–618.

Krätke, St. (1997): Regionalstrukturen Ost-Mitteleuropas im Transformationsprozeß. In: *PROKLA 107*, Vol. 27, No. 2: 291–316.

Krätke, M. (1997): Globalisierung und Standortkonkurrenz, in: *Leviathan*, Vol. 25, No. 2 (1997): 202–232.

Kuchle, H. (1996): Deutschlands Position auf dem Weltmarkt. In: *WSI-Mitteilungen*, Vol. 49, No. 5 (1996): 295–303.

Mahnkopf, B. (1992): Reunification et dualisation de la société; les syndicats allemands sous la pression de la déregulation, in: Allemagne d'aujourd'hui, special issue No. 121, July/Sep. 1992 *La Modernisation Est de l'Allemagne*: 84–100.

Mahnkopf, B. (1994): Ex Oriente Risk: The Impact of Unification on the 'German Model' of Industrial Relations, in: M. Tatur (ed.), Trade Unions in the Transition, *International Journal of Political Economy*, Vol. 14, No. 28, (1994): 39–72.

Matraves, C. (1996): German Industrial Structure in Comparative Pespective, discussion paper FS IV 96–25, *Wissenschaftszentrum für Sozialforschung*, Berlin.

Offe, C. (1997): *Varieties of Transition. The East European and East German Experience*, Cambridge (Polity Press).

Panitch, L. (1976): *Social Democracy and Industrial Militancy*, Cambridge (Cambridge University Press).

Panitch, L. (1996): Rethinking the Role of the State, in: J. H. Mittelman (ed.), *Globalization: Critical Reflections*, Boulder/London (Lynne Rienner): 83–113.

Pfeiffer, B. (1997): Das Ausbildungsangebot der westdeutschen Betriebe 1995 – Ergebnisse des IAB-Betriebspanels, in: *BWP*, Vol. 26, No. 2 (1997): 10–16.

Polanyi, K. (1944): *The Great Tranformation: the Political and Economic Origins of Our Time*, New York (Farrar and Rinehart).

Potratz, W./Widmaier, B. (1996): Industrie und Innovation in Europa: Verlust von Wettbewerbsfähigkeit durch Spezialisierung?, in: *WSI-Mitteilungen*, Vol. 49, No. 1 (1996): 1–10.

Priewe, J. (1997): Die technologische Wettbewerbsfähigkeit der deutschen Wirtschaft. Stärken, Schwächen, Innovationsdefizite, Discussion paper FS II 97–203, *Wissenschaftszentrum für Sozialforschung*, Berlin.

Sakamoto, Y. (ed.)(1994): *Global Transformation: Challenges to the State System*, Tokyo (United Nations University Press).

Schäfer, C. (1996): Mit falschen Verteilungs-'Götzen' zu echten Standortproblemen. Zur Entwicklung der Verteilung in 1995 und den Vorjahren, in: *WSI-Mitteilungen*, Vol. 49, No. 10 (1996): 597–616.

Scharpf, F. W (1987): *Sozialdemokratische Krisenpolitk in Europa*, Frankfurt/M./New York (Campus).

Scharpf, F. W. (1997): Wege zu mehr Beschäftigung, in: *Gewerkschaftliche Monatshefte*, Vol. 48, No. 4 (1997): 203–216.

Scherhorn, G./Haas, H./Hellenthal, F./Seibold, S. (1996): Informationen über Wohlstandskosten, Universität Hohenheim, Lehrstuhl für Konsumtheorie und Verbraucherpolitik, *Arbeitspapier* 66, Stuttgart.

Schroeder, W./Ruppert, B. (1996): *Austritte aus Arbeiausttgeberverbänden: Eine Gefahr für das deutsche Modell? Beitrittsaustritte aus regionalen Arbeitgeberverbänden der*

Metall- und Elektroindustrie (1990–1995), Marburg (Schüren).

Seitz, K. (1992): *Die japanisch-amerikanische Herausforderung, Deutschlands Hochtechnologie-Industrien kämpfen ums Überleben*, München (Bonn Aktuell).

Simons, R./Westermann, K. (eds.) (1997): *Standortdebatte und Globalisierung der Wirtschaft*, Marburg (Schüren).

Soskice, D. (1996): German Technology Policy, Innovation, and National Institutional Frameworks, discussion-paper FS I 96–319, *Wissenschaftszentrum für Sozialforschung*, Berlin.

Streeck, W. (1995): German Capitalism: Does it Exist? Can it Survive? in: C. Crouch/ W. Streeck (eds.): *Modern Capitalism or Modern Capitalisms?*, London.

Streeck, W. (1996). Gewerkschaften zwischen Nationalstaat und europäischer Union, Vortrag aus Anlaß des 75. *Gründungsjubiläums der ADA*, Frankfurt/M., mimeo.

Vitols, S. (1995): German Banks and the Modernization of the Small Firm Sector: Long Term Finance in Comparative Perspective, Discussion paper FS I 95–309, *Wissenschaftszentrum für Sozialforschung*, Berlin.

Wever, K. S./Allen, Ch. S. (1992): Is Germany a Model for Managers?, in: *Harvard Business Review*, Sept./Oct. 1992: 36–43.

Wuppertal Institut für Klima, Umwelt, Energie (1996): *Zukunftsfähiges Deutschland. Ein Beitrag zu einer global nachhaltigen Entwicklung*, BUND/Misereor(ed.), Basel/ Boston/Berlin (Birkhäuser).

Zinn, Karl-Georg (1997): Globalisierungslehre ist Mythenbildung, in: *Gewerkschaftliche Monatshefte*, Vol. 48, No. 4 (1997): 251–256.

EAST ASIA'S TUMBLING DOMINOES: FINANCIAL CRISES AND THE MYTH OF THE REGIONAL MODEL

Mitchell Bernard

At the height of the Vietnam War in the late 1960s it was common for East Asian elites and their counterparts in the US foreign policy establishment to use the image of falling dominoes to portray the grave threat posed by the spread of a 'monolithic communism' from country to country across the region.[1] Thirty years later it seems preposterous to have supposed that anti-colonial wars of national liberation led by Leninist parties in some of the world's poorest countries could have toppled most of the authoritarian, pro-capitalist regimes in Southeast and Northeast Asia. In other words, the dominoes never fell; that is, until 1997. It was not a mythical monolithic communism that ultimately brought the dominoes of the region tumbling down, but the contradictions of dependent capitalist development and the pressures of the globalisation of production and finance. The economic boom associated with 'export-oriented development' has given way to widespread currency depreciation, plummeting asset prices, the disappearance of liquidity, ever-increasing insolvency, rampant unemployment and the accompanying social unrest that has led, among other things, to the resignation of the region's longest ruling authoritarian, Indonesian president Suharto. These are the manifestations of a region in obvious crisis, a far cry from the miracle depicted in the World Bank's 1993 celebration of export-oriented capitalist 'development' in East Asia.[2]

This crisis, like crises more generally, provides a vantage point from which to see clearly into the processes and complex relationships that have given the region its shape. Contradictions that are otherwise present, but not always discernible, become exposed. Crises also offer new opportunities for reconfiguring power and reorganizing the material and ideational practices and institutional arrangements that buttress it, although as Marx reminded us, these opportunities are constrained by the limits of what is 'possible'. In the current conjuncture, elites, and the intellectuals who serve their interests, tend to regard crises as moments of disequilibrium to be 'managed' and rendered stable. In the discussion of East Asia's financial crisis, this managerial inclination is reflected in the 'debate' among academic neo-classical economists and their counterparts inside international financial institutions (IFIs) and agencies of the advanced capitalist states.[3] In these accounts, the crisis is portrayed as essentially excessive foreign borrowing coupled with a mis-allocation of these funds by domestic banking sectors lacking accepted standards of prudential supervision.[4] Financial reform is held out to be the next inevitable step in the region's modernisation, coupled with the removal of obstacles to the deepening of market regulation of ever greater aspects of social life, a remaking of the role of the state to facilitate this end and the strengthening of the real social power of investors under the banner of democratization and reform.

The financial crisis also presents an opportunity for those opposed to this neo-liberal managerialism to rethink the contradictory nature of capitalist development in the region, its specific class relations and state forms, and its articulation with various aspects of globalisation. Capitalist development across East Asia came to be marked by a series of political and ecological impasses that could only be transcended by a remaking of the social order, and in most cases by a recasting of the relationship between transnational and local forces. The crisis has created the context for precisely such a reordering. But this in no way means that the region was locked in some sort of static pattern. The regional 'model' vilified under the rubric of 'crony capitalism' by neo-liberals, and celebrated for the successes of the 'developmental state' by neo-institutionalists, never existed in a generic form. The terms of its transformation were already being contested and struggled over by specific social forces responding to already existing contradictions well before the devaluation of the Thai baht in July, 1997.

It is important to point out that prior to the crisis, many on the left also heralded capitalist industrialization in East Asia as a more progressive variant of capitalism than the neo-liberalism that has emerged in most advanced capitalist countries over the past two decades. The centrality of the state in the region's various political economies was seen as inherently 'progressive' merely because the state, even an avowedly capitalist one, is not 'of the market'. East Asia appeared to be the only region in the world where, according to some left-inclined observers, the forces of globalisation, particularly of finance, seemed to be kept at bay through the 1980s and into the 1990s by the existence of 'strong states'.[5] The second pillar of a progressive reading of East Asian capitalism was the idea that the configuration of state-society relations that existed around the region (especially in Japan and the first generation of so-called Newly Industrialising Countries [NICs]) managed to produce flexible institutions and practices that amounted to progressive *and* internationally competitive social relations of production. These two features were the basis for the argument put forward by some authors, such as Linda Weiss and Paul Hirst & Grahame Thompson, that while neo-liberal globalisation might be irreversible, East Asia showed that certain kinds of states can promote the interests of nationally-based capital in a *progressive* way.[6] This led to the conclusion that elites in other 'developing countries' should adopt this 'model' of political economy, and that the left in advanced capitalist countries should also espouse what Gregory Albo has critically referred to as a 'progressive competitiveness' alternative to neo-liberalism.[7]

This reading of East Asian capitalism and its appropriateness as an alternative to neo-liberalism has obviously been undermined by the financial crisis, as people within the region who have long been identified as 'progressive', such as Korea's newly elected President Kim Dae-Jung and Indonesian labour leader Mochtar, embrace major components of IMF-imposed restructuring. But even prior to the onset of the crisis, this so-called 'progressive' view based on the combination of industrial policy and flexible production, rested on a naive and superficial reading of the region's political economy. It assumed that there was a single region-wide 'model' that could be identified and extracted from divergent historical contexts even though key features of this 'model' were absent from the actual historical experiences of many of the countries in question.[8] More importantly, the state-centric focus on 'shaped advantage' and export competitiveness obscured the class and ecological bases of East Asian industrialisation and the contradictions and limits this produced. In the 1980s, with the erosion of the material basis of corporatism in Northern Europe, East Asian capitalism appeared to offer a new, more economically robust alternative to Anglo-American neo-liberalism that helped sustain the illusion that capitalism could be *both* internationally competitive and allow for a high degree of social solidarity.

In this essay I will explore the contradictions of East Asian capitalist development by treating it dialectically and locating the recent 'crisis' in its larger context. I will ask three inter-related questions: How should we best theorize dependent capitalist development in the region? What were the contradictions that precipitated the crisis? And to what extent does this moment of crisis represent a discontinuity? Posing these questions in this way implies rejecting the more conventional readings of the financial crisis of 1997-8 as representing either the end of a golden age of 'growth' or economic miracle, or merely a 'financial' crisis amenable to correction through a painful but short-lived implementation of 'structural adjustment' that will return the region to the *status quo ante* once its financial structures are modernized. While the events of 1997-8 represent both a financial crisis *and* a structural disjuncture, the question is not just whether or not economic growth resumes, but what kinds of political economies will emerge out of the restructuring, including the pattern of state-society relations, the nature of class power and the way globalisation and the rights of investors that it promotes coexist with 'democracy'.

If the crisis reflected the impasse of export-oriented dependent capitalist development, both in its internal dimensions and in its incorporation into the 'globalising' capitalist world order, in its 'resolution' there also lies the potential for reconfiguring domestic structures of power and re-organizing the way various fractions of global capital are inserted into the region's equally various political economies. Neither the crisis nor its aftermath can accordingly be conceived of as existing merely in the realm of 'finance'. It is as much a crisis of production and political regulation; the crisis marks the end of an export-oriented, dependent capitalism that was instantiated in locally specific ways. This assessment raises two further questions which I will return to by way of conclusion: first, is this a 'universalizing moment' for the region, with the weakening of the deep-rooted structural and ideological resistance to neo-liberalism that has characterised the region's political economy? Second, what does this crisis portend for dissident forces and the possibilities of a deepening of democratic practices that transcend mere electoralism.

I. RE-THINKING DEPENDENT CAPITALIST DEVELOPMENT

In speaking of 'dependent capitalist development' I am not referring to 'dependency theory', with its state-centric conception of underdevelopment whereby post-colonial countries remain structurally locked into the periphery by virtue of their dependent place in a 'world system' dominated by a core country or region. There is a lengthy tradition of writing on East Asian political economy that has framed the development of the region in just such core-periphery terms.[9] Among the many problems inherent in such a framework are its inability to deal with questions of agency, or with concrete class relationships and state forms; the historical variability of world order structures; and, most importantly, its treatment of problems that are associated with *capitalism* as problems of *national dependency*.

Dependent capitalist development transpires inside actual social formations. Irrespective of the extent of transnational pressure and control, each social formation contains a nationally specific configuration of class forces and form of state. They emerge from the local nature of class struggles and the way the internal balance of social forces shapes the production, appropriation and distribution of surplus in relation to the local ecological base. What makes this form of capitalism 'dependent' is not the structural dependence of a 'peripheral' state on a 'core' state, but the way that state elites and the dominant classes or class fractions within states maintain and reproduce their own social control through specific relationships with agents of transnational capital or with state elites in advanced capitalist countries. Local elites are dependent on flows of money, technology, military assistance and legitimating ideologies from advanced capitalist countries, but at the same time they possess an autonomous local base of political and social power, including their power to regulate the exploitation of local workers or peasants and the appropriation of local ecological assets to maintain levels of profit as well as levels of consumption, both in the advanced capitalist world and among local urban-based elites.

This analysis concurs with the position on globalisation advanced by Leo Panitch in his essay on 'globalisation and the state' in the 1994 *Socialist Register*. Panitch, building on Poulantzas' theorization of the internationalization of the state, argued that 'even an internal bourgeoisie implicated multiple ties of dependence in the international division of labour and in the international concentration of capital still maintained its own economic foundation and base of capital accumulation at home and abroad, as well as exhibited specific political and ideological features with autonomous effects on the state.'[10] While Panitch was not explicitly concerned with the relationship between globalisation and the state outside North America and Europe, his argument that globalisation involves a social and institutional restructuring that is largely internal is important in allowing us to think through the link between globalisation and dependent capitalism. This takes us a long way from the mechanistic, top-down 'neo-Marxist' formulations of dependency and underdevelopment of the 1970s, where the 'local' was thought of as structurally determined by a more or less fixed international location.

An important aspect of East Asia's dependent capitalist development is that it has ushered in a rapid industrialisation across the region and with it, a reduction in the levels of absolute poverty for many people and the creation of diverse new social relations that are unambiguously capitalist. The idea that the hallmark of dependency was the way it necessarily acted to inhibit the advent of capitalist industry was always a crude overstatement, to say the least. The important questions are what is the specific nature of the dependency, what kind of social order does it give rise to, and to whose benefit; and looking at the matter in this way forces us instead to turn our attention toward the manifold contradictions that are produced by the specific ways that dependent capitalism is locally instantiated.

This more dialectical formulation allows us to avoid the reified and oft-repeated misconception that there is some kind of a 'regional' East Asian model or, at a minimum, variants of a model, e.g., the NIC 'model' in Korea or a 'second tier' NIC model in Thailand or Malaysia.[11] To acknowledge that the region's various countries were not made by uniform external forces or by a uniform historical legacy allows us to accept the fact that dependent capitalist development has taken a number of forms. This point is both theoretically and empirically important because of the frequent attempts to identify *the* central component of an East Asian 'model', ranging from the neo-classical emphasis on free-trade and macro-economic probity and the neo-institutionalist focus on state capacity to promote 'late' development; to the unlikely convergence of some Japanese economists and 'world systems' theorists in the claim that it was the workings of the product cycle, in the guise of Japanese investment, that diffused a homogenous industrial structure to country after country;[12] and most recently, to attempts to see the region as a model of crisis-inducing 'crony capitalism'.

While attempts to construct a region-wide model of developmental capitalism highlight the limitations of ignoring diverse national contexts, they do - inadvertently - point to the significance of the broader 'macro-region' as a component of dependent capitalist development. While recent theorizations of globalisation have gone a long way to clarifying the relationship between the local and the global, they have not adequately dealt with the renewed prominence of macroregionality.[13] This refers not to any convergence of the region's different societies, but to the way different societies with their different class structures are connected to each other. This involves various types of formal and informal arrangements, depending on specific trans-regional class alliances and on the kind of institutions that exist within the relevant national social formations. It is, however, difficult to draw a formal distinction between the macro-regional and the domestic realms. Rather, regionalised structures and practices have constituted integral components of individual social formations without in any way implying any homogeneity of the social formations involved.[14]

Region-formation is also an important but often under-theorized component of globalisation. Locating national social formations in a regional context does not mean that regions are antithetical to either the local or the global. Rather, regions lie at the intersection of the local and the global. Regionalisation can in fact be a manifestation of global processes such as the transnationalization of capitalist production, the organization of credit or the diffusion of commodified culture. They may be manifestations of globalisation yet acquire regionally specific characteristics.

II. DEPENDENT CAPITALIST DEVELOPMENT AND THE EAST ASIAN BOOM

The region's political economies were forged by the confluence of three processes: the particular forms of state and class configurations that emerged from de-colonisation, the advent of the Cold War in East Asia, which enmeshed the state elites in America's anti-communist alliance, and the regionalisation of Japanese industrial capital in a manner that integrated fractions of local capital with their Japanese counterparts. It is important to explore how these three processes were intertwined.

The case of Thailand: Globalisation, regionalisation and dependent capitalism in East Asia's first domino

Thailand's dubious distinction of being the first of the East Asian dominoes to fall is particularly illuminating as to the tenuous nature of Southeast Asia's capitalist boom. Long looked upon as a bastion of corruption and rent-seeking by transnational capitalists and technocrats in the Bretton Woods institutions, Thailand came to be praised by the World Bank at the height of the boom as a paragon of '...outward looking orientation, receptivity to foreign investment and a market-friendly philosophy backed up by conservative macro-economic management and cautious external borrowing policies.'[15] While openness to foreign capital did make Thailand a bastion for Japanese manufacturing, precipitating the late-1980s boom, this same openness was ultimately instrumental in Thailand's collapse. But this openness needs to be read in conjunction with the changes in the configuration of power within Thailand.

In what is otherwise a very insightful account of the Thai bubble of the 1990s, Walden Bello also begins with the role of foreign capital.[16] He does so because he views Thai 'dependence' on foreign savings, which he contrasts to the case of Korea, as having fomented the crisis in the first place.[17] But while various fractions of global capital were indeed central agents in the bursting of the Thai speculative bubble, the origin of the crisis lay in the way these forces of globalisation were intertwined with the Thai power structure. The configuration of power inside of Thailand, and in particular, the nature of Thai capital and its links to the state, is a good illustration how capitalism takes root in different locations in different ways, how the local bourgeoisie emerge from locally specific contexts and how struggles to appropriate social power are ultimately local affairs.[18] The Thai bourgeoisie that grew rich on quixotic high-tech gambits, real estate speculation, maniacal property development and the denuding of the country's forests and littoral may have been tied to Japanese developers and bank-rolled by transnational lenders, but their formation and ongoing reconstitution as a class have been determined by the way capitalism and the modern Thai state emerged and have been constantly reconfigured.

It is a supreme irony that while Thailand avoided colonisation, it entered the post-World War II period with a political economy of a type more commonly associated with neo-colonialism than did a country like Korea that had experienced Japanese colonization. An ethnic Chinese commercial bourgeoisie had emerged in the late nineteenth century with a material base predicated on royal monopolies and on serving as intermediaries for British traders and financial capitalists operating under unequal treaties. These merchants were able to parlay their roles as tax 'farmers', rice millers and timber and mineral exporters into burgeoning financial empires.[19] The royal court-based elites were content to cede control of the financial, processing and marketing functions to these politically dependent merchants. In an effort to minimise foreign indebtedness and build up exchange reserves as a way of fending off the imperialists they also permitted the opening of new agricultural land rather than trying to expand production by undertaking large-scale infrastructure improvements.[20] This interaction of imperialist pressures with the domestic class structure helped create several long-term structural features of the Thai political economy: a merchant bourgeoisie caught between the state and foreign capital, and a fiscally conservative Thai state vulnerable to foreign pressure.

After World War II, five main Sino-Thai banking groups emerged to dominate Thai finance and commerce. With their roots in shipping, trading, insurance and rice milling, these banking interests forged an alliance with a succession of military governments who needed private financing for their statist projects.[21] Tariffs were levied on imported manufactures but with the aim of generating state revenue rather than promoting 'import substitution industrialization' as was the case in other parts of East Asia and parts of Latin America. Light manufacturing came to be controlled by the Sino-Thai financial conglomerates which realised rents from production for a protected domestic market. With the demise of the British presence in Southeast Asia and with the rise of the army as the dominant institution in society, Thailand's key external link was increasingly with the US army. The Vietnam War and the US decision to make Thailand the centre of its broader regional operations, combined with Thailand becoming a key destination for mass tourism, proved pivotal in the terms of Thailand's incorporation into the postwar capitalist world order.[22] Coinciding with the American escalation of the Vietnam war came the ascension to power of Field Marshall Sarit who presided over the Americanisation of the Thai army and put in place conditions that would make Thailand attractive to foreign capital.

American army investment in war-related infrastructure and an influx of holiday-makers into Bangkok precipitated a development boom in the late 1960s, characterised by real estate speculation and the increased concentration of land in the hands of those with access to capital and 'inside' information. The beneficiaries were not merely the privileged Sino-Thai commercial capitalists, but also top-level bureaucratic and military officials as well as rural economic elites. The boom began the long process of dispossessing subsistence farmers of their land, spawning a burgeoning class of agricultural tenants and an exodus of rural youth into Bangkok to form the beginnings of a Thai working class. They provided the cheap labour for tourism and other service industries and ultimately for the industrial boom of the late 1980s and early 1990s. While Thailand was eventually to become a central export platform for Japanese industrial capital, during the 1970s Japanese industries sought to overcome their own domestic crisis of over-production by taking advantage of Thailand's protected market and the historic absence of any indigenous industrial capitalists. They did this by forging alliances with prominent Sino-Thai capitalists who facilitated their presence inside Thailand's high tariff walls as vendors of locally-assembled manufactures to Thai elites, and suppliers of locally-made inputs for local production.[23]

Prior to the boom of the mid-1980s Thailand was affected first by the surging price of oil which it imported, and subsequently by the dramatic downturn in commodity prices which deleteriously affected commodity exports. When monetarist policies in the United States drove up interest rates, Thailand, like other neighbouring countries, became saddled with an unsustainable debt burden. In a move reminiscent of Latin America and Sub-Saharan Africa, Thailand was forced in 1982 to become a ward of the IMF, and subject to a structural adjustment programme. Two components of this restructuring were central to the boom and bust of the subsequent ten years; the changing role of capital vis-a-vis the state, and a more explicit attempt to promote export-oriented manufacturing.

The first change involved the privatisation of public enterprises and state promotion of a more formal role for business associations in policy-making and decisions concerning the allocation of public assets.[24] A key element of this restructuring involved senior officers in the Thai army converting their political power into private economic assets and corporate directorships.[25] This coincided with the increased importance of elections by the second half of the decade and with it a more influential role for 'party politicians' many of whom, like the recently deceased former Prime Minister Chatichai, were ex-Generals or state technocrats. This shallow electoralism, held up by neo-liberal apologists of globalisation as part of the 'third wave' of democratisation,[26] actually increased the influence of regional capitalists and more generally increased the power of capital both by enhancing the monetary rewards that induced businessmen to enter parliamentary 'politics', and by offering new degrees of influence to those able to finance electoral campaigns and the day-to-day maintenance of a power base.[27]

While the first component of restructuring created the class conditions for a domestic economic boom, the second change paved the way for the influx of Japanese capital. The IMF made its adjustment loans conditional upon the creation of certain conditions attractive to foreign industrial capital; currency realignment and tariff reduction.[28]

This combination of a reconfigured class structure and forced liberalisation created the structural basis for Thailand's emergence as a low-wage 'export platform'. But it was the rapid appreciation of the Japanese yen in 1985 and the subsequent lowering of Japanese interest rates two years later that precipitated the diffusion of labour-intensive Japanese manufacturing throughout Southeast Asia, and especially to Thailand.[29] As Bello points out, this influx of Japanese industrial capital, supplemented by Taiwanese investment, precipitated a manufacturing boom that undermined the leverage the IMF was able to exert on the Thai state, ensuring that structural adjustment in Southeast Asia was short-lived and partial.[30] Massive infrastructure projects that the World Bank held hostage to structural adjustment in the early 1980s, for example, were subsequently funded through Japan's development assistance in the late 1980s without any of the bank's neo-liberal conditionality.[31]

The Bangkok metropolitan area, replete with a spate of new factories, a large influx of unskilled workers from the provinces and world-class traffic congestion, had literally overnight become a major platform for assembly-intensive products manufactured for re-export to third countries. In the period from 1985-1992 over US $5.2 billion in Japanese investment poured into Thailand, precipitating a dramatic rise in exports. Not only was much of this increase in production attributable directly to Japanese capital, but hitherto domestically-oriented corporations like Siam motors came to rely so heavily on Japanese capital and technology that two mainstream observers, Hatch and Yamamura, liken Thailand's most prominent industrialists to 'compradors' of the colonial era.[32]

The Thai boom, however, entailed more than just the regionalisation of a division of labour. Yen appreciation meant that assets in other Asian countries appeared ludicrously cheap to Japanese developers. The Japanese state and tourist agencies also heavily promoted cheap holidays and the regionalisation of golf, Japan's prime form of corporate leisure. Developers soon followed Japanese industrial capitalists with a wave of investments in Thai golf courses, resorts, theme parks and retailing. By 1988 service and real-estate related investment had climbed to a quarter of Japan's total stock of investments in Thailand.[33] With restrictions on foreign ownership of real-estate, Japanese developers and tourist corporations allied themselves with Thai capitalists and army generals who controlled the construction industry. Military elites took equity positions in joint-venture developments, obtained licences to 'develop' protected forests and coastlines and used the coercive power of the state to appropriate land from peasants.

Finally, Japanese trading companies allied themselves with Thailand's Sino-Thai oligopolists whose roots lay in agro-business, buying up large amounts of land, and introducing export-oriented mono-crop agriculture and aqua-culture to meet the exploding demand for exotic fruits, vegetables and seafood in Japan.[34] Besides causing severe ecological damage, this 'booming' agro-business furthered the proletarianisation of the Thai peasantry.[35] Formerly self-sufficient rice producers were now 'freed up' either to stay in their villages as agrarian wage labourers or to migrate to the greater Bangkok area to work in foreign-controlled or joint-venture factories or in the ever-expanding tourism and sex trade. The precipitous increase in exports of manufactures and agricultural produce, the escalation of asset prices, especially the cost of land, the expansion of an urban technocratic and professional class and the massive influx of foreign visitors to Thailand created a euphoria among transnational 'development' technocrats and industrial and financial capitalists, prompting many to hold Thailand up as East Asia's next full-fledged 'tiger'.[36] Less discussed of course were the ecological and class bases underlying this boom. Also attracting little attention at the time was the bursting of Japan's asset bubble in early 1990 which led to a collapse of asset prices in Japan, the beginning of a decade-long deflationary spiral and, for Thailand, the gradual drying-up of the flow of Japanese investment. The entire Thai power bloc - the expanding bourgeoisie, the state technocrats and the upper echelons of the military - were all caught up in a speculative frenzy and the zeal of capitalist growth. Lacking the capital to sustain it, they threw themselves into the embrace of global finance.

It has been argued so far that the contradictions creating the context for the financial crisis were deep-rooted and structural, lying in the way the patterns of accumulation reflected nationally specific structures of power and the way shifts in these structures, in particular the harnessing of state power to the interests of fractions of local capital in the 1980s, combined with distinct forms of incorporation into the global political economy.[37] This articulation between local structures and global processes was in turn partially mediated through the regional diffusion of aspects of Japan's political economy. This regionalisation helped Thailand reflate following the collapse of commodity prices in the early 1980s. It was both made possible by the reconfiguration of the Thai power structure and contributed to its continuing transformation. The ensuing boom created the demand for foreign money among capital-poor Thai elites on the one hand, and the perception that Thailand was merely the latest example of the Asian miracle among global lenders on the other.

'Global finance', 'liberalisation' and the fall of the first domino

Before discussing the way that globalisation of finance has affected Thailand, the making of Thailand's debt crisis and the unravelling of dependent capitalist development, it is necessary to digress briefly to consider the nature of 'global finance' that the political economies of Southeast Asia encountered. While neo-liberal technocrats have dwelt on improvident lending by local financial institutions, political elites across East Asia have decried the impunity with which speculators can target a currency. Chalmers Johnson, in his analysis of the crisis, uses the terms 'global financial system' and 'global lenders' interchangeably.[38] This lack of clarity necessitates making two points to clarify what I mean when I refer to 'global finance'.

First, reference to 'global finance' represents a reification of finance capital. The globalisation of finance that has accompanied the demise of the Bretton Woods system of fixed exchange rates and the dismantling of national regulatory frameworks has given rise to a hierarchy of forces. Each fraction of finance has its particular form of agency that embodies specific sets of interests and relationships. Each has been able to insinuate itself into local arrangements in specific ways. A key element of globalised finance is its fragmentation, reflected in the de-centralization and privatization of the global organization of credit and the mechanisms for recycling capital.[39] This is crucially tied to the changing location of power at global, regional and national levels.[40] New forms of intermediation make the channels of credit and networks of monetary agents that link savers and borrowers more complex, more de-centralized and less subject to any sort of public or social control.

If we disaggregate these manifold agencies we can delineate a pyramid-shaped array of investor interests, with those having the greatest stake in a particular country, owners of a stock of fixed assets, at its base and those with no stake at all, hedge funds managers who merely speculate in currencies, at its apex. Located in the middle are institutional investors such as mutual and pension fund managers, foreign commercial and merchant banks, local banks and financial institutions, IFIs and state aid-granting agencies. Each of these interests has a distinct structural relationship to each national political economy.

Secondly, finance has been globalised in ways that at least partially reflect the regionalisation of production. In East Asia the regionalisation of Japanese capital helped precipitate a regionalisation of Japanese credit allocation in two ways. One was through the lending activities of Japanese banks that directly financed the activities of Japanese affiliates in Southeast Asia. The other was through the emergence of Tokyo and Hong Kong as regional centres of credit organization.

The Thai boom generated a prodigious demand for financing at precisely the time that institutional investors such as mutual funds were emerging as increasingly important sources of credit. North America's protracted recession at the beginning of the 1990s pressured fund managers to 'discover' higher yielding investment opportunities in 'emerging markets'. In order to attract highly coveted capital from abroad the Thai state put in place conditions to attract a range of foreign financial interests. Between 1990 and 1994, it undertook several significant initiatives to deregulate the financial system and make it accessible to foreign capital.[41] The first was the deregulation of domestic finance by removing constraints on portfolio management, loosening rules on capital adequacy and expanding the permitted field of operations of commercial banks and financial institutions. The second was the dismantling of all significant foreign exchange controls and the establishment of the Bangkok International Banking Facility (BIBF) in 1993. Under the BIBF Thai and foreign banks were permitted to engage in offshore borrowing in foreign currencies, to convert those funds to Thai baht and re-lend them to local borrowers. BIBF dollar loans soon became the conduit for most foreign capital flowing into Bangkok, amounting to about $50 billion over a three-year period. The third element of financial liberalization was the informal near-pegging of the baht to the US dollar by the Bank of Thailand. A fourth initiative involved maintaining interest rates at levels significantly higher than in advanced capitalist countries. Finally, although not part of the liberalization programme of the Thai state, the consistent and fulsome praise for this liberalization by the IFIs, as illustrated by the World Bank statement cited above, constituted an explicit vote of confidence that encouraged foreign investment and lending.

These initiatives served the interest of various fractions of local and transnational financial capital in different ways. Institutional investors poured money into local equity and bond markets. Mutual funds, which were primarily American-based and managed out of Hong Kong, were driven to the region by low real interest rates and, in the early 1990s, declining rates of return in the stock market at home. Fund managers sought open equity and bond markets and often demanded exchange rate stability as a pre-condition for market entry. The influx of these institutional investors resulted in a dramatic increase in the capitalization of equity markets throughout Southeast Asia. Bello notes how foreign investors became the largest buyers of equities on the stock exchange of Thailand while on the Jakarta exchange, the influx of foreign money increased its capitalization almost four-fold, from 69 trillion rupiah (US $23.4 billion) in 1993 to 260 trillion rupiah in 1996, with foreign trading accounting for an astronomical 85% of the volume.[42]

Foreign banks took advantage of the arbitrage opportunities provided by interest rate differentials. In this regard, cheap money in Japan came to play a central role in a regionalised organization of credit, with Japanese, European and American banks borrowing in Japan and lending to local financial institutions throughout the region in what came to be known as the 'carry trade'.[43] Japanese banks also used Hong Kong as a base for the provision of non-governmental project finance in infrastructure and power generation, indirectly promoting the rise of 'regional' investment houses based in Hong Kong such as the now defunct Peregrine Investments. In fact, the rise of Hong Kong as a centre of regional finance during the early 1990s is directly attributable to the regionalisation of Japanese finance.[44]

With the collapse of domestic Japanese demand in the 1990s and a seemingly intractable financial crisis at home, there was little demand for credit inside Japan. Japanese financial institutions had not fared well in their forays into South America, the US and Western Europe in the late 1980s, and had a collective sense that Asia was more familiar and safer territory due to cultural similarities and the greater influence there of Japanese capital.[45] From the setting up of the BBIF mechanism, Japanese net bank lending in Thailand by banks reporting to the Bank of International Settlements was $63 billion, of which more than 80% went to Thai financial institutions.[46]

Financial liberalization, of course, directly benefitted local Thai capital as well. This was particularly true for banks and finance companies which were now unencumbered by regulation. Once it became known in financial circles that the Bank of Thailand was planning to issue highly coveted new bank licences, finance companies competed with one another to establish themselves as major 'players' by borrowing large sums of 'carry trade' money through the BBIF and re-lending them locally, focusing on short-term investments, particularly in property development.[47]

Easy credit and willing foreign buyers of stocks and bonds also facilitated the emergence of a new stratum of would-be industrialists who entertained visions of translating cheap money into high-tech industries or Chinese empires. The historic political inability of the Thai state to direct lending for industrial policy purposes and the willingness of local banks to lend on easy terms allowed the owners of a host of emerging companies, like Shinawatra, TT & T, and the then celebrated and now defunct Alphatech, to parlay their political connections into lucrative licences for local control of new-fangled services such as mobile phone networks and satellite television broadcasting.[48]

The first visible weaknesses appeared in 1994 when the People's Bank of China devalued the Chinese renminbi to promote labour-intensive exports. This was followed by a 1995 agreement between the Japanese Finance Ministry and the US Treasury to depreciate the Yen against the dollar.[49] These exchange rate shifts did not upset the baht-dollar peg that provided financial investors with 'stability' but they did undermine the viability of cheap Thai exports. The ten-year increase in Thai exports peaked in 1995, forcing the Bank of Thailand to use its reserves to defend the peg.

By the end of 1995 it was already clear to local developers that there were no buyers for their luxury housing and modern office space. The stock of vacant units in Bangkok already had an estimated value of $20 billion. In June 1996 the Bank of Thailand began to prop up local banks by taking a thirty-two percent position in a prominent local bank on the verge of failing.[50] By early 1997 non-performing bank loans to Thai institutions stood at over $3 billion. The final blow to this elaborate house of cards was an intimation by Japanese Ministry of Finance officials that an interest rate hike might be necessary to strengthen the Yen which had fallen a full 40 yen, to 127 to the dollar, in the preceding two years.[51] The possible removal of one of the pillars of the 'carry trade' created the impetus for a run on the baht and the collapse of Thai asset prices. Commercial and investment bankers immediately began to call in their Thai loans. This sent local lenders who had borrowed in dollars but had lent in local currency scurrying to exchange baht for dollars or Yen. As local investors began to dump equities, institutional investors sold off all of their Thai holdings, precipitating a collapse of asset prices. The last act in the drama was the desperate but ill-advised attempt by Bank of Thailand to preserve the peg by borrowing money from the same lenders who were dumping its currency. The sight of an under-funded central bank defending an over-valued currency that the entire world was selling off presented an irresistible opportunity for hedge funds. Selling the baht 'short' constituted a bell-weather for other financial interests, triggering a further round of capital flight, and a withdrawal of virtually all lines of credit to Thailand. By the beginning of July the Bank of Thailand was left with no choice but to float the baht. When the Thai finance minister's request for a loan was turned down by Japanese financial officials, there was little alternative but to call in the IMF. Fifteen years after its last economic debacle, Thailand was once again subjected to IMF structural adjustment.

III. PARTIAL LIBERALIZATION AND THE IMPASSE OF OLIGOPOLISTIC CAPITAL IN KOREA

Before considering IMF restructuring and the broader implications of the crisis it is important also to look briefly at the Korean 'crash'. The composition of the Korean ruling bloc and its matrix of structures differ significantly from those in Thailand and other Southeast Asian countries. While Thailand featured an open capital market, a fixed exchange rate, and an absence of industrial policy-oriented, state-directed lending, Korea had neither a fixed exchange rate nor inflows of 'hot' money. If Thai bureaucratic elites hoped that foreign capital would do what the state and the local bourgeoisie could not (i.e., foment an industrial transformation of the country) Korea, whose state had long channelled lending into heavy industry, and whose bourgeoisie was dominated by oligopolistic industrial capital that exported capital-intensive products world-wide, encountered no such problem. Yet Korea, the 'classic NIC', celebrated by state institutionalists and progressive competitive social democrats alike, was no less an example of dependent capitalist development. Korea went from OECD candidate-member to the recipient of the single largest financial bailout in the history of multilateral lending in a mere two years!

Korea's financial crisis again is as much a manifestation of the impasse its dependent capitalism had reached prior to the implosion of December 1997 as it is a debt crisis. An understanding of this impasse once again requires a mapping of the domestic class structure and the nature of state-society relations, as well as Korea's global and regional linkages and the contradictions inherent in these relationships.[52]

Prior to the mid-1980s, Korea's political economy does bear some resemblance to the neo-institutional accounts of Korean political economy.[53] A powerful class of 'political capitalists' emerged in the 1950s, acquiring the privatised assets of the vanquished Japanese colonial regime. In return for funding of authoritarian politics, they were granted privileged access to foreign capital, which at the time meant US aid, and scarce commodities that they were able to parlay into industrial conglomerates known as *chaebol*.[54] For more than two decades after the advent of military rule in 1961, Korean finance was characterised by the tight relationship between the state and these capitalists. The state borrowed money from abroad and funnelled it through state-controlled banks at low interest rates to the *chaebol* to develop industries that it designated strategic. In the 1970s the state took advantage of its strategic alliance with the United States to gain access to large amounts of petrodollars that were available at negative interest rates.[55] It channelled these funds to the *chaebol* to promote rapid heavy industrialization and to maximize manufacturing exports. Allocative decision-making was made by the newly-formulated Planning Council which reported directly to the president.[56] In addition to being dependent on state-controlled finance, the *chaebol* became intertwined with Japanese industrial capital, developing a lasting dependence on Japan for technological know-how and intermediate inputs. This pattern of political economy precipitated what continues to be a key contradiction in Korean capitalism even in the aftermath of the crash; because this low-cost financing was geared to creating industrial capacity rather than profitability, the *chaebol* had staggering debt-to-equity ratios and a large accumulation of non-performing loans. The size of the debt and the potentially devastating social impact of the bankruptcy of any of the largest employers in the country required the socialisation of this high-risk industrial expansion.

This structure of industrialization was also a structure of political rule. The strategy of creating economies of scale in capital-intensive industries meant that there were insufficient funds available for the remainder of Koreans who were forced to borrow informally at excessive interest rates.[57] It was underpinned by state-controlled corporatist unions, strict enforcement of ideological conformity and overt suppression of labour protest. Dependent development was also characterized by the inability or unwillingness of Korean capital to externalize the ecological costs of rapid industrialization, resulting in devastating levels of air, water and soil pollution that earned Seoul the dubious honour of being the world's second most polluted city after Mexico City.[58]

This phase of Korea's political economic development, which has been reified in the neo-institutionalist 'development' literature as the East Asian developmental model, could not survive the passing of a specific set of historical circumstances. By the early 1980s, cheap foreign money and the ability to keep foreign capital at bay, two of the pillars of Korea's political economy, were removed: i.e., the USA's embrace of monetarism, and pressure by the Reagan administration to force open Korea's financial markets to ensure that it didn't become 'the next Japan'.

Internally, a new military regime led by Chun Doo-hwan seized power in response to a triple crisis of hyper-inflation, local recession and the assassination of President Park Chung-hee. The Chun regime, deprived of any domestic legitimacy by its bloody suppression of the Kwangju uprising, relied on support from the Reagan administration which viewed the new regime as a useful ally in the 'Second Cold War'. It undertook a reconfiguration of the Korean ruling coalition by distancing itself from the *chaebol* in order to tap into the anti-*chaebol* attitude of a rising stratum of middle-class managers, professionals and technicians.[59] The Chun regime also endeavoured to differentiate itself from its fallen predecessor by shifting the locus of economic decision to the more technocratic Economic Planning Board, privatizing state-owned banks, increasing interest rates to attract the high rates of household savings into the banking system, and promoting equity markets as a continued source of cheap funds for the *chaebol*. It did so while resisting American pressure to grant US financial institutions meaningful access. Bank autonomy was, however, constrained from the outset. Banks were instructed by the Ministry of Finance both to favour lending to small and medium enterprises over the *chaebol*, and to reschedule debt payments and grant new credit to the same *chaebol* for industrial upgrading.[60]

Further change accompanied the opening up of the political system in the late 1980s. Former political and bureaucratic elites were not strong enough to maintain the previous state structure in the face of nation-wide mass-protests. But neither were the 'democratic forces', notably labour and the middle class, strong enough or sufficiently united to dislodge the ruling elites.[61] The state came to reflect a grafting of the least progressive of the democratic elements. i.e., the reform politicians, onto the existing structure. These politicians quickly distanced themselves from the working class and sought to build electoral bases of middle-class support by pledging liberalisation and democratisation of the state and economy. Their ascendancy was highlighted by the advent of Kim Young-sam as Korea's first civilian president in 1993. For their part, the *chaebol* became increasingly uncomfortable with the heavy-handed attempts of the new regime to extract money to fund the new electoral politics. *Chaebol* owners began to argue for an end to state micro-management of industry.

From the late 1980s through the middle 1990s the impasses of Korean capitalism were to prove unsustainable. The end of military rule opened up the space for organized labour to demand large-scale wage increases and improvements in the abominable working conditions workers were subjected to. A proliferation of 'social movements' across the country also demanded the environmental regulation of industry and clamoured for the state to force capital to pay for the clean-up of local pollution. Korean capital now came to regard itself as 'burdened' by the high cost of local money, excessively high labour costs and unreasonable social regulation. The advent of Southeast Asia, and subsequently China as new sites of low-cost production, followed by currency devaluations in China, further undermined the *chaebol* strategy of low-wage, capital-intensive mass production. The final straw resulted from the strategy of channelling funds into the expansion of capacity to assemble random access memory chips. Both industrial capitalists and state elites were counting on this as the sector in which Korean capital was at long last to break its dependence on Japanese and American technology. However, in January of 1996, a glut of memory chips led to a precipitous fall in unit prices, accompanied by dramatic reductions in Korean exports.[62]

This confluence of events created an impetus on the part of Korean capital to both reduce costs and find new avenues of profit generation. This included renewed demands to gain access to cheaper money abroad and the adoption of a 'new management strategy' that would roll back many of the gains recently made by labour. The state negotiated three compromises with the *chaebol*. First, without changing the basic domestic financial structure and without allowing anything more than partial and modest incremental increases in foreign access to the Korean financial system, the state relaxed its limitations on foreign borrowing by Korean firms and ceased monitoring these borrowings. Second, the state completely abandoned its role of co-ordinating industrial investments. Finally, the state agreed to make Korea's labour market more 'flexible', thereby removing the restrictions on the unilateral laying-off of core blue collar workers.[63]

The first two of these compromises led directly to the debt crisis and the third led to the general strike of January 1997. Unlike countries such as Thailand which were wholly dependent on opening their capital markets to attract pools of portfolio investment, Korea was able to finance most domestic investment through domestic savings. The problem was the high cost of domestic money. By 1996, with Japanese interest rates the world's lowest, Korea's fledgling merchant banks and finance companies, with no experience raising funds offshore and a paucity of staff skilled in assessing credit worthiness and risk evaluation, began borrowing prodigious amounts of money from Japanese banks and the Japanese branches of US and European banks. These transactions, no longer scrutinized by the Korean state, featured poor maturity structures, with over 70 per cent carrying less than one year's maturity and more than half with a maturity of 90 days.

The domestic corollary of unregulated foreign borrowing was the availability of easy credit in Korea. As export earnings dropped, the major *chaebol* embarked on a course of rapid and ambitious expansion of capacity.[64] But equally important was the prolific lending to medium-sized companies that sought profits outside of manufacturing, venturing into a range of service-related and speculative activities.[65] The result of these patterns of off-shore borrowing and easy domestic credit was that by 1997 over $150 billion in debt was owed by Korea's financial institutions to foreign banks and more than $300 billion in debt was owed by Korean companies to Korean financial institutions. When the state refused to allow a major *chaebol*, Kia Motors, to go bankrupt, the bond rating agency Standard & Poors downgraded Korean debt, and hedge funds, fresh from their killing in Southeast Asia, moved in to attack the won. Over the ensuing few weeks the primary holders of Korean debt, the foreign banks, insisted on calling roughly 75 per cent of the loans due, precipitating a run on the Korean won and a precipitous asset deflation as $1 billion a day flowed out of Korea. Korea had quickly gone from being insulated from the flows of 'hot money' and their destabilising effects in the early 1990s to becoming yet another ward of the IMF.

IV. IMF RESTRUCTURING AND THE FUTURE OF EXPORT-ORIENTED DEPENDENT CAPITALISM

IMF austerity programs increased in severity and scope as the dominoes continued to tumble. However in all instances the Fund sought to remake the respective financial systems by demanding the closure of suspect financial institutions, the establishment of new regulatory practices and the complete opening of the capital market, including the right of foreign capital to attempt hostile mergers and acquisitions.[66] It also ensured a prolonged deflation and continued liquidity crisis across the region by insisting on capping public spending, reducing the role of the state and maintaining high domestic interest rates. In addition, the IMF assured foreign banks that their outstanding debts would be compensated in full and then, in conjunction with the US Treasury and the Japanese Ministry of Finance, proceeded to broker the rolling over of some of the debt from short- into long-term debt. This was done by compelling various states to socialize private debt. If this were not sufficiently intrusive, the Fund further took it upon itself to demand the breaking up of cartels, the privatization or dismantling of state-owned enterprises, the creation of flexible labour markets in Korea and the elimination of food subsidies in Indonesia, even as millions of subsistence farmers faced drought, crop-failure and possible starvation.

The actions of the IMF in orchestrating rescue packages and imposing structural adjustment have already come under heated attack on a number of counts: the thinly disguised advancement of American interests; its acting as a collection agency for bankers who profited greatly from imprudent lending; paying lip-service to country-specific conditions while insisting on 'one size fits all' neo-liberal programmes; and characterizing the crisis as 'financial' in its analysis while in practice demanding comprehensive restructuring of public and private institutions and state-society relations.[67]

While all of these criticisms have merit, they all point implicitly to the real issues that revolve around the refashioning of social power. As Robert Wade points out, the IMF has used this crisis to promote the interests of a 'Wall Street-Treasury Complex', the goal of which is nothing short of the institutionalization of a global regime of complete, unfettered capital mobility that further enhances both the structural and direct power of financial investors.[68] This will be further enhanced by the opportunities that structural adjustment creates for the widespread transfer of local assets, particularly in Korea, to foreign capital.

Related to this attempt at global reordering is the local struggle to reconfigure power. IMF conditionality creates an opening for the obliteration of class compromises or impasses that underpinned social order. By making the flexibilization of Korean labour markets part of IMF conditionality, for example, the Korean state and Korean capital can use the 'national crisis' as a pretext to attempt what they were politically unable to accomplish one year earlier, the diminution of the power of organized labour. This highlights a point that was made at the outset of this essay, that the imposition of IMF-mandated austerity on the majority of the population, like globalisation, has to be put in place locally and under the auspices of state power and with the support of key social forces. IMF programmes that have already depressed wages and wiped out millions of jobs have been legitimated by appeals to national solidarity. In countries like Thailand, while the urban middle class hail the crisis for bringing about a new 'democratic' constitution and weakening the role of the military, a large part of the migrant working class have been thrown out of work and in the absence of any social welfare system, have been forced to seek refuge in their home villages in the impoverished Northeast of the country.[69] However, land speculation and export-oriented cash cropping have increased peasant vulnerability to fluctuations in food demand by breaking down forms of subsistence agriculture and making it difficult to welcome back returning family members.

Just what are the implications of this crisis and of IMF restructuring for East Asian dependent capitalist development? What has likely come to an end is not some 'East Asian miracle'. Many of the region's capitalists will undoubtedly prosper and as long as global finance remains unaccountable to anybody but shareholders, global investors will almost surely return to the region once asset values have been driven down far enough and investor confidence has been restored. What is more plausible is that export-oriented dependent capitalist development as a continuing alternative to more liberal forms of capitalism has become unsustainable. There are several reasons for this. The first relates to the old fallacy-of-composition problem that was frequently raised in the 1970s and 80s, i.e., that export-oriented development based on the export of labour-intensive manufactures is viable only when it is practiced in a handful of countries with small populations. But as an increasing number of low-wage countries with large populations such as China engage in export-oriented manufacturing, the proclivity in capitalism toward over-production is quickly realized. The often-asked question, who will buy all these cheap exports, remains pertinent. In this regard, the dramatic disruptions of the Thai and Korean economies by the surge in Chinese exports in the mid-1990s was only the beginning. The effective nationalization of debt coupled with the political economy of forced austerity will make state elites desperate to promote exports just to generate the hard currency to repay the debt plus interest. This could possibly lead the region into a vortex of competitive devaluations.

Second, Japanese capitalism's own impasses, and the prospects of domestic restructuring in Japan, will ensure that the role previously played by Japanese capital in the formation of trans-regional class alliances with local capitals will not likely continue in the same organizational forms. It is indeed ironic that the contradictions in Japanese capitalism contributed to the tumbling down of the regional dominoes and promises to exacerbate and prolong the crisis that began in 1997. In fact the IMF-imposed neo liberal restructuring is predicated on a regional solution, i.e., a Japanese reflation to counter the deflation being exported from the rest of the region in the form of lower-cost exports. However Japan is mired in its own bad-debt crisis, Japanese industrial capital is still burdened with excess capacity from the late 1980s, and a collapse in domestic demand since 1991 has loosened long-term sub-contracting relationships and is precipitating a discernible increase in unemployment and under-employment, especially among young people.[70] Far from the prospects of Japanese imports rescuing the region and vindicating the imposed austerity, regional imports to Japan actually declined as a dramatically depreciating Japanese yen further contributed to the threat of a regional spiral of currency depreciations.[71]

Third and perhaps most importantly, structural adjustment is aimed at breaking the non-arms-length nexus between the state and capital as well as between fractions of finance capital and commercial/industrial capital. It is these relationships that contributed to East Asia being the region of the world most resistant to market 'freedoms' such as mergers and hostile acquisitions by foreigners, bankruptcies, and precipitous layoffs of core workers. Restructuring is aimed at making all fractions of capital subject to the discipline of the maximization of shareholder value and profitability. Here it must be remembered that the kind of financial system associated with Anglo-American style equity markets that is being prescribed for the entire region is itself based on a mythology that direct equity market-centred financing represents a less politicised, more 'efficient' form of finance. As Doug Henwood has show, contemporary equity markets are much more institutions for configuring the ownership of large corporations than institutions concerned with raising funds for productive investment. This has been reflected in the prevalence of mergers and acquisitions in the United States and in the transfer of family- and state-owned enterprises in 'peripheral' countries into the hands of private shareholders.[72] This appears to be precisely what is likely to emerge in East Asia as restructuring gathers momentum. The collapse of asset prices and dramatic currency devaluations make assets, particularly in Korea, a bargain for North American or European corporations, no longer barred from acquiring local assets. Furthermore, the IMF requirement of high domestic interest rates and tight fiscal policy has created a deflationary environment in which the Korean state and Korean capital have been desperately selling off assets in return for any infusion of funds.[73]

Finally, the crisis has highlighted the glaring class contradictions that were already prevalent but muted by authoritarian political power: the centrality of the state in all aspects of social life, the defeat of the left, virtual full employment and the continuation of some traditional forms of social solidarity. The weakening of all this, plus the harshness of more liberal forms of finance, is likely to exacerbate class conflict. But since restructuring is ostensibly promoting more transparency and accountability it is worth also speculating about democracy in the era of restructuring. The resignation of president Suharto and the promise of open and fair elections at the national level in Indonesia may help institutionalize procedural democracy as liberals suggest, but electoralism is likely to offer little more than a new mechanism for elite control that uses elections as a legitimating device while at the same time suppressing the demands of popular sectors. To be reminded of the limits of electoralism, we only need to be reminded of how all three candidates for the Korean presidency felt compelled at the height of the campaign to publicly profess support for the terms of IMF conditionality. Moreover, given how intractable the region-wide deflation will likely be, it is difficult to envisage democratically elected elites allowing any space for independent labour organizations or local ecological movements that threaten to disrupt accumulation and drive up costs. Here again we need look no further than the great democrat Kim Dae-jung and the way he has allowed labour to sit at the table solely to ensure that the mass layoffs of Korea's unionized workforce are accomplished relatively smoothly. President Kim's appeal to workers in his nationally-televised 'town-hall meeting' to accept layoffs and other hardships, illustrates how the coercion of neo-liberal restructuring can readily be modulated into modern, democratic 'public-opinion management' practices.[74]

Despite the warranted pessimism, there is perhaps a progressive moment that comes out of the crisis. The region's melt-down opens up space for people once again to entertain alternative conceptions of 'development' and the range of possible political strategies to achieve their implementation. Alternative thinking had been blocked by the widespread acceptance of the illusion of permanently high growth rates and ever improving material circumstances. In the short-term there is likely to be a good deal of support among a stratum of the elite and the middle class most adversely effected by liberalization, within each of the domino countries, for some modest reimposition of controls on capital, such as the adoption of the Tobin tax on cross-border flows of capital. There may even be support for promoting social welfare through a modicum of redistribution, especially in Korea, as previously secure workers are thrown out of work in increasing numbers without either a social safety net or a traditional extended family support network to fall back on. But even modest departures such as these require dissident forces to think beyond the restoration of some variant of state-centred dependent capitalism as a desirable alternative to the imposition of neo-liberalism. Trade union leaders desperate to protect jobs, and left-leaning intellectuals, have responded to the crisis by constructing a nationalist politics of resisting foreign-imposed austerity in alliance with the very domestic capitalists at whose hands they have been marginalized or oppressed. They have also called for the nationalization of private debt even though it places a long-term burden on the bulk of the population and makes the state even more susceptible to the pressure of creditors. Similarly, many foreign state-institutionalists, like Robert Wade and Chalmers Johnson, argue for a return to the 'developmental state' with its capacity to formulate industrial policy and to mobilize high rates of household savings for 'national development'.[75]

Ultimately any momentum for financial or other social re-regulation that might emerge in opposition to IMF-sponsored austerity needs the support of a coalition of social forces for a different conception of development. This requires a basic acceptance that a return to the *status-quo ante* is neither possible nor desirable. The recent boom and bust shows clearly that the hitherto widely accepted notion of growth based on export promotion, the suppression of labour and rapid ecological depletion as a recipe for 'sustainable' development, is a grand illusion. But any political project that seeks to challenge elite power while promoting social justice and ecological sustainability must begin by exposing the false idea that neo-liberalism and state-centred capitalism constitute the only possible options. The roots of the current crisis lay, as we have seen, in local and global structures of power and how they shaped production and the accumulation of surplus. A progressive project would have to be built around a challenge to and a re-fashioning of these structures of power. The latter would require a democratization of the state, the re-orienting of local production toward local demand, and the socialization of decisions about technology and the relationship between production and local and national ecological carrying capacities. It would also require a commitment to an alternative solution to the debt crisis; one that avoids the protracted transfer of funds to a transnational coalition of creditors.[76] While the balance of class forces obviously militates against this as a political project likely to compete successfully with the elite-driven nationalist or neo-liberal alternatives in the short-term, its social basis has to lie in worker and peasant collective action to gain more control over their work contexts, and in the assertion by local communities of greater control over the way the state, national and foreign capitalists acquire and appropriate locally-based assets. It is therefore hardly surprising that despite the increased prevalence of electoralism in Korea and Thailand, and its possible deepening in post-Suharto Indonesia, these are precisely the terrains of greatest resistance, where the struggles for and against real democracy are being waged most vigorously.

NOTES

I would like to thank Stephen Gill and Eric Helleiner for their helpful comments and suggestions.

1 Throughout this essay East Asia refers to both Northeast and Southeast Asia.
2 World Bank, *The East Asian Miracle: Growth and Public Policy*, New York: Oxford University Press, 1993.
3 For several examples of the burgeoning literature from varied perspectives see Lester Thurow, 'Asia: The Collapse and the Cure', *The New York Review of Books*, February 5, 1998, pp. 22-26; 'The Currency Crisis in Southeast Asia And the Republic of Korea', Asia Development Bank, Manila, 1998; Paul Krugman, 'What Happened To Asia?', http://web.mit.edu/krugman/www/DISINTER.html; and Walden Bello, 'The end of the Asian miracle', *The Nation*, 12-19 January 1998.
4 A representative example is the Asian Development Bank's report on the crisis. See *The Currency Crisis in Southeast Asia and the Republic of Korea* (Manila: Asian Development Bank, 1998).
5 For a view of the East Asian state as a bulwark against globalisation which did not, however, automatically assume its progressive character, see Manfred Bienefeld, 'Capitalism And The Nation State In The Dog Days Of The Twentieth Century' in R. Miliband & L. Panitch eds., *Between Globalism And Nationalism, Socialist Register 1994* (London: Merlin Press, 1996), pp. 94-129.
6 Linda Weiss, 'Globalization and the Myth of the Powerless State', *New Left Review* 225 (September-October 1997), pp. 3-27. Also see P. Hirst and G. Thompson, *Globalization in Question* (Oxford, Polity Press, 1994).
7 For an important critique of the general principal of 'progressive competitiveness'

see Gregory Albo, "Competitive Austerity' and the Impasse of Capitalist Employment Policy' in R. Miliband & L. Panitch (eds.), *Between Globalism And Nationalism, Socialist Register 1994* (London: Merlin Press, 1996), pp. 148-57. For a critique of the empirical and theoretical appropriation of a reified Japanese 'model' as something 'progressive' see Paul Burkett & Martin Hart-Landsberg, 'The Use and Abuse of Japan as a Progressive Model' in L. Panitch (ed.), *Are There Alternatives? Socialist Register 1996*, pp. 62-92.

8 There are a number of ways that a regionalised model of East Asian capitalism has been constructed. For an extended critique that takes class-formation seriously see M. Bernard, 'States, Social Forces, Regions and Historical Time in the Industrialization of Eastern Asia', *Third World Quarterly*, 17:4, pp. 649-665. There are analysts such as Linda Weiss who distinguish between states that are 'rent-seeking' and those which have the capacity to promote 'competitiveness'.

9 For an example that focuses on Japan as core and the rest of the region as periphery see Rob Steven, *Japan and the New World Order* (London: MacMillan, 1996). For an example of dependency writing focused on the Asian NICs see Walden Bello & Stephanie Rosenfeld, Dragons in Distress (San Francisco: Food First Publications, 1991).

10 Leo Panitch, 'Globalisation and the State' in R. Miliband & L. Panitch (eds.), *Between Globalism And Nationalism, Socialist Register 1994* (London: Merlin Press, 1996), p. 67.

11 For a discussion of why social formations in Southeast Asia are not merely fledgling versions of Korea or Taiwan that takes class-formation seriously see M. Bernard, 'States, social forces and regions in historical time: toward a critical political economy of Eastern Asia', *Third World Quarterly*, 17:4 (1996), pp. 649-665.

12 On this point see M. Bernard & J. Ravenhill, 'Beyond Product Cycles and Flying Geese: Regionalization, Hierarchy and the Industrialization of East Asia', *World Politics*, 47 (1995), pp. 171-209.

13 For a more elaborate discussion of 'region-formation' see M. Bernard, 'Regions in the Global Political Economy: Beyond the Local-Global Divide in the Formation of the Eastern Asian Region', *New Political Economy*, 3:1 (November 1996), pp. 335-354.

14 This point is more fully developed in M. Bernard, 'States, Social Forces, Regions'.

15 *World Development Report, 1996*, World Bank.

16 Walden Bello, 'The Rise and Fall of South-east Asia's Economy', *The Ecologist*, January 1998, pp. 1-9.

17 *Ibid.*, p. 1.

18 R. J. Muscat, *The Fifth Tiger: A Study of Thai Development Policy* (Armonk, NY: M.E. Sharpe, 1994).

19 For a description of the Thai bourgeoisie and their emergence see A. Suehiro, *Capital Accumulation in Thailand, 1855-1985* (Tokyo: UNESCO Centre for East Asian Cultural Studies, 1989). On the origins of capitalism in Thailand more generally see Chaiyan Rajchagool, *The Rise and Fall of the Thai Absolute Monarchy* (Bangkok: White Lotus, 1994).

20 R. Doner and D. Unger, 'The Politics of Finance in Thai Economic Development' in S. Haggard et al., eds., *The Politics of Finance in Developing Countries* (Ithaca, N.Y.: Cornell University Press, 1993), pp. 95-6.

21 Akira Suehiro, 'Capitalist Development in Postwar Thailand' in R. McVey (ed.),

Southeast Asian Capitalists (Ithaca: Cornell Southeast Asia Program, 1992), pp. 42-50.

22 For a discussion of Thailand and the affects of the Vietnam War see from Benedict Anderson, 'Withdrawal Symptoms: Social and Cultural Aspects of the October 6 Coup', *Bulletin of Concerned Asia Scholars*, 9:3 (1977), pp. 13-30.

23 On the successive stages of regionalised production see M. Bernard, 'The Pattern and Implications of Trans-National Production in Eastern Asia', *Eastern Asia Policy Paper Series, No. 2*, University of Toronto - York University Joint Centre for Asia Pacific Studies, 1994.

24 On the new decidedly non-clientalistic role of capital in Thailand during the 1980s see Anek Laothamatas, *Business Associations and the New Political Economy of Thailand* (Boulder, Colorado: Westview Press, 1992).

25 It is instructive to note that the Thai army features one general for every 300-350 troops, ten times the ratio in advanced capitalist countries. In fact foreign military analysts assert that only about half of the 600 generals in the Army and Supreme Command Headquarters in Bangkok actually occupy military positions. See Stan Sesser, 'The Course of Corruption: Will Democracy Survive in Thailand — and Southeast Asia?', *Mother Jones*, 18:3 (October-December 1993), p. 46.

26 For a classic example see Samuel Huntington, *The Third Wave: Democratization in the Late Twentieth Century* (Norman, Oklahoma: University of Oklahoma Press, 1991).

27 See Benedict Anderson, 'Murder and Progress in Modern Siam', *New Left Review*, 181 (May-June 1990), pp. 39-42.

28 On Thailand and structural adjustment see R. J. Muscat, *The Fifth Tiger*.

29 For data on the regionalisation of Japanese production see M. Bernard and J. Ravenhill, 'Beyond Product Cycles and Flying Geese: Regionalization, Hierarchy and the Industrialization of Eastern Asia', *World Politics*, Vol. 47 (January 1995), pp. 171-209. For a descriptive account of attempts at macro-economic coordination among the advanced capitalist countries see Yoichi Funabashi, *Managing the Dollar: From the Plaza to the Louvre* (Washington DC: Institute for International Economics, 1989).

30 Bello, 'The Rise and Fall of South-east Asia's Economy', p. 2.

31 Takashi Shiraishi, 'Japan and Southeast Asia' in P. Katzenstein & T. Shiraishi (eds.), *Network Power: Japan and Asia* (Ithaca: Cornell University Press, 1997), p. 190.

32 Hatch & Yamamura, *Asia in Japan's Embrace* (Hong Kong: Cambridge University Press, 1996), p. 80.

33 Inoue Reiko, 'An Army of Japanese Tourists', *AMPO Japan-Asia Quarterly Review*, 22:4 (1991), p. 4.

34 On the political, social and ecological consequences of Japan as an food-importing 'super power' see Gavan McCormack, *The Emptiness of Japanese Affluence* (Armonk, N.Y.: M.E. Sharpe, 1996), pp. 113-149.

35 On the proletarianisation of rural Thailand see Philip McMichael, 'Agro-food Restructuring in the Pacific Rim' in Ravi Arvind Palat (ed.), *Pacific-Asia and the Future of the World System* (Westport, Conn: Greenwood Press, 1993), pp. 103-16.

36 R. J. Muscat, *The Fifth Tiger*.

37 For a detailed mapping of this process in the Malaysian context see Terence Gomez and Jomo, K. S., *Malaysia's Political Economy: Politics, Patronage and*

Profits (Cambridge: Cambridge University Press, 1997).
38 Chalmers Johnson, 'Cold War Economics Melt Asia', *The Nation*, February 23, 1998, p. 17.
39 Randall Germain, *The International Organization of Credit* (Cambridge: Cambridge University Press, 1997), pp. 103-136.
40 See Elmar Altvater, 'Financial Crises On The Threshold Of The 21st Century' in L. Panitch (ed.), *Ruthless Criticism Of All That Exists, Socialist Register 1997* (London: Merlin Press, 1997), pp. 48-74.
41 The details of financial reform are dealt with in fuller detail in Bello, 'The Rise and Fall of South-east Asia's Economy'.
42 On Thailand see *Ibid.*, p. 4. On Indonesia see *Far Eastern Economic Review*, 25, September 1997, p. 43.
43 For a good discussion of how the 'carry trade' worked see Louis Uchitelle, 'Borrowing Asia's Troubles', *New York Times*, 28 December 1997, pp. 4-1 & 4-6.
44 See Henry Sender, *Far Eastern Economic Review*, April 16, 1998, pp. 12-3.
45 *Far Eastern Economic Review*, 25 September 1997, p. 43.
46 *Ibid.*, p. 43.
47 Peter Warr, 'What Happened to Thailand', *The Asia-Pacific Magazine*, No. 9/10, pp. 30-1.
48 For a discussion of Charn Uswachoke and his attempt to turn Alphtech into Thailand's first integrated circuit manufacturer using cheap money and foreign technicians, see Ted Bardacke, *Financial Times*, 4 March, 1996, p. 9.
49 Chalmers Johnson, 'Cold War Economics Melt Asia', pp. 16-19.
50 Michael Vatikiotis, *Far Eastern Economic Review*, May 21, 1998, p. 62.
51 *International Herald Tribune*, 11 December, 1997, pp. 1 & 4. For spot market exchange rates for May 1997 see *Far Eastern Economic Review*, May 8, 1997, pp. 56.
52 A more detailed treatment of the Korean case can be found in M. Bernard, 'Globalization and the Political Economy of Financial Restructuring in Korea', paper presented at the Conference on East Asian Perspectives on World Order in the Twentieth Century, SUNY Buffalo, May, 1998.
53 These accounts are by and large economistic, synchronic and celebratory with regard to industrial production. Not surprisingly they tend to occlude any treatment of class conflict, ecological degradation and the brutality of a hyper-militarized authoritarian state. The best of these is J. E. Woo's *Race to the Swift: State and Finance in Korean Industrialization* (N.Y.: Columbia University Press, 1991). More typical is Alice Amsden's Schumpeterian account, *Asia's Next Giant: South Korea and Late Industrialization* (N.Y.: Oxford University Press, 1989).
54 K. D. Kim, 'Political Factors in the Formation of the Entrepreneurial Elite in South Korea', *Asian Survey*, 16:5 (1976), pp. 465-77.
55 J. E. Woo, *Race To The Swift*, pp. 151-159.
56 B.S. Choi, 'Financial Policy and Big Business in Korea' in S. Haggard et al., eds., *The Politics of Finance in Developing Countries* (Ithaca, N.Y.: Cornell University Press, 1993), pp. 35-7.
57 *Ibid.*, pp. 159-60.
58 *Korea Newsreview*, 27, November 1993, p. 9.
59 On the politics of restructuring in the early 1980s more generally see S. Haggard and C. I. Moon, 'The State, Politics, and Economic Development in Postwar

South Korea' in H. Koo (ed.), *State and Society in Contemporary Korea* (Ithaca, N.Y.: Cornell University Press, 1993), pp. 81-88.

60 M. Bernard, 'Globalisation, the State and Financial Reform in the East Asian NICs' in G. Underhill (ed.), *The New World Order in International Finance* (London: MacMillan, 1997), p. 230.

61 J. J. Choi, 'Political Cleavages in South Korea' in H. Koo (ed.), *State and Society in Contemporary Korea*, p. 44.

62 *The Economist*, March 23, 1996.

63 On the details of the pre-IMF failed attempt to restructure labour laws see Hochul Sonn, 'The Late Blooming of the south Korean Labour Movement', *Monthly Review*, 49:3 (1997), pp. 117-129.

64 John Burton, *Financial Times*, October 25, 1995, p. 6.

65 For a detailed account of Korea's credit bubble see 'Kankoku keizai bubarru hokai', *Aera*, 27 July 1997, pp. 20-39.

66 Although the terms of conditionality have not been publicly disclosed a summary of the frameworks of restructuring can be found in publicly available documents. For an example see 'Republic of Korea: IMF Stand-by Arrangement: Summary of the Economic Program, December 5, 1997'.

67 It is interesting to note the number of critiques of the bank that are emanating from within the bastions of orthodoxy. See Martin Feldstein, 'Refocusing the IMF', *Foreign Affairs*, 77:2 (March/April 1998), pp. 20-33 and Martin Wolf, 'Same Old IMF Medicine', The Financial Times, January 1998, p. 12.

68 Robert Wade & Frank Veneroso, 'The Asian Crisis: The High Debt Model Versus the Wall Street-Treasury-IMF Complex', *New Left Review*, 228 (March-April 1998), pp. 18-20.

69 Ted Bardacke, *Financial Times*, 5 March 1998, p. 6.

70 James Kynge, 'Economic Clouds darkened summit skies', *Financial Times*, 17 December 1997, p. 6.

71 Paul Abrahams, 'Weakening yen threatens to take neighbours down with it' *Financial Times*, 28 May 1998, p. 4.

72 Doug Henwood, *Wall Street* (London: Verso, 1997), pp. 11-12.

73 Eight state-run corporations have been selected for overseas sales in the latter half of 1998, including key revenue generators such as The Korea Tobacco & Ginseng Corporation, and the centre-piece of industrialization in the 1960-70s, Pohang Iron and Steel Corporation. The state plans to raise $12-13 billion in foreign capital through the gradual sale of the assets or shares in these corporations.

74 See 'Kim Ready to Accept Layoffs as Cost of Business Reform', *Korea Herald*, 11 May, 1998, p. 1.

75 Robert Wade & Frank Veneroso, 'The Asian Crisis', pp. 3-23.

76 The experience of the Philippines in the post-Marcos period provides a striking regional example of the devastating social consequences of the state remaining steadfast in its determination to repay the entire amount of the external debt owed.

STATE DECAY AND DEMOCRATIC DECADENCE IN LATIN AMERICA

Atilio A. Boron

The debate about the scope and promise of capitalist democracy has been reignited by the Latin American experience of democratization in the 1980s. This could hardly be more welcome in a continent where the authoritarian imprint of capitalism has very deep roots and where bourgeois revolutions have been an exception. The authoritarian features of Latin American societies can be traced back to both their colonial heritage and to their dependent and reactionary mode of capitalist development, by and large based upon latifundia and servitude and not, as in the United States, on the impulses stemming from a myriad of free farmers (Boron, 1989). Little wonder that if in her almost two centuries of independent political life Latin America did not have a single capitalist revolution culminating in the implantation of a democratic regime: neither Mexico between 1910 and 1917, nor Guatemala in 1944, nor Bolivia in 1952, let alone Brazil in 1964, concluded their 'unresolved questions' by establishing a democratic regime. These 'revolutions' had as their overriding concern making room for the development of capitalism, not the construction of a democratic order.

Yet, despite the legacy of its traumatic history, in the early 1980s Latin America seemed ready to try democracy again. This trend was reinforced by the world-wide democratic thrust that started to gain momentum in an unprecedented manner. Impressed by these events, Samuel P. Huntington argued that the world was surfing on a 'third democratic wave' (Huntington, 1991). Others, like Francis Fukuyama, saw in these developments the clear signs of a victorious capitalism that, hand in hand with a no less triumphant liberal democracy, was heralding the 'end of history' (Fukuyama, 1992). In face of this supposedly definitive victory and the unchallenged hegemony of neoliberalism, as well as of what Norberto Bobbio called 'the harsh rebuttals of history' (Bobbio, 1976) – including the resounding failure of 'really existing socialisms' and the inability of social democracy to transcend capitalism – a significant section of the left has accepted a mistaken conception of democracy that rests on two premises. On the one hand, the supposedly linear and irreversible nature of democratic progress; on the other hand, the belief, both historically false and theoretically wrong, that democracy is a project that is coterminous with the mere establishment of adequate representative and governmental institutions. The heroic enterprise of creating a democratic state is reduced to the establishment of a system of rules and procedures unrelated to the ethical and social context proper to democracy and indifferent to the implications that deep-seated social contradictions and class inequalities have for the political process. Thus (mis)understood, democracy is completely 'depoliticized', becoming a set of abstract rules and procedures that only pose 'technical' problems.

It is rather puzzling that democracy, being such a simple and reasonable political programme, has been able to arouse throughout history fierce passions and dogged resistance, bringing about revolutions and counter-revolutions, bloody civil wars, protracted popular struggles and brutal repressions of all sorts. Was all this drama – the drama of the West since the time of Pericles – just the result of a simple *malentendu*? Wouldn't it be more reasonable to think instead that the implantation of democracy reflects a peculiar outcome of class conflicts, something that goes beyond an innocent procedural arrangement? Looking at the historical experience of Brazil, for instance, how could we possibly account for the fact that it was much easier to abolish slavery – and the Empire that rested on slave labour – than to democratize Brazilian capitalism?

Capitalist Democracy or Democratic Capitalism? A Short Theoretical Note.

A substantive caveat is in order before going on. Throughout these notes the expression 'democratic capitalism' will be used instead of the more common 'capitalist democracy'. The reason, briefly speaking, is quite straightforward: the latter expression conveys the wrong idea – but a rather apologetic one – that in this type of political regime the 'capitalist' side of it is just an adjective that barely qualifies the workings of a full-blown democracy. On the contrary, 'democratic capitalism' captures the real essence of these regimes by pointing out that the democratic features of it are, for all its importance, hardly anything more than political modifiers of the underlying undemocratic structure of a capitalist society (Boron, 1995b: 189–220; Wood, 1995: 204–237)

The belated triumph of Schumpeterian ideas, which downsize the democratic promise to its formalistic and procedural arrangements, mirrors the narrow scope and limits of democratic capitalism (early noticed by Marx in *The Jewish Question* and other essays) by ignoring both the ethical content of democracy – as a crucial constituent element of any discourse dealing with the organization of a good society – as well as the practical-historical processes of constituting 'real existing democracies'. It is of crucial importance to realize that Schumpeter-inspired 'procedural' theories of democracy imply a radical departure from the classic argument developed by Western political tradition from Aristotle to Marx. Authors as diverse as Plato, Aristotle, Machiavelli, Rousseau, Marx and Tocqueville all considered democracy to be something completely different from what mainstream political scientists imagine today. Tocqueville's introductory chapter to his famous *Democracy in America*, for instance, portrays the epic nature of democratization with these moving words:

> This whole book has been written under the impulse of a kind of religious dread inspired by the contemplation of this irresistible revolution advancing century by century over every obstacle and even now going forward amid the ruins it has itself created (Tocqueville, 1969: 12).

Despite the compelling force of Tocqueville's historical fresco mainstream political science still looks upon democracy from an incredibly narrow perspective, considering it as a method solely aimed at the formation of a government and no longer as a condition of civil society. Instead, the critical and substantive approach nurtured in the Marxist tradition considers democracy as a unique amalgam binding together three inseparable components:

(a) first, democracy requires a social formation in which a given level – historically variable, of course – of material welfare and fundamental equality have been achieved, thus allowing for the full development of unique individuals and a plurality of expressions of social life;

(b) democracy implies the effective enjoyment of freedom by the citizenry, a freedom that has to be not only a formal entitlement but a living and practical day-to-day experience rooted in the main features of a given society. However, while necessary, these two social conditions are not sufficient to produce by themselves a democratic state. Other, not necessarily democratic outcomes would be conceivable as well. So, a third condition has to be met:

(c) the existence of a complex set of unambiguous institutions and rules of the game able to guarantee the relatively uncertain outcomes that characterize democratic states (Przeworski, 1985: pp. 138–145). This is the politico-institutional condition of democracy, a necessary one indeed; but not a sufficient one, because democracy is devalued as a political regime when it is embedded in a type of society, like capitalism, characterized by structures, institutions and ideologies antagonistic and/or hostile to its spirit.

A critical theoretical approach, therefore, would argue that a full-fledged democracy only exists when all these three conditions are met. As Adam Przeworski has observed, '(t)o discuss democracy without considering the economy in which this democracy is to function is an operation worthy of an ostrich' (Przeworski, 1990: p. 102). In practical terms democratic capitalisms, even the most developed ones, barely meet these standards: the institutional deficits of advanced democracies are very well known; and even more serious doubts are raised when minimum levels of social and economic equality are considered, or when the effective enjoyment of freedoms – distributed extremely unevenly among the different sections of the population – is taken into account (O'Donnell, 1994).

Democracy and Citizen's Confidence

Economic crises, a rebellious military, a despotic plutocracy, or a scheming American embassy have been crucial factors in explaining the long history of political instability and military *coups* in Latin America. In the past, every democratic step forward carried with it the menace of a blatant authoritarian regression. Nowadays, the situation has changed: important as they are, those factors have lost their critical importance. As some recent theorizing on democracy has argued, the major threat now besieging democracy is a much subtler and, perhaps, a more formidable foe: the loss of purpose and meaning of democracy itself due to its lack of depth, its poor quality, its unfairness and its incompleteness (Agero, 1994: pp. 5–7). In other words, the dangers come now from the inside rather than from the outside of our embattled and faulty democracies, downgraded to an abstract and empty set of rules deprived of much meaning for the citizenry and thus leading towards institutional decay (Haggard and Kaufman, 1992: p. 349), or towards 'delegative democracies' whose perverse form of endurance should be clearly distinguished from genuine democratic consolidations (O'Donnell, 1992: pp. 6–10).

The right to participate in the election of their government, granted by universal suffrage, confers on the citizens an aura of dignity and self-respect which is one of the landmarks of democracy. However, when democratically elected governments break the 'representative covenant' and display a total lack of compassion in face of the sufferings of their fellow-citizens it is highly likely that most of the latter will be inclined to think that democracy is just a sham. Of course, the erosion of a government's legitimacy does not mean that democracy as a political regime will necessarily succumb. However, if several successive governments – in many cases, from different political parties – prove unable to cope with democratic shortcomings and institutional decay, then the future of democracy will certainly be anything but bright.

The Western political tradition speaks with a single voice: contrary to other, non-democratic, regimes the stability of democracy is to a large extent contingent on popular confidence and citizens' beliefs. But Latin American democracies have proved progressively unable to stop the erosion of such confidence. Public opinion data for several Latin American countries are revealing. The proportion of those who feel dissatisfied with democracy ranged between 40% in Peru and Bolivia to 59% in Brazil and 62% in Colombia (Haggard and Kaufman, 1995: pp. 330–334).

Neoliberal Policies and Democratic Consolidation

Neoliberal economic reforms have become a major factor in the loss of democratic credibility. Accepted as an unchallenged dogma, neoliberalism was instrumental in the swift abandonment of time-honoured ideological tenets and policies. Latin America shares with Eastern Europe and Russia the dubious honour of being the part of the globe where the ideological influence of the Washington Consensus is felt with greatest intensity (Boron, 1995a: pp. 90–97). Even a moderate leader like Chile's former president Patricio Aylwin recognized that in his own country, usually regarded as a model to emulate, the most pressing issue confronting democracy was to redress the 'social debt' caused by neoliberal 'market-friendly' public policies.

Moreover, the ideological success of neoliberalism far exceeds the modest accomplishments – at inordinate social cost – it obtained in the terrain of the economy. The case of Chile is particularly instructive. By 1988 – i.e. after fifteen years of economic restructuring! – the real wages of Chilean workers were not much higher than they had been in 1973, notwithstanding the immense social costs implied by an average unemployment rate of 15% through most of this period. Between 1970 and 1987 the percentage of households under the poverty line increased from 17% to 38%, and in 1990 the per capita consumption of Chileans was still inferior to that of 1980 (Meller, 1992). After celebrating the 'important gains' experienced by urban minimum wages in Chile between 1990 and 1992 a recent CEPAL report concludes that they have now recovered the purchasing power they had achieved . . . in 1980! (CEPAL, 1994: p. 10). As was pointed out by Luiz C. Bresser Pereira, 'Chilean society probably would not have tolerated these transitional costs if the regime had been democratic' (1993: 38). Commenting on similar developments, Tomas Moulian observed in a recent book that despite official propaganda 'Chile is one of the few countries where the income of the top 20% of the population has gone up between 1960–69 and 1994, from 36.6% of the national income to 45.8%'. Moulian also noted that in a sample of 62 countries Chile's index of social equity ranked 54th, in a cluster formed among others by South Africa, Lesotho, Honduras, Tanzania, Equatorial Guinea, Panama, Guatemala and Brazil. After reviewing many specific studies Moulian concluded that the data for 1978–1994 'show a systematic and significative deterioration of the income distribution' (Moulian, 1997: pp. 93–95).

In Mexico, the social and economic involution experienced after more than a decade of orthodox adjustments is unconcealable. Official data show that per capita national income fell 12.4% between 1980 and 1990 despite the reformist rhetoric used by PRI governments to sell their conversion to neoliberalism (Altimir, 1992). In those years poverty increased significantly: between 1982 and 1988 real wages went down by 40% and have remained very close to that level ever since. Moreover the traditionally high level of Mexican unemployment went up and per capita consumption in 1990 was 7% lower than in 1990 (Bresser Pereira, 1993). According to Castañeda, 'when in 1992 the Mexican government published the first statistical accounts of income distribution in 15 years the data were terrifying' (Castañeda, 1993: pp. 283–4). However, official optimism was not disturbed by these revelations. It took the insurrection in Chiapas, two political assassinations, a huge trade deficit and, finally, the collapse of the Mexican peso in December 1994 to make the local elites and their advisors realize that things were pretty much out of control. The new emergency package launched by President Ernesto Zedillo was bound to exact, as usual, renewed hardships from the poor: governmental officials anticipated that the purchasing power of salaries was likely to decline another 32%, bringing greater personal sufferings and deprivation to most of the 90 million Mexicans (DePalma, 1995: A 1/10).

Monetary stabilization, the opening up of the economy, balanced budgets, deregulation, privatizations, the downsizing of the state and the free rein given to market forces do not seem to be enough to ensure self-sustained growth, let alone a more equitable income distribution or, last but not least, a supply of other non-commodifiable but essential values for a democracy such as justice, fairness and well-being (Bresser et al, 1993: pp. 203–205; Przeworski, 1992; Dahl, 1992). As Western European experience since the second war clearly shows, and as the most recent experience of Japan and south east Asia convincingly proves, capitalist development requires an appropriate mix of public policies, and this calls for a state endowed with effective capacities of intervention in (and regulation of) markets (Blackburn, 1991).

In this regard it is worth reminding ourselves that the accomplishments of Chile's economic restructuring – much praised by ideologues of the Washington Consensus, despite looking rather unimpressive when compared with South East Asia or China – has had as one of its most eccentric features the preservation of the strategic copper industry in government's hands, an embarrassing relic for the neoliberal blueprint, to say the least. Nationalized during the Allende years, state-owned copper firms account for about a half of all Chilean export revenues. This significant amount of cash goes directly to the treasury and not, as in Argentina, Brazil and most Latin American economies, into the pockets of private businessmen, thus strengthening the public finances and the capacities of the state apparatus. In 1995 the state-owned Corporacion del Cobre transferred to the Treasury 1,764 millions of dollars of its profits, a figure far superior to the taxes paid by all private firms in Chile (IHN, April 6, 1996). This economic 'aberration' is deliberately disregarded by neoliberal economists, who tirelessly preach that all forms of public property are inefficient or inflationary. In addition, the size of the Chilean state – measured by the ratio of public expenditures to GDP – grew continuously in the last decade, as did strict state regulations concerning the financial markets, two features clearly at odds with the neoliberal creed. Last but not least, the export performance of Chilean agriculture is closely related to the emergence of a new class of rural entrepreneurs, a by-product of a radical programme of agrarian reform launched by the socialist government of Salvador Allende in the early seventies. To sum up, Chilean economic restructuring does not seem to be a shining example of neoliberal policies (Bresser Pereira, 1993: p. 38). Yet, all these 'peculiarities' of the Chilean model have apparently passed unnoticed by the otherwise alert economists of the World Bank. In a recent official document – which includes a section called 'Chile as a Model' – the Bank's Chief Economist Sebastian Edwards fails to mention these facts even in a modest footnote (Edwards, 1993: pp. 34–35).

Some of the results of this 'free-market fundamentalism' have been quite uniform throughout Latin America. Both of the two countries the World Bank and the IMF used to regard as major 'success' stories – Chile and Mexico, the latter being now quietly removed from the list – as well as the other countries of the region, show the same results: the application of neoliberal policies has vastly increased the numbers of those living under conditions of 'extreme poverty', and widened the gulf separating rich and poor. For the sake of brevity, let us hear what an organization like CEPAL, little inclined to rhetorical excesses, has to say in this connection:

> Poverty is the greatest challenge for the economies of Latin America and the Caribbean. Between 1980 and 1990 it worsened as a result of the crisis and the adjustment policies, wiping out most of the progress in poverty reduction achieved during the 1960s and 1970s. Recent estimates place the number of poor at the beginning of this decade, depending on the definition of poverty, somewhere between 130 and 196 million... Recession and adjustment in the eighties also increased income inequality in most of the region. In the countries with the most highly concentrated income distribution, the richest 10% of the households receive 40% of the total income (CEPAL, 1994: 1).

Moreover, the deregulation of markets and privatization have also magnified the bargaining power of a handful of privileged collective actors who have direct access to the upper echelons of the government and the central bureaucracy, further aggravating inequalities. The impoverished and fragmented societies resulting from both the crisis and the conservative response to it do not constitute the most fertile soil for the flowering of democracy, or for upgrading the quality of Latin America's 'democratic governance'. The structural imbalance between: (a) a handful of very powerful bourgeois actors and 'market forces' reigning without adequate counterweights; (b) large sections of demobilized, disorganized, mostly apathetic, depoliticized or submissive populace; and (c) increasingly impotent democratic states, threatens to prevent the genuine consolidation of new democracies in the South.

The Withering-away of the Sovereign State: Fiscal Crisis and Globalisation

The unprecedented empowerment of private interests at the expense of everything public places Latin American democracies under the Damoclean sword of capitalist coalitions which can easily, and at almost no cost to themselves, destabilize the political process when they see fit. As a result, weak democratic states can only produce feeble and ineffective governments which, in due course, tend to aggrandize the social, economic and political weight of very rich and well-organized private collective actors (Przeworski, 1985: pp. 138–139). Given that capitalist economies are extraordinarily sensitive to the economic calculations and initiatives of entrepreneurs and that the weakened national states have left themselves with very few instruments of market regulation and control, most governments prefer to make sure of being able to count on the 'business community', even at the expense of declining levels of popular legitimacy and support. The outcome of this policy choice is a weakened democratic regime, where democratic arrangements are increasingly perceived as political rituals deprived of any relevance to the everyday life of the citizenry. The popular devaluation of democracy goes hand in hand with an analogous downgrading of politics, seen as a selfish game played by professional and corrupt politicians and wealthy and powerful notables with total disregard for the common citizen.

As a result, Latin American democracies find their state capacities progressively deteriorating and are unable to provide the collective goods needed for the bare reproduction of civilized life: health, education, housing, social security, food programmes, and so on. In this section we will examine two specific causes of this state enfeeblement: on the one hand, the persistence of the 'tax veto' still successfully wielded by capitalists throughout Latin America; and on the other, the effects of globalisation.

(i) The 'tax veto'

The Latin American rich refuse to pay taxes. They react with anger and contempt when governments try to tax their properties, profits and earnings. Even modest taxes on their private boats, airplanes, sport cars, fancy summer homes or other luxurious items are regarded as 'communist' confiscations. For them, the American IRS and Stalin's Politburo are twin institutions aimed at the destruction of private property and capitalist civilization. This 'tax veto' is an aberrant social and economic tradition dating back to colonial times, and it has periodically created unbearable pressures on the state budget. Because of outrageous legal loop-holes, systematic tax evasion, and the successful resistance of capitalists to modernizing and democratizing the tax system policy-makers have routinely tried to solve the fiscal crisis by cutting expenditures or, when possible, raising new indirect and socially regressive taxes. In both cases, the burden of the financial adjustment has rested on the shoulders of the workers and the poor. In Argentina, for instance, a research study sponsored by the World Bank proved that, in the late 1980s, the tax burden on the richest 10% of the population was equal to 27.0% of its total income, while the taxes paid by the poorest 10% of the population amounted to 29.3% of their earnings. Unfortunately, in this matter at least, the 'structural reform' launched by Menem in the 1990s only served to make things even worse (Santiere, 1989: p. 27).

With the debt crisis the chronic underfinancing of the state in Latin America became a source of major and urgent national and international concern. Why? Because heavily indebted countries, especially those which signed the Brady Plan, from then on had to run consistent budgetary surpluses in order to repay the principal and interest on an ever-growing external debt. Therefore, amidst the severe crisis of the 1980s Latin American states reinforced the recessive trends of the economy with fiscal policies that depressed even more the purchasing power of large sections of the population and shrank the incomes of the middle classes while creating (in accordance with fashionable 'supply-side' economics) new tax incentives for the rich. Harsh cuts in social expenditures and in public spending generally became one of the key elements of the neoliberal blueprint.

Yet the theorists of the Washington Consensus conceal the fact that the critical situation of the state accounts in Latin America is not caused by overgrown governmental expenses but by the chronic inability of governments to collect taxes from the wealthy. In this matter the World Bank's schizophrenia is notorious: while the research of its own experts conclusively proves the preposterous regressiveness of Latin American tax systems, the Bank's leaders exhort our governments to 'reduce the tax burden' in order to attract private investment. Despite the allegations of the neoliberal zealots, the tax burden (measured as a percent of the GDP and excluding social security contributions) of the more developed countries of Latin America is around 17% while in the OECD countries the proportion is more than twice as much, averaging 37.5%. Taxes on capital gains and profits, which in the OECD countries reach an average level of 14% of the GDP, are only 4% in Brazil, 3% in Argentina, Chile and Uruguay, and 1% in Bolivia (CEPAL, 1992, p. 92). It is astonishing that Latin American governments that were strong enough to dismantle and/or sell at very low prices large – and sometimes very efficient – public enterprises, shut down governmental agencies, terminate social programmes, privatize all kind of public services, destroy labour unions, savagely cut the public budget, and overwhelm public resistance to these policies, could at the same time present themselves as surprisingly weak and frail when faced with the task of organizing an equitable and progressive tax regime. The class selectivity of the neoliberal state is blatant: strong to promote the market forces and to advance the interests of big capital, weak to defend the public interest or to be responsive to the needs of the poor.

The outbreak of the debt crisis in Latin America hastened the relentless disarticulation of the state apparatuses and the retreat of the governments from policy-areas in which their contribution had been very important for large sections of the popular classes. If these countries fail to break the tax veto the reconstructed Latin American democratic capitalisms will bear much more resemblance to corrupt and mafia-ridden 'free-market' Russia than to tidy Switzerland or Austria.

(ii) Globalisation and External Vulnerability

The process of economic globalisation has only made things worse: the tax veto coupled with globalisation has led to a radical weakening of the national states' administrative and decision-making capacities, a decline in the quality of governance and growing levels of vulnerability in face of an increasingly complex domestic and international environment. Latin America's new democracies are first and foremost responsive to the interests of foreign creditors and key sections of international capital and its watchdogs, the World Bank and the International Monetary Fund; second, they respond to domestic 'market forces', a euphemism for big capital and the firms, local or foreign, that operate in our markets; third, and much later, to the citizenry at large. It is very hard to conceive of a solid democracy that does not reach a minimum threshold of national sovereignty. Otherwise states are deprived of the means to make autonomous decisions in crucial matters that will inevitably have severe distributional impacts. The globalisation of economic activities has also sometimes caused the new Latin American democracies to transfer decision-making powers in a growing number of sensitive areas to transnational firms and international financial institutions under the guise of commercial agreements, 'conditionalities' and 'country risk' evaluations. Monetary, industrial, commercial and fiscal policies, hitherto by and large decided within the national boundaries of Latin America, are today settled in New York, Washington, London, Paris, or Tokyo, far removed from the reach, let alone the control, of the citizenry. In short, given the formidable reach of globalisation, and the reinforcement of financial dependence due to the external debt, a weak state increasingly deprived of decisional autonomy is likely to decay.

These processes of globalisation and state enfeeblement are, moreover, far from neutral in their distributional impact. Local capitalists and their metropolitan partners obtained several gains from the downsizing of the old developmentalist state: first, they significantly reinforced their economic predominance by drastically reducing public control of the markets and economic activities, and undermining both the consistency and the scope of the public sphere itself. Today, Latin American societies have become highly 'privatized': the state has retreated to minimal functions, and former collective goods (health, nutrition, education, housing, occupational training, and so on) have become individual problems that must be solved according to the egotistic rules of the market place. The name of the game is the survival of the fittest; the poor, the elderly, the children, the sick, the homeless, the unemployed and unemployable are the new clients of the Red Cross and a host of other non-governmental organizations. Private charity and altruistic associations are substituted for supposedly cost-ineffective social policies and state intervention. Secondly, the wholesale privatization of state-owned enterprises and state-administered services has transferred highly profitable monopolies to capitalists and guaranteed the repayment of the foreign debt by irresponsible, corrupt and *de facto* military rulers. Neoliberalism supplied the general justification for the transfer of public assets and state-owned enterprises, paid for with public savings, even in areas considered untouchable until a few years ago, like electricity, aviation, oil and telephones. Thirdly, these reforms have changed the balance between state and markets so dramatically in favour of the latter that any future government sensitive to popular demands, or inspired by even some vague reformist vocation, will immediately realize that it lacks some of the most elementary instruments of public policy-making as well as the efficient administrative cadres needed to carry out these tasks. This is why one of the most urgent tasks facing Latin American societies is the reconstruction of the state. As a former minister of industry in Venezuela rightly observed, by the end of the 1990s 'Washington may encounter some surprises to the south. Latin America, which has spent the last 10 years demolishing the state, will spend the next 10 rebuilding it' (Naim, 1993: p. 133).

Civil Society and Democratic Governance in Peripheral Capitalism

Even in Western Europe the social involution resulting from the relative rolling-back of the gains made during the heyday of the welfare state has prompted some scholars to talk about a 'two-thirds' society: a wide sector roughly comprising one third of the population has been progressively excluded from the benefits of material progress, doomed to become an underclass or a decaying segment of modern society, unable to be 'reconverted' and reinserted in the formal labour markets of advanced capitalism (Gorz, 1989). The economist Richard Freeman recently suggested in the *Harvard Business Review* that the United States may be moving toward an 'apartheid economy,' in which 'the rich live aloof in their exclusive suburbs and expensive apartments with little connection to the working poor in their slums' (Freeman, 1996, p. 120).

Yet this is not only a question of the immorality of social exclusion. The enduring legacy of neoliberalism is also a society whose social integration has been debilitated by the impact of unfettered market dynamics, worn out by the tremendous cleavages and inequities that characterize 'really existing capitalism'. Therefore, contrary to what is expected in at least Western European societies, it is not unlikely that in Latin America – a continent where the benefits of the welfare state arrived belatedly and in homeopathic doses – the 'two-thirds' are more likely to consist of those condemned to exclusion and marginality, while just one third, the bourgeoisie and the upper sections of the middle classes, will enjoy the charms of economic well-being and 'postmodernity'.

A society of this type is scarcely appropriate to sustain a democratic order. Paradoxical as it may seem, slave-owner Brazil and colonial Mexico were far more integrated as societies than their late twentieth century capitalist successors. The exploitation of the subordinated classes demanded, in those pre-capitalist modes of production, some forms of sociability, structural integration, and inter-class relationships that are largely absent in Brazil or Mexico today. The *fazendeiro* and the slaves, the landowner and the indigenous peasant, were antagonistic poles but both belonged to the same society. Their contradictions developed within a single social and economic structure, unified by the exploitative bonds of slavery and servitude and by a host of other social relations. Whereas, at the end of the twentieth century the Latin American bourgeoisie (and its allied social groups and classes) and the masses living in appalling poverty belong, on the contrary, to two entirely different social universes. The perverse fragmentation of modern capitalism has created dual societies in which people coexist only in an illusory manner thanks to the vicarious integration provided by television. In fact, rich and poor increasingly tend to live socially, culturally, economically and ecologically in worlds apart.

Referring to the case of the United States, Robert Reich, the former Secretary of Labor in the Clinton Administration, has remarked that as a result of neoliberal policies there are in America people living in the same society, but in two completely different economies (Rifkin, 1995: p. 180). The assertion is even truer in Latin America, where the bourgeoisie and the 'winners' in the game of capitalist restructuring seek refuge in exclusive residential districts, protected by sophisticated surveillance systems and a small army of security guards of all sorts. Their children go to private schools and bilingual institutes along with others of the same social class and then are sent to continue their education in American colleges and universities. If ill, the bourgeois will travel to Houston or Miami to see his/her doctor; for their entertainment they prefer New York, London or Paris. The source of their wealth is a global process of capital accumulation undertaken in a broad array of highly diversified economic activities where physical contact with a member of the labouring masses is an extraordinary and highly unlikely event. What economic and social relationship, if any, can exist between this social creature, the 'end-of-the-century bourgeois,' and the millions of 'wretched of the earth' that make their living selling candies, gums, cigarettes, and other cheap goods in the busiest intersections of our decaying cities? Or as fire-eaters or ragged clowns on downtown sidewalks? Or as occasional windshield cleaners at congested traffic lights? Or as precarious and informal workers who are barely able to speak the language of the country, have few skills and no formal education, have never seen a doctor, and live in tin and cardboard shacks? As Darcy Ribeiro once noted, not only do these people not fight against capitalist exploitation, they have a fervent desire to become an exploitable labour force. They are more than willing to do whatever is necessary in order to get an entrance ticket, albeit an expensive one, to the worst echelons of the system.

But, for this to be possible they first have to acquire the qualifications that may convert them into a 'usable' and exploitable labour force, an almost impossible task when neoliberal restructuring is destroying the state and dismantling social services, including public education and health; and there is no other place in which these masses may obtain the minimum training needed for entering into the formal labour market. For growing sections of Latin American societies class exploitation is not their most immediate problem. Their handicap is precisely their inability to become exploited.

Democratic governance, the art of good government, brings us back to Plato's metaphor of the statesman as the helmsman: is a good helmsman likely to be elected by these kinds of desperate boat passengers? Reacting to this question, conservative thinkers would argue in favour of some more or less subtle form of popular disenfranchisement, in order to let 'responsible' people conduct the business of government without interference from the rabble. Discussing the governability crisis of the early seventies Samuel P. Huntington wrote that the problems besieging industrialized countries were not capitalism's fault but the consequence of democracy's excesses (Huntington, 1975: pp. 73, 106–113). His thesis was wrong then and it is wrong again now. The main problem undermining democracy and democratic governance at the end of the century is precisely capitalism – the ways in which capitalist production and bourgeois societies have evolved – and not the supposedly inevitable self-destructive tendencies of democracy (Galbraith, 1992; Chomsky, 1996).

Of course, to address these challenges requires much more than delicate political engineering. An adequate institutional setting, a reasonable compromise between the elites, the improvement in the quality of political leadership and the betterment of the public policies carried out by the emerging democracies would be good, but not enough. Much more fundamental changes are required in the very structure of capitalist societies, and to this effect a radical programme of social and economic reform is badly needed. Improved democratic institutions and practices must always be welcome as valuable assets, but it would be naive to expect from them a miraculous cure for the deep-ingrained ills of Latin American capitalism. Political reform must go hand in hand with social and economic reform: a progressive tax reform, which is the cornerstone of any programme of social and economic transformation; the restructuring of the state, aimed at enhancing its capacity of effective intervention to regulate markets, and provide public goods essential for the bare survival of the poor, the children, the unemployed, the women, the elderly and the peasant populations; the deepening and strengthening of democratic institutions, bringing new life to a political scene dominated by empty structures and inconsequential political rituals, and significantly upgrading the popular responsiveness and accountability of governments; finally, a programme of social and economic reconstruction able to heal the wounds left by years of irresponsible and disastrous neoliberal witchcraft. A whole programme of structural reforms aimed at the radical transformation of capitalist formations must take precedence over the repayment of an illegitimate foreign debt, the preservation of budget equilibria, or the maintenance of a 'friendly atmosphere' for investors.

Obviously enough, neoliberals strongly disagree with this. In a notorious interview given to the Chilean conservative newspaper *El Mercurio* during the Pinochet years, Friedrich von Hayek asserted that, for a while, he was ready to sacrifice democracy and political rights in exchange for a governmental programme committed to the unfettered development of capitalism. In the end, Hayek ventured, economic freedoms would reassert themselves and open the door to democracy and political liberty. For socialism, on the contrary, democracy, liberty and justice are higher and more cherished values than free markets and profits. Political liberty is a necessity, John Stuart Mill used to say; economic liberty is a convenience. The goal of a reform-minded democratic leadership in Latin America should be, first of all, to make our countries safe for democracy, freedom and justice. Nothing more, but also nothing less. Marx believed that democracy was incompatible with capitalism and that, in the end, the former would prevail over the later. Tocqueville expressed as a concern what for Marx was the possibility of a victorious and liberating outcome. If democracy is, in Tocqueville's words, that 'irresistible revolution advancing century by century over every obstacle and even now going forward amid the ruins it has itself created', will it respectfully stop at the gates of the capitalist society? It does not at all seem likely.

REFERENCES

Agero, Felipe (1994) 'Democratic Governance in Latin America: Thinking about Fault Lines', Miami, North-South Center.

Altimir, Oscar (1992) 'Cambios en las desigualdades de ingreso y en la pobreza en America Latina', Buenos Aires, Instituto Torcuato Di Tella.

Blackburn, Robin (1991) 'Socialism after the Crash', *New Left Review,* No. 185, January–February, pp. 5–66.

Bobbio, Norberto (1976) 'Esiste una dottrina marxista dello stato?', in Federico Coen, ed., *Il marxismo e lo Stato* Roma, Quaderni di Mondoperaio.

Boron, Atilio A. (1989) 'Authoritarian ideological traditions and transition towards democracy in Argentina', *The Institute of Latin American and Iberian Studies*, Occasional Paper No. 8, New York, Columbia University.

Boron, Atilio A (1995a) 'A sociedade civil depois do dilœvio neoliberal', in Emir Sader and Pablo Gentili, eds., *Pos-Neoliberalismo. As politicas sociais e o Estado democratico*, Rio de Janeiro, Paz e Terra, 1995.

Boron, Atilio A. (1995b) *State, Capitalism, and Democracy in Latin America*, Boulder and London, Lynne Rienner Publishers.

Bresser Pereyra, Luiz C. (1993) 'Economic reforms and economic growth: efficiency and politics in Latin America' in L. C. Bresser Pereira, J. M. Maravall and A. Przeworski, eds., *Economic Reforms in New Democracies. A Social-Democratic Approach*, Cambridge, Cambridge University Press, pp. 15–76.

Castaneda, Jorge (1993) *La Utopia Desarmada*, Buenos Aires, Ariel.

CEPAL (1994) *Panorama Social de America Latina* Santiago, CEPAL.

CEPAL (1992) *Equidad y Transformacion Productiva. Un Enfoque Integrado*, Santiago, CEPAL.

Chomsky, Noam (1996) *Class Warfare*, Monroe, Maine, Common Courage Press.

Chomsky, Noam (1996) *Powers and Prospects. Reflections on Human Nature and the Social Order*, Boston, South End Press.

Dahl, Robert (1992) 'Why free markets are not enough', *Journal of Democracy*, Volume 3, No. 3, July, pp. 82–89.

DePalma, A. (1995) 'Mexicans ask how far social fabric can stretch', *New York Times*, New York, A 1/10.

Edwards, Sebastian (1993) *America Latina y el Caribe. Diez a–os despues de la crisis de la deuda*, Washington, D.C., Banco Mundial.

Feinberg, Richard (1990) 'Comment', in John Williamson, ed., *Latin American Adjustment: How Much has Happened?*, Washington, D. C.: Institute for International Economics, pp. 21–24.

Freeman, Richard (1996) 'Toward An Apartheid Economy,' *Harvard Business Review* (September–October).

Fukuyama, Francis (1992) *The End of History and the Last Man*, New York, The Free Press.

Galbraith, John Kenneth (1992) *La Cultura de la Satisfaccion* Buenos Aires, Emece Editores.

Gorz, Andre (1989) *Critique of economic reason*, London, Verso.

Haggard, Stephan and Robert R. Kaufman, eds., (1992) *The Politics of Economic Adjustment. International Constraints, Distributive Conflicts, and the State*, Princeton, N.J., Princeton University Press.

Haggard, Stephan and Robert R. Kaufman (1995) *The Political Economy of Democratic Transitions*, Princeton, Princeton University Press.

Meller, Patricio (1992) 'Latin American Adjustment and Economic Reforms: Issues and Recent Experience', Santiago, CIEPLAN, mimeo.

Moulian, Tomas (1997) *Chile Actual. Anatomia de un Mito*, Santiago, ARCI/Ediciones LOM.

Naim, Moises (1993) 'Latin America: Post-Adjustment Blues', *Foreign Policy*, Fall, No. 92, pp. 133–150.

O'Donnell, Guillermo (1992) 'Delegative Democracy?', Working Paper No. 172,

Kellogg Institute.

O'Donnell, Guillermo (1994) 'The State, Democracy, and some Conceptual Problems', in William C. Smith, Carlos H. Acu–a and Eduardo A. Gamarra, eds., *Latin American Political Economy in the Age of Neoliberal Reform*, Miami, North-South Center, pp. 157–169.

Przeworski, Adam (1992) 'The Neoliberal Fallacy', *Journal of Democracy*, Volume 3, No. 3, July, pp. 45–59.

Przeworski, Adam (1985) *Capitalism and Social Democracy*, Cambridge, Cambridge University Press.

Przeworski, Adam (1990) *The State and the Economy under Capitalism*, London & New York, Harwood Academic Publishers.

Rifkin, Jerome (1995) *The End of Work. The Decline of the Global Labor Force and the Dawn of the Post-Market Era*, New York, G.P. Putnam's Sons.

Wood, Ellen Meiksins (1995) *Democracy against Capitalism. Renewing Historical Materialism*, Cambridge, Cambridge University Press.

World Bank (1991) *World Development Report, 1991. The Challenge of Development*, Oxford, Oxford University Press.

COMRADES AND INVESTORS: THE UNCERTAIN TRANSITION IN CUBA

Haroldo Dilla

Much to the delight of technocrats and businessmen, the Cuban government has made what it calls economic reform its immediate priority. It was not as if it had very many choices. The disintegration of the Eastern bloc economies and later of the Soviet Union was a serious blow to the Cuban economy. Between 1986 and 1989 it had been virtually stagnant, and the brutal decline which began in 1990 meant that by 1993 the accumulated contraction of GNP had come close to 40%. The situation of the external sector was even more complex; suddenly, the country lost 85% of its traditional (and often preferential) markets, almost all its long and medium term lines of credit and its main sources of technology. Its capacity for imports fell by nearly two thirds.

In this situation, the customary hostility of the Cuban political leadership to the market gave way to a pragmatic acceptance of a series of linked realities. Cuba had to enter the capitalist world market, on a strictly competitive basis; for that to happen it would have no choice but to restructure many of its most basic economic and social organizations. In a memorable speech on July 26th 1993, the Cuban President, Fidel Castro, recognised the limiting conditions of the immediate programme of action: the preservation of the gains of the revolution in anticipation of better times, when socialist construction could resume its course.

Despite the bureaucratic obstacles placed in its way, and frequent setbacks, the process of economic liberalization and adjustment has been surprisingly rapid. The opening to foreign investment began in 1987; in 1995, a specific regulatory law gave investors broad legal protection. In 1992 a sweeping constitutional amendment was approved which recognised the right to private ownership of the means of production and opened the door to the decentralization of state enterprises by abolishing the state monopoly over foreign trade. One year later, in the midst of a dramatic collapse in GDP, ordinary Cubans were given permission to hold dollars and other strong currencies which could be spent in a chain of shops which until then could be used only by resident foreigners, tourists and a small local elite. During the same period, a significant proportion of state lands passed to cooperatives or, in a smaller number of cases, to small farmers. Self-employment in the service sector was also encouraged by the passage of favourable legislation.

In 1994 a process of budget adjustment, price increases and the imposition of taxes began with the aim of reducing a vastly excessive liquidity. In the second half of the same year, even though the state authorized a free market in food, throughout the eighties official discourse had repeatedly denounced the very notion. For just as the basket of basic necessities was slowly being reduced, a substantial proportion of popular consumption was taking place in a free dollar market which paid no regard to the wages earned by workers. Steps taken through 1996 and 1997 simply served to consolidate the processes already under way by successive changes in legislation and transformations of economic institutions: free trade zones were recognized in four areas of the country, the customs laws were modified, the banking system was reorganized, etc.

The Cuban political leadership has repeatedly proclaimed the achievements of its policy of opening to the market throughout this tough period. The economy was rescued from collapse, and after 1995, began to register significant rates of growth. And it must be acknowledged that this closed one option to which the U.S. extreme right and its associates in Miami aspired – a great march against a revolution in full economic collapse. Considering that these results have been achieved in the midst of a confrontation with the United States, whose economic blockade and politics of intervention have been the catalyst for the crisis, they can clearly be seen to merit recognition as having a historic national and international significance.

In the second place, the official line is that the recovery has been possible without recourse to orthodox neo-liberal measures, without sacrificing the public health service, education or social security, whose budgets have been maintained or have actually increased (they represent 60% of public spending), and preserving a clear and distinct role for the state. This too is undoubtedly a recognisable achievement that confirms the social commitment embedded in the programme of the revolution.

A number of questions remain, however, for any observer who remains convinced of the historical value of the Cuban revolutionary heritage. The process of liberalization and economic adjustment in Cuba differs from other similar processes elsewhere in Latin America not only for the reasons referred to earlier, but because what has happened in Cuba is not simply an adjustment to an existing standard capitalist mode of operation but a radical restructuring of the political economy, the forms of social regulation and cultural-ideological production. This is a qualitative transformation of profound significance; the slow commercial colonization of socialized areas of the economy has posed challenges at many levels to the most central of all political questions – the distribution of power. If we take as axiomatic the fact that a combination of militant anti-imperialism and the provision of free social services does not amount to socialism, we are left with a question as to the real depth of these systemic changes: first, at the social (and more specifically the class) level and, second, at the level of the rearticulation of the whole of political life.

It is central to this writer's thinking that the reforms are producing a recomposition of social classes as a consequence of the emergence of a technocratic-entrepreneurial bloc, and that that process is to the detriment of the popular classes. This tendency towards the restoration of capitalism in the country (in the name of socialism and under the direction of the Communist Party) is not inevitable. Therefore a second central idea informing this essay is that alternative paths exist that would permit the maintenance of socialism, and that they are inseparable from the articulation of the Cuban revolutionary agenda with an alternative left project at the international level. This would imply a major renovation of the political system in the direction of genuine popular power.

A subsidized utopia?

The dynamics of Cuban society between 1959 and 1989 were dominated by two contradictory tendencies: social levelling and social mobility. The first prevailed through the early years as a consequence of the radical reality of the revolution. It led to the virtual liquidation of the bourgeoisie and a significant proportion of the middle class, who either emigrated or underwent a process of proletarianization. Gradually, the society came to be organized around social and state ownership of the means of production. At the same time, this social levelling was accompanied by the rising social mobility of the majority of the people, particularly during the seventies, through state programmes for the provision of jobs and social services. By way of illustration – in 1953 57% of the population lived in urban areas, around 25% of the population were illiterate and only 11% had intermediate or higher education qualifications. By 1989, the last year in which annual statistics were published, 73% of a population of 10.5 million were living in urban areas – and some 38% in cities of over 100,000 population.[1] Illiteracy was by then a distant memory; over half the population had reached sixth grade of secondary education and there were around half a million technicians and professionals. Over 140,000 people, in addition, were involved in higher education.

This intense social mobility, while it led to an objective differentiation between social subjects, did not have corresponding effects on the self-identification of social sectors; that identity was determined by other factors, including the tendency to emphasize the concept of 'el pueblo' (the people) as the sociopolitical subject of social transformation and national defence. The political system acknowledged this through its adoption of the Leninist model of sectional organization which acted as 'transmission belts' between the people and the 'vanguard' organized in the Communist Party.[2] The result, inevitably, was a high level of concentration of political authority, given the monopoly of the revolutionary political class in the regulation of social life, in at least three senses.

First, the power to assign resources through a single, centralized and directive planning mechanism was reinforced by Cuba's entry into the Soviet economic bloc at the beginning of the seventies (from then until 1987 the Cuban economy experienced extensive growth with relatively abundant resources within the framework of a political economy characterised by undemanding production targets, equitable distribution and subsidised consumption). Second, the Leninist model of political organization, lubricated by a high level of political consensus, became a powerful mechanism of social control, not only with regard to the repression of counter-revolutionary tendencies (which were insignificant in real terms after the early sixties) but above all in relation to popular mobilizations on the one hand and the socialization of values and political behaviour on the other.

Third, and no less significant, was the capacity of the political leadership to produce a credible legitimating ideology which functioned as a kind of teleological paradigm in relation to both internal and external factors. This ideology exhibited a certainty that left little possibility for doubt about the actual, the possible and the best. It was coherent, given the close interrelation between the perceptions of day-to-day reality emanating from the social structure and official discourse; and it was accessible to the ordinary citizen, sharing values at the heart of national political culture which emphasised ethical principles like patriotism, internationalism and social justice as the motor of politics. Capitalism and all its organic components – the bourgeoisie, consumerism, inequality, the market, etc. – were fiercely anathematized and regarded as part of a past that would not be given a second opportunity.

Yet this structure contained within it serious contradictions between the declared goal of the socialization of power and the gradual appropriation of that power by a bureaucratic layer that had first emerged during the sixties and whose power was definitively consolidated in the subsequent decade through the so-called 'institutionalization' process. In systemic terms, the establishment of this bureaucratic layer could only be achieved by extending clientelistic relations, slowing down the socialization of power and consequently paralyzing the socialist development project itself.

History has exposed both the virtues and the drawbacks of this way of regulating social and political life. In a society with a low level of what Giddens has called 'universalization and social reflexivity', such a system of political regulation could function effectively;[3] among other things, it made possible a successful confrontation with the very real aggression from the north, it facilitated the mobilization and equitable distribution of disposable resources and it promoted a culture of political solidarity and a vast network of mechanisms of social participation and political mobilization. But its own achievements implied its approaching obsolescence, especially as people's mobility and high qualifications began to clash with the rigid mechanisms of socio-political control, producing dysfunctions like apathy and anomie. Economic reforms have dealt with the rest. The market, a discreet actor in earlier decades, began to play an increasingly key role in the allocation of resources and the distribution of the meagre surplus – and consequently in the reshaping of the relations of power. And ordinary Cubans began to realize to their astonishment that the future was nothing like as certain as the official discourse had suggested for so long.

Society, politics and the relations of power in the new era

It has been one of the constants of the official Cuban discourse that the political structures should be periodically renewed; on the other hand, this has been limited by a number of other factors, ranging from the inviolability of certain precepts, like the single party, to the refusal to countenance any changes induced by external pressures – an understandable refusal, of course, given the U.S.'s commitment to changing the Cuban political system to the point where it could resume its role as a decisive actor in the internal affairs of the country.

1990 was a crucial year in the dynamics of political renewal. It was not exactly a good year; since 1987 the economy had shown a stubborn tendency to decline which could not be reversed even by the 'rectification' proclaimed by the political leadership. The ideological constructions around the irreversible nature of socialist progress had sustained some heavy blows as a result first from the effects of perestroika and second by the less than edifying spectacle of the collapse of the Berlin Wall. Then, in the latter half of 1989, Cuban society was shaken by a public exposé of corruption among high officials of the armed forces and security services as well as civilian agencies.

The need to recover consensus and reaffirm the legitimacy of the regime was recognised as urgent by the political class on the eve of the Fourth Congress of the Cuban Communist Party scheduled for 1991.[4] The Party therefore called for a public debate whose purpose would be to '...make possible a consensus based on a recognition of the diversity of views that exists within the population and strengthened by democratic discussions within the Party and the Revolution, above all in the search for solutions, the examination of the means of achieving our socio-economic objectives, and in general in the perfection of our society.' For several months, Cuba experienced the freest and most democratic public debate in its history. Millions of people in thousands of settings (schools, labour halls, community centres) exercised their right to criticise, to propose solutions or simply to offer opinions on questions ranging from daily life to public policy. The results of these debates were never published, but the various reports and comments reflected a demand for profound renewal of the system within the framework of an enduring commitment to social objectives and national independence. The Cuban political class had access to more than enough information to judge the state of mind, aspirations and opinions of the majority of the Cuban people.

The political changes that occurred in the two subsequent years tried to take these demands into account, but rarely managed to be more than a pale reflection of the intensity of the earlier debates. In the first place a substantial constitutional reform was enacted which modified some 60% of the original document. Although most of these changes referred to the economic sphere (the system of property ownership, the decentralization of foreign trade, etc.), others, at least theoretically, touched on what Azcuy has called the 'hard core' of the 1976 Constitution:[5] the declaration of the non-denominational character of the State and the prohibition of any discrimination against religious believers; the removal of all references to democratic centralism and the unity of power; the removal of the strictly class-based definition of the social base of the State; the organization of direct parliamentary elections; etc. A subsequent Electoral Law reaffirmed the latter provision. It had the virtue of reaffirming that the Communist Party would not intervene in the selection of candidates or the elections themselves, and of reinforcing the role of the social and mass organizations in these areas; but it limited its democratic impact by placing restrictions on the principle of competition which had been the cornerstone of the much-vaunted local elections. At the same time new sub-municipal structures – the popular councils (*consejos populares*) – were created which came to play an important role in mobilizing local resources, in local decision-making and in some cases in drawing up community projects with a strong element of participation and self-management.

But what some sectors had envisaged as the auspicious beginning of the construction of a pluralist, participatory democracy, a political response to questions about socialist continuity under new social conditions, proved to be a series of changes on matters of detail that had more to do with good government than with democracy. In other words, if politics is not only, nor even principally, a question of norms or institutions but above all, according to Held, a question of the interaction of actors and subjects through the control of mechanisms of resource and value allocation, then we can affirm that politics in Cuba began to suffer a slow decline with the imposition of a new model of accumulation whose most crucial expression was the reorganization of the social networks of power.[6] Thus the formal changes that can be carried out today will be very different from those that may be realized in the future, when the configuration of forces has changed significantly. A brief analysis of the process of social reconfiguration will show a double tendency: the strengthening of a technocratic-entrepreneurial bloc that benefits from its links to the market and has real possibilities of becoming the hegemonic social layer; and at the same time, the fragmentation and weakening of the popular sectors.

Recycling the elites

From the point of view of this essay the most obvious result of the process of opening and reform has been the creation of an incipient new social bloc, which we shall call 'technocratic-entrepreneurial', within which three basic components can be identified. The first is located within the ambit of foreign investment. According to available statistics, in 1990 there were no more than twenty or so foreign investors. In 1994 there were 176 joint foreign enterprises, with investments of the order of $1.5 bn.[7] These involved 36 countries and 26 areas of economic activity. At the same time, 400 commercial companies were functioning inside Cuba.[8] By the end of 1996, the number of foreign investors had risen to 260, some of which were beginning to establish themselves in the newly-created free-trade zones (*zonas francas*). In the same year, 800 foreign firms were operating.[9] As the organs concerned are joint enterprises with the State, this sector is closely tied to a layer of entrepreneurs and local businessmen who share experiences, lifestyles and aspirations substantially different from the rest of the population.

The second component of this emerging bloc is formed by directors of state enterprises who have found themselves a favoured place in the world market and achieved a considerable autonomy as a result. Their new functions are incompatible with the traditional image of a public administrator within a centralized planned economy locked into the tragic triad of knowing nothing, doing nothing and wanting nothing. In his place there arises a new type of local entrepreneur more concerned with profit maximization than any other political considerations. The number of firms within that layer will also increase as the reform process continues.

A third (potential) component of this bloc is represented by those people (wealthy peasants, commercial intermediaries, service providers, etc.) who have accumulated large sums of money and other property through speculation on the black market, frequently at the expense of state resources. Given that most of these fortunes were illegally acquired, it is impossible to quantify their economic potential. But we can make an estimate by analyzing current bank accounts, where approximately 60% of the liquid cash is deposited and which in recent years have demonstrated a disquieting tendency towards concentration. According to figures issued by the Cuban National Bank and other official agencies, in late 1994 14.1% of the total accounts contained 77.8% of the total amount of savings. A year later,

13.1% of the accounts contained 83.7% of the total and by 1996 the concentration had reached the point where 12.8% of the total number of accounts (some 600,000 accounts) represented 84.7% of the total, some 6.6 billion pesos.[10] More significant perhaps is the fact that in the same year 2.7% of accounts contained 43.8% of all savings.

With the liberalization of markets in agricultural and industrial products, and the extension of self-employment, this sector has not only grown and 'laundered' its fortunes, but has also established increasing control over the circuits of circulation and realization in the internal market. In a not too distant future this sector will become an investor in small and medium enterprises and will become contractors to the formal sector of the economy, which will in turn expand its potential for accumulation.

It will come as no surprise that the social origin of these groups, and particularly of the first two, is the traditional civilian and military bureaucracy and their families, as well as young technocrats recruited and patronized by them. Even the third group reveals the close connection between the most prosperous private enterprises – restaurants and tourist accommodation – and retired top bureaucrats and their families, for both these activities require comfortable, centrally located accommodation of a type usually assigned by the State to this social layer. Pareto would undoubtedly have felt entirely vindicated by these developments.

The fragmentation of the popular sectors

Before 1989, the Cuban working classes were a relatively homogeneous sector. In that year, some 3.5 million people, 94% of the workforce employed in the civil sector consisted of wage earners in the state economy, the majority of whom were organized into trade unions supported by a very paternalistic labour code. Self-employed workers were just a few thousand in total, and the peasantry, independent or cooperativized, was numerically small and shrinking. The crisis, and the process of adjustment and liberalization, have substantially changed that picture. The wage earning sectors and the working class in particular have suffered an absolute reduction in their numbers as a result of the opening of new and more lucrative employment opportunities in the private or cooperative sector and the reduction in the number of supernumeraries in state enterprises themselves. In 1996 the wage-earning sector absorbed 78% of the economically active population, 16% less than eight years earlier.[11]

No less significant has been their loss of economic power as a result of the dollarization of the prices of a substantial number of consumer goods and economic services and the continuation of wage levels designed for subsidised consumption. In this sense, salaries in the state sector have been subject to a regime of super-exploitation to the point where the price of labour is lower than the cost of its reproduction. According to unofficial calculations, a Cuban family of four in which at least two people are working and receiving an average salary would require double their earned income in order to guarantee a minimum consumption of food, hygiene products and commercial services.

In real life, this situation is assuaged in various ways. Around 20% of wage earners working in areas privileged by the new economic dynamic (tourism, advanced technology, export industries) receive wages in cash or in kind in addition to their official salary; the effect is a virtual restructuring by international capital of the working classes and the wage earning sector in general. In other cases, these same workers have developed areas of self-employed activity, whether formally (26% of the licences issued in 1996 went to state employees for example) or informally. But such people also frequently have recourse to other expedients, not linked to work, which in turn generates a growing social anomie. One such instance is the receipt of economic help from relatives abroad. Another, no less relevant, is corruption. There is no need to go further into the ethical and ideological implications of these modes of survival. Another significant social tendency is the proliferation of unwaged individual and cooperative modes of production.

At one level it is worth examining the situation of small peasants and agricultural producers combined in cooperatives who for one reason or another have not managed to save. As we noted earlier, these sectors underwent a gradual and absolute reduction from the triumph of the revolution in 1959 onwards, so that by 1970 they represented 11% of employees in the civil sector, falling to only 5% in 1989.[12] With the creation in 1993 of Unidades Básicas de Producción Cooperativa (UBPC – Basic Units of Cooperative Production) the situation underwent a dramatic reversal; even though there are no official figures, it is estimated that some 300,000 joined the ranks of the agricultural cooperatives and that they now work 30% of the land. Another 50,000 people received individual land titles. The self-employed sector in the cities grew to a similar degree. These activities had expanded earlier, through the seventies, but their growth was cut off between 1986 and 1989 during the so-called period of rectification, when such pursuits were considered incompatible with socialist aims. In the summer of 1993, self-employment was officially rehabilitated as a means of generating employment and limiting the reach of the black market. Although the 'self-employed sector' hides several real fortunes accumulated by those who have won the best positions and successfully evaded the government's rising tax demands, the vast majority of operations covered by this law are small individual or family units whose net incomes, even though they are higher than the earnings of most workers in the formal sector, do not allow of any capital accumulation.

In February 1994 there were 142,000 legally self-employed people in Cuba; by June the figure reached 160,000 and by January 1996 it had risen to 208,346. In 1997 it was reported that the number had fallen to around 160,000. Yet none of these figures truly reflect the dynamics of the process. By the end of 1997, 401,847 applications had been received and some 158,597 people had left their jobs – an indicator of profound instability. Only 0.9% of the total worked in the most lucrative sector, the private restaurants; 27% ran small food or non-alcoholic drink vending stalls. At that time 26% of self-employed people still worked in the formal sector at the same time, while 30% were unemployed, 18% were housewives (a euphemism which often means an unemployed woman) and the rest were retired. 73% of licence holders were men, which leads one to assume that women played a subordinate supporting economic role. It is interesting to note that 80% of those holding licences had reached ninth grade in education.[13]

Finally, Cuban society is now beginning to move from a situation of full employment (legitimately considered a major achievement of the revolution even if its price was a notorious economic inefficiency) to one in which unemployment is a structural feature. In 1994 open unemployment reached 8.4% of EAP and in 1997 7%, which some analysts have interpreted as a positive indicator. But it does not suggest an irreversible downward move.[14] The administration of unemployment by the state has been made possible by a gradual application or even postponement of the rationalization of the numbers of workers in state enterprises. Against that, the labour market has started to provide new employment options, particularly in the emerging private sector. It is calculated that 70% of the decline in state employment has been absorbed by the self-employed sector; and it is likely that the future authorization of small and medium businesses will open new escape valves from the same sector. But it will not be an unlimited supply of jobs, for the unemployed will continue to increase in number even if the economy maintains a reasonable level of growth, precisely because it is a precondition of economic reproduction in the new model of accumulation that supernumeraries be expelled from the workforce.

Rethinking the future from the left

Rethinking the future from a left wing perspective is a necessity that goes far beyond the national frontiers of Cuba. The resistance of the Cuban people, their struggle for national independence and their defence of the social gains they have made has won them the admiration of the whole world and motivated a solidarity movement of enormous moral and political significance.The intransigent anti-imperialism of its leadership is equally worthy of recognition. All of this is important, but not sufficient.

For Cuba could come to constitute a component of an anticapitalist project in formation that, even though it may have different concrete expressions in each national situation, will only be visible on the international level. If that is to happen, however, Cuba must not only safeguard both its independence and its social advances, but must also continue to develop new concepts of development and of politics and to create a genuinely popular power, democratic and pluralist. Cuban society has ample reserves in this respect: a strong network of popular participation, a political culture permeated by a sense of solidarity and cooperation, a social subject both educated and committed to values that are essential to socialist objectives, and a political class important segments of which have a sense of responsibility and a high level of social sensitivity. On the other hand, there is no shortage of obstacles in the way, the most significant of which are precisely those conditions that the country faces that make it particularly difficult to achieve economic recovery, and its asymmetrical relationship with the capitalist world market, all exacerbated by the effects of an immoral U.S. blockade that functions at both the economic and the political level. Given the proven non-viability of autarky, Cuba's insertion into the world capitalist market is an inescapable condition of its national survival. This does not imply a fatalistic acceptance of the rules of the game of globalization, however; still less does it mean that it is impossible to find alternative paths that will substantially modify the currently dominant scenarios. A realistic judgment, however, cannot avoid the fact that, whatever the measures adopted, this insertion will produce a dramatic alteration in the relations of power and the operating code of the State. This leads to the conclusion that there is a pressing need for a redesigned politics that should be governed by three key principles, contradictory but not mutually exclusive. First, it should guarantee the unity of the nation in face of imperialist intervention. Second, it should strengthen 'the people' and their organizations and acknowledge the increasing complexity of the subject called 'the people'. Third, it should respond to social diversity on the basis of popular hegemony and the negotiated subordination of the emerging sectors that do not fall within that rubric. In summary, it would be a paradigm of a socialist politics that recognised the existence of contradictions and conflicts in a complex society and provided the mechanisms for resolving them in a democratic manner to the benefit of popular hegemony and national independence.

Towards a new associationism

The strengthening of the popular subject automatically assumes the autonomy of its organizations. The transmission belt model was a positive contribution to revolutionary ends in historical conditions that no longer exist. In the new situation, the popular organizations will tend to occupy contradictory spaces, even in relation to the policies dictated by the State.

At one level, the existing sectional organizations would need to be stimulated. The Federation of Cuban Women (FMC), for example, has had a prominent role to play in the social mobilization of women; it should now resume its role on the basis of a feminist perspective challenging the structures of gender oppression that permeate Cuban society and which could easily be reinforced by the exigencies of a model of accumulation one of whose pivotal impulses is the degradation of the female workforce through prostitution, the *maquilas* (assembly plants), etc. Something similar could happen with the trade unions. As long as they were operating in a subsidized economy and under the protection of a paternalistic labour code, the trade unions could maintain their legitimacy even while playing a quite discreet role in the labour process. Insofar as the new model of accumulation imposes an intensified exploitation of labour, however, and raises the costs of its reproduction, the site of labour will again become a place of alienation and contradictions where representation can only be effectively sustained by militant trade unions with the legal capacity to use all types of pressure, including the strike weapon.

All this has a cost. Let us admit, for example, that more belligerent trade unions could provoke reservations on the part of unsophisticated foreign capitals seeking to maximize profits in the shortest possible time. But this is an inescapable cost, and in any case it is not necessarily this type of capital that should invest in a country whose economic 'attractions' are rather more sophisticated than a cheap and docile work force.[15]

In the second place, the potential for the popular organizations in contemporary Cuba is not solely to be found in the traditional social and mass organizations. In the last five years, Cuban society has seen the emergence of a range of 'associations', some with strong public involvement, whose common denominators have been their commitment to national independence and a renewed socialism. They include civic associations, NGOs, academic organizations and community movements. In their totality they have generated interesting debates around a new vision of development which embraces issues like the environment, gender, popular participation, local culture, etc. The community movements in particular have attempted in practice to offer an alternative form of development and coexistence based in the community, overcoming in this way the traditional division between market and state that has absorbed public discussion in Cuba for so many years.[16] Paradoxically, all these movements have been boycotted by the bureaucracy, to the point where the top echelons of the party issued a document declaring their intention to administer the dynamic of these associations in the framework of a 'socialist civil society' whose parameters of inclusion and exclusion were never been defined, thus leaving them at the mercy of whatever arbitrary criteria were produced by the bureaucratic organs.[17] The official justification for this action was the argument that the interventionist policies of the United States certainly included utilizing civil society in Cuba as a means for undermining the system, repeating the formula used in some eastern European countries. And it is certainly the case that a strategy of intervention has been in place since 1980, as both Torricelli (1992) and Helms-Burton (1996) have shown, which envisaged a second level of operations directed at coopting specific social and political sectors including (though not exclusively) the components of civil society.[18] So it is perfectly understandable that the Cuban state should have attempted to protect national sovereignty from the subversive attentions of the United States, and that it should create, to that end, preventive bureaucratic 'filters' and hurdles. But it seems absurd that it should do so by imposing bureaucratic trammels and controls on organizations that expressed in their declarations and their practice the same total rejection as the state of all North American attempts at intervention and subversion.[19] Perhaps the reaction of the state against 'civil society' is not expressing only the patriotic zeal of the political classes or the traditional reticence of the bureaucracy to share its legitimate competence in matters of social control. It may also relate to its disposition to present to international capital a 'country in good order', incompatible with the existence of combative autonomous organizations.

Finally, the strengthening of the popular subject cannot be limited to the revitalization of existing organizations, but must also extend to the emergence of associations organic to the new actors and social layers subordinated in the process of accumulation. A first paradigmatic case is that of the thousands of self-employed workers. Their intermediate position in the emerging social structure objectively conditions their political ambivalence towards the continuity of socialism. As suggested previously, the majority of these workers depend basically on their own labour power and even while the present anomalous economic conjuncture ensures them relatively high earnings, they have no capacity for accumulation. The quality of their life continues to depend largely on the provision of social services and the state's commitment to social welfare. But at the same time, they tend to limit their world view to the wretched little world of personal gain from what are objectively 'their business activities'. They therefore see certain social obligations – paying taxes for example – as unjustified demands that represent obstacles in the way of their enrichment. The refusal of the last Communist Party Congress (1997) to allow the formation of small and medium enterprises in fact represents a block on what might have been an incentive to cooperatives and other associations of service providers.

A similar case, in terms of its possible political implications, is that of workers in the agricultural cooperatives, above all those generated by the Basic Units of Cooperative Production [UBPC], created (as we noted earlier) in 1993 as a decentralizing response on the part of the state to the need to achieve better agricultural yields.[20] The nearly 20% of state land ceded to these groups of workers represented the most audacious step towards socialization taken by the Cuban revolution in recent years. It has to be recognized, however, that the creation of the UBPCs lacked from the outset any clear political vision, with the result that they are still marked by an air of pragmatism and utilitarianism. The UBPCs were founded with bureaucratic constraints that prevented them having free access to the market and tied them to the bureaucratic structures of the state enterprises. From late 1994, access to the market was made possible, which has undoubtedly generated a partial dynamization of these institutions. But without other political actions, that dynamization could take a specific course to the detriment of the potential role of the UBPCs as areas of socialist property and to their levels of internal democracy. Avoiding these effects will not depend on economic success (though this is indispensable), but on the general political model into which these cooperatives are inserted.

Independent workers – whether self-employed, cooperative or linked in the future to small and medium enterprise – thus represent a challenge for a political class accustomed to centralized vertical control. Current policies have tended to insert these workers into the existing trade unions, which is obviously dysfunctional for the trade unions, the self-employed and cooperative workers, and has yielded very limited effects. Everything leads us to think that it would be better to stimulate the organization of these sectors into organizations of their own, capable of representing their specific interests within the system, even where that implies a new way of thinking and of doing politics.

Only on the basis of empowering people in the various social spheres will it be possible to design an alternative economic model combining forms of popular economy[21] with mechanisms of co-management and self-management based on a decentralized model – whether in the framework of state, private or mixed property. And at the same time such a model should embrace consumer organizations which, supported by the relevant legislation, can counter the predatory effect of the market (whether privately controlled or under the control of the state) on the levels of consumption of the population.

The same political design should address the necessary but subordinate role of the technocratic-managerial sectors. The importance of these emerging sectors does not derive from their number; in fact they probably do not number more than a few thousand people occupying still unstable locations on the social scale, lacking their own organizations and without a coherent sectoral consciousness. Their ascendance is linked to qualitative considerations, their positioning in the most dynamic areas of the economy, which provides them with 'exchangeable political goods' vis à vis the political class and the traditional bureaucracy. It is a bipartite, complementary relationship, though one not without its contradictions, in which the emerging sectors provide the traditional elite with the economic surpluses necessary for the reproduction of their project for power, at the same time as this guarantees the social peace indispensable for the new model of accumulation. And in the last instance, we should not forget that the new technocrats and entrepreneurs come from the very heart of the traditional bureaucracy and have been formed by its current politics, which places them within a very selective network of personal relations and access to resources (informational, material, etc.).

Their qualitative relevance may also be seen in their possession of a high capacity for ideological and cultural production, for which they need only present themselves before society as symbols of personal success in relation to the market. This has already had an impact on the attitudes and behaviour of significant popular sectors, for whom what was once seen as deviations from the norm (influence-peddling, corruption or marginality) are now evaluated as signs of success or simply as a legitimate form of resistance for purposes of survival. Its paradigm could only be a sweetened Chinese model, speaking volumes about economic and consumerist successes but silent about its depressing consequences in social, political, cultural and ecological terms.

Here, rather than among the insignificant dissident groups, which the system has been able to accommodate with no major problems, is to be found the real social base for a Cuban thermidor, and for what could be a greater problem in the future – the roots of a tropical mafia which is already beginning to acquire influence.

The principal limits to its evolution into a hegemonic bloc are formed by an alliance of the popular classes with the political elite that emerged from the revolution. As I noted earlier, the signs of caution manifested by the political leadership (and particularly by those who represent its historic direction) in the face of the advance of the market and the reform process, whatever technical value they may merit, express the enduring character of this basic social commitment, which is not open for negotiation given the need to maintain national unity in the face of U.S. hostility. The result is that at the present stage of the Cuban reform process there is still a strong compartmentalization of economic activities and a fragmentation of markets, which makes horizontal relations between the different components difficult even within each sector. It is not hard to see, however, that these structural conditions will be diluted by the force of the market if each popular block does not undergo renewal, see itself as an autonomous force and develop its own political positions. In formal terms, that would imply institutional, normative and procedural changes, none of which have anything to do with North American demands for a liberal democratization of the system.

The construction of democratic institutions

The first link in the chain would be more efficient and more participatory municipal subsystem, the first space for a concert of interests and political negotiation(s).[22] Cuban local spaces have ceased to be simple vectors of a centrally planned balanced regional development. In their stead, local spaces have begun to experience uneven development relative to their position within the network of economic imperatives set out by the world market. Tourist areas, mining zones, and free trade zones are new variables fragmenting the national space and diversifying localities. Local societies themselves are transformed with the appearance of economic and social agents that generate new relations of power. In this context there is little room left for the traditional ways of nourishing democratic decision-making in the central planning process: the aggregation of the people's demands and their transmission along vertical tracks. A future planning process must be indicative, decentralized and pluralist. Cuban local space should become the first site of democratic planning.

At the macro level, the way in which representative government organs are constituted now demands redefinition. Until now this has functioned on the basis of a popular vote organized by territories only, in the case of local and provincial assemblies that do not admit competitive elections. This has meant on the one hand a lack of representation in local government of groups of workers located in the territories and the underrepresentation of marginalized groups like women. On the other hand, it has brought the erosion of the deliberative capacities of the representative institutions and the recourse to legal fictions in an attempt to ensure that representation where it is necessary. A new design would suggest the composition of these institutions on the basis of different criteria that would satisfy the demand for territorial, sectoral and interest group representation. Of course that would also involve the real validation of a legal precept that conferred on the representative organs the major powers of the state in each territory. Until now the representative organs have had little involvement in legislation, few meetings – rarely more than four days a year – and a disquieting unanimity in their vote on every issue that was discussed.

Equally relevant is the establishment of civil liberties, rights and duties, clearly established in law and institutionally supported. Cuban revolutionary society has been prodigal in the elaboration of lists of social and economic rights that could be not be made to disappear by 'the magic of the market' and they must be defended as real advances of the revolution. Nevertheless, at the same time declarations of civic and political rights have been few and far between, vague and dependent on their implementation by the state. This has produced disgracefully arbitrary decisions to the detriment of individual and collective rights, and of public debate and ideas that dissent from the monolithic desires of the political class. We should recall here how classical Marxism described the society that could replace capitalism: '...an association in which the free development of each is the condition for the free development of all'.[23]

The Cuban Communist Party could not stand apart from this transformation; in fact it must be its protagonist. For only the Communist Party, the organization central to the political system with more than half a million members educated politically into a commitment to socialism, can set in motion the changes that are indispensable with a minimum risk of disruption, and in the process consolidate a genuine popular power. But that would imply in turn the transformation of the Party. A new form of organization and a new function would have to evolve which corresponded more closely to the range of different interests that would already have been acknowledged in the social and political field. In an optimum scenario, the result would be a more democratic party, more open to debate and permitting internal tendencies within the framework of unity around strategic propositions. It is not too dangerous to suggest that this could lead to a multiparty system, particularly if the Communist Party ceased to play a vanguard role. In this sense, a displacement of the political system in the direction suggested could assist the emergence and development of other parties responsible and loyal to the continuity of the system.

For nearly forty years the Cuban people have paid dearly for the sin of wishing to put in place an alternative project of national independence and socialism in what the United States has always considered to be its backyard. For many years it has had to pay the price of the undeniable advantages that Soviet support brought with it. Today it continues to bear a double cost for persisting in its objectives, returning thus with singular brutality to the historic tragedy of socialism in one country. The continuity of socialism, of a socialism at once renewed and rooted in a global anticapitalist strategy is not entirely impossible. But neither is it guaranteed by what used to be referred to as the 'general laws of history'. On the other hand, Cuba could certainly face a restoration of capitalism, in which case we would have to see the costs of the last forty years as an investment in the future rebirth of a left alternative. And above all we must continue to advance, as Don Quixote enjoined his squire, even if it provokes howls of protest from ex-bureaucrats turned entrepreneurs, ex-dogmatists turned liberals or simply from those who imagine that we really are arriving at the oft-predicted end of history.

Havana, April 28, 1998 (Translated by Mike Gonzalez)

NOTES

The author is a research fellow at the Instituto de filosofoía in Havana. The views expressed here are entirely his own and do not reflect those of the institution where he is currently employed.

1 Figures derived from the Annual report of the National Committee of Statistics (1989) and from the Report on the results of the 1981 Census of Population and Accommodation (Havana, August 1983).
2 I have discussed this specific form of societal organization in 'Cuba ¿cuál es la democracia deseable' in H. Dilla (ed) *La democracia en Cuba y el diferendo con los Estados Unidos* (1996) Havana, Centro de Estudios sobre América.
3 Anthony Giddens *Más allá de la izquierda y la derecha* (Beyond left and right) (1996) Madrid, Ed. Cátedra.
4 'Llamamiento al IV Congreso del Partido' in *Cuadernos de Nuestra América*, Havana, July-December 1990.
5 Hugo Azcuy 'La reforma de la constitución socialista de 1976' in H. Dilla (ed) *La democracia en Cuba y el diferendo con los Estados Unidos* (1996) Havana, Centro de Estudios sobre América.
6 David Held *Modelos de democracia* (1992) Mexico, Alianza Editorial.
7 A note of caution: since 1989 no systematic social statistics have been published in Cuba, so that the analyses that follow are based on partial studies and observations that are always open to an element of doubt.
8 These figures were presented at the 12th Havana International Fair. The opening ceremony of the fair was conducted by a high political official who assured the assembled business people that 'We can offer you an orderly country, a coherent and irreversible policy of openness to capital investment and a cohesive and extensive economic infrastructure. Our productive sector is developing in the direction of efficiency, our workers are industrious and self-sacrificing, as well as highly educated and technically skilled. Our society suffers from neither terrorism nor drugs. We can therefore offer you a sovereign nation with an honourable and incorruptible government' *Cuba Foreign trade*, Havana, July-December 1994.
9 *Granma* 14th December 1996.
10 There were only 4,500 personal bank accounts in hard currency containing some 9.5 million dollars. See Alejandro Beruff 'Las finanzas internas de Cuba' in *CEEC Balance de la economía cubana* (mimeo) (1997) Havana.
11 Vivian Togoros 'Enfoque social del desempeño de la economía cubana en 1996' in *CEEC Balance de la economía cubana* (mimeo) (1997) Havana.
12 Juan Valdés *Procesos agrarios en Cuba* (1997) Havana, Editorial de Ciencias Sociales.
13 For an extremely suggestive critical analysis of these phenomena see Tania García

'¿Cuentapropismo o economía popular?', a paper presented to the workshop on 'Municipios Economía local y Economía Popular' at CEA, 7th-8th March 1996. Statistics on the number of self-employed should be treated with care. As usual in this segment of the labour market, behind every legally registered worker paying tax there are a number of others contributing their labour more or less continuously to private enterprise. This could multiply the real figure of people whose principal income derives from self-employment.

14 *Granma* 26th November 1997 quoted in V. Togoros op. cit. Official unemployment statistics are always lower than the real levels, for they always refer to people seeking work through the official agencies. But only part of the jobless population look for work that way. On the other hand there are no data for underemployment. Unemployment has particularly affected young people under 30 (60% of the total) and women.

15 An anecdote, by way of illustration: when the Melia chain opened its first hotel in Cuba, the Spanish management refused to accept a trade union. According to one Cuban assistant manager, the Spaniards finally accepted the union on the grounds that 'a well structured union could smooth activity' (*Granma*, 10th April 1991). Such a consensus is deeply disturbing. but in any event it has to be recognized that the trade unions are the sectoral organizations that have demonstrated the most courage and the highest level of organization in the face of structural adjustments and reforms. I have partially analysed their role in 'Comunidad, participación y socialismo: reinterpretando el socialismo cubano' in H. Dilla (ed) *La participación en Cuba y los retos del futuro* (1996) Havana, CEA.

16 Cf. H. Dilla, A. Fernández and M. Castro *Movimientos barriales en Cuba* (1997) San Salvador.

17 *Granma* 27th March 1996.

18 It was certainly more than a declaration of intent. Since the early nineties, several right wing North American foundations have tried to organize a common front against Cuba, though it must be recognised that they were concerned not only with intervening in civil society but also in influencing other sectors, including civil servants, the military and the security forces. For an analysis see Hugo Azcuy 'Estado y sociedad civil en Cuba' in *Temas*, Havana, no. 4, October-December 1995.

19 CEE Conclusion of the workshops 'Las ONGs en el mundo' Havana 1995.

20 For an empirically based analysis of the UBPC see Niurka Pérez and Cary Torres 'UBPC: hacia un nuevo proyecto de participación' in H. Dilla (ed) *La participación en Cuba y los retos del futuro* (1996) Havana, CEA.

21 For purely functional purposes I define popular economy here as the combination of productive or service activities carried out by individual or collective agents who depend (fundamentally) on their own labour power for the continuation of their activities and whose defining feature is self-regulation based on principles of solidarity and association. See José Luis Corraggio 'De la economía informal a la economía popular' in *Nueva Sociedad*, no. 131, May-June 1994.

22 Cf. H. Dilla 'Municipios y construcción democrática en Cuba' in FLACSO *Perfiles latinoamericanos* (1996) Mexico, Flacso.

23 K. Marx and F. Engels *Manifiesto del Partido Comunista* (The Communist Manifesto) (1976) Moscow, Editorial Progreso.

UNSTABLE FUTURES: CONTROLLING AND CREATING RISKS IN INTERNATIONAL MONEY

Adam Tickell

Introduction

> The essential building block of all markets, known as a risk, will remain a permanent fixture in the business world. The history of finance has demonstrated an unswerving ability to innovate in order to minimise risk and uncertainty. Derivatives, in all forms, are another example of this progression. While the products of innovation are susceptible to abuse, it is far worse to stunt the creative process through misguided regulatory practices (Burns, 1994, 9).

During the past two decades the global financial system has been transformed. Markets have opened, exchange controls have been removed, interest rates have become more volatile and financial institutions have become among the most important arbiters in the global political economy. These processes have, undoubtedly, contributed to the relative success of the liberal growth model which, although far more brutal to its losers than its Keynesian predecessor, is putting deep roots down into the capitalist earth. Yet these transformations in the financial arena have been accompanied by a sweeping away of many of the old securities that underwrote the Keynesian model. Increasingly volatile interest and exchange rates turn profits into losses as entirely external forces transform the cost of borrowing or the 'value' of their products. For example, a firm which priced exports at one exchange rate may see substantial profits turn into losses solely on the basis of revaluation of currencies. Banks and brokers responded to this environment by developing products which allow firms to 'hedge' their financial exposure and protect themselves against adverse market moves.

This essay explores the growth and implications of derivatives, arguing that although individual institutions tend to use them to offset or control risk, the aggregate impact of derivatives for the financial system is to increase it. The essay goes on to explore the emergence of concern among regulatory authorities, particularly following the collapse of Barings Bank, that derivatives have the potential to undermine global finance. While the putative regulatory order enhances control, I argue that ultimately it is based on a liberal logic which eviscerates itself.

Managing risk? The development of the derivatives markets

Derivatives have a relatively long history with sporadic examples of buying and selling commodities in the future dating back at least to London in the 1630s during the Dutch Tulip Bulb mania, and rice markets in Osaka in the 1650s (Chance, 1995). The development of modern derivatives, however, stems back to 1848. In the year that much of Europe was in turmoil as the emergent middle class flexed its muscles against the aristocratic remnants of feudalism, the inauguration of the Chicago Board of Trade (CBOT) laid the foundations for much of the late twentieth century financial system. As William Cronon's (1991) magisterial analysis of Chicago demonstrates, that city, at the centre of a vast agricultural hinterland, saw the development of 'to arrive' contracts which allowed grain traders to sell their grain at an agreed price and deliver it later. Such contracts rapidly became widespread as both farmers and traders realised that the contracts allowed them to hedge against the risk that prices would move against them, and in 1865 the CBOT adopted the first formal rules governing these futures contracts. Even in these early days, however, the Chicago futures market was a place where contracts were traded speculatively and 'men who don't own something are selling that something to men who don't really want it' (Rothstein, 1982, quoted in Cronon, 1991, 125).

While derivatives markets continued to develop fitfully during the late nineteenth century and for most of the twentieth, encountering prohibition, mild regulation and fraud along the way, it was not until global financial markets became more integrated and the most important international currencies floated freely that derivatives began to transmute into the complex variety seen today.[1] In 1972 the Chicago Mercantile Exchange[2] created the International Monetary Market which permitted trading in currency futures: these were the first derivatives contracts not to be based on physical products and laid the basis for the development of more esoteric and abstract contracts later on.

Although they have a series of common features, in that their principal rationale is to enable investors to manage risk by offsetting the effects of volatility in the financial markets, and also in that their value is 'derived' from the value of underlying assets, derivatives are really a large number of different financial instruments.[3] The most basic form of derivative is a variant of the form that developed in Chicago in the 1860s: the future.[4] A buyer of a future agrees to pay a given price on an agreed date for an asset (ranging from agricultural commodities to foreign currency), while the seller of a future agrees to sell on the same terms. Futures enable a buyer to lock into a given price and provide certainty. If, for example, a US firm planned to import $50,000 worth of goods from Germany in three months time, they could buy $50,000 worth of Deutsche Mark futures to protect themselves against any fall in the value of the dollar. In order to ensure that buyers of futures can afford to meet their commitments, they are required to deposit an initial margin payment before they are allowed to trade on an exchange. The margin payment is calculated to be high enough to cover the change in the price of the contract over one day, but varies according to the volatility of the market and the type of asset being traded. For example, trading government securities futures requires smaller margin payments than trading futures based on equities. The 'downside' of futures, as Chew (1996) points out, is that buyers are committed to them, even if prices move in their favour.[5] For example, in 1985 Japan Airlines contracted to buy dollars at a rate of ¥165.97/$1.00 but as the exchange rate was ¥99.4/$1.00 by the end of 1994, by purchasing the futures contracts the company paid ¥176 billion (US $1.8 billion) more than they would have done if they had bought foreign exchange when it was needed.[6]

A swap is an agreement to exchange cashflows between two parties and is effectively made up of a series of futures contracts. Interest rate swaps dominate the market and typically involve the 'counterparties' to the trade agreeing to exchange their interest rate liabilities. For example, if Firm A is borrowing money at variable interest rates it may wish to protect itself against rising interest rates. It can then agree to pay fixed interest rates by 'swapping' its borrowing for fixed interest rates with Bank B. Theoretically, at the start of the swap neither party is better off because the advantage either way is priced into the structure of the instrument. If interest rates begin to move upwards, Firm A has made a saving in its interest rate payments (and Bank B has lost money). If, on the other hand, interest rates fall, Firm A has committed itself to paying higher interest rates than it would have had to do so and makes a nominal loss.

The third common derivative tool is the 'option'. In exchange for a premium, options give buyers the right either to buy (in the case of a 'call option') or sell (in the case of a 'put option') an asset at a predetermined price. Buyers will exercise that right if – and only if – interest rates move in their favour. If interest rate moves are disadvantageous they can decide not to buy the assets. Sellers, on the other hand, expose themselves to theoretically unlimited risks in exchange for a premium (and will therefore hedge their exposure themselves). Sellers of options receive premium income for potentially limitless losses and for this reason most sophisticated options traders both assume that they need to trade sufficient options for premium income to be able to cover inevitable losses (in the same way as household insurance companies pay for claims by pooling the risk), and also limit their exposure to any one event (by, for example, hedging their own risk profile). For these reasons, options trading is not for the financial novice.

Banks and brokers have developed these three basic forms of derivative instrument into more complex variants, largely by combining features of each. Swaptions, for example, are options to buy swaps and allow purchasers flexibility effectively to terminate another swap contract. For example, if a firm has a ten year swap A which it believes it might wish to end after five years, it could buy the option to buy a swap (a swaption) which had the opposite characteristics of its original swap A and would therefore cancel the costs of A. However, if circumstances mean that it wishes to continue with its original swap, then it will not exercise its swaption. Other, more complex, derivatives include exotically named instruments such as 'butterflies', 'differential swaps', 'strangles', 'condors' and 'straddles' (Tickell, 1996).

Creating risk? The wider implications of derivatives growth

Since the early 1970s, and particularly during the closing two decades of the twentieth century, the use of derivatives has mushroomed and in a short period of time derivatives have gone from being an arcane and little-used instrument to becoming a ubiquitous feature of business life.[7] As Table 1 shows, the nominal value of derivatives contracts outstanding in 1995 was estimated at $30,602 billion, representing a growth of over 2,800% over a ten year period. Furthermore, these data under-estimate the total value of derivatives and a survey in April 1995 calculated the notional value of contracts at $47,500 billion, with an average daily turnover of $880 billion. Two thirds of transactions took place between counterparties based in different countries (Group of

Thirty, 1997). Care needs to be taken with these data. The statistics collected by central banks are not always comparable, either in definitional terms or in terms of the level of detail collected, while by expressing the statistics in terms of notional outstanding value a false impression of the risk profile of the instruments may be obtained (BIS, 1996a, 1996b). In particular, the Bank for International Settlements estimates that the cost of all of the over-the-counter derivatives contracts would 'only' be approximately 4% of the notional value.

This rapid growth has taken place because, as we have seen, derivatives allow institutional investors, corporate treasury departments, and bank risk management departments to hedge risk. Although in principle this is a zero-sum game at the level of the financial system, because if company A gains from a futures contract, company B loses, the reallocation of individual risks among a larger number of firms means that one-off shocks may be more easily coped with. Second, some derivatives provide signals to the wider financial markets which, advocates claim, reduces uncertainty and offers potential benefits of specialised knowledge. In the case of commodities, rising futures prices may be a stimulus for increased production (Parsons, 1988), while differences between the prices of options and the underlying asset reveal to participants in the financial markets what informed opinion is about the expected volatility of the asset price. Third, derivatives significantly reduce the costs of diversifying portfolios, because investment managers can expose themselves to derivatives based on baskets of stocks rather than on a smaller number of more volatile stocks. Fourth, derivatives are relatively cheap because they effectively operate on leverage. Until the completion date of the contract, investors only need to pay a small fraction of the value of the underlying assets, in the form of the margin payment. US Treasury futures, for example, require an initial margin payment of only 1.5% of the value of the Treasury Bonds. This means that buying $1 million of Treasury futures costs only $15,000 up front. If Treasury Bonds appreciate in value during the lifetime of the contract, the investor realises the gains for a very small initial payment. If, however, the bonds fall in value during the contract period, the purchaser of the derivatives has to make extra margin payments in order to prove that they can cover any losses. Furthermore, futures are a risky purchase because if the value of the underlying instrument moves against the buyer, they are legally committed to buying them at what could turn out to be a considerable loss (see Chew, 1996; Parsons, 1988; Grossman, 1988; Gibson and Zimmermann, 1994).

However, despite their risk management function, derivatives have managed to achieve something of a bogey status since they first entered the public consciousness during the early 1990s. This is because they not only allow institutions to offset risk, but have also been implicated in a series of high-profile losses which have undermined the financial viability of companies, banks and government entities (see Table 2). Kelly and Hudson (1994, 2) for example, have argued that institutions 'do not use [derivatives] markets merely to reduce their exposure to risk, but are assuming risk in the hope of financial gain, placing in jeopardy our homes, our retirement incomes and the money we set aside' (see also GAO, 1994a, b). In one sense, much of the public concern is misplaced. In conditions of a perfect market derivatives are unable to effect the price of underlying assets (such as exchange or interest rates); all they can do is to allocate risk between different players in the market and as they spread that risk more widely they should provide a wider systemic stability.

Yet perfect markets do not, of course, exist.[8] Derivatives are traded in real markets where some players have some specialist knowledge, for example, that others do not have, while the very complexity of some instruments may lead to 'market risk' (Merton, 1995). Market risk develops because the value of a derivative depends on the price of a number of different underlying variables (such as exchange rates, interest rates and commodity prices). This means that it is difficult to predict what the impact of changes in the prices of these variables will be on the derivative without knowing the detail of the instrument's structure. Despite the increasing sophistication of models, there continue to be inaccuracies in the measurement of risks inherent in specific instruments (Duffee, 1996), and institutions expose themselves to changes in value which may not be easy to predict. Furthermore, derivatives are more prone than other financial products to liquidity and credit risks. Liquidity risk arises from the potential that a derivative will not easily be traded during times of particular volatility in the markets, although there is little evidence that it has been a major problem to date. Credit risk, on the other hand, is more common and occurs when the counterparty to a trade is unable to meet its obligations. Although this is a feature of any bi-lateral contract, the opacity of some derivatives, the potential for high gearing and the non-linear risk structure implicit in many of them (Bond et al, 1994) means that credit risk is a particular problem of derivatives. These difficulties can be exacerbated if institutions are unable to specify their total exposure to particular events and also, as Cohen

(1995, 2011) argues: 'given the complexity of some instruments, it is economically feasible for only a relatively few individuals at a company to understand such transactions, and if one or more leave, the company's ability to manage its risk will be compounded.'

In spite of these extra risks that the increased use of derivatives represents to individual institutions, liberal commentators have scorned suggestions that additional controls need to be introduced. While practitioners and regulators have argued that they are analogous to electricity, because they are necessary to modern life but dangerous in the wrong hands (see Lackritz, 1995; Levitt, 1995), *The Economist* magazine maintains that:

> derivatives are simply another financial and managerial tool which financiers and managers need to use properly. True, some of those instruments are too powerful for inexperienced or unsupervised hands. Their innards can sometimes be complicated. But then the same could be said for motor cars, and few people would advance that as an argument for more traffic lights.[9]

This is a seductive argument but it is, for two reasons, fallacious. First, the analogy is a poor one: the powerful and potentially dangerous nature of cars does not call for traffic lights, but for driving tests and speed restrictions and laws, conventions and mores which regulate drivers. Second, and more important, calls for derivatives to be further regulated stem not from their capacity to undermine an individual financial institution (the equivalent of a car crashing into a tree), but from the potential for more widespread financial problems (a multiple high-speed pile-up). As an IMF study put it, derivatives reinforce the on-going process of global financial integration:

> Derivative instruments tend to strengthen market linkages between individual financial institutions in ways which are difficult to quantify. Consequently, disruptions or increased uncertainty in one market may now be more likely to spill over into other derivative markets and into cash markets (quoted in Gibson and Zimmerman, 1994, 10; see also GAO, 1994a; Group of Thirty, 1997).

A systemic crisis could be triggered by one of three things: default by a major player; a sudden shift in the prices of derivatives in the financial markets sufficient to undermine the viability of a major player; or the inability to net out obligations and receipts. Derivatives are traded in two ways: on organised and regulated exchanges, such as the London International Financial Futures Exchange (LIFFE) or the Chicago Mercantile Exchange (CME), and 'over-the-counter' (OTC). Exchange-traded derivatives are less flexible than OTC products, have standard structures, require that money is placed with the exchange as a guarantee and that extra margin payments are made against adverse market moves. Furthermore, the organised exchanges cooperate closely with clearing houses in attempts to ensure financial stability in such a way that margin payments by traders are made when deals go against them so that, in effect, the exchanges become counterparties to the trades. Although this has not always proved effective, most spectacularly in the Barings case, it remains a considerable strength of exchange, as opposed to OTC trading of derivatives.

Over-the-counter derivatives are tailored products which have no protection from the exchanges and are held off balance sheet. As a result, they are cheaper and more flexible, but their risk profile is higher and the products can be less easily sold to third parties. To liberal commentators, critics of OTC markets miss the point:

> the nimble nature of the OTC markets readily permits – indeed actively encourages – the introduction of new products... Any attempt to stifle the innovative thinking of the many highly intelligent figures involved... is an utterly moronic piece of reactionary thought worthy of the worst moments of twentieth century socialism. If a company wishes to risk its capital by creating a new product, then let it (Black and Young, 1997, 2).

However, concern about the absolute and relative growth of the OTC markets is not confined to left-wing commentators (such as Atkinson and Kelly, 1994; Kelly and Hudson, 1994), but includes senior regulators and participants on organised exchanges. This is because the OTC markets are less liquid than exchanges and during periods of turbulence they have enhanced the potential for a widespread collapse of market liquidity and backwash throughout the whole financial system.

If derivatives have increased potential instability in the international financial system, they are not alone in doing so. The breakdown of Bretton Woods and the development of a liberal, market-dominated system since has also contributed to growing connections between financial markets, which has resulted in local perturbations being rapidly transmitted throughout the world. In October and November 1997, for example, successive bursts in the bubble economies of east and southeast Asia came to a head when shares on the Hong Kong stock market collapsed, precipitating large falls in all the world's stock exchanges and stimulating fears of a global financial meltdown.[10] Furthermore, during the 1990s it has become clear that other factors have exacerbated the levels of systemic risk in the international financial system.

First, there has been the emergence of large, integrated financial conglomerates with highly complex financial and corporate structures. One of the contributory factors in the collapse of Barings, for example, was the lack of clarity in the reporting lines engendered by the complex nature of the bank's corporate structure (Board of Banking Supervision, 1995; Ministry of Finance, 1995). Second, an increasing share of international financial transactions is dominated by a small number of institutions from a small number of countries which have the geographical networks, specialist knowledge and technological expertise to command market power and manage internal risk. There is heavy industrial concentration across a range of different international market sectors and that some firms have a strong presence in many markets.[11] Furthermore, the trend is towards greater concentration, as the costs of running an integrated global presence (in terms of technology and labour costs) squeeze out smaller participants. In foreign exchange, for example, the top ten dealers have increased their market share from 31% in 1990 to 43% in 1997 and by the end of the century over 75% of the market is expected to be controlled by the top 15 firms.[12] Such concentration contributes to instability because if one of the dominant institutions were to get into difficulty the contagion effect would be more serious than in a less concentrated market:

> These institutions tend not just to be each other's largest counterparties, but also to have extensive dealings with many of the same customers around the world and to be members of the same clearing houses and exchanges. While mutual credit exposures with individual firms may not be excessive, direct and indirect credit risk exposures within this group are so complicated and opaque and change so rapidly that it is virtually impossible to monitor them in anything like real time. Accounting and disclosure practices have not begun to keep pace. Risk exposures can build up undetected by existing monitoring systems (Group of Thirty, 1997, 8).

Such developments have not occurred in a vacuum and there have been a series of parallel developments which have acted as buffers for the financial system and prevented a systemic meltdown at the first sight of crisis. At the level of the firm, risk management systems have become much more sophisticated, some derivatives have become better understood and some of the lessons of the collapse of Barings have been learnt. Furthermore, there is some evidence that financial companies have sought to diversify their derivative portfolios in order to reduce their exposure to particular events (see, for example, Group of Thirty, 1997). At the level of the financial markets, too, there have been developments which offset derivative risks. Technological development has enabled the exchanges to monitor exposure levels more effectively while private sector solutions, both sublime and ridiculous, are emerging which aim both to root out rogue traders (for example, Arthur Andersen have a unit which, as a sideline, provides an investigation into potentially fraudulent trading activity) and offset the impact (through, for example, specialist insurance policies).

Controlling risk? Regulating derivatives markets

While firm- and market-level measures are reducing the potential risks in the system, it is incumbent on bank supervisors to attempt to control the excesses of the financial markets. Although it is true that the globalising tendencies in finance have undermined some of the authority and power of national regulators, this is only a partial process and supervisors remain active in attempting to prevent crises in the financial markets. However, while they have retained this power, it is also important to remember that national-states actively encouraged the internationalisation of finance in general, and the development of derivative markets in particular, which is contributing to increased levels of systemic risk.

The collapse of the post-war financial order, when money was largely national in character and currencies were little traded and largely at fixed exchange rates, undermined the basis of the international regulatory environment (Leyshon and Tickell, 1994). From the development of the Eurodollar markets, in which banks could evade US regulatory jurisdiction of their dollar holdings, in London in the 1960s, international banking began to cease being solely an ancillary to trade and investment and began to develop its own dynamic. In the United States these pressures, as well as intensified competition from non-bank financial institutions that had been stimulated by the 'May Day' deregulation of the New York Stock Exchange in 1975, encouraged banks to lobby Congress to relax the regulatory 'burden', in the face of opposition from the Federal Reserve Board (see Helleiner, 1994; Hawley, 1984). The lobbying was hugely successful, leading to the Depository Institutions Deregulation and Monetary Control Act (1980) and the Garn-St Germain Depository Institutions Act (1982), both of which dismantled bank regulations, and the establishment of international banking facilities (IBFs) in 1981 as a direct challenge to the Euromarkets. As Eric Helleiner has emphasised, the failure of the Federal Reserve to dictate the US regulatory environment was a defining moment in the history of international finance for three reasons. First, it demonstrated that financial institutions could arbitrage between national regulatory systems and choose the one most conducive to their business aims. If one state attempted to impose a more burdensome regime than was to be found in other major financial arenas, it could find its business progressively seeping to other states. Second, the establishment of IBFs, free from tax and domestic US regulatory restrictions, led directly to competitive deregulation in countries which wished to compete with the US and UK as hosts for financial institutions. Third, the failure of a conservative approach to bank regulation and macro-economic management heralded the development of neo-liberal financial regulation. Therefore, by the early 1980s the three pillars of the emergent 'pro-market' regulatory order were born: regulatory arbitrage; regulatory competition; and regulatory neo-liberalism.

Although the thrust of regulatory change during the 1980s and 1990s was to remove domestic restrictions,[13] the period since the breakdown of the Bretton Woods system has also seen the fitful emergence of international supervisory co-operation. Under the auspices of the Bank for International Settlements, which was founded in 1930 to manage the international payment system but has since emerged as the 'central banker's central bank' and as the pre-eminent body for international monetary collaboration, bank supervisors agreed where ultimate responsibility for international banks lay under the Basle Concordat of 1975 (Kapstein, 1994; Helleiner, 1994; Roberts, 1998). More importantly, concern in London and Washington that the quality of bank assets had deteriorated as a result of liberalisation led them to draw up proposals for minimum capital adequacy standards. As Helleiner (1996) points out, if the UK and US had imposed new rules unilaterally it would have materially harmed the competitive position of their national institutions in the capital markets, particularly vis à vis Japanese institutions. They were, in this respect, as vulnerable to the effects of geographically uneven regulation as any other state. However, because both London and New York occupied pivotal roles in the international financial system, US and British officials were able to threaten other nations with exclusion from the two cities unless they adopted similar measures. The result was that the BIS issued the Basle Accord on capital standards in 1987 (BIS, 1997b) which, according to Ethan Kapstein, became the 'cornerstone of a new regulatory order' (1992, 283).

In many respects the Basle Accord was indicative of the new

regulatory order. First, although the committee which set it up had no status under international law and their agreement was not *legally* binding on signatories, its sponsorship by leading financial nations gave it *de facto* power and it rapidly became set in national regulations (Roberts, 1998).[14] Second, the Basle Accord 'was only brought about because two of the key nation states in international finance were able to impose their beliefs on others. Countries without their privileged locations in the international financial system would not have been able to do so,[15] nor would unilateral action by the UK and the USA have proved effective. Finally, it underwrote the 'pro-market' nature of international regulatory co-operation. This is limited in expectations and aims, as Helleiner points out:

> . . . increasingly specific norms, rules, and decision-making procedures were established concerning lender-of-last-resort, regulatory and supervisory activities in order to prevent further crises. These provisions greatly assisted central banks in co-operating by altering expectations, making information available, and institutionalising patterns of co-operation. Equally important, they did much to alter market behaviour and instilled confidence among private operators by demonstrating the seriousness with which financial officials were attempting to handle potential problems. Still, the regime's strength should not be overstated. It was focused only on the narrow task of preserving global stability through lender-of-last-resort, regulatory and supervisory activities... (1994, 190).

This new supervisory regime, therefore, embodies a broadly liberal assessment of how governments can and should intervene in an era of financial openness. In an era of open financial markets, regulatory arbitrage means that unilateral intervention is likely to be ineffective, while the emergent hegemony of liberal ideas means that any more radical proposals for intervention, such as the 'Tobin Tax' (see Eichengreen et al., 1995) on foreign exchange transactions, were easily dismissed during the 1980s and early 1990s.[16]

Until the collapse of Barings Bank, however, regulators were seemingly unconcerned by the growth of the derivatives markets. What regulations there were tended to be variable, subject to undercutting and not always legally binding (see Group of Thirty, 1997). While regulators were clearly aware of the growth of derivatives, critical voices about the capacity of supervisors to understand it tended to be marginalised. For example, no action followed the recognition by Charles Bowsher, US Comptroller General, that:

> [The] nature of derivatives activities clearly demonstrates that [regulation] has not kept pace with the dramatic and rapid changes that are occurring in domestic and

global financial markets. Banking, securities, futures and insurance are no longer separate and distinct industries that can be well regulated by the existing patchwork quilt of Federal and State agencies.[17]

Similarly, a highly critical report by the General Accounting Office in 1994 was shrugged off by the Federal Reserve and dismissed by the ISDA as representing 'good facts and bad conclusions' (see GAO, 1994a, b; ISDA, 1994). Indeed, as derivatives were the fastest growth component of the financial sector, supervisory authorities positively encouraged product innovation in the exchanges within their jurisdiction while also promoting exchanges internationally (Cerny, 1993). For example, when in 1991 the House of Lords ruled that debts incurred by British local authorities in the swaps market had been illegally incurred, the governor of the Bank of England lobbied ministers to introduce retrospective legislation in order to preserve the integrity of the markets (see Tickell, forthcoming).

At least part of the explanation for this regulatory neglect has been the growth of practices which made it genuinely difficult for regulators to dictate the rules of the game. Since the development of the Euromarkets, financial institutions have practised 'regulatory arbitrage' (Cerny, 1993; Leyshon and Thrift, 1997; Moran, 1990). There are two components to this. On the one hand, they have developed new products which attempt to circumvent the existing rules while on the other they have sought out jurisdictions with a relatively light supervisory touch in order to reduce the costs of compliance or to carry out activities that are restricted elsewhere. The avoidance of regulation is a major spur to product innovation (McBarnet and Whelan, 1991; Shah, 1996b; Miller, 1986) and means that as fast as regulations are framed to deal with one product, another product may be devised which evades the new rules. Furthermore, the complicated internal structure of such products means that supervisors may face problems in determining their risk structure (to firms and at the systemic level) and, therefore, be unsure about the appropriate response. Until the collapse of Barings, supervisors were increasingly sanguine about financial innovation as a means of regulatory avoidance. For example, Peter Cooke, who for years was one of the most influential architects of the post-Bretton Woods regulatory era, recently said that:

I do not think [regulatory] avoidance is important at all. At the end of the day, these are all tricks that one would expect banks to play, seeking to probe or bend the law in their favour. [New products] are developed by clever lawyers and bankers seeking to sell new products so that they can earn their fees and commissions. If the

> new instrument patently breached the rules, then one would have to take steps to stop it, but I think the degree of difference between various tiers is pretty marginal in terms of the broad brush of capital regulation (quoted in Shah, 1996c, 381-382).

Firms also avoid regulation by exploiting space: that is, they locate activities in markets where regulation is less, rather than more, restrictive or where the levels of monitoring are lower. While in rare cases this may reflect a cavalier attitude to risk, it more usually reflects the ideological near-hegemony of liberal approaches to regulation (see, for examples, Kaufman, 1997; Kaufman and Benston, 1995; Fox, 1995) and the intensely competitive nature of some product areas. Even after two decades of regulatory change, geographical arbitrage remains a potent force. For example, it was widely reported during early 1998 that a major American bank was planning to relocate its wholesale banking and dealing activities to London because the New York regulatory environment was proving so burdensome (Warner, 1998). Whether the press briefings for the stories reflected real plans or pressure on US authorities to remove regulation is, to some extent, irrelevant. In a very real sense they represented a set of political pressures on national authorities to deregulate further.

The collapse of Barings Bank in 1995, when a single trader managed to evade both internal controls and external supervision in order to effect a series of disastrous derivatives trades, proved to be a defining moment in international approaches to derivatives regulation. Although the British authorities initially attempted to isolate the impact of the event by claiming both that it was unique to Barings and that the involvement of derivatives was incidental (see Tickell, 1996), less publicly, supervisors began to take the potential threat from derivatives far more seriously. Within Britain, criticisms of the Bank of England's supervision of Barings by its own official inquiry and, more trenchantly, the inquiries by Singapore's authorities and the House of Commons Treasury Select Committee (BoBS, 1995; Ministry of Finance 1995; Treasury Committee, 1996) led to an audit of the Bank's internal supervisory culture. This review was carried out by external consultants and recommended a series of changes which strengthened the analytical basis on which judgements were founded (Davis, 1996; Bank of England 1996, 1997a, 1997b). In the longer term, however, a perception that the Bank of England was in part responsible for the events at Barings undoubtedly contributed to the wholesale restructuring of the supervisory systems as one of the first actions of the incoming Labour government in 1997.

If the collapse of Barings presaged a widespread restructuring of financial service regulation in Britain, its impact on the international regulatory arena was no less important. For arguably the first time, standing bodies of international regulators began to take seriously the possibility that Barings may have been a warning of worse things to come.[18] As Andrew Large, the chairman of the Securities and Investment Board, mused at the conference of the International Organisation of Securities Commissions (IOSCO):

> Fortunately the systemic impact of the Barings collapse was kept to a minimum by official actions and by the presence of a willing buyer... But what if Barings had had a balance sheet 10 times or 50 times its size?... What would have happened then? (see Large, July 1995, 7).

Within three months of the Barings incident, regulators of the major financial centres issued the 'Windsor declaration' which signalled their willingness to force greater disclosure of information about derivatives exposure, to ensure that derivatives exchanges shared information, and to develop co-operative structures so that regulators could successfully intervene during emergencies (BIS, 1996; Corcoran, 1997). Since 1995, the shape of the emergent regulatory framework for derivatives has become clearer and involves regulatory co-operation and moves towards harmonisation; an increased emphasis on risk management; and an increased emphasis on market disclosure.

First, national regulators have built upon the experience of co-operation over the capital standards and the 1992 'minimum standards agreement'[19] with agreements to share information about large exposures in order to gain a global picture of firms' activities. At a minimum, such co-operation should ensure that, if banks are honest in their reporting, supervisors are aware of any potential problems before they arise. For example, in 1996, 149 derivatives exchanges signed a memorandum of understanding which agreed the trigger points at which information would be shared. Implicit in regulatory co-operation is that regulators should eventually begin to harmonise their approaches to derivatives, in much the same way as the capital adequacy accord led to a de facto norm. One of the governors of the Federal Reserve Board, for example, has recently argued that:

> We need some level of regulatory conformity... Otherwise, the inconsistencies and incompatibility of rules and regulations across countries may make it difficult, if not impossible, for some firms to engage in global business activities... We must also recognise that technology and financial innovation are permitting banks today to become ever more adept at avoiding regulatory barriers . . . (Phillips, 1997, 2).

Any such harmonisation will be difficult to achieve and it is important to recognise that regulatory reform remains contested. At the international level, national regulators play off their own sectional interests against their perception of systemic risks and against competitor nations. The global dominance of markets in the UK and the USA remains, in part, a regulatory creation and supervisors in those countries are acutely aware of the risks of harmonisation to nationally important industries.[20]

Second, national supervisors are increasingly beginning to emphasise risk management (for example, the BIS and IOSCO, 1995a; SIB, 1996; Bank of England, 1997b). This approach attempts to cover all types of derivative instruments and situate them within the total portfolio of the firm in order to assess the net value of the firm's exposure that would be jeopardised in the event of credit, liquidity or market problems. Furthermore, the BIS and IOSCO have issued a joint paper which sets out how supervisors should assess these risks, explicitly stating that qualitative as well as quantitative judgements need to be made. However, it would be a mistake to interpret such moves as being against the grain of pro-market regulation. The BIS/IOSCO paper emphasised that the 'two committees are aware of the potential costs associated with requests for additional information on institutions derivatives activities and recognise that additional information requirements should only arise where there is a clear supervisory need' (1995a, para 14).

Third, supervisors argue that there is a need for firms to disclose their derivatives activities to the market. This, it is argued, will benefit firms because they will be able to assess the credit-worthiness of their counter parties. As formalised in another joint report by BIS and IOSCO (1995b), during the latter half of the 1980s and 1990s it appeared as if any problem could be solved through market disclosure (see, for example, Casson, 1996; Financial Regulation Report, 1997). As Susan Phillips, of the Federal Reserve Board, has argued, this is a voluntaristic approach: 'Each institution should tailor its risk measurement and management process to its own needs. While adhering to basic principles, each institution must determine for itself the proper incentives and techniques for managing its affairs' (1997, 3). Although such disclosure is voluntary, the report maintained that:

> An institution that provides little information about its risk profile may be susceptible to market rumours and misunderstandings by market participants in times of stress, which could possibly result in a loss of business with counter parties, a higher cost of capital and funding difficulties (BIS and IOSCO 1995b, 54).

How, then, should we interpret the emergence of international co-operation in regulating derivatives? Since the demise of the Bretton Woods era it is clear that financial markets have undermined the material and intellectual capacity of states to control them. In his examination of the ways in which globalisation and arbitrage undermined regulatory systems after 1975, Phil Cerny suggested that:

> States are like lumbering giants, vastly powerful when roused, but often easy to get around, disable with a hundred darting blows from different directions (or a few well-aimed stones from a sling shot) and topple over in a dazed condition. This is especially true given that the state is not true Leviathan, but an unevenly developed and organised structure in which the right hand does not usually know what the left hand is doing and the co-ordinating function does not usually resemble a brain (1993, 79).

Yet perhaps we should understand the new cooperative spirit as being an incremental attempt to wrest power back from these markets. While the scope for regulators is limited, such an analysis would suggest that they have accepted that any intervention must work with the grain of the market. To extend Cerny's metaphor, perhaps the crises at Barings and elsewhere finally roused the giants who, even if they cannot finally defeat their foes, can hold them in check. There is some truth in this analysis. The emergent framework of pro-market regulation undoubtedly strengthens the international financial system and makes it more resilient in the face of systemic problems. While not undermining the competition state, the regulatory framework is increasingly setting standards below which national rules must not fall (although at the same time this baseline normalises the standards of liberal participants). And yet, this explanation remains partial for two reasons.

First, it is important to recognise that pro-market regulation is inscribed with a series of ideological understandings about the role of the state. It is not just that the state's capacity to intervene effectively in financial (and other) markets has been eroded (although this is the case, [Clark, 1998]); so have the ways of thinking about the state's role. In this sense discourses which emphasise that states have little power end up naturalising the very processes they describe. Therefore, the development of a transnational financial policy community centred on the BIS, which is largely technocratic and free from democratic accountability, serves not only to set the tone for the international co-operation, it also sets the parameters of thinking. In the case of derivatives trading, the policy discourse still largely adheres to liberal understandings of market rationality (exemplified by the emphasis on disclosure as a means of overcoming market imperfections).[21] A recent example of the way in which technocrats have internalised a liberal logic was shown by the response to moves to increase the supervision of over-the-counter derivatives by the Commodity Futures Trading Commission – a Federal Government agency. Echoing industry claims that even a review of OTC markets would raise serious problems, Alan Greenspan, chairman of the Federal Reserve Board, argued that:

> There appears to be no reason for government regulation of off-exchange derivative transactions between institutional counterparties. Private market regulation appears to be achieving public policy objectives quite effectively and efficiently... Participants in these markets have been savvy enough to limit their activity to contracts that are very difficult to manipulate. Institutional participants in the off-exchange derivative markets also have demonstrated their ability to protect themselves from losses of fraud and counterparty insolvencies.[22]

Second, despite the progress made, derivatives regulation remains timid. Regulators continue to rely on firms opting to disclose information to the markets and on peer pressure to force companies to do it. However, although there is evidence that large firms are conforming (see, for example, BIS and IOSCO, 1996a), progress is slow. Furthermore, there is evidence of 'creative compliance' in the interpretation of accountancy rules (Smith, 1992; Shah, 1996a). Finally, the emphasis on disclosure means that credit 'rating agencies are likely to play a major role in helping the market to enforce standards' (BIS 1997b, 168-67). These organisations, particularly 'Moody's Investment Services' and 'Standard and Poor's', are rooted in an Anglo-American financial orthodoxy and make judgements on the integrity of debt issued by financial institutions, corporations and local and national governments, summed up in an investment grade. Credit rating agencies have increasingly assumed a governance role in international finance and effectively pass judgement on the soundness of managerial practices. This exercises a powerful disciplinary force on institutions which stray from the norm. Yet, as Sinclair (1994) has argued, it is a form of governance which may be fragile, is unaccountable, and excludes alternative ways of seeing the world. It is, of course, entirely in keeping with a regulatory order which understands markets as being essentially rational. There is one problem with relying too heavily on the credit rating agencies: their predictive capacity. While the agencies have proved adept at making judgements in the majority of cases, when faced with less predictable events or fraud, the grades are less reliable. For example, shortly before the bankruptcy of Orange County in 1995, both Moody's and Standard and Poor's issued very strong grades for the municipality;[23] while high grades were also issued on the sovereign, financial institution and corporate debt of East and South East Asian countries prior to the crisis of 1997. To rely on such institutions as the cornerstone of international derivatives regulation is taking great risks with the integrity of the international financial system.

Conclusion

This essay has argued that supervisors were late to wake up to the increased instability engendered by the phenomenal growth of derivatives markets and that the shock waves from the collapse of Barings finally created a sense of urgency. The regulatory 'solution' to the derivatives problem, which is simultaneously being promulgated in national and international fora, is based on three principles: increased co-operation; risk management; and market disclosure. While this approach has undoubtedly strengthened the system compared with its predecessor (i.e. benign neglect), it remains to be seen whether it is adequate to the task. Arguably, however, the rule-based framework is problematic, in part, because it fails to take account of a qualitative shift in the broader culture of finance where power has shifted towards traders (as they account for a greater proportion of profits), while simultaneously this group has become more risk tolerant (Clark, 1997; Tickell, 1998b; Hilton, 1998).

In privileging non-state authority, the international policy community has internalised an (accurate) assessment of the difficulties of reining in the markets and their belief in the desirability and rationality of efficient markets, and concluded that strong regulation is impossible. Although the over-arching presumption of free trade to the detriment of cultural specificity or environmental interests within the World Trade Organisation may be deplorable, its fast and effective dispute resolution mechanisms, and its strongly-framed laws, suggest that alternative models for financial regulation are possible. Coming in the wake of the derivatives debacles of the 1990s, the Asian financial crisis truly shook the mantra of liberal economists and during 1998 the builders of the international disorder fell over themselves to call for a 'new architecture for the international financial system' (see, for example, Alan Greenspan [Chair of the US Federal Reserve Board], 1998; Michael Camdessus [Managing Director of the IMF], 1998; Robert Rubin [US Treasury Secretary], 1998). And yet it is clear that the foundations will be shallow and follow the model set in derivatives regulation. As a paper by the G-7 finance ministers – the most powerful finance ministers in the world – put it in May 1998:

> We have identified the need for action in five key areas:
> - enhanced transparency;
> - *helping countries prepare for integration into the world economy and for free global capital flows;*
> - strengthening national financial systems;
> - ensuring that the private sector takes responsibility for its lending decisions;
> - enhancing further the role of the International Financial Institutions and co-operation between them (G-7, 1998, 1, emphasis added).

In other words, the solution to the problems created by the inappropriate application of liberal economic dogma is more of the same.

An alternative approach would recognise that the changes in the international financial system did not appear from nowhere but, following from the logic of the argument of this essay, were politically and economically constructed; that powerful national states positively encouraged the growth of derivatives markets; and that such markets are potentially destabilising. While it is true that once these decisions have been made it is hard to push the genie back into the bottle, it is not impossible to restrict the ease with which money can flow and to prevent the speculative trading of derivatives. National governments and their representatives in international bodies must tackle the emergent culture of finance which rewards traders with astronomical bonuses – encouraging risk-taking – by setting punitive rates of tax; and, in general, priorities that set the needs of finance over the needs of people must be challenged. Even modest proposals are not trivial tasks, they require that the most powerful forces in capitalist countries be undermined; that the discourses accepted even by social democrats be exposed for the camouflage for liberal ideology that they are; and that the inevitable job losses in finance be accepted as a price worth paying for the long-term benefit of society. As William Lyon McKenzie King, Canada's long-serving Prime Minister recognised in 1935:

> Once a nation parts with its currency and credit, it matters not who makes the nation's laws. Usury, once in control, will wreck any nation. Until the control of currency and credit is restored to government and recognised as its most conspicuous and sacred responsibility, all talk of the sovereignty of parliament and of democracy is idle and futile (quoted in Stewart, 1997).

Table 1: Market for selected financial derivatives (billion US dollars)

	1986	1987	1990	1991	1992	1993	1994	1995	1996	1997
Futures	583	724	1541	2251	3019	5103	5945	6074	6180	7752
Swaps	500	867	3450	4449	5346	8475	11303	17713	20730	23700
Options	with futures		750	1268	1615	2668	2918	3112	3704	4429
Swap		180	561	577	635	1398	1573	3705	4722	5033
Total	1083	1771	6302	8546	10615	17643	21739	30602	35337	40914

Notes:

Only includes ISDA data and under-reports. Only reports one side of contract.
Data for 1995 are not fully comparable with earlier periods due to a broadening of the reporting population.

Source: Bank for International Settlements (1990-7) *International banking and financial market developments* (Basle, BIS); International Monetary Fund (1996) *International capital markets: developments, prospects and key policy issues* (Washington, IMF).

Table 2: High profile derivative losses

Date	Organisation	Estimated cost	Ostensible cause
1994	Glaxo	£115 m	Bond losses after getting into derivatives contracts 'without knowing what they meant'.
	Alied Lyons	£150 million	Gambled that the dollar would fall during and after the Gulf War. It rose.
	Kashima Oil	Y152.5 billion (US$1.57bn)	Foreign exchange loss.
1994	Atlantic Richfield Co	$23m	Derivative-related losses incurred by its Money Market Plus Fund.
	IG Metall-gessellschaft	$2.2 billion	Losses on energy products-linked derivatives.
	Gibson Greetings	$23 million	Sued Bankers Trust claiming poor advice on swaps dealings. Bankers Trust New York Corp settled the suit.
1994	Orange County	$1.5 billion	Betting against rising interest rates.
1995	Barings	£900m	Betting against changing stock markets and failure to disclose.
	Chile Copper Corp	$175 million	The trader responsible said he initially made a mistake and the losses mounted as he played the markets to try to recoup his losses.
	Proctor and Gamble	$102m	Sued Bankers Trust after lost money on two interest rate swaps.
'early 1990s'	Union Bank of Switzerland	£500,000	Trader disobeyed instructions forbidding him to increase market positions in warrants and convertibles and then hid illicit trades.
1996	Sumitomo/ London Metal Exchange	£1.6 billion	Illegal trading of copper futures. Sumitomo admits liability.

March 1997	SBC Warburg	'multi-million'	SFA investigate Warburg over an apparent mishandling of the sale of £300m of European shares for an investment trust.
March 1997	Government of Belgium	$1 billion	Trading exotic instruments in London.
March 1997	NatWest	£90m	Trader made a series of disastrous trades in interest rate options. Bank admits that there were errors in its control systems.
Jan. 1998	Union Bank of Switzerland	$690m (est.)	Sold securities which gave investors the right to force UBS to buy bank shares at a set price (which would fall if prices edged down). Prices collapsed as result of Asian banking crisis.

Source: author's database.

NOTES

An earlier version of this paper was given at the annual conference of the RGS/IBG in Guilford, 1998 and at seminars in Aberystwyth, Kings College London, Portsmouth and York University, Toronto. I would like to thank participants on these occasions for their comments and ESRC for its support.

1 Trading futures and options was variously banned in Japan, parts of Europe and in some states in the USA (including in Illinois for a very brief period in 1867); the US government laid down limited restrictions on grain futures in 1922 and banned trading options on futures in 1936; Congressman Gerald Ford successfully introduced legislation in the 1950s which continues to prohibit trading futures contracts on onions; and during the early 1900s America was beset by a spate of fraudulent bucket shops which took money from private customers for futures transactions and then closed (see Chance, 1995).

2 The CME was formed in 1919, but its predecessor organisation – the Chicago Produce Exchange – dates back to 1874.

3 Among the large body of literature which explores the derivatives markets see, for example Wall and Pringle, 1988; Cooper and Mello, 1991; Chew, 1996; Winstone, 1995. There are also some excellent Web sites which provide relatively non-technical descriptions of derivatives (see particularly 'Derivatives Research Unincorporated' (http://www.vt.edu:10021/business/finance/dmc/dru or, for a 'leave the markets to run themselves' spin, see 'Applied Derivatives Trading' at http://www.adtrading.com).

4 Futures are traded on major exchanges, such as the Chicago Mercantile Exchange or the London International Financial Futures Exchange (LIFFE) and have standard contractual terms. Similar contracts, known as 'forwards' are traded over-the-counter (OTC) and customised according to agreements between buyers and sellers.

5 Indeed, this is the reason that futures contracts are sold. Sellers simply take a different view of the likely movement of the underlying asset.

6 J. Kelly 'Accountancy: the risk that lurk off the balance sheet' *Financial Times* July 18, 1996, page 22.

7 Indeed, firms in the USA have even been sued for *not* using derivatives to manage their risks. In 1992 the Indiana Court of Appeal ruled that the directors of a grain

elevator co-operative had breached their fiduciary duty by not selling the co-operatives' grain in order to hedge their product against any potential fall in prices (Chew, 1996).

8 Because markets are not perfect, some derivative instruments do affect underlying asset prices. However, contrary to expectation, most evidence suggests that options contracts and, at least, equity index futures simultaneously increase the price of underlying assets and reduce price volatility (see DeTemple and Jorion, 1990; DeTemple and Selden, 1991; Robinson, 1993; Bach, 1994; Elfakhani and Chaudhury, 1995). However, as I argue below, perhaps a more important and less benign impact is that increased use of derivatives may help to explain greater risk tolerance among market participants which increases market volatility overall (see also Gibson and Zimmerman, 1994).

9 'Derivatives: the beauty in the beast' *The Economist* 14 May 1994.

10 See, for example, 'Rescuing Asia' *Business Week* 17 November 1997.

11 In 1997, the transactions of the ten largest financial institutions comprised over 42% of all foreign exchange deals, over 67% of all bookrunning for international equities, over 52% of all bookrunning for international bonds, and over 31% of issuing and management of international bonds. These statistics are based on data from *Euromoney*, November 1997, except the estimate on foreign exchange dealings, which is based on the Euromoney Foreign Exchange dealing poll, May 1997 (calculated from a sample of 194 of the largest institutions and based on volume of business placed).

12 'Foreign exchange dealing poll' *Euromoney* 1997.

13 It continues to be so. For example, the IMF continues to pressure countries to liberalise their financial markets, while the General Agreement on Trade in Services, negotiated under the auspices of the World Trade Organisation, is providing a baseline for regulatory reform (see WTO, 1997; Sorsa, 1997).

14 For example, it formed the basis for European capital standards under the single market programme (see Tickell, 1998a).

15 The capital standards were set at a level which most US and UK banks had already met and which effectively penalised more cautious institutional environments such as Germany and Switzerland.

16 Although it remains the case that regulators do not share the views of extreme free-marketeers, who advocate minimal regulation (i.e. Kaufman, 1997) and criticise international co-operation as being monopolistic and anti-competitive (Duffield and Giddy, 1993; Meltzer, 1988).

17 Charles A Bowsher, *Risks and regulation of financial derivatives: hearing before the Senate Committee on Banking, Housing and Financial Affairs* 103d Congress, 2nd Session, May 29, 1994. The speaker was the Comptroller General of the US.

18 The BIS had in fact, begun to address the question, but most suggestions had argued that whatever problems there were would best be addressed within the markets, rather than through active regulatory intervention (see Group of Thirty, 1993; ISDA, 1994). Even a BIS economist has recently admitted that the 'private sector has played the leading role' (White, 1996, 12).

19 This agreement set a baseline for regulatory standards in supervising international banks (see BIS, 1997b; White 1996).

20 Compare, for example, the rhetoric of Tietmeyer (1997), the head of the Bundesbank, with that of Arthur Levitt, chairman of the Securities and Exchange Commission, in *The Insurance Accountant*, (1997).

21 Of course, it remains the case that discursive representations become effective through their mediation with extra-discursive mechanisms (for example, Jessop, 1990; Sayer, 1993).
22 Quoted in J. Seiberg 'Fed chief hints favor for a bill that limits derivatives regulation' *The American Banker* February 24, 1997, p. 2; 'Deregulating futures trade wins backing of Greenspan' *Baltimore Sun* February 22, 1997, p. 20C.
23 'SEC says ex-assistant treasurer lied to Moody's, Standard and Poor's' *The Bond Buyer* February, 1997

REFERENCES

Atkinson, D. and Kelly, R. (1994) *The wrecker's lamp: do currency markets leave us on the rocks* (London, Institute for Public Policy Research, 30-32 Southampton Street, London WC2E 7RA).

Bank of England (1996) *Review of supervision* (London, Bank of England).

Bank of England (1997a) *A risk based approach to supervision: the RATE approach* (London, Bank of England).

Bank of England (1997b) *Banks' internal controls and the Section 39 process: a consultative paper* (London, Bank of England).

Benston, G. and Kaufman, G. (1996) 'The appropriate role of bank regulation', *Economic Journal*, pp. 106, 688-697.

BIS [Bank for International Settlements] (1996) *66th annual report* (Basle, BIS).

BIS [Bank for International Settlements] (1997a) *67th annual report* (Basle, BIS).

BIS [Bank for International Settlements] (1997b) *Compendium of documents produced by the Basle Committee on Banking Supervision Volume One: basic supervisory methods* (Basle, BIS).

BIS and IOSCO [Bank for International Settlements and International Organisation of Securities Commissions] (1995a) *Framework for supervisory information about the derivatives activities of banks and securities firms* (Basle, BIS).

BIS and IOSCO [Bank for International Settlements and International Organisation of Securities Commissions] (1995b) 'Public disclosure of the trading and derivatives activities of banks and securities firms', Reprinted in *Compendium of documents produced by the Basle Committee on Banking Supervision Volume Two: advanced supervisory methods* (Basle, BIS, 1997).

BIS and IOSCO [Bank for International Settlements and International Organisation of Securities Commissions] (1996) 'Survey of disclosures about the trading and derivatives activities of banks and securities firms', Reprinted in *Compendium of documents produced by the Basle Committee on Banking Supervision Volume Two: advanced supervisory methods* (Basle, BIS, 1997).

Black, S. and Young, P. (1997) 'Exchanges vs OTC trading', *Applied Derivatives Trading*, 20 (November), Available from http://www.adtrading.com/adt20/exchotc.hts.

BoBS [Board of Banking Supervision] (1995) *The report of the Board of Banking Supervision into the circumstances of the collapse of Barings* (London, HMSO HC673).

Bond, I., Murphy, G. and Robinson, G. (1994) *'Potential credit exposure on interest rate swaps', Bank of England* ,Working Paper Series 25.

Burns, J. P. (1994) 'Should the derivatives markets be regulated?', *Applied Derivatives Trading, 8* (http://www.adtrading.com/adt8/burns.hts)

Camdessus, M. (1998) 'Toward a new architecture for a globalised world'. Address at the Royal Institute for International Affairs May 8th, and available from the International Monetary Fund, 700 19th Street, N.W., Washington, D.C. 20431 (http://www.imf.org).

Casson, P. (1996) 'Market risk, corporate governance and the regulation of financial firms', *Journal of Financial Regulation and Compliance*, 4, pp. 134-143.

Cerny, P. (1993) 'The deregulation and reregulation of financial markets in a more open world', in P. Cerny (ed.) *Finance and world politics* (Aldershot, Elgar) pp. 51-85.

Chance, D. M. (1995) 'A chronology of derivatives', *Derivatives Quarterly*, 2, Winter, pp. 1-8.

Chew, L. (1996) *Managing derivative risks: the uses and abuses of leverage* (London, Wiley).

Clark, G. L. (1997) 'Rogues and regulation in global finance', *Regional Studies*, 31, pp. 221-236.

Clark, G. L. (1998) 'The retreat of the state', *Working Paper*, WPG 98-2 (available from School of Geography, University of Oxford, Oxford, OX1 3TB).

Cohen, S. S. (1995) 'The challenge of derivatives', *Fordham Law Review*, 63, pp. 1993-2029.

Corcoran, A. M. (1997) 'Populism, demographics and the end of geography: the challenge to regulators of the cyberage', *Applied Derivatives Trading*, 19 (http://www.adtrading.com/adt19/corcnet.hts).

Cronon, W. (1991) *Nature's metropolis: Chicago and the Great West* (New York, WW Norton).

Davis, H. (1996) 'Culture of regulation', *Financial Stability Review*, 1, pp. 7-11.

Dufey, G. and Giddy, I. (1983) 'Trends in international banking and implications for regulation', in E Roussakis (ed.) *International banking* (New York, Praeger) pp. 482-497.

Duffee, G. R. (1996) 'On measuring credit risks of derivative instruments', *Journal of Banking and Finance*, 20, pp. 805-833.

Eichengreen, Tobin, J. and Wypolsz, C. (1995) 'Two cases for sand in the wheels of international finance', *The Economic Journal*, 105, pp. 162-172.

Financial Regulation Report (1997) 'Derivatives disclosure: current developments', *Financial Regulation Report*, February.

Fox, J. (1995) 'Banks say too much capital required by market risk rules', *American Banker*, 22, September, p. 3.

GAO [General Accounting Office] (1994a) *Financial derivatives: action needed to protect the financial system* (Washington, GAO) GAO/GGD-94-133.

GAO [General Accounting Office] (1994a) *Response to the International Swaps and Derivatives Association position paper* (Washington, GAO) GAO/GGD-94-163.

George, E. A. J. (1997) Speech given at a dinner with the Lord Mayor for Bankers and Merchants of the City of London at the Mansion House, 12 June, and available from Bank of England, Threadneedle Street, London.

Gibson, R. and Zimmermann, H. (1994) 'The benefits and risks of derivative instruments: an economic perspective', *International Finance and Commodity Institute Paper, 1* (IFCI, 11 route de Drize, 1227 Geneva, Switzerland).

Greenspan, A. (1998) 'Remarks before the 34th Annual Conference on Bank Structure and Competition of the Federal Reserve Bank of Chicago', May 7th, and available from Board of Governors of the Federal Reserve System, Washington, DC 20551 (http://www.bog.frb.fed.us).

Grossman, S. (1988) 'An analysis of the implications of stock and futures price volatility of program trading and dynamic hedging strategies', *Journal of Business*, 61, pp. 275-298.

Group of 7 (1998) 'Strengthening the architecture of the global financial system', Report of G7 Finance Ministers to G7 Heads of State or Government for their meeting in Birmingham, May 1998.

Group of Thirty (1993) *Derivatives: practices and principles* (Washington, Group of Thirty) 1990 M. Street, NW, Suite 450, Washington, DC 20036.

Group of Thirty (1997) *Global institutions, national supervision and systemic risk* (Washington, Group of Thirty) 1990 M. Street, NW, Suite 450, Washington, DC 20036.

Hawley, J. (1984) 'Protecting capital from itself', *International Organisation*, 38, pp. 138-165.

Helleiner, E. (1994) *States and the emergence of global finance* (Ithaca, Cornell University Press).

Helleiner, E. (1996) 'Post-globalisation: is the financial liberalisation trend likely to be reversed?', in R. Boyer and D. Drache (eds.) *States against markets* (London, Routledge) pp. 193-210.

Hilton, D. J. (1998) 'Identifying successful traders and dealers'. Paper given at the Centre for the Study of Financial Innovation, March.

ISDA [International Swaps and Derivatives Association] (1994) *The GAO report on financial derivatives: good facts and bad conclusions – an ISDA position paper* (New York, ISDA), 1270 Avenue of the Americas, Suite 2118, Rockefeller Center, New York, NY10023.

Jessop, B. (1990) *State theory* (Cambridge, Polity).

Kapstein, E. B. (1992) 'Between power and purpose: central bankers and the politics of regulatory convergence', *International Organisation*, 46, pp. 265-287.

Kapstein, E. B. (1994) *Governing the global economy: international finance and the state* (Cambridge, Harvard UP).

Kaufman, G. (1997) 'Bank failures, systemic risk and bank regulation', *Cato Journal* 16.

Kelly, R. and Hudson, A. (1994) 'Hedging our futures: regulating the derivative markets', *Fabian Society Discussion Paper*, 18 (London, Fabian Society, 11 Dartmouth St, SW1H 9BN).

Lakritz, M. (1995) 'Testimony' before the House Subcommittee on Capital Markets, Securities and Government Sponsored Enterprises, Committee on Banking and Financial Services, Washington, July 27.

Large, A. (1995) 'Regulation for a global marketplace'. Speech given at the 20th Annual conference of IOSCO, 12 July and available from the SIB, Gavrelle House, 2-14 Bunhill Road, London, EC1Y 8RA.

Large, A. (1995) 'The UK's experience of financial service regulation'. Speech given at the University of South Africa, 31 October and available from the SIB, Gavrelle House, 2-14 Bunhill Road, London, EC1Y 8RA.

Levitt, A. (1995) 'Municipal bonds and government securities markets', Testimony before the Committee of Banking, Housing and Urban Affairs, United States Senate, January 5.

Leyshon, A. and Thrift, N. J. (1997) *Money/Space* (London, Routledge).

Leyshon, A. and Tickell, A. (1994) 'Money order? The discursive constitution of Bretton Woods and the making and breaking of regulatory space', *Environment and Planning A*, 26, pp. 1861-1890.

Moran, M. (1990) *The politics of the financial services revolution* (London, Macmillan).

McBarnett, D. and Whelan, C. (1992) 'International corporate finance and the challenge of creative compliance', in J. Fingleton and D. Schoenmaker (eds.), *The internationalisation of capital markets and the regulatory response* (London, Graham and Trotman) pp. 129-142.

Meltzer, A. (1988) 'The policy proposals in the AEI studies', in W. S. Havat and R. M. Kushmeider (eds.), *Restructuring banking and financial services in America* (Washington, American Enterprise Institute).

Merton, R. C. (1995) 'Financial innovation and management and regulation of financial institutions', *Journal of Banking and Finance*, 19, pp. 461-481.

Miller, M. (1986) 'Financial innovation: the last twenty years and the next', *Journal of Financial and Quantitative Analysis*, 21, pp. 459-471.

Ministry of Finance (1995) *The report of the inspectors appointed by the Ministry of Finance* (Singapore, Government of Singapore).

Parsons, J. E. (1988) 'Bubble, bubble, how much trouble? Financial markets, capitalist development and capitalist crises', *Science and Society*, 52, pp. 260-289.

Phillips, S. M. (1997) 'Remarks on whether national financial market regulatory systems should be harmonised in the light of international competition', *BIS Review*, 11, pp. 1-5 (http://www.bis.org).

Roberts, S. (1998) 'Geogovernance in trade and finance and political geographies of dissent', in A. Herod, G. O'Tuathail and S. Roberts (eds.), *An unruly world?* (London, Routledge), pp. 116-134.

Ross, S. A. (1989) 'Institutional markets, financial marketing and financial innovation', *Journal of Finance*, 44, pp. 541-556.

Rubin, R. (1998) Speech at Mansion House, London, May 8th. Available from http://www.treas.gov/press/releases/pr2428.htm.

Sayer, A. (1993) 'Postmodern thought in geography: a realist view', *Antipode*, 25, pp. 320-344.

Shah, A. (1996a) 'Creative compliance in financial reporting', *Accounting, Organisations and Society*, 21, pp. 22-39.

Shah, A. (1996b) 'Regulatory arbitrage through financial innovation', *Accounting, Auditing and Accountability Journal.*

Shah, A. (1996c) 'The dynamics of international bank regulation', *Journal of Financial Regulation and Compliance*, 4, pp. 371-385.

SIB [Securities and Investment Board] (1996) *Equity related derivatives: inside information and public disclosure issues* (London, SIB, Gavrelle House, 2-14 Bunhill Road, London, EC1Y 8RA).

Sinclar, T. J. (1994) 'Passing judgements: credit rating processes as regulatory mechanisms of governance in the emerging world order', *Review of International Political Economy* 1, pp. 133-159.

Smith, A. (1996) *Accounting for growth: stripping the camouflage from company reports* (London, Century).

Sorsa, P. (1997) 'The GATS agreement in financial services: a modest start to financial liberalisation', *IMF Working Paper WP/97/55* (Geneva, IMF).

Stewart, W. (1997) *Bank heist: how our financial giants are costing you money* (Toronto, Harper Collins).

Tickell, A. (1996) 'Making a melodrama out of a crisis: reinterpreting the collapse of Barings Bank', *Environment and Planning D: Society and Space*, 14, 1, pp. 5-33.

Tickell, A. (1998a) 'Europe in the world economy: financial integration and uneven development', in R. Hudson and A. Williams (eds.) (London, Sage).

Tickell, A. (1998b) 'Globalization and the culture of finance', Paper presented at the annual conference of the Association of American Geographers, Boston, March 1998, and available from the author at Department of Geography, University of Southampton, Southampton, SO17 1BJ.

Tickell, A. (forthcoming) 'Creative finance and the local state: the Hammersmith and Fulham swaps affair', *Political Geography.*

Tietmeyer, H. (1997) 'Globalisation of financial markets and the need for international standards and harmonisation of prudential agreements'. Speech presented at the 'Financial stability and prudential standards' conference, Hong Kong, September 22 and available from Deutsche Bundesbank, Wilhelm-Epstein-Str. 14, P.O.B. 10 06 02, D-60006 Frankfurt am Main, Germany.

Treasury Committee (1996) *Barings Bank and international regulation* (London, HMSO, HC65-1).

Warner, J. (1998) 'US forced to ease regulation as banks head for London', *The Independent*, February 2, p. 19.

White, W. R. (1996) 'International agreements in the area of banking and finance', *Bank for International Settlements, Working Paper 38* (Basle, BIS).

WTO [World Trade Organisation] (1997) *Opening markets in financial services and the role of the GATS* (Geneva, World Trade Organisation) (http://www.wto.org).

GLOBALISATION, CLASS AND THE QUESTION OF DEMOCRACY

Joachim Hirsch

I

The postmodern has abandoned class. Class theory is no longer 'chic', to say nothing of class politics. The dominant social theories now accept as fact what democratic theory once treated as fiction: an individualised 'civil society' where social inequalities are seen not so much a problem as a structural necessity and as providing the basic incentive to compete in a society primarily oriented to 'success' in the global market. The prevailing academic interpretations of our era certainly contradict the reality of a capitalism in which national and international inequalities become ever more conspicuous, in which neo-liberal strategies of crisis management have not only deepened existing forms of exploitation but generated new ones through 'rationalisation' and 'structural adjustment', and in which the pressure of international accumulation increasingly works its unmediated effects on national political and social processes (Hirsch 1995).

The removal of class from academic discourse, just when globalisation is so palpably restructuring social relations and international conflict in the context of economic dependency and exploitation, has certainly got something to do with the state of class theory itself, not least with its traditional focus on class and class conflict within the arena of the nation-state. The widespread diminution of class themes in postwar theoretical discourse had a lot to do with the political-economic structure of 'Fordist' capitalism, which was distinguished by its strong focus on domestic markets, the development of widely inclusive mass production and consumption, the expanded domain of national state regulation, sustained economic growth, a system of progressive social security provision and finally, the institutionalisation of class conflict. The vision of a state interventionist, egalitarian and politically integrated society appeared to have obviated the question of class struggle as a pressing social problem. It is clear today that this was nothing more than an short episode in the history of capitalism.

Nevertheless, social transitions, crises and the conditions for social reproduction have changed so much that class theory needs new categories and perspectives. While Marx in *The Eighteenth Brumaire* long ago identified decisive contradictions in the relationship between the class structure and institutional forms of liberal democratic politics, these appeared in some way to be resolved by the socially co-operative arrangements of Fordism. The revolutionary and reforming struggle of the working class, from which Fordism emerged, may be understood as society's reaction to self-destructive tendencies inherent to capital, as Polanyi (1990) suggested. This illustrates the paradoxical situation whereby the class struggle, as it were, 'rescued' capitalism. Today, the problem of social continuity in reaction to the self-destructiveness of capitalist market economies is posed in renewed and sharper form, following the crisis of Fordism, global capitalist restructuring, and the withering of traditional labour movements.

The existence of liberal democratic institutions and procedures at the level of the nation-state was an essential precondition for the labour movement's 'reformist' struggles. A relatively closed and secure national society also became an unspoken basis for most liberal democratic theory. It made the notion of a clear relationship between those governing and those governed - voters and their representatives - conceivable, lending significance to concepts such as 'participation' and 'democratic legitimation' (Held 1991). A democratic process which can empower citizens and ensure popular control over political institutions is, in principle, possible only when social and political membership is clearly defined and only when a democratic government possesses the capacity of a sovereign entity. The cornerstone of all legal, political and democratic theory, the concept of a social contract, had its decisive justification and foundation in the correspondence between a 'people' and a 'government'. Of course, the reality of this supposed unity of governed and governing has never fully materialised. It has always been true that many of those living within a state's boundaries never had more than formal access to civil rights, that the possibilities for political co-operation were limited by social irregularities and relations of economic control and that the scope for state action was restricted by economic power structures. Moreover, as the politics of each nation-state had consequences beyond their borders, internal social transitions were also determined by international power relations.

But the liberal democratic assumption of a system of nation-states is clearly undermined when subjects cannot vote on political decisions because they do not have rights of citizenship; when people live outside state borders; or when the relevant decisions do not fall within the institutional remit of the nation-state. It would appear that the process of economic globalisation and the concomitant structural transformation of the nation-state have finally put an end to what was at all credible in liberal democratic theory. Categories such as 'the people, 'the electorate', 'responsibility', 'participation' become deeply problematic (Held 1991: 197). 'Membership' - whether it is within a powerful interest group, a security enclave, the richest segments of society, or even a community club or cultural grouping - becomes increasingly indeterminate at both national and international levels.

The social structure of 'post-Fordism' is marked by the link between growing social division at the national level and the expanding movements of refugees and emigration internationally (Narr/Schubert 1994: 74ff). As a consequence, the notion of a unitary national society is increasingly invalidated. More than ever, claims for nationhood and community cannot conceal the extent to which their own material bases have come into question. These developments appear to the indefatigable positivists of mainstream sociology as some autonomous process of 'individualisation', 'multiculturalism' or a 'pluralisation of lifestyles'. In contrast, a critical perspective requires an appreciation that these developments are rooted not so much in the self-defining behaviour of individuals, or in a generalisation of postmodern values, as in the dynamic process of global accumulation and the massive restructuring that is bound up with it.

The transformation of working relations is crucial. The process of rationalisation set in motion to bring order to the crisis of Fordism resulted, in most advanced capitalist countries, in a degree of structural long-term unemployment which would earlier have been ruled out as destabilising of the liberal democratic political system. The reason for this development lies in the fact that the traditional Keynesian mechanisms for global regulation no longer hold. A policy concerned principally with increasing the value of capital assets and securing international competitiveness *must* consciously and strategically factor in mass unemployment in spite of all rhetorical assurances to the contrary. Ultimately, it serves to break resistance to the widespread restructuring of the production process. However, the greater the growth in unemployment and the loosening of the social security system, the less likely it is that social provision will be able to shelter the so-called 'victims of modernisation' who have been left out of work. Marginal work and unemployment become ever more associated with material deprivation. The permanent split between employed and unemployed has become as striking a feature of society as the division between privileged elite employees and marginalised casual workers.

'Deregulation' is the antidote widely proposed by economic 'experts'. What is intended is the loosening or dismantling of tariffs and legal restraints, the direct abolition of standardised work practices in addition to an indirect deregulation of employment relations by means of a growing disparity in pay and increased pressure for mobility. This strategy aims to boost profits through a marked decrease in average net income and the intensification of work; in other words, a fundamental redistribution of social wealth. Whatever the 'success' of this restructuring, its recognised consequence in every case is the expansion of the industrial reserve army and intensification of social divisions.

The effects of rationalisation and deregulation set by the world market are manifest in an industrial 'human resource' strategy less concerned with a stable core workforce than with an ever more mobile and easily serviceable 'flexible core labour reserve', which may be supplemented by short or part-time employees, by subcontracted firms or by personnel supplied by employment agencies. Drawing on labour from companies operating in low wage areas reinforces this trend. Recourse to 'just-in-time' production methods - involving economically dependent service and supply subcontractors operating with tight cost margins - increases the numbers of poorly paid and socially uninsured workers. The difference in the level of security enjoyed by the marginalised, mass workforce dependent on low pay, and the relatively privileged core of workers, in regular employment, is gradually being eroded. The heavily regulated and relatively secure employment status enjoyed by so many qualified males during the Fordist phase of metropolitan capitalism has been steadily disappearing. All workers stand in an increasingly comparable relation to a 'productivity' and 'quality' dynamic which is underpinned by enforced pressure for loyalty, service and conformity (Elam 1994; Tomaney 1994).

Evidence of marginalisation may be seen, for example, in the rapid increase in the numbers of German workers without employment guarantees or social security provisions. The phenomenon of the 'new self-sufficiency', i.e. a shift from formal salaried work to self-employment brought on by the pressure of rationalisation and mass unemployment, must be added to the picture. This self-employment is associated not only with demanding performance and mobility requirements, but also with an increasing frequency of employment-related injuries. Income for almost half of those self-employed is, moreover, below the national average in Germany.

The worsening economic, social and political inequalities of post-Fordist accumulation, and the greater dependency, pauperisation and political repression which correspond to these conditions, intensify the pressures of enforced emigration and refugee movements. Despite increased control mechanisms, much of this migration flows into expanding cities and provides the market there with cheap, possibly illegal labour, deprived of adequate political and social rights (Castells 1994). The fact that international capital was always founded on 'combined' forms of production, control and exploitation (Balibar/Wallerstein 1992: 215ff) becomes even more apparent in the urban centres in the wake of globalisation.

The resultant splintering of the social structure is such that the existing models of class and strata no longer have any great explanatory efficacy. Faced with the divisions between multinational and local companies, pioneering high-tech firms and dependent suppliers, specialist service providers and traditional branches of industry threatened with extinction, it is ever more difficult to speak of capital ownership itself as giving rise to a single class. At the same time, marginalised workers in their varying forms, together with the apparently 'self-employed', are growing in numbers even as a relatively privileged stratum of highly qualified and remunerated employees, working internationally in the high-tech, finance and management sectors, comes into being. Such a large chasm has opened between those core employees in international management, communications, financial and service sectors, on the one hand, and the rest of the traditional workforce, the semi-sufficient and self-employed, those farmers not already ruined by agricultural big business, those on low-pay, part-time and job-share schemes and the world of immigrants and black labour, on the other, that the difference between working-class and middle-class has become more tenuous.

This does not, of course, mean that collectivities which have defined themselves through similarities in their everyday activities, lifestyle and perceptions of the world will disappear. In some social science research, particularly in the field of voting behaviour and consumer trends, it has become conventional to distinguish between different social 'milieux' instead of classes or strata. Bourdieu's notion of 'habitus' is one example: the method and style by which people understand and form their social existence in a way which, though not wholly independent from material circumstances, is actively constructed by specific socio-cultural conditions. Interestingly, the concept of milieu can be traced back to work carried out by the commercial market research agency (SINUS) which distinguished working milieux according to the following categories: 'new', 'distinguished conservative', 'technocratic liberal', 'alternative', 'lower middle class', a milieu 'of social mobility', a 'hedonistic milieu', a 'traditional' and, finally, a milieu 'without traditions'. In contrast another research group led by Michael Vester divided society into a different typology of milieux: 'progressive, successfully modern', 'the classless modern', 'the sceptical modern employee' and a 'contented established conservative centre' - a group which corresponds to roughly a quarter of the population (Vester 1993; compare Schulze 1992). Both these investigations come to the conclusion that society is polarising towards the top and the bottom, permitting the emergence of a wide range in the middle which is highly diverse in its social practices and conditions.

It is questionable whether such analyses possess any validity beyond their principal aim - providing statistics about group-specific consumption and voting patterns (compare Ritsert 1988a). Motivated by the objective of generating commercially applicable data about social and political behaviour, researchers cannot avoid distilling out relatively stable 'milieux'. The question arises, however, whether these milieux are not mere intellectual constructs which only superficially describe the real fragmentation of society. This is suggested by the fact that immigrant and refugee populations, who are neither entitled to vote nor offer strong consumer profiles, are as a rule excluded from such investigations. And just how little can be understood about contemporary social patterns from these conceptualisations is indicated by the increasing unreliability of their election forecasts.

Nevertheless the basic observation of such research - that the social structure is becoming ever more differentiated due to economic shifts without, however, being simply defined by an abstract concept of 'individualisation' - remains correct. Objective disparities in socio-economic conditions, though expressed in different ways socio-culturally, remain decisive for understanding and social positioning. In view of the growing commercialisation of lifestyles, social differentiation theory - the attempt to demonstrate social belonging and differentiation by means of objective consumption - appears ever more important. Wearing particular brand names becomes an expensive passport to social inclusion.

Social milieux which come into being like this, however, are not independent of their underlying class structure - in the sense of 'objective' material conditions and possibilities - although they are less and less defined by these alone. This is why the concept of a 'pluralistic class society' describes social reality more adequately than talk of an 'individualised' society 'beyond class and social rank' (Beck 1986). Nevertheless, between socially advanced 'boutique bourgeois' workers, on the one hand, and exploited low-cost workers or refugees forced into the underground economy (whether self-employed or officially remunerated) on the other, there still exists an important cultural and social divide.

The notion of a 'two thirds society' describes a situation in which an impoverished and socially excluded 'third' of society stands in contrast to the comfortable majority which politically dictates crucial social developments on the basis of its numerical supremacy. This description is misleading not only because it still posits the existence of relatively homogenous social groups but also because it misrepresents the ratios involved. What Robert Reich sees as a split in US society between an elite twenty percent and a downwardly mobile, or already marginalized, eighty percent, is probably closer to reality (Reich, 1991).

The model of consumption typical of Fordism is placed under severe pressure by these developments. Increased differentiations in wealth, enforced by conspicuous displays of social difference, impact upon consumption patterns. Mass consumption is nevertheless a notable feature of post-Fordist capitalism. Consumption patterns and lifestyles become increasingly differentiated as a result of material inequality and a marketing strategy which seeks to overcome market saturation by individualising and pluralising the products on offer. This differentiation is made possible by means of flexible post-Fordist mass production, which puts the producer in a position to reproduce the same product in a virtually infinite variety of styles. Consumption shifts its focus, in the main, towards profitable capitalist goods and services, videos and computers, electronic communications, clothing, fast food and cars, whilst collective consumer interests such as housing, health, culture and education, the environment and so forth become more restricted and uneconomic thanks to the dismantling of state social provision. Car ownership can easily become bound up with broader living conditions, so that the attempt to escape poorer conditions results in congestion and pollution. Amongst an apparently endless variety of products, a new form of social deprivation is spreading - the lack of collective goods - which obviously affects most of all those who do not have sufficient income to purchase products and services in the market.

The cycle of consumption remains unbroken; it follows a logic which means ever more work in order to buy ever less useful, and also ever more damaging, goods (of which the private car is the symbol par excellence). However, a contradiction arises as a growing portion of society come to exist at the fringes of this hi-tech consumer world as a result of their low pay and unemployment. Whilst one group works longer and more intensively, in order to consume more post-Fordist products of conspicuous consumption, the other works less and less to buy post-Fordist mass products. Italian designer clothing labels and their Hong Kong or Chinese imitations exemplify this difference.

II

Capitalist society is fundamentally determined by the contradictory interrelation of classes and a market-based society. In effect, this means that social status is still decided as much by the individual's objective position in the production process as by his or her standing as a free and equal subject of the market. Under the conditions of post-Fordist restructuring, this relationship takes on a particular dynamic. The transition to a service sector society means a further push in the direction of an all-embracing capitalism. As the class compromises brokered by the trade unions and the 'people's parties' (*Volksparteien*) continue to disintegrate and as the socioeconomic layers of society drift further apart, the dominance of the market has become more apparent. The market value of an individual's labour is becoming increasingly decisive, and without private access to capital, important products of high consumerism and thus social recognition remain out of reach. The tendency is for each individual to become an entrepreneur, even if only as a purveyor of his or her own labour. Whoever fails to provide the market with the required achievements is threatened by social marginalisation or descent into one of the many and diverse subcultural milieux.

The prevailing sociological term used to describe this process is individualisation (see especially Beck 1986 and 1993). As we have already established, this does not mean that collective social groupings no longer exist. Rather, the term implies that these groupings are subject to increasing differentiation. This development is not new; it was actually a fundamental characteristic of Fordist capitalism. Indeed, it is rather undergoing a certain degree of accentuation and modification. The dismantling of welfare-state security, the increasing commercialisation of social relations and the fragmentation of society combine with intensified economic pressure and ever greater social inequality. Seen in abstract terms, individualisation determines the life of a single female computer specialist just as much as that of an illegal immigrant who sells flowers and newspapers to pub customers at night. However, their respective social opportunities differ tremendously. Yet even the possibilities opened by gaining professional qualifications appear in a different light when certificates offer no more than an entrance ticket to a precarious job market. These prospects look just as poor for a taxi-driving sociologist as for an academically qualified cleaner. The motorcycle messenger, seemingly the very embodiment of mobility and freedom, is not merely working in an extremely unhealthy, rather dangerous and modestly paid job, but is also exposed to enormous risks in old age and in the case of sickness.

Without doubt, the progressive implementation and expansion of market-based society and the dissolution of tightly defined classes and social affiliations are raising individual opportunities and freedom of choice, when combined with a dose of good fortune and the ability to achieve. At least in developed urban areas, relative prosperity and the welfare security won by past struggles have allowed the struggle for sheer survival and the battle against material want to recede into the background of society's general consciousness. At the same time, conventional socio-cultural commitments have been weakened by accelerated capitalist modernisation and this has contributed to the process. The observation that subjective lifestyle shaping, self-styling and 'experience orientation' are becoming more important is certainly not totally misguided. Nevertheless, the catchword 'experience society' ('*Erlebnisgesellschaft*', Schulze 1992) is misleading, and not just because it obfuscates the underlying economic processes. If shaping one's individual lifestyle is becoming more important, this is not achieved, today at least, in the spirit of creative self-determination, but rather as a result of a passive response to an ever more differentiated and aggressively marketed capitalist supply of goods and services which flexible specialised production has generated. The subjective 'aestheticisation of everyday life' (Schulze 1992) shows clear signs of a 'totalising aesthetic of the product'. 'Experience' is above all *consumption*, empirical investigations have shown. Thus the individualisation and pluralisation of society not only remain entrenched within capitalist one-dimensionality, but this one-dimensionality actually appears to be strengthened by it. The pluralisation or individualisation of society must not be understood in the final instance as an objective trend, but must instead be seen to have arisen out of changed societal perceptions, where the individual's power to shape his or her own destiny *appears* to be enhanced despite the persistence of social inequality and traditional socio-cultural affiliations falling by the wayside. It is not least the consequence of political and ideological developments in which the capitalist unravelling of institutionalised class compromises plays just as big a role as the critique launched by the social protest movements against bureaucratic and standardised mass consumer society. The existence of a neoliberal hegemony since the collapse of the Fordist social project is pivotal, in which capitalist restructuring and social critique have both played an important role. This complex of economic, political and ideological processes and struggles contributes considerably to the legitimation of current societal upheaval.

Real freedom always presupposes a certain degree of equality and security which can be translated into a materially founded common community. At the same time it includes the right to and the possibility of difference, for example in relations between the sexes or through the expression of different cultural orientations and ways of living. The contradictory relationship between freedom, equality and difference is becoming ever more critical in the process of radical escalation towards an entirely market-based society (Balibar 1993: 99ff). The creation of nationally bound, and thus relatively homogeneous, societies was an important prerequisite for capitalist development. Now it is becoming apparent that the growth of a global capitalist economy is beginning to reverse this process, i.e. money relations are not only undermining their own natural foundations, but also the social preconditions which have existed until now. The disappearance of a 'community' - which under prevailing economic conditions has to discipline and 'normalise' its members through the application of force - can indeed be greeted as a movement towards liberation. The irony, however, is that those who are driving the restructuring process with such determination are precisely those who consider this development to signal at the same time a dangerous erosion of values.

The relationship between political democracy and economic class structure thereby takes on a new and explosive character. If one assumes that capitalist society derives its staying power from the fact that political and social forms are developed by society to preserve itself and its ecological foundations against the threat posed by commodification, and this presupposes, in turn, the existence of minimal democratic structures and meaningful participation, then the consequences of globalisation are somewhat alarming. They point above all to the undermining of democracy at its very foundations: at the level of the nation-state. The danger of societal self-destruction at the hands of society's own economic dynamic is ever present today - catastrophe after catastrophe, global environmental disaster, mass poverty, military conflict and latent or open civil war are all evidence of this fact.

III

The burning question remains that of finding a foundation for an emancipatory, democratic social movement, whose horizons extend beyond factional and defensive warfare. This assumes, of course, that opposition from the exploited and oppressed within a globalised capitalism will continue to be characterised by partial, isolated forms of resistance, which often pit groups in struggle against one another. Chances seem slim that such struggles could be unified into a common front against international capital. To conceive of liberation in terms of an heroic final battle between opposing classes would certainly be to repeat a mistake. Real revolutionary processes have little to do with masses united under a General staff, or with the expression of simple antagonisms, but are rather produced when contradictions and conflicts are distilled: they come about when varied interests and oppositions disregard existing differences to form a movement. This does not take the form of an idealized process of unification, but is an historical process in which people reflect on their different experiences, build understandings with others, and make difficult compromises. Central to this process is that people struggle, that a rebellious consciousness is sustained and prevented from regressing into nationalism or sexism.

As the grip of global capitalism tightens, posing new challenges to those seeking to beat an independent path in national politics and development, the prospects for struggles which confine themselves to the national arena dwindle. Precisely because capital is organized systemically on an international scale, emancipatory possibilities today require the cultivation of a new internationalism; an internationalism which, if only because the scope of state power is dwindling, must be based on organisational forms that are autonomous and capable of extending solidarity to overcome conditions of social and political fragmentation. Restricted to the national state level, social movements fail not merely because of this reduced sphere of action, but also because a nationally oriented politics runs the risk of embroiling itself in spatial competition which threatens to deepen inequalities between regions.

Of course, objective commonalities such as exploitation and deprivation are a basic prerequisite for social movements and struggles. But experience of these social conditions is extremely diverse, particularly at the international level, and movements only become powerful once they succeed in developing convincing concrete utopias. If a new class politics is to emerge under these conditions it will develop on the basis, not so much of objectively given experiences, but rather, of a politically constructed vision and project. What is necessary, first and foremost, is a search for visions of a better world in which the bonds of dependency, instrumentalism and extra-human modes of coordination may be broken. Traditional models of social democracy offer no answer to this problem. It is no longer merely a question of material prosperity and distribution, but also one of freedom and human dignity. A new 'International' must therefore take the form of a radical movement for democracy and human rights. Such a movement can develop most quickly through a growing network of autonomously organised and internationally active organisations and groups of organisations. This has already been witnessed in certain fields, such as around ecological, women's, peace and human rights concerns (see Hirsch 1995a: 183ff and Hirsch 1995b). Whilst starting points for an international movement are already evident, they are still largely absent from trade union politics. Of vital importance to these new organisations and projects is their autonomy from the national state and party apparatus which is necessarily subject to the logic of the competition and commodification.

This new politics called for here demands a recognition of existing differences - diverse historical traditions and ways of living as well as divergence of material interests. Given increasing social inequality, stark disparities in material standards of living, and often conflicting political frameworks, a new internationalism will be possible only after dispelling the illusion of a common ground, so that diverse starting points and interests may be appreciated and respected. If interests and goals are not identical, critical engagement over differences and the building of compromise is required. The success of this dynamic process requires, finally, that struggles are conducted in the first instance *locally*. In sum, it should be underlined that the question of class theory and class politics has to be understood more than ever using the Gramscian concepts of politics and hegemony. A revolutionary movement should be seen, not as a simple class movement, but as a process of building a new hegemony which embraces very different – and of course conflicting – interests and actors, which is rooted in concrete experiences in alternative social practices, and which aims at a thoroughly new and still unknown model of a truly free society. We cannot, of course, look to any narrowly defined proletarian party process - a notion that was in any case questioned from the start - as our model. What that means in concrete political and organizational terms remains open to further theoretical consideration and, above all, to a critical engagement with concrete movements in struggle around the world: from Mexican Zapatistas and Brazilian landless people, to French transport workers or airline pilots. A totally new conception of both the form and content of revolutionary politics is needed.

As social polarization has dramatically increased in the wake of capitalist crisis and restructuring, a reinstatement of class struggle to the central place it once held within critical theory is needed. A theory of society with critical and revolutionary aspirations must be capable of adapting to the changing historical circumstances it seeks to understand. Class politics in globalised capitalism cannot be expected to conform to models generated out of the historical experiences of the nineteenth and early twentieth century. The aim is no longer one of liberation from poverty through industrialisation and technical progress spawned by capitalist development. The problem is not the 'fettering', but rather, the catastrophic liberation, of productive forces. State power structures are characterised much less by the existence of opposing camps than by the increasing totalitarianism of neoliberal one-dimensionality. To this extent the 'democratic question' is more central now than ever before. Given the technical possibilities available to humanity, social emancipation today must refocus on the task of abolishing the conditions in which the individual exists as a wretched, degraded and servile being, to quote Marx once more. However, what this means practically is rather more complicated than Marx imagined.

The utopia which was once called socialism or communism has disappeared just as much as its concrete historical manifestations. It must be recognised that social liberation does not mean the implementation of a ready-made social model. Social liberation must rather consist in creating space for the realisation of, not one, but a multiplicity of different life-plans and conceptions of society. Such objectives are not served by any traditional concept of a homogeneous class movement. They must be achieved through a multiplicity of social forms. It must be realised that capitalism, which is only now showing its true colours, cannot be shaped, formed or harnessed to collective purposes. Democratic politics, if it is to earn its name, must aim not just to modify existing societal conditions, but actually to remove them. It is a matter of revolutionising economic, social and political relations in their entirety in a way which would transcend all traditional notions of a socialist revolution.

At the same time, conditions for such a revolution have never been so diverse. In the centres of capitalism at least, the option of a political revolution along traditional lines is neither plausible nor desirable. In contradistinction to many peripheral countries, it is not a question there of creating the economic and social preconditions for a reasonably functional liberal democracy. What is required instead is a revolution in life patterns, social relations, modes of consumption, ways of working and conceptions of progress. At the same time, capitalist state rule has become all-inclusive, pervading all aspects of life, and has thus become progressively 'totalitarian'. Precisely as a result of this, it has become technically and politically vulnerable to an extent never witnessed before. Elections to positions of state power do not have any of the revolutionary potential that mass acts of refusal do, actions which reject day-to-day conformity with the system, based on a practical awareness that not everything needs to be tolerated. It must be understood that capital is not constituted by objects or people, but is rather a set of social relations in which everyone is involved, and which everyone reproduces through their everyday practical behaviour. The state and political parties form part of these relations. Globalisation and neoliberalism are not simply imposed on us from outside. They are produced and stabilised by everyone through everyday practices, ways of living, modes of consumption, relations between the sexes and current value systems. As for effecting a radical change to this situation, the ruling engine of economic and political development can be derailed more readily, the more comprehensive and complicated its machinery becomes. And through this very process, new and genuinely democratic politics and institutions can be formed.

The contradiction inherent in talk of a 'class society without classes' is only an apparent one. Capitalism denotes a society in which exploitative material relations and their attendant social conflicts represent the motor of development and structural change. This is particularly evident in the crisis of Fordism and subsequent global restructuring. Analysis of capitalism must be class analysis (Ritsert, 1988b). At the same time, objective class conditions manifested in the process of production and appropriation of societal surplus are being overlaid by a multiplicity of cultural, ethnic, racial, national, gender and social divisions and differences. This is a fundamental characteristic of capitalist society, but in the current process of restructuring, it is proving to have an even greater influence. This is why material socio-economic position provides ever fewer clues to social consciousness and political behaviour. In terms of the distribution of individual opportunities, class affiliation nevertheless does still have a profound effect. But increasingly cultural and political relations are superseding economic class position - exemplified by the impact of the consumer and media industries and the structure of the international political system - so that class is submerged ever more deeply beneath multiple layers of social relations and political consciousness, nearly beyond the point of recognition.

Seen in this light, an anti-capitalist revolution has perhaps never been as attractive an option as it is today, particularly if it seeks to incorporate broader social antagonisms such as relations between the sexes and between human beings and nature. The globally networked and technologically advanced capitalist system is not only always teetering on the edge of crisis, but is also more economically and politically vulnerable than ever before. But taking advantage of this vulnerability will require overcoming capital's cultural hegemony. Today, people appear less able than ever to look beyond their everyday bread-and-butter social obligations, to develop a sense of the opportunities of which they are continually stripped and to perceive the affront to human dignity experienced every day within the lives they are forced to lead. The ideological hegemony of the capitalist way of life has probably never been so anchored in our group consciousness as it is today. Increasing social fragmentation combined with growing inequalities at the national and international level do not necessarily act to counter this hegemony. Indeed, these factors can actually consolidate its power in direct proportion to the level of general acceptance that there is no alternative to current social relations.

A real revolution must therefore encompass more than social and the political transformation: it must be a cultural revolution as well. This cannot mean the same thing everywhere, but at the same time, much can be learned from the traditions and experiences of others. In this way, the diversity, decentralization and multiplicity of struggles should be seen as more than the unfortunate necessary result of diverse economic and political structures; rather they are potentially positive factors in the development of revolutionary theory through the practical struggles of our time.

REFERENCES

Balibar, E 1993: *Die Grenzen der Demokratie,* Hamburg.

Balibar, E and Wallerstein, I 1992: *Rasseklasse Nation. Ambivalente Identitäten,* 2. Edition, Hamburg.

Beck, U 1986: *Risikogesellschaft,* Frankfurt am Main.

Beck, U 1993: *Die Erfindung des Politischen,* Frankfurt am Main.

Castells, M 1994: 'European Cities, the Informational Society and the Global Economy', in: *New Left Review,* N.204.

Elam, M 1994: 'Puzzling out the Post-Fordist Debate', in Ash, A (Ed.), *Post Fordism,* Oxford.

Held, D 1991: 'Democracy, the Nation State and the Global System', in: Ders (Ed.) *Political Theory Today,* Cambridge.

Hirsch, J 1986: *Der Sicherheitsstaat,* 2. Edition, Frankfurt am Main.

Hirsch, J 1995a: *Der nationale Wettbewerbsstaat, Staat, Demokratie und Politik im globalisierten Kapitalismus,.* Amsterdam/Berlin.

Hirsch, J 1995b: 'Nation State, international regulation and the question of democracy', in *Review of International Economy,* V.2, N.2.

Marx, K 1969: *Der achtzehnte Brumaire des Louis Bonaparte,* in: MEW, Bd. 8, Berlin.

Narr, W-D & Schubert, A: *Weltökonomie. Die Misere der Politik,* Frankfurt am Main.

Polanyi, K 1990: *The Great Transformation. Politische und ökonomische Ursprünge von Gesellschaften und Wirtschaftssystemen,* 2. Edition, Frankfurt am Main.

Reich, R 1991: *The Work of Nations,* New York.

Ritsert, J 1988a: *Über die Aeronautik von Heißluftballons. Sozialwissenschaftliche Studientexte,* Special Edition 2, Frankfurt am Main.

Ritsert, J 1988b: *Der Kampf um das Surplusprodukt,* Frankfurt am Main.

Roth, K-H 1994: 'Die Wiederkehr der Proletariat und die Angst der Linken', in Ders (Ed.) *Die Wiederkehr der Proletariat,* Cologne.

Schulze, G 1992: *Die Erlebnisgesellschaft,* Frankfurt am Main.

Tomaney, J 1994: 'A New Paradigm of Work Organization and Technology?', in Ash, A (Ed.), *Post-Fordism,* Oxford.

Vester, M et. al. 1993: *Soziale Milieus im gesellschaftlichen Strukturwandel,* Cologne.

THE CHALLENGE FOR THE LEFT: RECLAIMING THE STATE

Boris Kagarlitsky

For Marxists, the question of the state has always been above all a question of power. Marx and Engels spoke of state institutions as a system of organized and legalized class coercion. Lenin not only saw in the question of power the main question of any revolution, but also reduced it to the seizure and subsequent transformation of the 'state machinery'. By the 1970s, however, it had become obvious that the state no longer enjoyed a monopoly on power. Michel Foucault shook the thinking of the radical intelligentsia by showing that power is dispersed, and does not by any means reside only where people are accustomed to look for it. This was inevitably reflected in the strategy of the left. Realizing that the state did not possess the totality of real power in modern capitalism, people on the left became disillusioned with the possibilities which the state offered. But if the state does not dispose of all power, that does not mean that the question of power can be decided outside of and apart from the state. Too few on the left have posed the question of using the state as a bridgehead in the struggle for real power. Yet without this, any discussion on reforms loses its meaning.

A theoretical argument which is more and more often invoked in order to justify inaction holds that the national state is now losing its significance. The weakening of the role of the national state in the context of the 'global market' is an incontestable fact. But it is equally indisputable that despite this weakening, the state remains a critically important factor of political and economic development. It is no accident that transnational corporations constantly make use of the national state as an instrument of their policies.

It is clear that the left needs to have its own international economic strategy, and to act in a coordinated way on a regional scale, but the instrument and starting-point of this new cooperation can only be a national state. In a country where unique resources are present (and many countries including Russia, Mexico and South Africa have such resources), and where regional business interests are concentrated, even large transnational corporations will prefer to make concessions to the state sector rather than to place at risk the very possibility of their participating in this market.

Among many left thinkers, a healthy skepticism with regard to the possibilities of the state has very quickly been replaced by completely absurd theories in the spirit of 'stateless socialism'. In the 1950s, when socialists posed the question of nationalization, liberal ideologues stressed that public ownership was not as important as the mechanism of control. In the 1980s, however, massive privatization began, leading to the destruction of the state sector on a world scale, after which a significant sector of the left has not only failed to resist privatization, but has in practice become reconciled to its results.

For the most part, left thinkers have become reconciled to the image of the state as a demoralized bureaucratic machine that is unable to carry out effective management and which merely swallows taxpayers' money. It has to be recognized that such images do not appear out of thin air. But in most countries it was not the left that created the state bureaucracy, even if the left figures in the consciousness of millions of people as the servant and defender of bureaucracy. At the same time the right effectively exploits for its interests both the annoyance of citizens with the state, and their no less powerful demand that the state defend them against foreign threats. Such threats more and more often turn out to consist not of hordes of foreign warriors, but of mountains of foreign goods, crowds of half-starved emigrants, and a mafia that is rapidly internationalizing itself – in short, the natural consequences of the economic policies pursued by the right itself.

The problem of the state becomes insoluble for the left from the moment when it rejects the idea of the radical transformation of the structures of power. The established state structures start to appear unshakeable. They can either be accepted or rejected. On the symbolic level, many on the left do both. Practical politics, which unavoidably give rise to constant changes in state structures and institutions, becomes a monopoly of the right. The democratization of power and the participation of the masses in decision-making cannot in themselves guarantee that social reforms will be successful. But if progressive social forces, on coming to power, do not begin promptly to democratize the institutions of the state, this can only end in the degeneration and ignominious collapse of left governments.

Globalisation and the left

Globalisation has become a key idea of neo-liberalism in the 1990s, against a background of the downfall of all other ideologies, and the thesis of the 'impotence of the state' has acquired three bases. On this view, governments are regarded as powerless in relation to transnational corporations (such as Microsoft, Ford or the Russian Gazprom); to international financial institutions such as the World Bank and the International Monetary Fund; and finally, to inter-state formations such as the North American Free Trade Association (NAFTA) or the bodies created on the basis of the Maastricht Treaty in Europe.

Globalisation, however, is nothing qualitatively new in the history of bourgeois society. Capitalism was born and grew to maturity as a world system. It was only toward the end of the eighteenth century that national capitalism, rooted in the social structures of particular Western countries, began to develop. This national capitalism, like modern nations themselves, was not a precondition for but a product of the development of capitalism as a world system. At the end of the twentieth century, capitalism is again becoming directly global. This does not put an end to national societies or states, although they are in profound crisis, as they also were in early capitalism (as the world systems school has rightly noted).

'Modern states are not the primordial frameworks within which historical development has occurred,' notes Wallerstein. 'They may be more usefully conceived as one set of social institutions within the capitalist world-economy, this latter being the framework with which, and of which, we can analyze the structures, conjunctures, and events.'[1] Or as James Petras puts it:

> In the twentieth century 'globalisation' was intense until 1914, followed by a prolonged period of shift to national development during the late 1920s to the mid-1940s, followed by an increasing and uneven effort from the 1950s to the 1970s to return to globalization. The overthrow of nationalist and socialist regimes and the increased competitiveness of Asian capitalism in the 1980s has led to the current period of 'globalization', a phase which is itself today under increasing attack from within most countries, North and South. Thus globalization is not the 'ultimate' phase of capitalism but rather a product of state policies linked to international economic institutions.[2]

The development of capitalism is always cyclical, and there are no grounds for asserting that the changes that have occurred in society by the end of the twentieth century are in principle 'irreversible'. Nevertheless, we should not lose sight of the qualitative differences between globalisation and the preceding periods of internationalization of capitalism. Thanks to technological progress and victory in the Cold War, the capitalist world system for the first time in its history has really become a world system. The prediction by Marx and Engels in the Communist Manifesto, that capitalism would overcome all state and national boundaries, has been realized in full measure only a hundred and fifty years later.

Encountering the phenomenon of globalisation, left analysts have become divided into two camps. Some have seen globalisation as an inevitable process, technologically preordained and impossible to resist, while others have viewed it as a product of the political will of the bourgeoisie, almost as a conspiracy, which can be thwarted with the help of a counterposed political will. But one has the impression that what many on the left have analysed is not the real process of globalisation, but the bourgeois concept of it. The real processes occurring in the world economy have not been the topic of the great theoretical discussion, but merely the background to it, or illustrations.

Meanwhile, every attempt to examine concrete processes of globalisation using particular countries as examples has prompted the conclusion that technology, though not neutral, is not all-powerful either. The new informational and productive potential acquired by transnational corporations in the late twentieth century has indeed created the preconditions for globalisation, and also predetermined the success of the West in the Cold War. But the technologies are continuing to develop, opening up new possibilities, including possibilities for resisting capitalist globalisation.

The thesis of the 'impotence of the state' is, then, not so much an observation of fact as a self-fulfilling prophesy. A state that acts strictly according to the rules dictated by neo-liberal ideology and the International Monetary Fund does in fact become impotent. It is true that this 'impotence' is of a very peculiar kind. Anyone who tries to issue a challenge to the existing order discovers that the state remains quite strong enough to take up the struggle in defence of that order.

Despite the fact that international financial institutions have acquired enormous influence, they cannot pursue their policies except through the agency of states. Governments, especially left-wing ones, love to explain their own decisions as the result of 'external factors'. Even the leaders of the South African Communist Party, outraged by the government's neo-liberal budget, explain to their supporters: 'The limitations of the budget should not be blamed on the minister of finance or upon the government in general. They are limitations that are symptomatic of any economy that remains hostage to powerful domestic and international private sector forces.'[3] In fact, everything is somewhat different. The Bulgarian trade union leader Krascho Petkov states:

> Without denying the importance for eroding social welfare and workers' living standards of the structural adjustment programmes and also of the traditional monetarist approach of the international institutions, it is necessary also to note the 'services' performed in this area by national governments. The ignoring or underrating of international standards and rights, and the undervaluing of the role of social policy, are often the result of national initiatives, and not of foreign influence. In this case the governments are merely hiding behind the demands of the international financial institutions, while the latter in turn are not objecting openly.[4]

For the left, the whole point of conquering power must be to change the rules of the game, and at the same time to destroy the present complex of relations between national governments and international financial and political institutions. For many of these institutions, hostility and serious non-compliance on the part of national governments would be a real catastrophe, especially if the dissatisfied states tried to set up their own parallel international structures or to transform the existing ones. It is precisely because many radical alternatives lie directly on the surface, ready to be picked up, that excluding any thought of the possibility of new approaches on the national and international levels is a matter of life or death for neo-liberals. Tons of paper, countless hours of television time and enormous intellectual efforts are spent simply in order to suppress the discussion of alternatives

The strength of the International Monetary Fund and of other international financial institutions consists above all in the fact that they coordinate their actions on an international scale, while their opponents are isolated. Consequently, the answer to the policy of financial blackmail should not be to renounce reform, but to search for allies in the international arena, combining this with a clear policy of change and with reliance on the mass movement within the country.

An understanding of the fact that integration is essential cannot reconcile serious left thinkers either to the European Union and the Maastricht Treaty or to the Commonwealth of Independent States. On the contrary, it is necessary to wage an irreconcilable struggle against the present international order in the name of the principles of democratic integration. The decisive role in this struggle will be played by the processes occurring within the framework of the 'old' national states.

Ultimately, all international institutions represent continuations of national states, rest upon them, and are powerless to act without them. This applies to the European Union, to the United Nations Organization, to NATO, and even to the International Monetary Fund and the World Bank, which at times are perceived as independent global entities. The dominant forces here are not private banks, but creditor states. In this sense the global role of the IMF bears witness not to the strengthened role of elemental market forces, but on the contrary, to the strengthened global economic role of the states of the centre in relation to those of the periphery. Even private transnational companies live in symbiosis with the state; without government support they could not maintain and develop their complex global structures. They need the military strength of the state to preserve the complex rules of the game and to defend their interests. While skimping on the social sphere, governments are forced to spend greater and greater sums on international punitive expeditions.

Globalisation makes companies not only larger, but also more complex, and often more vulnerable. This is why the demand is voiced for the standardization of laws, for introducing uniform social norms, and for opening markets. It is untrue that transnational capital does not need the state. Without the participation of the state transnational capital could not keep its indispensable markets open and its own national borders closed; nor could it manipulate the price of labour power and raw materials. Capitalism is impossible without laws, and laws do not exist outside of states. Even the notorious 'international law' does not exist independently. It is imposed through the efforts of particular states, which depending on their interests and capabilities serenely tolerate some breaches and harshly punish others.

During the 1980s and 1990s the scale of state intervention in economic, social and cultural life has not diminished, but on the contrary has grown. 'Deregulation' is also a form of interventionism, albeit a perverted one. Now, however, this intervention has been aimed at destroying the public sector, at reducing living standards, and at removing customs barriers. Practice shows that keeping markets open demands no less activity from governments than protectionism. All that happens is the restructuring of the government apparatus and a change of priorities. 'However paradoxical it might seem,' wrote *Nezavisimaya gazeta*, 'under the conditions of the market economy the administrative globalism of the Russian government sometimes surpasses the gigantomania that afflicted the economic structures of the USSR. It will be recalled that the exorbitant cost of the mistakes made by the Soviet managerial hierarchy was one of the main reasons for the crisis of the national economy.'[5] Neo-liberal policies have not resolved this problem.

Moreover, privatization and liberalization have placed still more power in the hands of the central bureaucracy. The 'young reformers' Anatoly Chubais and Boris Nemtsov, supported by the experts of the International Monetary Fund, have arbitrarily spent billions of dollars and reorganized government structures as if they were playing with a child's constructor set, without accepting the slightest responsibility for the consequences of their decisions. 'In the present Russian government,' *Nezavisimaya gazeta* continues, 'the cost of an error by the reformers has reached unbelievable levels, since decisions by Chubais and Nemtsov draw tens of millions of dollars into play. Meanwhile, unlike the situation in the centralized economy of the USSR, the reformers are permitted to act without any outside control.' Immense power has become concentrated in the hands of a narrow group of people who manage the financial flows within the state. 'In Russia the formation of a monopoly on the taking of decisions which affect the lives of tens of millions of people is close to complete.'[6]

Almost nowhere has neo-liberalism led to a sharp reduction in the size of the government apparatus. The case of Russia, which in cutting the public sector to a tenth of its former size increased the state apparatus by approximately three times, is of course something exotic. Nevertheless, it is not unique. Throughout the world, while some government services have shrunk, others have grown. Cuts in spending on social needs are accompanied by increases in spending on the repressive apparatus, the privatization of the public sector dramatically increases the load on the taxation service, and so forth. In the longer perspective, a balanced budget is an unattainable goal, while the financial crisis of the state cannot in principle be overcome within the framework of such a model.

Liberals have been able to revise the priorities of the state, and these priorities can also change under pressure from workers. For this to happen, political will is indispensable, and this will is realized through the medium of power. The 'impotence of the state' is, as already noted, largely a propaganda myth. But in order for the state to be able once again to carry out its regulatory function in the interests of workers, it must itself be radically transformed and in a certain sense globalised (through democratically organized inter-state associations). Left organizations, struggling under changed conditions, no longer need only mutual solidarity but also the direct coordination of their actions, making it possible to campaign effectively on the international level. Inter-state associations can become agents of regulation. It is possible for the public sector to receive a new impulse for its development on the inter-state level. However, integration carried out within the framework of a neo-liberal strategy will never bring us closer to this goal. International structures created within the context of a neo-liberal project cannot simply be improved and reformed. The road to a new type of integration lies through an acute crisis, and possibly through the dismantling of these structures.[7]

The Contradictions of neo-liberalism

Many today adhere to the simplistic notion that transnational companies are homogeneous and monolithic bodies with ideally disciplined executive structures, a clear vision of their tasks, and efficient decision-making processes. This strongly recalls the idealized vision of Soviet centralized planning – only now, the structures are global and private. In reality, what happens with transnational corporations is the same as with all hyper-centralized systems, including the Soviet Gosplan: they start becoming differentiated, and interest groups, sub-elites and feuding clans take shape within them. The people at the lower levels of the hierarchy manipulate information in order to obtain decisions to their advantage from the officials higher up. Anyone who has dealings with the offices of transnational corporations in the countries of Eastern Europe hears from their employees the usual complaints against the centre, which does not understand local conditions, obstructs work and stifles initiative. Only the centre is now located not in Moscow, but in Washington or Western Europe.[8]

From the very beginning neo-liberalism was a hegemonic project in precise accordance with the concepts of Western Marxism. The technological changes that brought shifts in the structure of society in the 1980s could not fail to provoke a crisis of hegemony as well. This crisis was used by international financial institutions and neo-liberal ideologues in two ways. On the one hand, the traditional class hegemony in the world of labour was undermined, and on the other, the transnational corporations managed to bring a 'new class consciousness' to the world of capital, consolidating it around themselves. The differences and contradictions remain, but as in any class project, the part is subordinate to the whole, the particular to the general.

It is this unprecedented consolidation of elites that has given the neo-liberal project its astonishing strength. The various groups have continued to struggle among themselves, but within the framework of a common orientation. Changes of government have not led to changes of course, and clashes of interest have been confined to lobbying. The problem of neo-liberalism lies in the fact that its structure of dominance is inevitably superimposed on the far more complex and diverse structures of various societies. Hence neo-liberalism, without claiming to make human society united or homogeneous (this would undermine the ability of capital to practise global manipulation), strives to simplify the task before it, to make all societies alike, structurally similar, and thus easily understood and managed on the basis of common rules. This runs up against the elemental 'resistance of the material'. Precisely the same rejection of an alien model undermined the communist bloc.

The economy can be global, although the significance and potential of national economies should not be underestimated. The desire of peoples to retain the symbols and institutions of 'their own' states is due not only to traditionalism, nationalism or 'sentimentality', but to an instinctive understanding that if these symbols and institutions are lost, the final possibility for these peoples of influencing their own fate will be lost as well.

Transnational bureaucracies are extensions of state structures, and have quite obvious national roots. But they are not democratic institutions. Transnational capital and its bureaucracies are marginal in their relation to any society, including even those of the countries of the 'centre'. However, they are far from marginal in relation to the state. Moreover, the state is becoming more and more an organ for the defence of these 'new marginals' from society. 'In reality the financial groups, the manipulators of high technology, have one common feature above all: a total absence of vision or strategy. They act on a world scale, but do not master anything,' says the French weekly *L'Evenement du jeudi*. 'When the states no longer organize the social space, the true master of the universe becomes uncertainty.'[9]

The question at issue is the very survival of democracy. There are no democratic institutions on the global level. Capital is being globalised, but not people. However cosmopolitan our culture might be, the overwhelming majority of people remain physically restricted by their conditions of daily life, bound to some particular place. National society and the state remain the level on which social change is really possible and necessary. It is quite another matter that under the conditions of globalisation not only revolution but also reform cannot be successful unless it spreads to a whole number of countries. This, of course, is nothing new either.

The neo-liberal governments that are destroying the welfare state explain to the population that under the new conditions the country can no longer permit itself the former level of social welfare. Defenders of the welfare state recall in turn that practically all the countries where in the late 1980s or 1990s social programmes and regulation were declared 'impermissible luxuries' are now much richer than at the time when these measures were first introduced. In principle, such discussions are pointless; both sides are right. The irrationality of modern capitalism makes itself evident in the fact that the accumulation of wealth by 'society' does not in principle guarantee a happy life to society's members.

State borders are a particularly important element of regulation within the framework of the neo-liberal project, though this is the skeleton in the closet about which no representative of the establishment wants to speak. If the movement of capital about the world is becoming more and more free, the mobility of labour power, by contrast, is limited. The frontiers between the countries of the 'centre' are dissolving, but between the 'centre' and the 'periphery' (and in a number of cases between different countries of the 'periphery') they are becoming more strict. From being the subjects of economic activity, workers as a result are becoming exclusively its objects, 'labour resources', just as passive a material as, let us say, genetically engineered plants. Through the same process 'social partnership', which presupposes at least a formal equality of capital and labour, is becoming pointless as well. The globalisation of the economy has rendered the old social democratic compromise pointless. Enterprises work for the world market, but society remains national. The growth of wages does not guarantee demand for a country's own goods along the lines of the old Fordism.

The fate of democracy

The theorist of the left wing of the German 'greens', Elmar Altvater, argues that the left has not yet learnt to orient itself in the 'new political landscape'.[10] Instead of complaining about the internationalization of capital, they would do better to struggle for 'social regulation yielding global results [Auswirkungen].' Such regulation, however, is impossible on the basis of the old state methods; it has to rest on 'global civil society'.[11] Meanwhile Altvater recognizes that 'despite all the economic globalisation no world society has arisen.'[12] Consequently 'global civil society', if it exists anywhere except in the imagination of theoreticians, is not representative of real society. Only an insignificant minority of people are drawn into the various 'free associations', particularly on the world level. This slogan is as utopian as it is elitist. Regulation does need to become regional and global; however, this cannot be on the basis of 'civil society', but must be on the basis of democracy and civil equality of rights, something which is impossible outside the state.[13] Beginning on the local level, regulation requires a system of local self-government and national organs of representative authority. Having grown weak as a result of the process of globalisation, the state when it is forced to reckon with the consequences of this process is capable of winning back its lost positions. But even if state intervention becomes a popular idea again, the question of its forms and class nature remains open.

In 1995 the London *Economist* noted with satisfaction that recent history was 'littered with examples of markets forcing governments to change policy.'[14] In reality, this seemingly self-evident assertion is a complete lie. Modern history knows hardly a single case in which government policy has changed under the influence of the 'invisible hand of the market' alone, that is, simply as a result of a series of misfortunes resulting from objective causes. Regardless of whether a particular programme was effective or not, its implementation took place long before it was possible to speak of the 'test of the market'. Government policies have changed in response to the demands of particular transnational corporations, international financial institutions and more powerful states. The obvious economic failures of neo-liberal regimes in Eastern Europe and Latin America have never led to a correction of course. On the contrary, the more obvious the failure of neo-liberalism has become, the more resolutely its prescriptions have been enacted.

Even the attack on the French franc by money market speculators, after the socialists came to power in the early 1980s, was not caused by a decline in the French economy, but by a clear, conscious wish to put pressure on the socialists not to implement radical policies. In other words, it was a form of class struggle by the bourgeoisie. It is quite obvious that any change in any of the relevant conditions can inspire such resistance, just as all reforms are associated with difficulties. There is nothing remarkable in this. All that is extraordinary is the readiness of the modern left to give in at the first sign of discontent from the financial oligarchy, while neo-liberal governments are quite ready to press ahead with their policies even when these have obviously failed and the dissatisfaction is near-universal.

So long as workers with the help of the state do not succeed in changing the rules of the game, imposing countervailing limitations on capital, there cannot be any kind of balance, and consequently even the most moderate reformism is impossible. The weakness of the left arises from its unwillingness to use the force of the state against the bourgeoisie. The growth in the influence of transnational structures requires the creation of a counterweight. But at the same time the new situation demands the radical transformation of the state, of its institutions and of its social nature. Traditional bourgeois democracy has shown that it cannot act as a serious counterweight to transnational capital, and it is therefore essential to step outside these bounds.

The theory of the 'objective impotence' of the state would be correct if the state had suffered a defeat from the 'invisible hand of the market'. However, the role of 'objective limiting factor' in most cases is played not by elemental economic processes, but by the actions of international financial institutions and... other states. 'The rule of money is no longer mediated primarily by the market,' Simon Clarke notes. 'The rule of money is directly imposed on capitals and on the state by the banks and financial institutions.'[15]

The Italian Marxists Pietro Ingrao and Rossana Rossanda urge their readers not to forget that even in the age of transnational corporations governments wield enormous power not only in the military-technical field but also in the economic one.[16] The scrupulously moderate Will Hutton also reminds us that the state has a significant ability to practise regulation on the international level as well: 'Globalisation is still limited by the power of national governments and vested interests of individual economic systems. It is true that the financial markets have greater power of veto than they used to, and compel more conservative economic policies, but considerable latitude remains.'[17] On the one hand, the state and national capital are quite able to use their policies to influence the decisions of transnational companies. On the other hand, the state can influence them through its participation in international organizations. 'In a number of key areas, ranging from the regulation of capital flows to fish stocks, the individual nation state can *augment* its individual powers by pooling sovereignty and delegating authority to supranational agencies.'[18] Hutton prefers not to remind his readers, however, that all this would have a certain point only if these agencies were themselves radically democratized.

In most cases the supposed 'impotence of the state before the market' is in fact a manifestation of the impotence or weakness of some states in the face of others, whose governments have taken on themselves the role of high priests and interpreters of the 'logic of the market'. This is shown to perfection by the discussions surrounding the common European currency. At a meeting of representatives of the European Union in Lisbon the conservative government of Germany literally compelled its partners to agree to limit their budget deficits to three percent as an essential condition for the introduction of a common monetary unit. No-one managed to establish why the figure was three percent, and not four or two and a half. Any such criterion, like the planning targets of the Soviet era, is a product of formal bureaucratic thinking that has nothing at all in common with the 'logic of the market'. Adam Smith's 'invisible hand' is nowhere in evidence here.

The practice of liberalizing the European economy also clearly refutes the myth concerning the organic link between freedom and the market. The more the powers of the state are transferred to specialized private structures and independent (although formally state or inter-state) financial institutions, the more the sphere of democracy is narrowed. Involvement by the population in making decisions is reduced to a minimum, and once a choice has been made it becomes 'irreversible'. It is worth recalling that during the 1970s theoreticians of the 'open society' spoke of the possibility of reversing decisions as one of the most important advantages of democracy over 'communism'. Yet in the 1990s, as recognized by ideologues of reforms in both Eastern Europe and the West, a major goal was to ensure that these reforms were 'irreversible'. Within the framework of neo-liberal strategy, euromoney is becoming yet another factor of irreversibility, undermining democracy in the process. If the population loses access to the making of decisions, the financial bureaucracy acquires independence from the population: 'Without a direct link between money and citizens, Europe is heading into a terrible regression.'[19] It is striking how on the international level the capitalism of the end of the twentieth century is precisely reproducing all the contradictions and vices of the bureaucratic centralization which a few years earlier led to the downfall of the Soviet system.

The institutions of popular representation are in profound crisis. This applies both to the 'old' democracies of the West and to the former communist countries which borrowed parliamentary corruption without parliamentary culture. During the 1970s European left theoreticians spoke of a transition that was supposed to be occurring from bourgeois democracy to 'advanced democracy', which was no longer an instrument of class domination. This transition has not been successfully carried through anywhere, ever. After the fall of the Berlin wall, amid declarations of the triumph of freedom, the reverse process got under way even in the most developed countries. From constituting an association of citizens, democracy is being transformed into a form of interaction of elites. To use Aristotle's term, an oligarchy.

In many parts of the world the 1990s saw the setting up or revival of democratic institutions, but the ease with which this occurred testified to the weakening of their real role. They no longer hindered anyone, and did not place difficult problems before the elites. They ceased to exert decisive influence on the life of society, and thus no longer posed a danger to the ruling classes even in states that were experiencing serious social crises. The weakening of the labour movement aided the implantation of this 'inoffensive democracy'. But wherever parliaments or municipal organs created serious problems for the neo-liberal project, they were mercilessly disbanded, as happened with the Greater London Council, the Peruvian Congress and the Supreme Soviet of Russia. If it was necessary to shoot, the elites shot. If they had to break the law, the law was broken. If it was necessary to rule by decree, this was done. And all this occurred within the framework of 'democratization'. Unlike earlier times, the disbanding of representative organs was not followed by the installing of repressive dictatorships. In most cases new organs, more in line with the neo-liberal project, were simply established in place of those that had been abolished.

Eastern Europe is orienting itself toward Western Europe, and Western Europe in turn is becoming more and more like America. During the 1980s European political life offered a significantly richer choice of alternatives than its American counterpart. During the 1990s this situation has changed. The European elites have become increasingly oriented toward to the transatlantic political model. As the American political scientists Daniel Hellinger and Dennis R. Judd have noted, the present-day elites are interested in democracy only as a means for legitimizing their power. The political system is thus evolving in the direction of oligarchy, while elections, free discussion and the struggle between parties are turning into a 'democratic facade'.[20] A regression is occurring from a democratic to a liberal state. Will Hutton sees the same process occurring in Britain: 'If the only choice – forced on political parties by the new power of veto of the global capital markets, which threaten a run on the currency of countries whose policies they dislike – is some variant of the new conservatism, then political debate becomes a charade.'[21]

Christopher Lasch characterized the policy of the elites, aimed at excluding the masses from decision-making, as 'the abolition of shame'.[22] The integrating mechanism of capitalist democracy was being destroyed. 'Those who saw themselves losing out in the market economy saw government as a positive force working to keep them included when it came to harvesting the economic fruits of capitalism'.[23] State redistribution is always one of the foundations of democracy under capitalism. To a significant degree, its abolition robs bourgeois democracy of meaning, transforming it into oligarchy or an 'intraparty' democracy of the elites.

The 'new democracies' are afflicted by the same ailments as the old. Corruption is eating away at their political institutions. Disillusionment with democratic institutions, with elections and parliamentarism, is on the rise even in countries that have long traditions of the struggle for freedom. 'Compared to the military-dominated regimes of the past, the current civilian government seems to be plagued by an even greater number of audacious and reckless irregularities and a rising tide of suspicion over the links between economics and politics,' South Korean journalists wrote in the late 1990s. 'Compounding this frustration is the fact that the same people who dedicated themselves to democratization during one of the nation's darkest periods have become just as corrupt as those whom they once denounced.'[24]

Corruption is indeed becoming a global phenomenon, and this is closely linked to the changes occurring in the economy. The defence mechanisms devised by democratic systems during the epoch of early or welfare capitalism are no longer working. New forms of graft and new temptations are appearing. As the state becomes more and more 'open' to the outside, it simultaneously becomes less and less susceptible to control by its own citizens; as a result, new opportunities for abuses proliferate. The ideology of the neo-liberal market, by destroying non-market ethical norms, also plays a role here.

The principles of citizenship are also under threat in areas where at first glance it might seem that only 'technical' problems are involved. For example, the concepts of national security that have arisen during the epoch of globalisation are becoming a direct threat to democracy. The replacing of mass conscript armies with professional armed forces, something now occurring in more and more countries, is incompatible with maintaining the principles of citizenship. Universal liability for military service has historically been inseparable from democracy.

If the national wars of the past (including wars of conquest) had clear goals and were fought against familiar adversaries, international police operations are 'special' not so much because they require special methods as because their aims are not fully understood by society, and most importantly, because these operations are not perceived by society as being of its own doing. Even if society passively supports military actions (as during the war in the Persian Gulf and the bombing of Bosnia), mobilizing the population and consolidating society on this basis is impossible. The interests of transnational corporations in remote regions are not fully clear even to important sectors of the bourgeoisie, and still less are they recognized as corresponding to these sectors' own interests.

Placing its stake on professional police forces, the neoliberal state does not become stronger. High-technology equipment is not a mark of strength, but represents an attempt to make up for the weakness that flows from the impossibility of using a mass army. The more complex the system, the more it is vulnerable, not simply to the blows of the enemy, but also to the constantly increasing likelihood of organizational and technical breakdowns, professional errors and so forth. From this also stems the fear, well known to historians of the seventeenth and eighteenth centuries, of using expensive forces in conflicts fraught with the danger of heavy losses.

If professional armies in the countries of the centre become police forces, in the countries of the periphery and semi-periphery modern-day feudal militias arise on the same basis, and can easily be used against one another. Where, as in Russia, general liability for military service remains, the army is divided into elite professional units and a mass of downtrodden recruits who serve not even as cannon fodder, but simply as slaves for the military elite. Under such conditions neither the slogan of 'defence of the fatherland' nor traditional antimilitarism can meet the needs of the left. The primary place is assumed by the fight to stop the armed forces being turned into a modern version of a feudal levy or into the local detachment of the 'world police'. This means returning to the traditional idea, from the time of the early bourgeois revolutions, of the army as an organization of armed citizens.

A new state system

The crisis of citizenship cannot be overcome in isolation from the social crisis to which it has given birth. The question of what to do with the institutions concerned is insoluble unless the social relationships are altered profoundly; what is necessary is to change the nature of the state in social, not just 'civic' terms. This also implies extensive institutional change in the spirit of 'radical democracy', but much more than simply that.

Paradoxically, the collapse of the old model of the state under the pressure of globalisation is opening up prospects for a radical reform of the institutions and structures of power. The journal *Viento del Sur*, which is close to the Zapatistas, wrote that the neo-liberal experiment had given birth to such a profound crisis of the Mexican state that neither a change of government nor electoral reform would any longer be of help. The crisis could be solved only 'with the overcoming of this state form through a new social pact that establishes a different state.'[25] This applies not only to Mexico according to *Viento del Sur*. The entire capitalist periphery (and not only the periphery) is faced with the need to establish a new state system, based not on national self-assertion but on democratic participation, on the political self-assertion of society itself.

> Very briefly, neo-liberalism and economic globalization as they are now operating can only be combated if in every nation-state the majoritarian society creates a political regime that serves its interests and which guarantees that this society can ensure (and not merely influence) the choosing of the public policies needed for the prosperity of the majority. In order to turn back the perverse process of neo-liberalism and economic globalization, it is not enough simply to win control over governments through the action of political parties; it is necessary to substantially modify the democracy of elites that has held sway within capitalism (when there has been democracy at all), and which includes the party leaderships. The political system has to ensure that society is always present and watchful, so that the government, however legitimate it might be, acts in the real interests of those it represents. Only if popular society wins control over the terrain that corresponds to it in each country, including in the countries that provide the base for the huge corporations that dominate the world economy, will a struggle against neo-liberalism and economic globalization be possible on a planetary scale.[26]

The strategy of the left has, then, to consist not of defending the old state, but of using the crisis of this state to ensure that the basis for new institutions is laid both on a national and also on an international, inter-state level.[27] What is required is an all-permeating democratization that encompasses not only the structures of political power, but also the institutions of social security, self-government, the public sector, and all the mutual connections between these various structures and institutions.

The traditional argument of radical democrats has been that liberal democratic institutions are good, but that it is possible and necessary to expand the sphere of freedom still further. In the late twentieth century this line of argument has lost its earlier force. It is necessary to go beyond the traditional institutions of formal democracy, not because we can in theory create something better, but because these institutions in their earlier form no longer work in any case. If the left does not take on itself the task of radically reforming the state, then this goal will sooner or later be urged by the radical right. If democracy does not affirm itself as an extra-market – and to a significant degree anti-market – system, the masses will follow those who call for restricting the elemental forces of the market in the name of authority, hierarchy, the nation and discipline.

In the epoch of globalisation, capitalism has become more destructive and dangerous than ever. The question is 'not whether we can expect a better or worse world from the global market, but whether we can expect a world at all.'[28] However, it is precisely globalisation that also creates the prospects for a genuinely international and universalist left movement, for the rethinking and refounding of state institutions – in brief, for radical reforms on an unprecedented scale.

The destinies of capitalism and democracy have finally parted company. In this situation, it becomes clear that the left is and always has been the only real champion of democracy. The majority of left-wing politicians see their mission consisting solely in maintaining and defending parliamentary institutions and the constitutional rights of citizens. This is essential, but it is quite inadequate. Such a defensive policy is doomed. Only if we realize the anticapitalist potential of democracy can we win this struggle.

NOTES

1 Immanuel Wallerstein, *Unthinking Social Science*, Cambridge, MA, Polity, 1991, p. 57.
2 James Petras, 'The process of globalisation: The role of the state and multinational corporations', *Links*, n. 7, July-October, 1996, p. 60.
3 *Green Left Weekly*, 26 March 1997, p. 21.
4 *Rabochaya politika*, 1996, n. 6, p. 42.
5 *Nezavisimaya gazeta*, 15 May 1997.

6 *Ibid.*

7 For example, the first attempts at a real union of Russia and Belarus provoked an acute crisis not only of the mongrel Commonwealth of Independent States, founded in place of the Soviet Union, but also of the Russian state itself; it became obvious that the Russian regions were demanding a status analogous to that of Belarus. See the discussion of integration in the books: Pyat' let Belovezh'ya, *Chto dal'she?* Moscow, Gorbachev Foundation, 1997; A. Vygorbina, *Dva podkhoda k sblizheniyu. Nezavisimaya gazeta-Stsenarii*, 15 May 1997.

8 The American economist Doug Henwood has shown that the portrayal of transnational companies as 'global assembly lines' is also exaggerated. Compared with 1977, the interfirm transfer of partly finished goods to or from foreign manufacturing affiliates has increased from 12 per cent of US trade to... 13 per cent! It is true that the share of US GDP represented by trade rose during this period from 17 to 24 per cent, but it nevertheless remains less than in other countries. Interfirm transfers of the global assembly line type rose from 2 per cent in 1977 to 3.2 per cent in 1994 (see *Left Business Observer*, 14 May 1997, n. 77). In other words, the globalisation of real production in uneven (it is less in large countries with developed internal markets), and on the whole is significantly less than ideologues have assumed.

9 *L'Evenement du jeudi*, n. 617, 1996, p. 47.

10 Pietro Ingrao, Rossana Rossandra, *et al.*, *Verabredungen zum Jahrhundertende. Ein Debatte uber die Entwicklung des Kapitalismus und die Aufgaben der Linken.* Hamburg, H. Heine, 1996, p. 193.

11 *Ibid.*, pp. 202-3.

12 *Ibid.*, p. 197.

13 At the international conference 'Globalisation and Citizenship', held in Geneva in December 1996 under the sponsorship of the United Nations Organization, it was noted that 'Although pressures from international civil society and interventions by intergovernmental organizations have broadened the range of rights and standards historically associated with citizenship, far less has been achieved at the level of enforcement. Indeed it would seem that the weakening of state structures in many countries has seriously undermined the possibility of enforcing global standards' (*UNRISD News*, n. 15, Autumn 1996/Winter 1997, pp. 1-2).

14 *The Economist*, Special supplement, 7-13 October 1995, p. 9.

15 Simon Clarke, *Keynesianism, Monetarism and the Crisis of the State*, Aldershot, Edward Elgar, 1988, p. 355.

16 See Pietro Ingrao and Rossana Rossanda, *Appuntamenti di fine secolo*, Rome, 1995; Ingrao, Rossanda, *et al.*, *op. cit.*

17 Will Hutton, *The State We're In*, London, Vintage, 1996, p. xxiii.

18 *Ibid.*, p. 342.

19 Patrick Viveret, *Iniciativa Socialista*, February 1997, n. 43, p. 52.

20 See Daniel Hellinger and Dennis R. Judd, *The Democratic Facade*, Belmont, CA, Brooks/Cole, 1991, p. 329.

21 Hutton, *The State We're In*, *op. cit.*, p. 17.

22 Christopher Lasch, *The Revolt of the Elites and the Betrayal of Democracy*, New York, W.W. Norton, 1995, p. 197.

23 Lester C. Thurow, *The Future of Capitalism*, New York, W. Morrow & Co., 1996, p. 242.

24 *Korea Focus*, v. 5, n. 2, March-April 1997, pp. 117, 119.

25 *Viento del Sur*, n. 8, Winter 1996, p. 3.
26 *Ibid.*, p. 57.
27 This is how the connection between globalisation and the reform of the state is interpreted in documents of the German Party of Democratic Socialism. See Alternative Politik und Globalisierung. PDS International, Informationsschrift der AG Friedens – und Internationale Politik. Extra. pp. 11-13.
28 Alan Freeman, 'The poverty of nations: Relative surplus value, technical change and accumulation in the modern global market', *Links*, n. 7, July-October 1996, p. 54.

THE PUBLIC SPHERE AND THE MEDIA: MARKET SUPREMACY VERSUS DEMOCRACY

Colin Leys

Introduction.

Democratic socialists have the greatest need of a robust, equal-access 'public sphere', in which the collective thinking of society can be carried on and in which state policy can be critically debated by everyone outside the inner circle of party, corporate and state power. It is here that public opinion is formed; and public opinion is, in the last analysis, the only real weapon the democratic left can deploy against the greater economic and social resources of capital. The left's need for such a 'public sphere' is especially great now, following the general defeat that has led to, and been consolidated by, the deregulation of capital. To recover from this defeat the left has to develop new ideas adapted to the new situation presented by globalised capitalism, and to win popular support for them; and this must ultimately be accomplished in the public sphere.

By the beginning of the twentieth century, however, the public sphere was already far from adequately meeting these requirements. According to Jurgen Habermas, who coined the term in his influential book, *The Structural Transformation of the Public Sphere*, published in 1962, it had been seriously eroded in the course of the nineteenth century;[1] with the widening of the franchise, popular education and the spread of mass culture it had become the target of heavy manipulation and commercial advertising and had ceased to be a forum for objective and critical debate. And in the present century, Habermas thought, matters had become steadily worse: the 're-feudalisation of society' - the creeping re-absorption of civil society by the state through bureaucratisation, commodification and the 'colonisation of the life world' had all but destroyed the public sphere. 'The main formative conversations of society' (as James Curran has called them) no longer really occurred in a setting in which the necessary facts were adequately presented and reflected on, and the views and interests of all citizens were accurately represented.[2]

This view was, as Habermas later admitted, somewhat overwrought: the eighteenth century public sphere was less perfect, and its twentieth century successor perhaps less imperfect, than his account allowed.[3] Still, the limitations to which he drew attention were real enough; and since then a drastic further regression has taken place. The media of communication have been far more deeply subordinated to market forces than ever before, and what is communicated through them has been subjected to an altogether new degree of commodification.

This is not just a question of a few 'media moguls' such as Murdoch or Berlusconi using their hugely enhanced market dominance to propagandise for their self-interested far-right views. It is also a matter of public service broadcasting's declining independence and dedication to public service values. In brief summary, the 'public sphere' as a whole has become increasingly *market-driven*, increasingly restricted to points of view *premised on market supremacy*, increasingly *visual* and increasingly *passive*; whereas the democratic left needs extensive coverage of political issues, critical analysis of them (which primarily visual treatments militate against), and an active not passive stance on the part of the public.

Moreover the restriction of the points of view that are reflected in the mainstream media to those based on market values has been given a further twist by the recent evolution of all West European socialist parties towards acceptance of markets (subject only to 'regulation'). This means that even public service broadcasters can now see themselves as being politically 'impartial' when confining the viewpoints expressed to those that are premised on market values, leading to what *Le Monde Diplomatique* calls 'la pensée unique':

> When one listens to the media, modernity is almost invariably equated with free trade, strong currencies, deregulation, privatisations... Outdated notions, on the other hand, are almost invariably associated with the welfare state, government in general (unless it shrivels into a lean law-and-order machine), unions (which are said to defend special interests, unlike those of, say, big business), the nation-state (guilty of fostering nationalism), the people (always likely to be entranced by populism).[4]

Public service broadcasters face a severe dilemma. The neoliberals' aim is to weaken the public service broadcasting sector, by cutting into its audience share with commercial sports and entertainment channels and thus delegitimising the obligatory licence fee or tax share which provides its revenue; then to reduce its tax income, or licence fee where one exists; and finally to privatise it, or force it to depend on voluntary subscriptions, like American public service broadcasting, and become marginal and irrelevant. Public service broadcasters no longer feel confident that the socialist or social-democratic parties are going to defend them. Will these parties insist that audience share is not to be the measure by which public service broadcasting is judged?

So far the left has, on the whole, not sufficiently grasped the seriousness of the problem. The aim of this essay is first to suggest why, then to describe in outline the way market forces are commodifying the media and closing down the public sphere, and finally to sketch very briefly the sort of alternative which the left needs to focus on and fight for.

Democracy and the changing media

One of the reasons why the left has been relatively slow to grasp the lethal significance of media commodification may be found in the special circumstances that prevailed in the post-war years, which were formative for so much of subsequent left thinking. These years were not only unique in the social-democratic hegemony that marked them, they were also unique in the combination of media forms that co-existed at that time.

In the era of modern democracy, the 'main formative conversations of society' have been conducted through approximately six successive - though sometimes historically overlapping – forms or media of communication: (1) public meetings, supplemented by pamphlets and non-commercial news-sheets – roughly from the origins of modern democracy in the eighteenth century to about 1970; (2) commercial newspapers - the period from about 1880 to the present during which, in Europe but not in north America, ownership was relatively dispersed and the left also had, for a while, its own mass circulation press, but which ended with a right-dominated and largely unregulated commercial press oligopoly; (3) public service broadcasting (first radio and then television) - from about 1920 onwards (supplemented by public service-regulated commercial broadcasting); (4) lightly-regulated or unregulated commercial radio and television broadcasting - from about 1980 onwards in Europe, but much earlier in the USA; and (5) 'multi-media' (i.e. increasingly integrated systems combining text, speech, sound, and still and moving images), largely controlled by a handful of transnational mega-firms - whose dominance is just beginning.

Of course the dominant media forms and combinations of forms have varied between countries, although all countries have experienced the dominant influence of meetings, and all are about to experience - or do already – the dominance of the multi-media oligopolies. In the period from about 1950 to 1980, however, there was a unique overlap of media forms: face to face meetings, a still partially pluralistic press, and vigorous public service broadcasting. Although there were problems with press concentration, and numerous shortcomings in the various national public service broadcasting systems, the combination of these three media systems provided the means for a collective discourse that was perhaps uniquely effective in the history of large-scale democracies.

Public service broadcasting commanded very wide audiences, with some programming – including newscasts and political discussions - that attracted mass viewing across all the social divides. This was perhaps especially true in Britain. A competing commercial TV sector was introduced there relatively early (in 1955) but under strong 'public service' regulation. Faced with this competition - but not with unfettered commercial competition - the BBC, which had already achieved a 'savvy mixing of low and high forms', found itself able to hold its own.[5] The result was a televised public discourse across the two sectors that was broadly shared by the whole population, and against which the notoriously partisan and untrustworthy 'infotainment' tabloids, and the often scarcely less partisan 'quality' press, were judged (in Britain nearly 80 per cent of people still think television news readers tell the truth, compared with only 10 who trust print journalists). In addition, people still attended public meetings where politicians were seen in the flesh and were expected to answer awkward questions, and whose proceedings were fairly fully reported in the press; and at this period many people still attended various other political meetings - of trade unions or party branches or pressure groups of all kinds - where the discourses of the mass media and the public performances of politicians were reviewed and criticised.

This era can easily be romanticised, but one indication that it was real enough is the way many people, including many on the left, have been slow to recognise the seriousness of its accelerating erosion now; there is still a strong tendency to think that the problems of the media will be solved as a result of a collective debate for which, in reality, the current media regime provides less and less room.

Yet the problem for socialism is obviously particularly serious; the formation of a new hegemonic project means the development of a persuasive critique of the dominant ideology and discourses, and persuasive visions and models of alternative social arrangements, which can be criticised, modified, and ultimately accepted by a majority in the 'collective dialogue of society'. This, however, cannot take place without access to the 'commanding heights of the media system', not least because meetings of all kinds have largely disappeared.[6] Their disappearance is partly due to the greater potency - greater reach, greater visual impact, and greater control - offered by radio and television, which has led politicians to prefer them to meetings; but it is also, and more fundamentally and lastingly, due to the fact that the mass media, and especially television, have radically altered the way we get political information and knowledge, and indeed our whole way of life, in terms both of the time the media absorb (the average Briton watches television for three hours a day, the average American for much more), and the outlook they normalise: '...we go out less purposively, and are willing, and indeed may feel we have to, spend more on what we do at home. People will pay a lot of money on entertainment technology that removes the need for them to leave their houses.'[7] The mass media culture has thus contributed significantly to the disappearance of meetings, while not itself constituting a substitute for the shared, engaged and interactive discourse that meetings made possible.

The commodification of the media

That the media should have been allowed to become primarily institutions at the service of capital accumulation and not at the service of democracy is, from a democratic perspective, an arresting fact, and one that we should pause over; something essential to democracy has been, in effect, given away. How did this happen? A general, obviously oversimplified, answer runs as follows. In the liberal reaction against autocracy, freedom from state control of thought and expression was seen as having to include freedom of publication; and a 'free press' - meaning freedom to print and distribute political pamphlets and 'news papers' - was a crucial part of this. But once industrialised production made it possible to make newspapers profitable, by aiming them at larger readerships and financing them out of advertising revenue, the 'freedom to publish' radically altered its meaning. It became freedom to make money and to exercise the political influence that successful commercial publishing afforded. As competition reduced the number and diversity of newspapers, anti-monopoly legislation was introduced; but even if this had been more effective than it was, focussing on the issue of how *many* owners there were has often tended to obscure the fact that market competition ultimately obliges all owners of mass-circulation papers to run them as businesses, not as a service to democracy. Survival depends on profitability, profitability depends on advertising, advertising depends on readership maximisation, and readership maximisation depends on entertainment - not political debate.

Moreover with the advent of globalisation and the dominance of discourses of 'national competitiveness', even the liberal discourse that underpinned anti-monopoly legislation has been progressively abandoned. The political arguments for media pluralism are increasingly brushed aside by purely economic arguments in favour of allowing some media companies to become national or regional 'champions', big enough to survive in global competition. The principle appears to be that it is better to be dominated by one or two domestic giants than one or two foreign-based ones; the requirements of national democracy are simply ignored. In the British case the ideological character of this argument is aggravated by the fact that Rupert Murdoch's News International, the leading candidate to be Britain's 'champion' (controlling half of Britain's land-based digital TV, all its satellite TV, a large part of its land-based analogue commercial TV and a third of national press circulation), is an American-owned, Australian-based company, which pays virtually no tax in Britain.[8]

Simultaneously with the abandonment of the principle of political pluralism in national media the original arguments for establishing broadcasting as a public service have also disappeared. It was initially agreed that a democracy could not allow private interests to exercise the power afforded by radio and television when only a few wavelengths or channels existed; there was also the argument, particularly strongly made in Britain, that these potent new media should be used to *educate* the new mass electorate. But frequency scarcity has been replaced by frequency abundance, thanks to the digital revolution and other technological changes; and the idea of a so-called 'mandarin' elite using the airwaves to educate the masses has also become unacceptable. As a result, public service broadcasting is being increasingly displaced by the commercial sector, partly by competition (see below) and partly by ideological erosion - the commercial sector attacks the whole idea of non-market public service. Rupert Murdoch, with characteristically populist arrogance, seeks to subvert the whole public service discourse by declaring that 'anybody who, within the law of the land, provides a service which the public wants at a price it can afford is providing a public service'.[9]

The speed with which global market forces are currently eroding the autonomy and quality of public service broadcasting, and driving what is left of it to mimic market-driven values, varies significantly from country to country; but the process is unmistakably at work everywhere and constitutes an increasingly serious obstacle to the construction of a new progressive project.

The logic of commodified media

It is first of all necessary to note the scale and the scope of the media industry. It consists of a set of interlocking markets, marked by constant technological change and political competition, and including: media hardware (from satellites and computers to walkmans) and software (for multimedia production and transmission, and for education and training) – in effect, the entire information technology market; print publication (newspapers, magazines); radio broadcasting; television production and broadcasting; film and video production and distribution; music performances and recording sales; advertising; and public relations. Thanks to the speed of technological change, which is fast eroding the boundaries between all these formerly separate sectors, no useful figures for the total weight of all these sectors in the economy currently exist; in Britain they certainly account for not less than 500,000 jobs – twice the number employed in the automobile industry – and are fast-growing.[10] In 1997 there were already some 250 television channels in Europe; the number was due at least to double by the end of the millennium.

The digital revolution also means that the media are increasingly integrated: music, sound, images, film, text and numerical data can all be received on a home computer; books and newspapers go onto CD-ROMs. This drives media companies to seek vertical and horizontal integration so as to maximize profits from the multiple upstream and downstream forms of exploitation that a product may lend itself to, and to protect themselves from the risk of technological obsolescence. Film studios seek to own video store chains, computer companies seek to own film libraries, etc.[11] As a result, a few increasingly transnational megafirms predominate: Time-Warner-Turner, Sony, Disney-ABC, Bertelsmann, Axel-Springer-Kirch, Fininvest and News Corporation. Some analysts even speculate that the time is not distant when, thanks to digitalisation, just one of these firms, News Corporation, will confront yet another, Bill Gates's software giant Microsoft, in a contest for ultimate control of the entire global media system.[12]

Some of these big companies use the media they control for direct political propaganda; this is notoriously true of the British press, and has been a factor keeping attention – especially the attention of the country's competing political elites, always preoccupied with the next election - focussed on the issue of monopoly. This was well illustrated by the British Conservative Party's anguish at the start of the General Election campaign in March 1997, when Rupert Murdoch instructed the editor of the *Sun* (with a circulation of nearly four million, and perhaps ten million readers) to switch the paper's support to the Labour Party; and the power of press barons has been the cause of successive attempts by the left in the British Labour Party to introduce legal barriers to the concentration of newspaper ownership. Significantly, the risk that any such effort would provoke a deadly partisan onslaught from the press owners in the name of 'press freedom' has always led the Labour leadership to quash such initiatives.[13]

But while this is manifestly undemocratic it is not necessarily the most serious problem. Although the tabloid press has political influence, it is not able to offset major shifts in opinion occurring in response to objective changes in people's everyday lives. In spite of the *Sun*'s hostility to Labour before March 1997, surveys showed that the proportion of its readers who supported the Conservatives had steadily fallen, from 45 per cent in 1992 to 25 per cent at the end of 1996;[14] so that in making its switch the *Sun* was simply trying not to lose its readers by coming round to the opinion that most of them had independently arrived at (it was also a response to the fact that since 1994, under Tony Blair's leadership, the Labour Party had moved so much closer to Murdoch's views, as the *Sun*'s editor condescendingly pointed out). From a democratic point of view the most fundamental problem is, in fact, precisely that the market sector, however many competitors there are, is indeed ultimately driven by its own logic always to put commercial criteria before all others in shaping media content; the aim is to maximize circulation for advertisers, and minimise costs, and this progressively diminishes the democratic process by reducing the vitality and scope of the public sphere.

Maximising circulation or audiences makes entertainment a priority. This extends both to the balance of content, and to the way content is placed or sequenced. In the US, the editorial and reporting costs of even major newspapers account for less than 20 per cent of the total. Advertising averages 75 per cent of total revenue and advertisements typically constitute about 70 per cent of total content, while entertainment accounts for most of the rest. In the case of provincial newspapers in Britain, where rationalisation on purely business principles has probably gone farthest, the share of editorial costs in provincial newspapers fell from 27 per cent in 1947 to 15 per cent in 1975. In the case of radio and TV, the need to hold audiences for advertisers means that any public affairs programmes that licensed broadcasters are obliged to broadcast tend to be placed in unpopular time slots and made as entertaining and undemanding as possible. In the USA, where regulation of commercial broadcasting is lightest, serious news and public affairs programmes, as opposed to the inexpensive coverage of human-interest court cases or disasters, have become rare.

Profit-driven cost-cutting reinforces all these tendencies. In newspapers it means that the decline in the ratios of editorial and reporting to advertising content involves severe cuts in editorial and reporting staff; in the ten years 1982-1992 the median editorial (i.e. journalist) staff on US dailies fell by almost a quarter and on weeklies, by over a third. In the 1980s, the editorial share fell much faster, accelerated by mergers and the use of the new technology. In one example four newspapers employing a total of 25 journalists were merged into one freesheet employing one reporter.[15] Journalists' pay has also fallen steadily, senior and experienced staff being replaced by young reporters on less than half national average wages. In Britain, the total editorial staffing of all papers is estimated to have fallen by at least 40 per cent between 1977 and 1993, while the total number of pages per issue increased by 72 per cent.[16]

Similar tendencies have been at work in broadcasting. Even so-called flagship programmes like BBC 2's *Newsnight* have cut and casualised staff and replaced senior reporters with cheap junior ones.[17] 'Tabloid' TV is on its way, to match the tabloid press. And as staff resources are cut, the uncritical use of news material supplied by outside sources increases, surrendering both the provision and the interpretation of news to government, party and corporate spin-doctors, whose use by all those who can afford them has steeply increased.[18] Globalisation, moreover, makes it easier to buy cheaper US-produced news services such as CNN with its US-determined agenda, or Sky News with its populist rejection of any overt 'mission to explain'; the ideal of the 'collective conversation' of a national society is increasingly displaced by that of a multiplicity of individuals passively viewing the world through the eyes of global business.

Two general features of market-driven media should also be noted: the drive to entertain, and the drive to widen audiences. Market research dictates the themes and treatments chosen to attract the readerships and audiences that, in effect, are being constructed for sale to advertisers.[19] This dictates the familiar 'dumbing down' tendency – reducing the intellectual demands made on the reader, listener or viewer, by ruthless simplification, and a heavy reliance on 'human interest' stories, the cult of celebrity – and emotional appeal – anxiety, shock and sex; and once habituated to this, audiences are seen as being resistant to anything else. A further twist has been provided by the development of a global market for feature programmes; producers are under increasing pressure to make programmes with international sales appeal. On this calculus what is specifically national, especially what is specifically political, in feature programmes, must be reduced, if not eliminated. The subordination of the public sphere to the market is here made explicit.

The impending digital revolution, in which a superabundance of new commercial channels will shortly be offered, promises a sharp acceleration of these processes. Audience fragmentation is inevitable, and in the anxiety this is creating among prospective new broadcasters they are all turning to the only two reliable audience-attractors – films and sport (in both of which, incidentally, Murdoch's News Corporation already has a very large if not dominant stake).

The political implications were illustrated rather dramatically by the party election broadcasts in the 1997 election in Britain, in which talks by party leaders were largely replaced by political soap operas or cartoons. A very similar effect, perhaps even more fatal to intelligent 'collective dialogue', is the declining length of 'soundbites' in political interviews (which are said to have fallen to an average of 7-8 seconds for the candidates in the last US Presidential election). In general, the end result can be seen in the US model of barely regulated television. Nicholas Fraser, a BBC editor, sums it up as a 'willingness to concede that "quality" is for rich people and trash is for the masses. This is an American attitude but it is becoming evident too in Europe... In the US, traditional broadcasting is known as "free TV". "Look, I wouldn't watch it," a mogul said to me, about his network's output. "Of course free TV is terrible - it's for poor people, not you and me".'[20] National political discussion clearly cannot be conducted in media conceived in these terms.

Some other politically significant effects of market-driven media also deserve to be noted. One is the one-directional nature of the communication; the reader/listener/viewer is passive and remote. Where a live audience is involved, spin-doctors do their best to ensure that awkward questions will not be asked. Even where politicians talk to professional interviewers on television, the agenda is at best set by the idea of 'impartiality' laid down in public service regulations, i.e. a 'balance' between the positions of the leaders of the major political parties, with other perspectives rarely represented.

Another problem is that television, which most people consider the most reliable source of news, famously works by means of the selection of images which often have little relation to the picture a balanced and critical analysis would produce;[21] moreover it can't be checked by re-reading what has just been said. Television also rarely provides any significant historical context. It might be argued, in fact, that its contribution to the deletion of historical context is one of television's most serious injuries to democracy. While public service broadcasting in Britain, at least, still produces excellent historical programmes, these tend to attract minority audiences; whereas the 'infotainment'-influenced format of even public service mass-audience news programmes tends to de-historicise all events.[22] By the time the introductory human-interest story has been told, there is little time to do more than 'position' the subsequent two minutes' worth of information with the aid of interpretive labels ('rebel', 'loyalist', 'Arab', 'hard-line' and the rest), which give the impression of history having been taken into account, while actually excluding it. A great deal depends, too, on the size and quality of the research teams employed. As these decline through cost-cutting, the historical sophistication of the programmes - the questions asked, the context provided - declines too.

A final political effect worth emphasising is the tendency of market-driven media to kill off intra-party debate. With the multiplication of radio stations and TV channels carrying news (including 24-hours news channels) competition drives producers to treat differences of opinion within parties, especially differences between senior party figures, as 'splits', with potentially negative electoral consequences. This drives parties to try to limit public policy discussion. In 1997 the British Labour Party made radical changes to its constitution so that annual conferences would in future avoid having controversial debates and so offer a target to the media; open debates by elected representatives of the membership were replaced by private discussions in 'policy forums' selected, not elected, from various parts of the party structure.[23]

Some objections

Against this general picture of market-driven media eroding and displacing the collective debate necessary for democracy (let alone democratic socialism), three arguments are advanced that need to be briefly considered here.

First, it is argued with some justification that commercial broadcasting has had beneficial effects in forcing much-needed improvements in state-controlled 'public service' broadcasting - breaking the monopoly of party and/or state bureaucrats over the news, forcing elite-dominated broadcasting organisations to cater to popular wishes, ending the reign of propaganda, didacticism and dullness. The force of this argument is undeniable, but it is not, on the other hand, an argument for allowing unregulated commercial broadcasting to undermine and eventually destroy public service broadcasting, and with it, the very existence of the public sphere on which democracy depends.

A second argument is based on technological change: the threat of unregulated commercial broadcasting is said to be exaggerated because channel superabundance may actually lead to a decline in overall viewing, and a lessening of its importance. In Britain, there was a drop of almost ten per cent in viewing time between 1985 and 1995, and the impending proliferation of channels through digitalisation could conceivably lead to a further fall. Polls indicate that people do not welcome it and many commentators think there could be widespread indifference. The trouble with this argument is that a decline in viewing does not entail an increase in some other form of collective discussion, and it is not obvious that any other is likely.[24]

The third argument, also based on technology, is that interactive TV, the internet, and multimedia will re-establish democratic debate by linking each citizen to every other. It seems unwise to count on this, having seen how the much-heralded democratisation of the press that was supposed to occur in the 1980s (through the lowering of production costs by the advent of computerised editing and typesetting) was successfully thwarted by the established publishers using their market power to raise the costs of entry to newcomers; it is worth noting that in Britain in 1997 the total number of internet subscribers was about one per cent of the electorate. And we can be sure that the much-hyped 'interactive' TV, when it comes, will really be 'responsive' TV, with viewers responding to agendas set by commercial interests, not TV meeting the needs of democracy. In general, technological change that is driven by the search for profits will not, by its nature, come to rest in a low-cost universally accessible system. The establishment of such a system - supposing it were judged desirable - would require a politically-determined decision, and public expenditure to make it genuinely universal.

The impact on public service broadcasting

The erosion of democracy that is occurring through the marketisation of the media has been significantly obscured by the existence of the 'public service' sector in broadcasting. In Britain at least, the left has tended to take comfort from the existence of this sector, even when it too has been hostile to the left (as for instance in the television treatment of industrial conflict in the 1970s, or the 'Bennite' left in the 1980s), feeling that over time it must respond to 'public opinion'. This view rests on a conception of public opinion being formed somewhere else – in some more primary or basic collective conversation that continues to take place independently of the media, if not in public or trade union meetings, then in homes and pubs. This view is not entirely mistaken. There is an ongoing process of grass-roots discussion, related to people's everyday experience; but it is easy to underestimate the extent to which the agenda and interpretations of the media set the agenda of this conversation too, and shape the way personal experience is interpreted. It also tends to overlook the extent to which public sector broadcasting is now itself being reshaped by the pressures of market forces.

As Curran has pointed out, different forms of public service broadcasting have different weaknesses in relation to market pressures, to which first international radio and now satellite TV broadcasting has increasingly exposed them all, regardless of national state policy.[25] State-controlled services tend to be boring and are usually distrusted, and hence succumb both to more entertaining commercial competition (the earlier success of radio stations like Radio Luxembourg is a case in point), and to political pressures to remove their protected status and even privatise them (as with France's TF1 television channel). Public service broadcasting parcelled out among political parties or religious or linguistic communities has stronger political defences but tends to ossify debate, and make broadcasting predictable and boring by giving fixed party or religious interests a sort of oligopoly – which itself is likely to prove vulnerable to market competition, as in the case of the satellite commercial channel RTL4's dramatic sweep of viewers in the Netherlands.

The quasi-corporatist or civil service model adopted in Britain avoids these weaknesses, but has its own limitations. In particular it suffers from being governed by unrepresentative, politically-appointed boards; the mandate to be politically impartial is, as already noted, interpreted as requiring it to be impartial only between the positions of the main parliamentary parties; 'diversity' of content is interpreted to mean diversity of cultural interests, not of ideological viewpoints; and universality of access is understood to mean that everyone should be able to receive broadcasts, not to have input into their content. These limitations are reinforced by broadcasters' tendency to restrict their sources of news and opinion to 'a small repertory of the powerful, authoritative and accredited', whose elite point of view the broadcasters themselves then tend to reflect.[26] (For example, the political editor of the *Independent* newspaper, Andrew Rawnsley, commenting on the 1996 party conferences on BBC Radio remarked that Labour had 'had its most successful conference for years, with the leadership in complete control'; no one on the programme questioned the elite standpoint implied in this.)

On the other hand the public service sector in Britain has notable strengths, and has to some extent withstood neoliberal political pressures. This has been due partly to a lingering attachment to mandarin values within the Conservative Party's leadership; partly to anxiety in the commercial sector about whether, if the BBC were obliged to depend on advertising revenue, it would capture so much of the available advertising spend (running at about £2.6 billion in 1997) that some of the commercial companies would go to the wall; and perhaps most importantly to the fact that the public service system was very popular, thanks to its professionally-driven excellence and its successful 'early compromise between elite and market values'.[27] As a result, the privatisers' attack in the 1980s was limited. The BBC was left with its licence fee revenue, but obliged to cut costs by casualising and reducing staff, outsourcing more of its production to the private sector, and subjecting all programming to more business-oriented, management-inspired criteria through the creation of an internal 'quasi-market'.

But what this story also shows is that even the most popular public-service system is only *relatively* robust in face of market pressures, which feed into its thinking and performance as the effects of *anticipated* competition, and the fear of being reduced or even abolished outright by a more hostile neoliberal government later. In the case of the BBC, the issue has become defined as one of whether its share of total viewing is sufficient to make it possible to go on requiring all TV owners to pay the BBC licence fee, which is in effect a hypothecated tax. New commercial channels are bound to draw away viewers from all existing channels, including the BBC's, and at some point the neoliberals will argue for making the licence fee voluntary or shifting to pay-per-view, as advocated by the *Economist*, or privatising it, as advocated by the Institute for Economic Affairs.[28] Competition from global commercial and pay-per-view TV, especially from Murdoch's three satellite companies (Sky in Europe, Fox in north America, and Star in Asia), has also dramatically altered the economics of sport and sports broadcasting rights, pricing the live broadcasting of more and more non-'ring-fenced' sports out of the reach of public service sector broadcasting, and pulling audiences with them.[29] The BBC has had to counter with more popular programming, while at the same time spreading its licence revenue ever more thinly to enter digital broadcasting and 24-hour newscasting, trying to economise by cutting staff, sharing resources between services, going 'bimedia' (i.e. making radio and television services share facilities) and expanding overseas sales.[30] In early 1998 a new schedule for Radio 4, the BBC's main national talk programme, included, among other things, shifting coverage of Parliament to less popular wavelengths and times. There could be no serious doubt that these measures eroded the fulfilment of the BBC's public service mandate.

In face of competition from satellite and cable the BBC shows signs of retaining its viewer share more successfully than ITV; and the inroads of the new subscription channels have been quite limited, though how long this will last as more channels are offered, and how far it is at the cost of reduced quality in the public service sector, remains to be seen.[31] The Channel 3 commercial TV companies, vigorously supported by the advertising industry, have predictably reacted to the new competition by lobbying to reduce the public service obligations laid on them.[32] The spiral continues, with the end already known, in outline, from North America.

Reclaiming the media for democracy

For a renewed collective debate about the fundamental principles of social organisation to be possible, and for a renewed socialist project to be articulated and get a hearing, a new media order is needed. The most comprehensive scheme is perhaps the one proposed by James Curran which envisages four distinct publicly-funded (or subsidised) sectors, alongside a purely market sector (like the barely-regulated satellite and cable broadcasting companies in Britain today), each one catering for a different facet of a modern, technically complex and diverse 'public sphere': a public service sector, a 'social' market sector, a professional sector and a 'civic' sector.[33]

The *public service sector* would be adequately funded from public sources and have a mandate to represent widely differing socio-economic interests and perspectives as well as cultural ones. It would be controlled by directors chosen by and publicly answerable to a broadly representative council;[34] but it would still be required to justify its funding by, among other things, maintaining a significant audience share - in other words, it should compete effectively for public attention and support, but on the basis of quality, not advertiser-driven, audience-maximising programmes.

This sector would be supplemented, second, by a *'social market' sector.* This would be advertising-funded broadcasting and publishing but subject to public-service regulation. The aim would be to combat the tendency to oligopoly and uniformity of the pure market sector, but not only (as with ITV in Britain today) by regulations to limit monopoly and cross-media ownership and to make it serve the public interest in various ways, but also by providing official assistance of various kinds which would be given to social forces that would otherwise be under-represented in the market sector, on the lines of the support currently given to minority publications in Sweden and Norway, or (through a different formula) to Channel 4 TV in Britain.

Third, a *professional sector* would serve the traditional conception of a 'fifth estate', providing fiction and drama programmes as well as public affairs, financed from an advertising tax but controlled and run by professional journalists and governed by professional journalistic values.

Finally a *'civic' sector* would consist of state-assisted channels, stations and publications controlled by popular bodies, from parties to minority organisations and community groups, catering primarily to the internal communication needs of these various sub-communities though also facilitating the contributions they can ultimately make to the wider national discourse.

Other elements of a democratised media system not included in Curran's model, but which should also, ideally, be generalised, include a constitutional right of reply to statements in the media that are misleading and tendentious; other public service obligations of various kinds laid on high-circulation newspapers, such as the obligation to carry party political statements in the same way that the regulated broadcast media are obliged to carry party political broadcasts, as proposed by Martin Linton MP, or the requirement to devote specified proportions of space to certain categories of 'public service' content, as proposed by Jean Seaton;[35] and laws protecting editorial and journalistic independence from owners and advertisers, rejecting the idea of absolute property rights over any medium of communication, and establishing a degree of internal democracy within press and broadcasting organisations.

Priorities for the left

This concluding section is necessarily very tentative, and is offered purely as a possible contribution to agenda-making.

In the first place, it probably needs to be recognised that while the media have played a crucial role in the marginalisation and ghettoisation of progressive ideas and perspectives, this could not have been so successful had these ideas and perspectives been inherently more convincing. The first necessity is for serious intellectual effort to evolve a coherent and believable new vision of a non-market society.

At the same time, even working out such a vision - as the European labour movement did over roughly a hundred years from 1850 to 1950 - itself depends on the media, and initially, especially, on a strong 'civic' sector (in the sense outlined in the previous section). In countries where this sector is poorly endowed, and where the governing parties are unlikely to help it, the labour movement seems the likeliest source of support. In Britain, where the Labour Party leadership have been frankly distancing themselves from the trade unions and 'repositioning' the party as a 'party of business', the unions need to think in terms of directing some financial support to the progressive media sector, perhaps beginning with a few magazines and 'talk' radio stations, where the set-up and running costs are relatively modest. At the same time, the lesson of so many failed left publishing (and broadcasting?) projects needs learning, that progressive media initiatives are a waste of money and energy unless they can compete on quality - i.e., in concept, form, content, and technique.[36]

Yet advocacy of a comprehensive media regime is also important. The ideals of democracy remain potent and can be attached to the demand for a democratic media regime. Potential support for it exists, as is shown by the European Parliament's narrowly-defeated effort to strengthen the TWF Directive in 1997.[37] What is needed is to concretise a vision of a functioning public sphere that will empower people concerned with the risks in their environment, the power of large corporations, the secrecy of officials and quangos, and so on, by making the media a real 'fourth estate' and a field open to individuals, groups and movements to speak and act in. From the outset, advocacy must articulate discourse on the media to the discourse of democracy, and disarticulate it from the discourses of industry and the market - speaking of deliberative democracy, not 'information policy', of recovering the airwaves from big business and restoring them to the constitution, and so on. There is scope for discursive initiative here.

The idea of a media regime in the service of democracy also has the merit of consisting, essentially, of a shelf-full of eminently practical measures, many of which already exist in some country or other (and which cannot therefore be dismissed as unrealistic), and almost all of which, as with freedom of information, have broad liberal appeal. Concentrating initially on campaigns to secure these would be educative in itself, and success would tend to make the achievement of other measures less difficult.

NOTES

This is a revised version of a paper originally presented to the Conference on Contemporary Political Thought: The Left in Europe of the 21st Century, organised by the Andreas Papandreou Institute of Strategic and Development Studies (ISTAME), Athens, 3-4 July 1997. Thanks are due to the Killam Foundation for support for the work on which it is based and to James Curran for invaluable guidance.

1 *Strukturwandel der Offentlichkeit*, published in English as *The Structural Transformation of the Public Sphere*, Cambridge: Polity, 1989.

2 The expression quoted is from James Curran, 'Media Soundings', *Soundings*, No. 5 1997, p. 132.

3 For a lucid summary and general critique of Habermas' thesis see Craig Calhoun, 'Introduction', in C. Calhoun (ed.), *Habermas and the Public Sphere*, Cambridge, Mass and London, England: The MIT Press, 1992, pp. 1-48; Habermas' response is on pp. 421-61. Nicholas Garnham's essay in the same volume ('The Media and the Public Sphere') also deserves attention.

4 Serge Halimi, 'When market journalism invades the world', *Le Monde Diplomatique*, June 1997 (English translation from http://www.monde-diplomatique.fr, courtesy of Alan Zuege).

5 Nicholas Fraser, 'A New Moronism', *Guardian* 2 June 1997. By 1996 BBC 1 and 2 together still had 43.6 per cent of total audience, Channel 3 (Independent TV) and Channel 4 combined had 47.3 per cent, and satellite and cable channels 9.1 per cent.

6 The phrase quoted is from James Curran, 'Media Soundings', in *Soundings* No. 5, 1997, p. 132. It is true that some of the functions formerly performed by meetings are now performed by conferences and workshops, but participation in these is generally limited to members of organisations who can afford the fees, which are often prohibitive; it seems undeniable that the participation of most people in any kind of political meetings – if not any kind of meetings at all - has drastically declined. This is not to say that people no longer discuss public affairs at all, as noted below; but there is an important distinction to be drawn between casual interpersonal exchanges and planned, more or less ordered and informed discussions, aimed at arriving at shared conclusions, or at least clarifying differences.

7 Jean Seaton, 'Sovereignty and the media', paper presented to The Sovereignty Seminar, Birkbeck College, 1997, p. 2.

8 T. Lennon, 'Wily Rupert is a safe bet', *Free Press*, March-April 1997; leading article, *Guardian*, 17 July 1996.

9 Murdoch, R., *Freedom in Publishing*, James McTaggart Memorial Lecture, London: News Corporation Ltd., 1989, p. 4.

10 The Policy Studies Institute has calculated the total employment of the 'cultural industry' at over 500,000 in 1994 (*Cultural Trends* No. 25). If we subtract employment in things like live concerts, libraries and museums that are included in this total, but then add employment in advertising and telecommunications and the production of telecommunications equipment, data processing equipment and other IT equipment, which it does not include, we seem bound to arrive at a still larger figure.

11 V. Mosco, *The Political Economy of Communication*, London: Sage, 1996, p. 145.

12 M. Tran (*Guardian* 22 May 1997) quotes the editor of *New Media Age* as saying: 'Gates wants to control cyberspace... He wants to be a big media player. He's scrambling for a way of taking MSN [Microsoft's online service] content to the TV. He's already bought up hosts of picture libraries and intellectual property... The future will see not Gates versus Larry Ellison [chairman of database software developer, Oracle]. It will be Gates vs Murdoch'.

13 The last general initiative of this kind was the Labour backbencher Chris Mullin's 1995 Media (Diversity) Bill, which would have made it illegal to own more than one national newspaper (and illegal for foreigners, like Murdoch and Conrad Black, who owns the *Telegraph*, to own more than 20 per cent of one). It would also have prevented any newspaper owner from having more than a twenty percent share in any television company. In 1998 a House of Lords cross-party amendment to the Blair government's Competition Bill sought to prohibit 'predatory pricing', which was being practised by Murdoch's *Times* and threatened the demise of at least one major national daily. The amendment, which had widespread support within the party, was also vetoed by the Labour leadership.

14 *The Free Press*, London: Campaign for Press and Broadcasting Freedom, 1997.

15 T.D. Humphrey, 'Britain's Provincial Press', unpublished paper, Department of Media and Communications, Goldsmith's College, University of London, 1997.

16 A. Davies, '"The Management of Reputation": Public Relations and Its Influence on New Production in the British National Press', unpublished paper, Political Economy Study Group, Department of Media and Communications, Goldsmith's College, 1996. The figures for numbers of pages are for eight national newspapers. In mid-1997 it was reported that the chief executive of the Mirror Group of

newspapers, David Montgomery, was planning to have all the papers in the group, which included both the tabloid *Mirror* and the up-market 'quality' broadsheet *Independent*, share reporters; there would be just one reporter per story, the 'editorial integrity' of each paper being supplied by its editors re-working the story (Roy Greenslade, 'Hack of All Trades', *Guardian* 23 June 1997).

17 In June 1998 the radio and television technicians' union BECTU closed down most of the BBC's live national programmes for 24 hours in a fight over the corporation's plans to move them into a new subsidiary company and make them all become 'multi-skilled', which the union saw as incipient privatisation.

18 In Britain by the end of the 1980s the government had become the biggest advertiser and employed 800 staff in the Central Office of Information and 700 press and information officers in fourteen departments, at a total cost of about £240 million p.a. (P. Golding, 'Political Communication and Citizenship: The Media and Democracy in an Inegalitarian Social Order', in M. Ferguson, (ed.), 1990, *Public Communication: The New Imperatives*, London: Sage, 1990, p. 95). Davies (op. cit.) summarises the rather scattered data on the rise of the rest of the 'public relations' industry in Britain, citing estimates of annual growth rates in the 1980s of 25-30 per cent. In 1991 Government accounted for about 15 per cent of the total PR workforce, companies for 28 per cent, consultancies for 53 per cent and non-profit organisations for five per cent.

19 D. Smythe, 'Communications: Blindspot of Western Marxism', *Canadian Journal of Political and Social Theory* Vol. I, 1977, pp. 1-27.

20 Fraser, op. cit.

21 According to Diane Mather, *Surviving the Media: How to Appear Successfully on TV, Radio or in the Press*, London: Thorsens, 1995, research shows that viewer reaction to a speaker is determined 58 per cent by appearance, 35 per cent by voice and only seven per cent by content.

22 On the way competition from the commercial sector affects public service news presentation see B. Pfetsch, 'Convergence Through Privatisation? Changing Media Environments and Televised Politics in Germany', *European Journal of Communication* 11/4, pp. 427-451.

23 '...when Labour is in government... the more controversial or significant the debates and other events at Party Conference, the more they attract sensational press attention. Gladiatorial contests and deeply divisive conflicts particularly capture attention, irrespective of their true significance; and the alleged power and influence of key individuals, unions or groups are emphasised... As far as possible, and without detracting from the democratic decision-making powers of the Conference, we need to beware of providing opportunities for external opponents and critics of the Party to pinpoint Conference as an example of difficulties for the Party in power' (Labour Party, *Labour Into Power: a framework for partnership*, 1997, p. 14). See also L. Panitch and C. Leys, *The End of Parliamentary Socialism: From New Left to New Labour*, London: Verso, 1997, Chapter 11.

24 An alternative argument, based on the British experience in particular, is that public service broadcasting, adequately funded from taxation, or funded by advertising but tightly regulated (and preferably both, to make each compete on quality), may manage to retain mass audiences, while the unregulated commercial sector fragments into dozens of minority-audience channels of all kinds. This, however, depends on a secure and sophisticated public service sector, which is currently under threat.

25 James Curran, 'Media and Democracy; The Third Route', in Michael Bruun Andersen (ed.), *Media and Democracy*, Oslo: University of Oslo Press, 1996; also Curran, 'Welfare vs Free Market', op. cit.

26 James Curran, 'Reform of Public Service Broadcasting', *The Public*, Vol. 3, No. 3, 1996, p. 14.

27 Curran, ibid., p. 11.

28 The *Economist*, 15 March 1997; M.E. Beesley et al., *Markets and the Media*, London: Institute of Economic Affairs, 1996, pp. 100-07. The privatising option assumes that advertising spending will grow fast enough to fund a privatised BBC without threatening existing commercial channels. As for the alternative of making the BBC depend on voluntary subscriptions, the BBC's Chairman, Sir Christopher Bland, has claimed, without giving his reasons, that the BBC would do well financially although it would cease to be a more or less universally watched service (*Guardian* 12 June 97). In light of the experience of Public Service Broadcasting in the USA this attitude on the part of the corporation's chairman ought to give rise to more concern than it seems to have; see James Ledbetter, *Made Possible By: the death of public broadcasting in the United States*, London: Verso, 1997.

29 Countries may designate certain national sporting events as 'crown jewels' for which the television rights may only be sold for 'free to air' (i.e. non-subscription channel) broadcasting.

30 In July 1997 the BBC announced plans to put Radio 4's early morning news and public affairs programme 'Today' and BBC1's 'Breakfast News' under the control of a single editor, foreshadowing the unification of their news staffs: 'the idea is the latest proposal to cut costs on the BBC's daily news output on television and radio to help finance the launch of a 24-hour TV news service. More than 100 jobs could go... although new posts are to be created on the 24-hour channel' (*Guardian* 16 July 1997). The Director General of the BBC told the House of Commons Select Committee on the National Heritage that the corporation was facing a £40 million revenue shortfall by the beginning of the next century.

31 The BBC gets £1.8 bn per annum from about 20 million people paying a £90 licence fee; ITV gets £1.7 bn from advertising; Murdoch's Bskyb satellite channel package costing £300 per annum is subscribed to by four million viewers, for a total of about £1.2 billion, much of which is spent on sports and film rights.

32 The Director General of the Institute of Practitioners in Advertising was quoted as saying that the BBC was 'behaving like a commercial competitor' and that the IPA 'would back [ITV's] attempts to move News at Ten [the main news programme, which the ITC requires to be at 10pm] to allow uninterrupted films and dramas at 9pm'(*Guardian* 28 May 1997). The attempt was unsuccessful in 1997.

33 See especially James Curran, 'Mass Media and Democracy', op. cit., pp. 105-12. For a more philosophical reflection on the principles of a democratic public sphere see also John Keane, *The Media and Democracy*, Cambridge: Polity Press, 1991, especially chapters 5 and 6.

34 On this see also R. Collins and C. Murroni, *New Media New Politics*, Cambridge: Polity 1996, pp. 150-54.

35 M. Linton, 'Winning Ways', *Free Press*, January-February, 1996; Jean Seaton, 'Down With Aunt Tabitha: A Modest Media Proposal', in Pimlott, B., and T. Wright (eds.), *The Alternative*, London: W.H. Allen, 1990.

36 The unions learned a painful lesson in this regard when a new left-wing Sunday

tabloid newspaper, the *News On Sunday*, was launched in 1987 with £6.5 million largely provided by them. The idea was that the new print technology had created the opportunity for new papers to enter the market by lowering the cost barriers to entry. The paper folded after 6 weeks. In 1996 Curran estimated that at least £20 million would be needed to establish a new national newspaper in Britain ('Welfare vs. Free Market', op. cit., p. 135).

37 The 1988 TWF directive laid down that all stations and channels broadcasting in the European Union must have 51 per cent domestic content - but with the proviso 'wherever practicable', added at the instigation of Mrs Thatcher, acting at the behest of President Reagan and the US film industry. This proviso effectively nullifies an important part of the directive's intentions and in 1997 the US film industry joined forces with European commercial broadcasters and the telecommunications industry to lobby successfully against its removal. On the other hand they were unable to get the directive abolished, as they wished. The directive also explicitly authorises states to prohibit the sale of exclusive broadcasting rights to national sports events. Furthermore a general Public Service Broadcasting Protocol to the EU treaties was adopted in 1997, which in principle protects the right of all EU states to define, fund and organise public service broadcasting without challenge from private sector interests on the grounds of its being an obstacle to free competition.

THE TALE THAT NEVER ENDS

Sheila Rowbotham

I compiled 'The Tale that Never Ends' to mark the anniversary of the Communist Manifesto and the revolutions of 1848. The title is from William Morris' poem 'The Pilgrims of Hope'.

It was read at *The Socialist Register*'s 'Celebrating and Moving On' event at Conway Hall, Red Lion Square, London on May 9th, 1998, by Tony Garnett, Jacquetta May, Maggie Steed and Harriet Walter. The compère was Roland Muldoon from Hackney Empire, and there were also readings, talks and songs from Julie Christie, James MacGibbon, Leo Panitch, John Saville and the Raised Voices choir. It was organised by *The Socialist Register* with help from the Lippman/Miliband trust, Merlin Press, Hackney Empire and *Red Pepper Magazine*. The publicity was done by Dave Timms.

'The Tale that Never Ends' draws on ideas and quotes which appear in *The Socialist Register 1998*, and I reproduced part of Paul Thomas' essay in the script. I was greatly helped by the wise ears of Tony Garnett, Jacquetta May, Maggie Steed and Harriet Walter in putting it together. Thanks to them and to everyone who helped up front and behind the scenes.

Part I: Manifesto!

'A spectre is haunting Europe – the spectre of Communism'.

Frederick Engels, *News from Prussia*, June 1844:

> 'In the manufacturing district of Silesia... very serious riots have occurred. The workpeople of the neighbourhood depend almost entirely upon linen-manufacture... Oppressed by competition, machinery and greedy manufacturers, they at last arose. The military... fired on the rioters... Several were killed... But the enraged crowd rushed on against the soldiers... the commanding officer, who had been dragged from his horse and severely beaten, retreated... The military were repelled by the people and could only restore the peace after receiving reinforcements...'

When Frederick Engels' reports on the Silesian weavers appeared in the Chartist newspaper *The Northern Star* he was in Manchester, working in his father's firm and studying workers' conditions for the book he was writing. A tall, slender young man of twenty-four, with a military bearing and a diffident manner, he spoke nearly perfect English. He hated the world of business and deserted the dinner parties for the Owenite Hall of Science, joining the Chartist movement which was demanding manhood suffrage. He also met exiled German working-class revolutionaries who belonged to a secret society, the League of the Just, in London. This group, which later became known as the Communist League, was to commission Marx to write the Communist Manifesto in the autumn of 1847.

Bruno Hildebrand, a German economics professor, describes one of their educational meetings:

> 'We went through a beer shop and up a staircase into a room furnished with tables and benches which could accommodate about 200 people... Men were seated in little groups eating a very simple dinner or smoking one of the pipes of honour... with their pot of beer in front of them... The door was always opening to admit new arrivals. The clothes were very proper... most of the faces were evidently those of workers. The main language was German, but we could also hear French and English. At the end of the room was a grand piano with some music books on it – and this in a London that was so unmusical showed us that we had come to the right place.
>
> 'The room... filled up... When a solemn silence had been established and everyone had taken his pipe from his mouth... Citizen Schapper delivered a report on the week's events. His speech was eloquent, very detailed and full of interest... a strong communist tendency was always plain and the proletariat was the constant theme running through the entire speech. I admit that I can stand a good dose of liberalism, but certain passages made my hair stand on end...'

In August 1844 Frederick Engels visited Karl Marx in Paris. Marx, who had recently married the aristocratic Jenny von Westphalen, was trying to earn his living through journalism. Gustave Meyer, Engels' biographer, writes:

> 'If the urgent active spirit of Engels was like the mountain torrent, Marx was like the storm which blows unheeding whether it destroys or builds... Engels was... a more practical man, quicker at finding his bearings. He had a feeling for 'what was in the air': he could take up material which lay ready to hand.. But Marx struggled with the spirit of his time as Jacob wrestled with the spirit of the angel.'

They found to their excitement that they had been moving in the same direction. Like many members of the German intelligentsia, Marx had been profoundly affected by the revolt of the impoverished Silesian weavers and was searching for a means of resisting the fearful power of capital which appeared to be sweeping all before it. Both men were convinced that the workers were the catalyst. Engels introduced Marx to his Chartist friends, George Julian Harney and Ernest Jones, as well as the German communist exiles. Frederick Lessner, a member of the communist group, recollected:

> 'Marx was then still a young man, about 28 years old, but he greatly impressed us all. He was of medium height, broad-shouldered, powerful in build, and vigorous in his movements. His forehead was high and finely shaped, his hair thick and pitch – black, his gaze piercing. His mouth already had the sarcastic curl that his opponents feared so much...'

Marx set up the Communist Corresponding Committee in Brussels, where he was now living. The idea was to keep everyone in touch.They were, however, an argumentative lot. And Marx presided with a heavy hand. Paul Annenkov, an admirer of Jenny Marx, describes how he dealt with an opponent, the socialist tailor Wilhelm Weitling, early in 1846:

> 'We took our places at the small green table. Marx sat at one end of it with a pencil in his hand and his leonine head bent over a sheet of paper, while Engels... made the opening speech... Engels had not finished when Marx raised his head, turned to Weitling, a handsome fair-haired young man in a coat of elegant cut and a coquettishly trimmed small beard, and said: 'Tell us, Weitling, you who have made such a noise in Germany with your preaching: on what grounds do you justify your activity and what do you intend to base it on in the future?'
>
> With a serious, somewhat worried face, Weitling started to explain that his aim was to open the eyes of the workers to the horrors of their condition.. He spoke for a long time... confusedly and not too well, repeating and correcting himself... He now had quite different listeners from those who generally surrounded him at his work... he therefore lost his ease of thought and of speech.
>
> Marx checked him with an angry frown... Marx's sarcastic speech boiled down to this: to rouse the population without giving them any firm, well thought-out reasons for their activity would be simply to deceive them... and assumed on the one side an inspired prophet and on the other only gaping asses.
>
> Weitling 's pale cheeks coloured... In a voice trembling with emotion he started trying to prove that a man who had rallied hundreds of people under the same banner in the name of justice, solidarity and mutual brotherly assistance could not be called completely vain and useless... his modest spadework was perhaps of greater weight for the common cause than criticism and armchair analysis of doctrines far from the suffering and afflicted people.
>
> On hearing these last words Marx finally lost control of himself and thumped so hard with his fist on the table that the lamp on it rung and shook. He jumped

up saying: 'Ignorance never yet helped anybody!'

We followed his example and left the table.'

Weitling to the German socialist Moses Hess, 1846:

> 'I see in Marx's head only a good encylopaedia, but no genius. He owes his influence to other people. Rich men back him in journalism, that's all.'

Marx and Engels were young, in a hurry and completely certain that they were right.

Karl Marx on his work with Engels during 1846 and '47:

> 'We published... a series of pamphlets... in which we subjected to a merciless criticism the mixture of French-English socialism... and German philosophy, which at that time constituted the secret doctrine of the League...'

But there was always some dreadful new theory to combat. They had no sooner sent the utopian theorists such as Fourier and Saint-Simon packing, when the son of a French cooper, Pierre Joseph Proudhon, who had refused to join the Corresponding Committee in May 1846, forestalled them by studying works on economics and coming up with a cooperative financial plan. The German working class Communists were impressed.

Engels to Marx, Paris, September 1846:

> 'This new nonsense is really nonsense beyond bounds... What these people have in mind is nothing more or less than to buy up the whole of France... and later the whole world by dint of proletarian savings... would it not be a much shorter road to... coin five franc pieces out of silver contained on the shine of the moon... And those blockheads... (I mean the Germans) believe this piffle. Blokes who cannot manage to keep six sous in their pockets for drinks on the evenings they meet in the wine saloon want to buy up toute la belle France... It is an outrage that one must still take up the cudgels against such barbarous balderdash.'

The League of the Just were upset by Marx's intransigence. Its leaders Karl Schapper, Josef Moll and Heinrich Bauer wrote to him in June 1846, pleading for tolerance and suggesting an international conference:

> 'We believe that.. different orientations to communism must be expressed... If intellectuals and workers from all lands met together, then there is no doubt that a lot of barriers which still stand in the way would fall. In this congress all... types of communism could be discussed peacefully and without bitterness and the truth would certainly come through and win the day.'

The first draft of the Communist Manifesto originated in this congress which was held in London in June 1847. It was called 'A Communist

Confession of Faith':

> 'Are you a Communist?'
> 'Yes'.
> 'What is the aim of the Communists?'
> 'To organise society in such a way that every member of it can develop and use all their abilities...'

Engels to Marx, June 1847:

> 'I dealt with it point by point... the lads declared themselves satisfied. *Completely unopposed*, I got them to entrust me with the task of drafting a new one...'

Engels urged Marx to attend the next congress, writing in November 1847:

> 'Think over the Confession of Faith a bit. I believe we had better drop the catechism form and call the thing: Communist *Manifesto*. As... history has got to be related in it, the form it has been in is quite unsuitable. I am bringing what I have done with me; it is in simple narrative form, but miserably worded, in fearful haste. I begin: What is Communism? And then straight to the proletariat – history of its origin, difference from former labourers, development of the antithesis between proletariat and bourgeoisie, crises, conclusions... I mean to get it through in a form in which there will be at least nothing contrary to our views.'

The artisan communists remained suspicious; there were complaints about an aristocracy of scholars. Jenny Marx encouraged Marx to become a member of the League and listened to the workers' grumbles with a certain sympathy, observing that when intellectuals met workers:

> 'They set off their learned bombs and wrap themselves up in a supernatural halo; they do not know how to gain the friendship of workers whom they repel instead of attracting.'

Jenny, now the mother of three small children, was no longer the sheltered beauty Marx had wooed in Trier. She was busy organising Christmas parties while copying out the Communist Manifesto. There was a world trade crisis, prices were rising. Marx had taken on too many lectures and was earning no money. Paul Annenkov provided money for the Marx family that Christmas. They celebrated New Year in style, dancing at the German Workers' Union banquet. The *Deutsche Brusseler Zeitung* reported:

> 'The banquet on New Year's Eve was another step toward fraternization and strengthening democracy in several countries. No discordant note disturbed this respectable and enjoyable party. A number of ladies in full evening dress took part

and we observed beautiful women applauding vigorously. The banquet was followed by music and then by a dramatic performance, where Madame Dr Marx showed a brilliant talent for recitation. It is very impressive to watch exceptionally gifted ladies trying to improve the intellectual faculties of the proletariat.'

What with one thing and another the Manifesto was still not finished. By January 26 Schapper, Bauer and Moll were exasperated:

'The Central Committee charges its regional committee in Brussels to communicate with Citizen Marx, and to tell him that if the Manifesto of the Communist Party... does not reach London by February 1st of the current year further measures will have to be taken against him. In the event of Citizen Marx not fulfilling his task, the Central Committee requests the immediate return of the documents placed at Citizen Marx's disposal.'

Marx finally sent the manuscript off to London at the end of January 1848. The Communist Manifesto was published the following month.

Manifestus:
struck by the hand
Manifestation:
demonstration
Manifestieren:
to declare
Manifestazione:
performance
Manifestino:
leaflet
pamphlet
broadside

Manifest: 'What is clear can be seen in all its bearings.. what is evident is seen forcibly, and leaves no hesitation in the mind; what is manifest is evident in a very high degree, striking upon the mind at once with overpowering conviction.' (Websters' dictionary).

The Communist Manifesto described the transformatory power of capitalism with eloquence and passion.

'*Constant revolutionising of production, uninterrupted disturbance of all social conditions, everlasting uncertainty and agitation distinguish the bourgeois epoch from all earlier ones. All fixed, fast-frozen relations, with their train of ancient and venerable prejudices and opinions are swept away, all new-formed ones become antiquated before they can ossify. All that is solid melts into air...*'

In writing their extraordinary synthesis Marx and Engels drew on their own experiences of a society in turmoil in which values were being overturned and on the workers' movements around them. Engels, on arriving in London, 1842:

> 'Hundreds of thousands of people from all classes and ranks of society... rush past each other as if they had nothing in common, nothing to do with one another... This isolation of the individual – this narrow-minded self-seeking – is everywhere the fundamental principle of modern society...'

'*... as the use of machinery and division of labour increases... the burden of toil also increases, whether by prolongation of the working hours, by increase of the work exacted in a given time or by increased speed of the machinery...*'

The Address of the Female Chartists of Manchester to their Sisters of England, Ireland, Scotland and Wales. Passed at a Public Meeting of their Sex, the Chartist Room, Tib St, Wednesday July 21st, 1841:

> 'Sisters, if ever there was a time when it was our duty to shake off our lethargy and engage in a grand struggle for liberty, surely it is now... Thousands of both males and females are walking the streets for want of employment... while we can scarcely get sufficient to keep body and soul together, for working twelve or thirteen hours per day.
>
> Should such a state of things exist, when there is sufficient for every man, woman and child in existence? Justice and common sense say no! ..Why is it that those who have produced everything that is valuable in society.. cannot get enough to quell the ravings of hunger? Why because they have no power to make the laws that influence the distribution of wealth...
>
> Up then brave women of England, Ireland, Scotland and Wales, and join us in the cry for the Charter, which will protect labour, and secure plenty, comfort and happiness to all!
>
> Sisters in the cause of democracy we remain,
> Yours, in the bonds of affection,
> The Female Chartists of Manchester.
> Hannah Leggeth, Treasurer.
> Sarah Cowle, Secretary.'

'*As the repulsiveness of the work increases, the wage decreases.*'

The French socialist Louis Blanc on how work is auctioned:

> 'A contractor wants a workman; three present themselves.
> 'How much for your work?'
> 'Half a crown: I have a wife and children.'
> 'Well and how much for yours?'
> 'Two shillings; I have no children, but I have a wife.'
> 'Very well; and now how much for yours?'

> 'One and eightpence are enough for me; I am single.'
> 'Then you shall have the work.
>
> It is done; the bargain is struck. And what are the other two workmen to do? It is to be hoped they will die quietly of hunger. But what if they take to thieving? Never fear; we have the police. To murder? We have the hangman. As for the lucky one, his triumph is only temporary. Let a fourth workman make his appearance, strong enough to fast every other day, and his price will run down still lower; there will be a new outcast, perhaps a new recruit for the prison.'

'The need of a constantly expanding market for its products chases the bourgeoisie over the whole surface of the globe. It must nestle everywhere, settle everywhere, establish connections everywhere.'

The Chartist Thomas Cooper addressed an immense crowd, standing on a chair outside the Crown Inn, Hanley, 1842:

> 'After we had sung 'Britannia's sons, though slaves ye be' and I had offered up a short prayer. I described how the conquerors of America had nearly exterminated the native races... I recounted how English and French and Spanish and German wars in modern history, had swollen the list of the slaughtered... I described our own guilty Colonial rule, and still guiltier rule of Ireland; and asserted that British rulers had most awfully violated the precept, 'Thou shalt do no murder'..'

'The bourgeoisie, wherever it has got the upper hand, has put an end to all feudal patriarchal relations... and left remaining no other nexus than naked self-interest.'

Engels in Manchester:

> 'One day I walked with one of these liberal middle class gentlemen into Manchester. I spoke to him of the miserable unhealthy methods of building that is to be found in the working-class districts and of the atrocious, disgraceful condition of those districts. I declared to him that never in my life had I seen so badly built a town. He listened to all this patiently and quietly, and at the corner of the street at which we parted he remarked: 'And yet there is a great deal of money made here. Good morning, Sir."

'It has drowned the most heavenly ecstasies of religious fervour, of chivalrous enthusiasm, of philistine sentimentalism, in the icy water of egotistical calculation.'

Paul Lafargue, *Reminiscences of Marx*, 1890:

> 'From time to time, he would lie on the sofa and read a novel; he sometimes read two or three at a time, alternating one with the other... In Don Quixote he saw the epic of dying out chivalry whose virtues were ridiculed and scoffed at in the emerging bourgeois world... He considered Balzac... as the prophetic creator of characters which were still in their embryo in the days of Louis Philippe and did

not fully develop until after his death, under Napoleon.'

'*The bourgeoisie has stripped of its halo every occupation hitherto honoured and looked up to with reverent awe. It has converted the physician, the lawyer, the priest, the poet, the man of science, into its paid wage-labourers.*'

Eleanor Marx remarked, in 1895, on her father's friendship with the German romantic poet Heinrich Heine:

> 'He would... make all sorts of excuses for Heine's political vagaries. Poets... were queer kittle-cattle, not to be judged by the ordinary, or even the extra-ordinary standards of conduct. My mother – for whose beauty and wit Heine had a profound admiration – was less lenient.'

'*The bourgeoisie has torn away from the family its sentimental veil, and has reduced the family relation to a mere money relation.*'

Marx to Arnold Ruge, 1843:

> 'I can assure you without any romanticism that I am head over heels in love'.

He had loved Jenny since he was a student. Though her father and mother liked him, he was seen as a wild young man with bad debts and no profession. The young couple had to wait for seven long years until they could marry and Marx had to sign a contract exempting Jenny for liability for his debts. They stayed in Kreuznach for their honeymoon. Jenny Marx's biographer H.E. Peters remarks:

> 'Jenny soon noticed that the honeymoon bedroom was turning into her husband's study. He had brought with him some twenty-four works in forty-five volumes dealing with French, English German and American history and he was studying them carefully. Jenny was surprised by the numerous notes he took. He made notes from almost every page, and his notebook from the time of their Kreuznach honeymoon comprises 250 pages.'

They settled in Paris, which Jenny found exciting, though she disapproved of the easy-going morals in their revolutionary bohemian circle. In the summer of 1844 Jenny was forced to return to her mother in Trier because her first baby was ill. Marx's journalism was just not providing enough money for them to survive. She feared that he would be seduced in worldly Paris.

> 'I know it is bad and stupid to torture myself with all kinds of worries and forebodings... however the spirit is willing but the flesh is weak.'

In The Communist Manifesto Marx was dismissing the charges of 'free love' which were associated with French socialism. His wife would have approved. For Jenny, the connection between dignity and virtue was one certainty of her upbringing which she would never relinquish – whatever happened:

> 'Lieutenant August Willich settled in with us as a communist *frère et compagnon.* He appeared in our bedroom early in the morning... and tried, with Prussian horse-laughs, to hold forth about 'natural' communism. But Karl made short work of his effort. And he did not fare any better with me when he tried to wheedle out the worm that is in every marriage'

'*... the real point... is to do away with the status of women as mere instruments of production.*'

In the early nineteenth century radicals frequently linked the oppression of women with slavery. In 1843, the French socialist Flora Tristan, an engraver and author of *Workers Union*, argued that women's emancipation was inseparable from that of the working classes. She called on workers:

> 'Free the last slaves remaining in France, proclaim the Rights of Woman.'

'*The bourgeoisie has called into existence... the modern working class – the proletarians... These labourers, who must sell themselves piecemeal, are a commodity.*'

The Chartist Ernest Jones' *Song of the Lower Classes*, 1852:

> 'We're low, we're low – we're very very low
> Yet from our fingers glide
> The silken flow – and the robes that glow,
> Round the limbs of the sons of pride.
> And what we get – and what we give,
> We know – and we know our share.
> We're not too low the cloth to weave -
> But too low the cloth to wear.'

'*... The workers begin to form combinations... they found permanent associations... Here and there the contest breaks out into riots... The organisation of the proletarians into a class, and consequently into a political party, is continually being upset again by the competition between the workers themselves. But it ... rises up again, stronger, fiercer, mightier.*'

Ernest Jones at a Chartist Council meeting, January 11, 1848:

> 'There are some gentlemen who tell the people that they must grow rich and then they will be free... Become rich! How? In the workhouse or the gaol? Become rich in the deer forests of our nobles? Become rich on six shillings a week? Become rich in the churchyards of famished Ireland ? (Applause) Go tell it to the unemployed

in Manchester – to the 20,000 destitute in Bradford. Go tell it to the Irish tenant dying by the light of his burning cottage set on fire by his landlord. Go tell it to the beggar at the doors of Grosvenor Square! Go tell him once for all to stay a slave; but do not insult his misery by telling him to become rich...

No, my friends, above all we need the vote... go in person and knock at the doors of St Stephen's, knock till your privileged debtors give you back, trembling, what they have owed you for centuries! So knock, and go on knocking until justice has been done. (Thunderous applause)'

'The Communists fight for the attainment of the immediate aims of the working class; but in the movement of the present, they also represent.. the future of that movement.'

Percy Bysshe Shelley, *The Mask of Anarchy*, 1819:

'Rise like Lions after slumber
In unvanquishable number,
Shake your chains to earth like dew
Which in sleep had fallen on you -
Ye are many – they are few.'

'The workers have nothing to lose but their chains. They have a world to win.'

George Julian Harney, 1846:

'The Fraternal Democrats call on all oppressed classes of every land... to unite themselves for the triumph of their common cause. 'Divide and rule' is the motto of the oppressor. 'Unite yourselves for victory' should be ours.'

'Modern bourgeois society... is like the sorcerer who is no longer able to control the powers of the nether world whom he has called up by his spells.'

'Workers of the World. Unite.'

Part II: The Pilgrimage of Hope

Alexis de Tocqueville, aristocratic conservative, Chamber of Deputies, Paris, January 29th, 1848:

'I am told that there is no danger because there are no riots; I am told that, because there is no visible disorder on the surface of society, there is no revolution at hand.

Gentlemen, permit me to say that I believe you are mistaken. True, there is no actual disorder; but it has entered deeply into men's minds. See what is preparing itself amongst the working classes... can you not see that their passions instead of political have become social?... Do you not listen to what they say to themselves each day? Do you not hear them repeating unceasingly that all that is above them is incapable and unworthy of governing them; that the distribution of goods prevalent until now throughout the world is unjust; that property rests on a foundation which is not an equitable one?

I believe that we are at this moment sleeping on a volcano.'

Jenny Marx, Brussels, early in February 1848:

'The police, the army, the militia, everybody was called up to serve; all were ready for battle. The German workers also thought it was time to look for weapons. Daggers, revolvers etc. were bought. Karl provided the means gladly, for he had just received some money.'

Alexis de Tocqueville, *Recollections*, The morning of February 24th:

'On leaving my bed-room, I met the cook, who had been out; the good woman was quite beside herself, and poured out a sorrowing rigmarole, of which I failed to understand a word except that the Government was massacring the poor people. I went downstairs at once, and had no sooner set foot in the street than I breathed for the first time the atmosphere of revolutions. The roadway was empty; the shops were not open; there were no carriages nor pedestrians to be seen; none of the ordinary hawkers' cries were heard; neighbours stood talking in little groups at their doors, with subdued voices with a frightened air; every face seemed distorted with fear or anger.'

Gustave Flaubert's novel *A Sentimental Education*, published in 1869, gives an account of romance amidst revolution:

'Men from the suburbs were going by armed with muskets and old sabres; some wore red caps and all were singing the *Marseillaise* or the *Girondins*. Here and there a National Guard was hurrying to his post at the town hall. Drums beat in the distance. They were fighting at the Porte Saint-Martin. There was something brave and martial in the air. Frederic went on walking. The ferment of the great city made him cheerful.

On the hill where Frascati's used to be he caught sight of Rosanette's windows; a mad idea crossed through his mind; his youth flared up. He crossed the boulevard.

The outer door was being closed; Delphine, the maid, was writing on it with a piece of charcoal: 'Arms already supplied'. She spoke rapidly: 'Madame is in such a state. She sacked the groom this morning for cheeking her. She thinks there's going to be looting all over the place. She's scared to death – particularly since the gentleman's cleared out!'

'What gentleman?'

'The prince'.

Frederic entered the boudoir. Rosanette appeared, in her petticoat, with her hair down her back, distracted with terror. 'Oh, thank you! You've come to save me. It's the second time and you never ask for your reward!' 'I beg your pardon', said Frederic, putting both arms round her waist.

'What! What are you doing?' stammered Rosanette, at once surprised and amused by his behaviour.

He answered: 'I'm in the fashion. I've reformed!'

> She allowed herself to be pushed down on to the divan, and went on laughing under his kisses...
>
> ... A sudden rattle of musketry made him wake with a start; and, in spite of Rosanette's entreaties, Frederic insisted on going to see what was happening. He followed the sound of the firing down the Champs-Elysées. At the corner of Saint-Honoré he was met by a shout from some workmen in blouses: 'No! Not that way! To the Palais Royal!'
>
> Frederic followed them. The railings of the Church of the Assumption had been pulled down... Suddenly, out of an alley, rushed a tall young man, with black hair hanging over his shoulders and wearing a sort of pea-green singlet. He carried a soldier's long musket; there were slippers on his feet and he was running on tiptoe, as lithe as a tiger, yet with the fixed stare of a sleep walker. Now and then explosions could be heard...
>
> Men addressed crowds at street corners with frantic eloquence; others, in the churches, were sounding the tocsin with all their might; lead was melted, cartridges rolled; trees from the boulevards, public urinals, benches, railings, gas jets were torn down or overturned; by morning Paris was filled with barricades. Resistance was not prolonged; everywhere the National Guard intervened; so that by eight o'clock, through force or by consent, the people were in possession of five barracks, nearly all the town halls, and the most important strategic points. No great exertion was needed; through its own weakness the monarchy was swiftly tottering to its fall.'

On the evening of 24 February, Thomas Frost, a young Chartist painter from Croydon, was attending a meeting of the Fraternal Democrats in central London. He wrote in his autobiography:

> 'Suddenly the news of the events in Paris was brought in. The effect was electrical. Frenchmen, Germans, Poles, Magyars sprang to their feet, embraced, shouted and gesticulated in the wildest enthusiasm. Snatches of oratory were delivered in excited tones, and flags were caught from the walls, to be waved exultingly, amidst cries of *Hoch! Elijeu! Vive la Republique!* Then the doors were opened, and the whole assemblage descended to the street and, with linked arms and colours flying, marched to the meeting-place of the Westminster Chartists in Dean Sreet, Soho. There another enthusiastic fraternization took place, and great was the clinking of glasses that night in and around Soho and Leicester Square..'

In Brussels crowds gathered in squares, in cafes and in taverns; young orators demanded 'liberté' and 'égalité'. The authorities decided it was time to get rid of foreign agitators and began compiling lists of known German communists. In Paris the workers demanded the right to work. Louis Blanc issued the decree of 25 February:

> 'The provisional government of the French Republic undertakes to guarantee work for all citizens. It recognises that workers must form associations among themselves in order to enjoy the legitimate profits of their labour.'

De Tocqueville:

> 'From the 25th of February onwards, a thousand strange systems came issuing pell-mell from the minds of innovators, and spread among the troubled minds of the crowd. Everything still remained standing except Royalty and Parliament: yet it seemed as though the shock of the Revolution had reduced society itself to dust, and as though a competition had been opened for the new form that was going to be given to the edifice about to be erected in its place. Everyone came forward with a plan of his own: this one printed it in the papers, that other on the placards with which the walls were soon covered, a third proclaimed his loud-mouthed in the open air. One aimed at destroying inequality of education, a third undertook to do away with the oldest of inequalities, that between man and woman.'

La Voix des Femmes newspaper, 29 March:

> 'It will no longer be permissible for men to say that they are humanity. Along with the end of servitude of labour will go the servitude of women.'

Radical and socialist women set up newspapers and clubs. They demanded equal civil and political rights, equal pay, an end to low pay. They advocated work sharing as a remedy for unemployment and the democratisation of the National Workshops which provided work. They proposed public restaurants, nurseries, free medical care, provision for pregnant women. They argued for divorce law reform, voluntary motherhood, communal houses and an end to male dominance. Women endorsed the right to work, but they were envisaging the right to live.

Jeanne Deroin; former dress-maker and self-educated teacher:

> 'Liberty, equality and fraternity have been proclaimed for all. Why should women be left with only obligations to fulfil, without being given the rights of citizens?'

Desirée Gay; milliner, influenced by the Owenites and Saint-Simonians. Led protests for democratisation of National Workshops:

> 'If men enter into associations to produce wealth and defend liberty, then women must join with them... putting equality and fraternity into practice.'

Pauline Roland; teacher, influenced by Saint-Simonians. Advocate of free sexual unions. Organiser of the Fraternal Association of Socialist Male and Female Teachers and Professors:

> 'Woman is a free person... she must create her life by means of her own work, her own love, her own intelligence.'

On the night of March 4 the Brussels police raided the Hotel Bois Sauvage, arrested Marx for providing money for arms and flung a distraught Jenny in jail.

> 'It was the place where they put up homeless beggars, rootless wanderers, unfortunate lost women. I am pushed into a dark cell. I sob as I enter, and one of my unfortunate fellow sufferers offers me her bed. It was a hard wooden bunk. I fall down on it.'

King Leopold the First of Belgium to his niece Queen Victoria:

> 'I am very unwell in consequence of the *awful* events at Paris.'

Queen Victoria to King Leopold:

> 'Since February 24 I feel an uncertainty in everything existing, which one never felt before. When one thinks of one's children, their education, their future – and prays for them – I always think and say to myself, 'Let them grow up fit for *whatever* station they may be placed in, *high or low*'. This one never thought of before, but I *do always* now.'

Revolution seemed to be infectious. From March 1848 rebellions erupted in the Austrian Empire, then in many of the German states; they spread though the Italian peninsula reaching the regions controlled by the Austrians. Nationalism mixed with liberal democratic demands for constitutional reforms and civil liberties. In the towns workers joined in, adding claims for free education and trade union rights. In Ireland, devastated by famine, there were sporadic revolts. The English responded by transporting the leaders of Young Ireland to Australia.

In April, Garth Wilkinson, a middle-class radical, reported to his wife:

> 'London is in a state of panic from the contemplated meeting of the Chartists, 200,000 strong on Monday; for myself, nothing that happened would surprise me...'

On April 10th London was packed with soldiers and police armed with cutlasses. The government had declared the demonstration illegal. The Chartist leaders were divided about what to do. Around 20,000 people assembled on Kennington Common, with a strong Irish contingent bearing banners 'Ireland for the Irish'. Their suffrage petition was presented. But the police broke up the demonstration to the House of Commons. Richard Whiting, then a schoolboy, recollected:

> 'When they came back at night, angry, hungry, footsore, they found the bridges barred and the sullen canon between them and the palaces, public offices, banks, and, what was more of a hardship... their miserable homes. They were filtered over in detachments at last and kept on the run till they reached their hovels dead beat.'

April 23. The first French national election based on universal manhood suffrage returns a moderate majority.

May 15. Parisian workers, frustrated by continuing inequality, invade the National Assembly, demanding that the terrified deputies should send help to the cause of Polish independence.

De Tocqueville:

> 'As always happens in insurrections, the terrible was mingled with the ridiculous. The heat was so stifling that many of the first intruders left the Chamber; they were forthwith replaced by others who had been waiting at the doors to come in. I saw a fireman in uniform making his way down the gangway that passed along my bench. 'We can't make them vote!' they shouted to him. 'Wait, wait,' he replied, 'I'll see to it, I'll give them a piece of my mind.' Thereupon he pulled his helmet over his eyes with a determined air, fastened the strap, squeezed through the crowd, pushing aside all who stood in his way, and mounted the tribune. He imagined he would be as much at his ease there as upon a roof, but he could not find his words and stopped short. The people cried, 'Speak up fireman!' but he did not speak a word and they ended by turning him out of the tribune.'

The new government announced on 21 June that young unemployed workers between 18-25 should join work teams in the provinces. The National Workshops were to be closed. That evening de Tocqueville met the novelist George Sand at a dinner; a supporter of revolution and a defender of women's rights, she was his political antithesis.

> 'I was strongly prejudiced against Madame Sand, for I loathe women who write, especially those who systematically disguise the weakness of their sex, instead of interesting us by displaying them in their true character. Nevertheless she pleased me. I thought her features rather massive, but her expression admirable: all her mind seemed to have taken refuge in her eyes, abandoning the rest of her face to matter... We talked for a whole hour of public affairs; it was impossible to talk of anything else in those days. It was the first time that I had entered into direct and familiar communication with a person able and willing to tell me what was happening in the camp of our adversaries. Political parties never know each other: they approach, touch, seize, but never see one another. Madame Sand depicted to me, in great detail and with singular vivacity, the condition of the Paris workmen, their organization, their numbers, their arms, their preparations, their thoughts their passions, their terrible resolves. I thought the picture overloaded, but it was not, as subsequent events clearly proved...'

When fighting broke out, Frederic, the hero of *A Sentimental Education*, is to be found making love to Rosanette outside Paris. He is too happy to heed the distant drums calling on the country people to defend Paris against the workers' uprising. However, when he sees the name of his friend Dussardier among the wounded in the newspaper, he is filled with remorse. Dussardier, a shop worker, had fought for the February revolution – now he is on the other side of the barricades. Frederic hastens back to Paris to look for him:

> 'The Place du Pantheon was full of soldiers lying on straw. Day was breaking. The camp fires were going out.
>
> The rising had left impressive traces in this district. The surface of the streets was broken from end to end into lumps and hummocks. Omnibuses, gas pipes and cart wheels were still lying on the ruined barricades; there were little black smears in certain places, which could only have been blood. The houses were riddled with bullets, and their inner framework could be seen through the splintered plaster. Blinds, hanging from a single nail, flapped like rags. Doors opened on to a void, where the staircase had fallen in. The inside of rooms could be seen, with their wall-paper in shreds; sometimes fragile objects had been preserved. Frederic noticed a clock, a parrot's perch, some prints.
>
> Carriages were moving down the boulevard, and women in front of doorways were making lint. But the rebellion was conquered or nearly so; so declared a proclamation by Cavaignac which had just been posted. A company of Mobile Guards appeared at the top of the rue Vivienne. The wealthier citizens shouted with enthusiasm; they raised their hats, clapped their hands, tried to kiss the soldiers, and offered them drinks, while women threw flowers down from the balconies.'

The National Guard and the Mobile Guards showed no mercy to the artisans, labourers and unemployed who had rebelled. Thousands were killed. Thousands more were later to be deported to Algeria.

Despite the repression, the French workers, women as well as men, continued to set up newspapers and create cooperatives. The agitation for the Charter continued in England. Far away in the United States, the first Women's Rights Convention was held at Seneca Falls on July 19th and a new movement came into being.

Marx and Engels still anticipated revolution. In May 1849 Jenny Marx, stranded in gossipy Trier, wrote to her friend Lina Scholer in America after Marx was expelled from Germany:

> 'Life is not a bed of roses here I can tell you that dear, faithful Lina. I am completely at a loss to know what lies ahead of us. My dear Karl remains confident and cheerful and considers all the pressures that we have to endure only heralds of a coming and complete victory of our view of life.'

Gradually the extent of the defeat became evident. In December 1848, Louis Bonaparte, the nephew of Napoleon, was elected president. His rule was secured through a coup d'etat and plebiscite in 1851. Marx commented sardonically in *The Eighteenth Brumaire of Louis Bonaparte*, 1852:

> 'Hegel remarks somewhere that all facts and personages of great importance in

world history occur, as it were, twice. He forgot to add the first time as tragedy, the second as farce.'

In 1851 Jeanne Deroin and Pauline Roland wrote from prison greeting the second American Women's Rights Convention.

'Sisters of America! Your socialist sisters in France are united with you in the vindication of the right of woman to civil and political equality. We have moreover the profound conviction that only by the power of association based on solidarity – by the union of the working classes of both sexes to organise labour – can be acquired, completely and pacifically, the civil and political equality of women and the social right of all.

Faith, Love, Hope and our sisterly salutations.'

Jeanne Deroin went into exile in Britain. Pauline Roland was deported to Algeria and died on her return journey to France. Exile, prison and death took a terrible toll on the revolutionaries of 1848. Those who survived faced derision in the conservative decades that followed. A new generation had little sympathy for fossilised romantic rebels. 'The reaction after '48' wrote Flaubert,' dug a gulf between one France and the other.'

At number 64 Dean St, Soho, Karl and Jenny Marx, their children, along with Helene Demuth, the servant who bore Marx's son Freddy, were crammed into two rooms in 1850. A Prussian spy has left us a description:

'Everything is broken, tattered and torn, finger-thick dust everywhere, and everything in the greatest disorder; a large old-fashioned table, covered with waxcloth, stands in the middle of the drawing-room, on it lie manuscripts, books, newspapers, then the children's toys, bits and pieces of the woman's sewing things next to it, a few teacups with broken rims, dirty spoons, knives, forks, candle-sticks, inkpot, glasses, dutch clay pipes, tobacco-ash, in a word all kinds of trash, and everything on one table; a junk dealer would be ashamed of it.'

Marx struggled to understand what had gone wrong. Surrounded by the children and domestic confusion, he wrote on. A decade of poverty was to follow. Three of their children died; illness, insecurity and privation became a way of life, as Marx grappled with the economic dynamics of this capitalism which was proving so tenacious, so contrary. In 1862, remorseful over Jenny's suffering, he told Engels:

'If only I knew how to start some kind of business! My dear friend, all theory is dismal, and only business flourishes. Unfortunately I have learnt this too late.'

After the defeat of the Paris Commune in 1871, Jenny reflected:

'In all these battles we women have to bear the hardest, i.e. the pettiest part. In the battle with the world the man gets stronger, stronger too in the face of his enemies, even if their number is legion; we sit at home and darn socks. That does not banish the worries, and little daily cares slowly but surely gnaw away the courage to face life. I am talking from more than thirty years experience and I can say that I did not give up courage easily.'

Marx could not see this future when he wrote his Manifesto. Nor could he have imagined what was to be done in the name of communism or comprehended how the meaning of his words would be turned inside out. The World Bank's World Development report for 1996, *From Plan to Market*, quoted The Communist Manifesto, while celebrating the transition to capitalist market economies: 'Constant revolutionising of production... all that is solid melts into air...' Capital it seems has had the last word.

History however keeps on happening and is apt to surprise us all, as that canny observer, Alexis de Tocqueville, understood so well. In the early 1850s, as he jotted down the notes which were to be published in 1893 as his *Recollections*, de Tocqueville wondered:

'Will Socialism remain buried in the disdain with which the Socialists of 1848 are so justly covered? I put the question without making any reply. I do not doubt that the laws concerning the constitution of our modern society will in the long run undergo modification... But will they ever be destroyed and replaced by others? It seems to me impracticable. I say no more, because – the more... I consider... the different forms even now taken by the rights of property on this earth – the more I am tempted to believe that what we call necessary institutions are often no more than institutions to which we have grown accustomed, and that in matters of social constitution the field of possibilities is much more extensive than men now living in their various societies are ready to imagine.'

The Communist Manifesto opens such a field of possibilities. Marx's message remains far too subversive for the World Bank; never settle down with the injustices to which you have been made accustomed. And as we read, his words are joined by thousands and thousands and thousands of voices from far away and long ago: Look; Listen; Criticise; Remember; Understand; Organise; Imagine; Create; Hope.

The socialist movement did revive in the 1880s – the 'grandchildren of the Chartists', Engels called them. And this time around they knew that defeats had to be taken into account. In his poem *The Pilgrims of Hope*, William Morris asks: 'How can I tell you the story of Hope and its defence?'

The very first 'pilgrim' in the poem is a French refugee from the 1848 revolution, who relates 'The battle of grief and hope with riches and folly and wrong.' His story becomes the source of renewal, 'the tale that never ends'.